W9-CLO-176

LORETTE WILMOT LIBRARY
Nazareth College of Rochester

Rochester City Ballet

KNOPF

75

YEARS·OF·PUBLISHING

The Ballets Russes

Colonel Wassily de Basil, 1934.

The Ballets Russes

Colonel de Basil's
Ballets Russes de Monte Carlo
1932–1952

Vicente García-Márquez

Alfred A. Knopf · New York 1990

DISCARDED
LORETTE WILMOT LIBRARY
NAZARETH COLLEGE

This Is a Borzoi Book Published by Alfred A. Knopf, Inc.
Copyright ©1990 by Vicente García-Márquez
All rights reserved under International and Pan-American Copyright
Conventions. Published in the United States by Alfred A. Knopf, Inc.,
New York, and simultaneously in Canada by Random House of Canada
Limited, Toronto. Distributed by Random House, Inc., New York.

Grateful acknowledgment is made to the following for permission to reprint
previously published material:

Robert Cornfield Literary Agency: Excerpts from Looking at the
Dance by Edwin Denby. Originally published in 1949 by Pellegrini Press,
and subsequently in paperback in 1968 by Horizon Press. Copyright 1949
by Edwin Denby. Also found in Dance Writings: Edwin Denby, edited by
Robert Cornfield and William MacKay, published in 1986 by Alfred A.
Knopf, Inc. Copyright © 1986 by Yvonne and Rudolph Burckhardt.
Reprinted by permission of the Robert Cornfield Literary Agency on behalf
of the Estate of Edwin Denby.
Methuen & Company: Excerpts from A Prejudice for Ballet by A. V.
Coton. Published by Methuen & Company, London, 1938. Reprinted by
permission of Methuen, a division of Octopus Publishing Group.
Times Newspapers Limited: Excerpts from ballet article by Ernest
Newman from Sunday Times (London), July 5, 1936. Copyright 1936
by Times Newspapers Ltd. Reprinted by permission.

Library of Congress Cataloging-in-Publication Data
García-Márquez, Vicente, [date]
The Ballets Russes : Colonel de Basil's Ballets Russes de Monte
Carlo, 1932–1952 / Vicente García-Márquez. — 1st ed.
p.   cm.
Includes bibliographical references.
ISBN 0-394-52875-1
1. Ballets Russes de Monte Carlo—History.   I. Title.
GV1786.B3G38   1990
792.8'09449'49—dc20   89-19984   CIP

Manufactured in the United States of America
First Edition

792.809449
Gar

A mis padres
A mi abuela

Contents

Acknowledgments

HISTORY is reinterpretation, and the historian writes with his perception of what has preceded. My intention in this book was to re-create the sensibility of the period as much as possible, and not just to document facts. I am aware that the intrinsic values and modes that make a period unique will always escape the historian and can remain only in the perceptions of its survivors. I wanted the protagonists to voice their feelings, reminiscences, and observations; and I wanted to frame these within a historical context. I wanted to bring these historical figures back on stage so that they could re-enact their world and experiences. Only then could the moment be partly reconstructed and perhaps made more believable.

The idea of writing this book germinated in Los Angeles through my friendship with Tatiana Riabouchinska. In the beginning she was elusive and avoided my persistent questions. She surprised me when, two years after our first meeting, she showed for the first time an earnest interest in guiding me through the records of the period. So it is to Riabouchinska that I offer the major credit for helping me to pursue this goal. She was to become to me, as I was to her, a devoted friend. Her intuitive understanding allowed me the freedom to discover for myself the answers I lacked. She was instrumental in re-creating this universe, but from a delicate distance, so as never to impose her views. Her library, which eventually was moved virtually *in toto* to my house, was my first working ground, while her films, books, photos, and memorabilia became my initial tools. She showed a selfless dedication during my eight years of intensive research, and bestowed upon me the privilege of my first contacts with Baronova, Toumanova, Massine, and Kochno, to all of whom I am forever indebted.

Irina Baronova is a miracle of human kindness and understanding. On a cobbled street in La Tour de Peilz, under the Swiss summer sun, she appeared to me for the first time as a vision of beauty, as the unattainable ideal. Throughout the years she has been an inexhaustible source of stimulation, and her impartiality of judgment and acute sense of observation will always be cherished.

If others attempted to recapture a world long past, Tamara Toumanova appeared as its living embodiment. In her presence the dividing lines of time are nonexistent. Outside her world, life became a delusion. Many have been my memorable hours in the company of Toumanova and her Mama, where every moment was imbued with intensity and fervor, where the trivial became relevant and legend became the absolute mode of existence.

Léonide Massine and Boris Kochno enlightened me with their appreciation of art. They were invaluable in my achieving a better understanding of their work. The time I spent with Massine at Isole dei Galli allowed me the opportunity to discuss his work with him in the place where much of it was conceived.

I am also grateful to Olga Morosova de Basil, who was most cooperative and kind during my frequent visits to Paris and who assisted me in every possible way.

I am further obliged to Georges Auric, Robert Bell (Boris Belsky), Alexandra Danilova, Adele de Angelo (Charaska), Edwin Denby, Patricia Denise (Alexandra Denisova), Claire H. de Robilant, Mary Ann de Vlieg, Vladimir Dokoudovsky, Sir Anton Dolin, Eugenia Doll (Delarova), Felia Doubrovska, Tamara Finch (Tchinarova), Florence Goldsborough, Vsevolod Grigoriev, Roland Guérard, Rosella Hightower, Jean Hugo, Roman Jasinski, Michel Katcharov, Irving Kolodin, Moscelyne Larkin (Moussia Larkina), Yurek Lazowski, Tatiana Leskova, Tania Lichine Crawford, Irene Lidova, Dame Alicia Markova, Tatiana Massine Weinbaum, Joan Miró, Geneviève Moulin, Vera Nemtchinova, Irina Nijinska, Anna Northcote (Severskaya), Lara Obidenna, Michel Panaiev, Celida Parera Alonso, Mrs. C. C. Powell, Paul Riabouchinsky, Dimitri Rostov, Elizabeth Ruxton (Lisa Serova), Igor Schwezoff, George Skibine, Gennady Smakov, Nina Stroganova, John Taras, Mme Constantin Terechkovitch, Eugenie Toumanova, Irina Vasilieva, David Vaugham, Nina Verchinina, George Verdak, Nina Youchkevitch, and George Zoritch.

I would also like to thank the following institutions: the archives of the Royal Opera House, Covent Garden; BBC Hulton Picture Library; the *Illustrated London News* Public Library; the Victoria and Albert Museum Theatre Museum; the Paris Opéra Library; the Bibliothèque National, Paris; the Emeroteca Nacional, Madrid; the Dance Collection of the Library of the Performing Arts at Lincoln Center, with special thanks to Rita Waldron for her assistance.

When one is writing a book, especially one's first, one encounters many people who are indispensable through its different phases, and I would like to express my gratitude to them: Fred and Elena Maroth; Parmenia Migel Ekstrom, who from our first meeting became a champion of the book-to-be and whose reading of the manuscript saved it from countless errors; José Manuel Pacheco, who read the final draft and offered constructive criticism that was enlightening and essential; and Kevin Boynton, who typed most of the manuscript, and whose editorial work on the text as well as his non-balletomane's observations on the content were most valuable. I am grateful to my friends in Europe and the United States who read some of the chapters and, above all, endured years of obsessive Ballets Russes conversations: in particular, Stephen Berg, Galo Bravo, Ana Maria Velasco, Henry McClenney, Elvia Quijano, Mario Piombi, Elyane Plard, Shela Xoregos, and Robert Gaston-Cottin. My eternal gratitude to Louisa Horton Hill, a perfect hostess during my long sojourns in New York, who made everything conducive to work. Lastly, my gratitude to Robert Gottlieb for his unconditional and wholehearted support, to Eva Resnikova, and to my editor, Susan Ralston, whose dedication and enthusiasm were essential in the creation of this book.

Introduction

HEN the Ballets Russes de Monte Carlo made its debut in the spring of 1932, hope for the continuity of ballet in Europe was resurrected. The advent of the new decade, ushered in by economic chaos, had witnessed the loss of the two individuals who had established international touring companies: Serge Diaghilev, who died August 19, 1929, and Anna Pavlova, who died January 23, 1931. The formation of the Ballets Russes de Monte Carlo by Colonel Wassily de Basil and René Blum marked the pivotal beginning of a new artistic freedom and aesthetic expression. The collaborations sponsored by the company resulted in a merger of the old and the new, a re-examination and re-elaboration of the scope of modern ballet. They revived the public's interest in nineteenth-century classicism, and also developed the integration of dance and music that had begun with *Les Sylphides*. Balanchine's *Cotillon* and Massine's *Jeux d'enfants*, both created in 1932 with libretti by Kochno, had no literal story and were consistently set in terms of dance. The following year Massine's *Les Présages*, set to Tchaikovsky's Fifth Symphony, opened a new chapter in ballet history as the first symphonic ballet in the West to explore a new structure, theme, and choreographic syntax. Also in 1933 came Massine's *Choreartium*, set to Brahms's Fourth Symphony, the first abstract ballet, which provoked international attention and controversy unequalled since that day in music and dance circles, a work that was vehemently championed by Ernest Newman. Massine's *Symphonie fantastique* (1936, Berlioz) was probably his greatest statement on his concept of the dance/drama.

Other Diaghilev collaborators contributed to the artistic eminence of the new company. Nijinska revived old ballets and produced one of her most classical and personal new ones, *Les Cent Baisers*, a ballet that stressed technical virtuosity and the dominating role of the ballerina. Fokine created three monumental productions in *Le Coq d'or*, *Cendrillon*, and *Paganini*. In 1941, Balanchine's *Balustrade*, set to Stravinsky's Violin Concerto, inaugurated, as *Cotillon* had done almost a decade earlier, a new phase of his creativity and announced stylistic preferences that were to characterize his future opus.

Also of vital importance was the emergence of David Lichine as the first Russian choreographer to develop in the West outside of Diaghilev's direct influence. And although today only his *Graduation Ball* is popularly revived, he produced a series of works of strong theatricality and originality in *Francesca da Rimini*, *Protée*, *The Prodigal Son*, and *Cain and Abel*.

With more than seventy ballets in the repertory, including twenty Diaghilev revivals supervised by their creators and two Petipa classics presented in abbreviated form, de Basil's company offered a comprehensive overview of ballet history. With this repertory the company traveled unceasingly throughout Europe and the Americas, as well as the Australasian countries. De Basil presented long seasons in these countries' major theaters, in addition to exhausting one-night stands in small towns. Thus the company became, unlike Diaghilev's elite-supported company, a self-supporting enterprise. Wherever they went, balletic values were established and the seeds sown for future schools and companies.

In the thirties, at the height of the personality cult, the Ballets Russes dancers entered the star system. The "baby ballerinas"—Irina Baronova, Tatiana Riabouchinska, and Tamara Toumanova—along with Alexandra Danilova, Léonide Massine, and David Lichine, excited awe and breathless adoration, and became symbols of a dazzling glamour. Their names and photographs were featured daily in social columns and in illustrated magazines from London to Bombay, from New York to Buenos Aires; their travels were reported in the international press and in newsreels.

No other ballet company in history has achieved the international prominence of de Basil's Ballets Russes de Monte Carlo. In its heyday, the company was the darling of the international elite, to which it represented the epitome of cosmopolitanism and sophistication. This was especially true of the British, who tried to remain as insulated as possible from a deteriorating world economy and its politics, as evidenced by Baldwin's tenure as Prime Minister, the euphoria of London social and cultural life, the Royal Jubilee, and the Empire Exhibition. And for the ever-growing general public, ballet was the entrée to a world of fantasy. In an era marked by depression, mental breakdown, civil war, Nazism, fascism, and anarchy, the glamorous Ballets Russes seasons were an opiate. The aura of sophistication and decadence in *Cotillon*, the frothy comedy of *Le Beau Danube*, the fairy-tale romance of *Les Cent Baisers* and *Cendrillon*, the neo-Romanticism of *Symphonie fantastique*, and the exoticism and splendor of *Le Coq d'or* were a neutralizing antidote to the progressively darkening cultural, social, economic, and political attitudes that were to lead to war. Only *Les Présages*, although it offered a hero who struggles with evil and is victorious at the end, reflected the alienation, anxiety, and confusion of the decade. True to its title, it presaged the cataclysm that was to ignite on September 3, 1939. In the meantime, the Ballets Russes de Monte Carlo kept dancing on the rim of the volcano.

In the early years of World War II, the company performed in Australia and the United States, and from 1942 to 1946 they remained in Latin America. Between seasons in the opera houses of the various capital cities, they journeyed through the jungles in precarious conditions to dance in quasi-primitive environments. There was an almost missionary quality to these travels.

At the war's end the company returned to the United States and then to Europe, where it survived until 1949. They had returned to a changed world, one that no longer needed an international company. Nationalism had come into vogue. An era had ended.

Chronology of the Ballets Russes

1932	January 5–April 9	Participation in the opera season at the Théâtre de Monte Carlo
	April 12–May 5	First season at the Théâtre de Monte Carlo
	June 9–21	First Paris season, at the Théâtre des Champs-Elysées
	October 14–December 1	Tour of Belgium, Holland, Germany, and Switzerland
1933	January 5–April 9	Participation in the opera season at the Théâtre de Monte Carlo
	April 13–May 9	Théâtre de Monte Carlo
	May 12–21	First Barcelona season, at the Gran Teatre del Liceu
	June 9–30	Théâtre du Châtelet, Paris
	July 4–October 30	First London season, at the Alhambra Theatre
	November 6–9	Golders Green Hippodrome, London
	November 10–December 9	Tour of England
	December 22	American debut at the St. James Theater, New York; beginning of first American tour
1934	January–April	American tour
	April 5–May	Division of the company into two groups. Second group, with Serge Grigoriev as régisseur and Bronislava Nijinska as choreographer, presents a season at the Théâtre de Monte Carlo
	May 9–25	Reunion of the two groups at the Gran Teatre del Liceu, Barcelona
	May 28–June 16	Théâtre des Champs-Elysées, Paris
	June 19–August 11	Royal Opera House, Covent Garden, London
	September 25–October 17	Inauguration of the Palacio de Bellas Artes, Mexico City. First Mexican season
	October 25–November–	Tour of Canada
1935	March	Tour of United States
	April 4–May 2	Théâtre de Monte Carlo
	May 3–26	Tour of Spain
	June 11–July 25	Royal Opera House, Covent Garden, London
	October 9–20	Metropolitan Opera House, New York
	October 21–	Tour of United States, Canada, and Cuba, including a second season
1936	May 8	at the Metropolitan Opera House
	May 19–June 7	Gran Teatre del Liceu, Barcelona
	June 15–July 29	Royal Opera House, Covent Garden, London
	October 1–15	Scala Theatre, Berlin
	October 29–November 8	Metropolitan Opera House, New York

	November 9–	
1937	April 13	Tour of the United States and Canada, including a season at the Metropolitan Opera House (April 9–13)
	May 5–19	Maggio Musicale, Florence
	June 9, 17	Collaboration with the Covent Garden Opera, Royal Opera House, Covent Garden, London
	July 1–31	Summer season at the Royal Opera House, Covent Garden, London
	September 6–October 9	Fall season at the Royal Opera House, Covent Garden, London
	October 21–31	Metropolitan Opera House, New York
	November 1–	
1938	March 11	Tour of United States and Canada
	March 28–April 30	Scala Theatre, Berlin
	May 1–5	Copenhagen
	June 18–August 13	Royal Opera House, Covent Garden, London
	September–	
1939	April	Theatre Royal, Sydney, followed by tour of Australia and New Zealand
	May 10–11	McKinley Auditorium, Honolulu
	June 12–July 29	Royal Opera House, Covent Garden, London
	December 30–	
1940	August	Theatre Royal, Sydney, followed by tour of Australia and New Zealand
1941	March	Tour of United States and Canada
	March 6–14	Palacio de Bellas Artes, Mexico City
	March 20–April 1	Teatro Auditorio, Havana
	June 25–26	Teatro Auditorio, Havana
	August 23–November 10	Tour of United States and Canada
1942	January 5–27	Palacio de Bellas Artes, Mexico City, and Teatro Degollado, Guadalajara
	April 10–May 25	Teatro Municipal, Rio de Janeiro, and Teatro Municipal, São Paulo
	June 12–July 12	Teatro Politeama Argentino, Buenos Aires
	July 15–August 2	Teatro S.O.D.R.E., Montevideo
	August 5–27	Tour of Argentina (Teatro Municipal, Rosario; Teatro Rivera Indarte, Córdoba; Teatro Municipal, Mendoza)
	September 1–October 4	Teatro Municipal, Santiago de Chile, and Teatro Municipal, Viña del Mar
	October 15–November 28	Teatro Colón, Buenos Aires
	December 4–	
1943	January 11	Teatro Griego, Córdoba
	January 16–February 16	Teatro Municipal, Viña del Mar
	March 14–April 4	Teatro Municipal, Lima
	April 13–18	Teatro Municipal, La Paz
	April 22–November 28	Teatro Colón, Buenos Aires, as part of the permanent company under the direction of Colonel de Basil

	December 29–	
1944	March 31	Teatro Municipal de Verano, Montevideo
	April 10–June 21	Teatro Municipal, São Paulo, and Teatro Municipal, Rio de Janeiro
	June 30–July 20	Teatro S.O.D.R.E., Montevideo
	July 28–October 1	Teatro Avenida, Buenos Aires
	October 2–9	Teatro Municipal, Santa Fe, and Teatro Municipal, Rosario
	October 11–17	Teatro Municipal, Santiago de Chile
	December 16–	
1945	January 16	Teatro Municipal, Lima
	January 30–February 24	Teatro Nueve de Octubre, Guayaquil, and Teatro Municipal, Quito
	March 6–June 20	Tour of Colombia (Teatro del Colón, Bogotá; Teatro Bolívar, Medellín; Teatro Apolo, Barranquilla; Teatro Heredia, Cartagena)
	July 1–August 19	Teatro Municipal, Caracas
	September 2–October 13	Teatro Nacional, Panama, and Colon
	October 15–November 9	Teatro Nacional, San José, Costa Rica
	November 11–13	Tegucigalpa, Honduras
	November 14–December 3	Teatro Municipal, San Salvador, and Teatro Municipal, Santa Ana
	December 4–31	Teatro Lux, Guatemala
1946	January–April	Palacio de Bellas Artes, Mexico City, followed by tour of Mexico: Monterrey, Laredo, Guadalajara, Vera Cruz, Jalapa
	May	Teatro Auditorio, Havana
	June 10–July 10	Teatro Municipal, Rio de Janeiro
	July 18–August 4	Teatro Municipal, São Paulo
	September 29–October 23	Metropolitan Opera House, New York: three Sunday programs (matinées and evenings) on October 27, November 3, and November 10
	October–	
1947	March	Last tour of United States
	March 20–29	Last season at the Metropolitan Opera House, New York
	July 22–September 14	Royal Opera House, Covent Garden, London
	October 7–17	Palais de Chaillot, Paris
	October 18–23	Théâtre Alhambra, Brussels
1948	April 21–June 30	Gran Teatre Liceu, Barcelona, and tour of Spain
	July 5–15	Coliseu Theatre, Lisbon
	July 20–November 8	Tour of Spain
	November 8	Final performance: Sala Augusta, Mallorca

Lineage of the Ballets Russes Companies

1909–1929   *Ballets Russes de Serge Diaghilev*

1929–1932   *Théâtre du Casino de Monte Carlo (Société des Bains de Mer)* and *Ballet of the Opéra Russe à Paris*

1932   *Les Ballets Russes de Monte Carlo*
Directors: René Blum and Col. W. de Basil
Artistic Advisor: Boris Kochno
Maître de Ballet and Choreographer: George Balanchine

1933 London   *Ballets Russes de Monte Carlo*
Director General: Col. W. de Basil
Artistic Director: René Blum
New York   *Monte Carlo Ballet Russe*

1934 London   *Ballets Russes de Col. W. de Basil*
Director General: Col. W. de Basil
Artistic Director: René Blum
Maître de Ballet and Artistic Collaborator: Léonide Massine
(Col. de Basil's act of putting his own name on the company caused the breach between him and René Blum)
New York   *Monte Carlo Ballet Russe*

1935 London   *Ballets Russes de Col. W. de Basil* or *Col. W. de Basil's Ballets Russes*
Founder and Director General: Col. W. de Basil
Maître de Ballet and Artistic Collaborator: Léonide Massine
New York   *Monte Carlo Ballet Russe*

DE BASIL'S COMPANY

1936 London   as in 1935
New York   *Col. W. de Basil's Ballets Russes*

1937 London   as in 1935
New York   *Col. W. de Basil's Ballet Russe*
        (de Monte Carlo)

1938 London   *Russian Ballet*, presented by
        Educational Ballets, Ltd.
        Directors: Victor Dandré
          (Chairman), W. G. Perkins,
          G. Sebastianov (Managing
          Director)
Australia   *Covent Garden Russian Ballet*,
        presented by Educational
        Ballets, Ltd.

1939 London   *Covent Garden Russian Ballet*,
        presented by Educational
        Ballets, Ltd.
Australia   *Original Ballet Russe**
        Director: Col. W. de Basil

* *This name remained in effect until the company disbanded in 1951.*

BLUM'S COMPANY

1936   *Ballets de Monte Carlo*
        Founder and Director: René Blum
        Maître de Ballet and
          Choreographer: Michel Fokine

1938   *Ballet Russe de Monte Carlo*
        Founder and Director: René Blum
        Artistic Director: Léonide Massine
        Managing Director: Serge Denham

The Ballets Russes

Monte Carlo, 1932: The company with Blum, Miró, and de Basil.

August 1929–
December 1932

> I do not think the Ballet will long survive. There is all the machinery, but no driving force. The man who built the machine is dead. . . .
>
> Without the puppet master who pulls the strings the members of the ballet are only lifeless toys.
>
> The puppets are sad little things just now.
>
> *Daily Express* (London),
> August 21, 1929

WHEN Serge Diaghilev died in Venice on August 19, 1929, Léonide Massine was working as a soloist and ballet master at S. L. Rothafel's Roxy Theatre in New York. Not long afterward, the choreographer was approached by the impresario E. Ray Goetz of Theatrical Attractions and Cole Porter, who had introduced Massine to Goetz, with the idea that Massine should take charge of the Ballets Russes and bring it to the United States. Although (according to Massine's then wife, Eugenia Delarova) Rothafel tried to dissuade him, the choreographer and Goetz, who was interested in backing the venture, persisted. Through Massine's contacts, Goetz was able to acquire most of Diaghilev's sets and costumes. By 1930, rumors of Massine's plan were all over New York, and John Martin, the dance critic of the *New York Times*, wrote to Massine inquiring about the possibility of forming a company "to reproduce the greatest successes of Diaghilev with American dancers."[1] The plans never materialized, however, and as a result of the Wall Street crash, Goetz wrote to Massine explaining that he preferred to wait until conditions improved.[2]

Typically, though, Massine did not give up. In 1931 he approached his European connections, including Sir Thomas Beecham and one of his highest hopes, René Blum, who was in charge of organizing the ballet seasons at the Casino de Monte Carlo.

The Depression had scarcely affected the principality of Monaco, and since Diaghilev's death, Blum had tried to fulfill his contract with the Société des Bains de Mer—the joint-stock company that owned the Casino—by hiring individual dancers and ballet companies. Nevertheless, Massine's proposal was turned down, indicating that, contrary to what many historians have stated,[3] Blum and Raoul Gunsbourg, director of the Casino Theatre, were not eager to revive the Ballets Russes. In a letter to Massine of July 8, 1931, Blum wrote of his skepticism about the idea of putting together the scattered remains of Diaghilev's company:

> The more I think about it, the more I recognize the unseemliness of an organization that would be nothing more than an extension of the former Diaghilev ballet without Diaghilev himself—that is to say, without the prestige of the wonderful man who created it and who was able to keep it going for fifteen years in Monte Carlo in the face of all adversity. Besides, I have explored the possibilities, and I have put the question to some people in Monaco; their response has been the same: give us something else.[4]

4

A month later, Blum wrote again to Massine: "A series of Diaghilev ballets is what I would like to avoid at all costs."[5]

A number of ballets had been produced on the Continent since Diaghilev's death in 1929, but they were isolated attempts lacking a cohesive aesthetic, and they represented nothing more than a repetition of the Diaghilev formula. Until her death in 1931, Anna Pavlova presented a series of seasons designed mainly as a showcase for her own talents. Ida Rubinstein had presented Massine's *Amphion*, to music of Honegger, at the Paris Opéra on June 22, 1931, the same year that Bronislava Nijinska joined the Opéra Russe à Paris.* Also in 1931, the Paris Opéra produced three Serge Lifar ballets: *Le Prélude dominical et six pièces à danser* (Ropartz), *L'Orchestre en liberté* (Sauveplane), and *Bacchus et Ariane* (Roussel). These works represented Lifar's attempt to develop a personal style, which he elaborated in his treatise *Le Manifeste du chorégraphe* (1935). The only other subsidized ballet company in Europe, Milan's La Scala ballet, relied on some Diaghilev revivals from the Fokine period or commissioned lavish spectacles such as Massine's *Belkis* (Respighi). The Royal Danish

---

*The Opéra Russe à Paris was founded in 1925 by the Russian singer Maria Kousnetsova and her second husband, Alfred Massenet (a nephew of the composer). Kousnetsova had created the non-singing role of Potiphar's Wife in the 1914 Diaghilev production of Richard Strauss's *The Legend of Joseph*. The Opéra Russe à Paris was disbanded in 1940.

Ballet, which was confined to its home base, relied solely on its Auguste Bournonville repertory. In England the first pioneering efforts to establish a permanent ballet company got under way with the inaugural dinner of the Camargo Society in 1930, with Adeline Genée presiding. Also in 1930, Marie Rambert's students produced the first works by Frederick Ashton and Susan Salaman at the Lyric Theatre, Hammersmith. In October the Camargo Society produced Ashton's *Pomona,* and the following year the Ballet Club was formed by Marie Rambert. Under Ninette de Valois, a permanent company, the Vic-Wells Ballet, was established at the Sadler's Wells, with Lydia Lopokova and Anton Dolin as guest artists.

In the spring of 1931, the ballet of the Opéra Russe à Paris was one of the dance attractions presented at the Casino. (Other attractions included Vicente Escudero, the Paris Opéra Ballet, the Boris Kniaseff Ballet, and Uday Shankar.) The Opéra Russe at the time had two directors: Prince Alexis Zereteli, a former manager of the People's Theatre in St. Petersburg, and Colonel W. de Basil, whose real name was Vassily Grigorievitch Voskresensky. The company was being represented by Zerbazon, a theatrical agency founded in 1925 by Zereteli, de Basil, and Ignaty Zon, a Russian émigré who had owned a *café chantant* in Moscow before the Revolution.

Nijinska had originally joined the Opéra Russe in the summer of 1930 to choreograph the ballet sequences in the operas *Ruslan et Ludmila, Rusalka,* and *Sadko,* and to create works for the all-ballet evenings that alternated with evenings of opera. For the Opéra Russe she created *Capriccio Espagnol* and *Etude* and staged her *Les Noces* and *Les Biches,* as well as Fokine's *Petrouchka,* in which she increased the virtuosity of the ballerina's variation, which she danced herself. During the 1931 Monte Carlo season, the leading dancers were Felia Doubrovska, Anatol Oboukhov, and Boris Romanov, who also replaced Nijinska as ballet master. He choreographed *Chout* (Prokofiev), *L'Amour sorcier* (de Falla), and a new version of Stravinsky's *Pulcinella.*

It was during this period that Blum and de Basil started to discuss the possibility of organizing a ballet company based in Monte Carlo. De Basil offered Blum the nucleus of a company (the Opéra Russe), with dancers, repertory, scenery, and costumes. In return, Blum was to provide the theater and its facilities and the financial support of the Société des Bains de Mer. According to Boris Kochno, who had been Diaghilev's secretary and librettist throughout the twenties, de Basil also offered to find patrons to support the enterprise. Their aim was to join forces to create an entirely new company—in fact, the early negotiations made no mention of a new "Ballets Russes," but spoke only of the "Ballets de Monte Carlo."[6] George Balanchine, who was to become ballet master, strongly objected to including the word "Russe" in the name of the new venture,[7] and Massine, in a letter to de Basil, said that he was pleased that de Basil had decided upon the title "Ballets de Monte Carlo."[8] As late as January 1932, a contract was signed between the Opéra Russe and the Société des Ballets de Monte Carlo, a subsidiary of the Société des Bains de Mer, by which the opera company would donate all its ballet scenery, costumes, and properties to the Ballets de Monte Carlo.[9] The Opéra Russe also forfeited its right to produce any future ballets and was bound not to interfere with the success of the newly organized

5

ballet company. When and how de Basil persuaded Blum to change the name to "Ballets Russes de Monte Carlo" is unclear. It was not until April 20, 1932, that both men registered a corporation in Monaco, and even then the identity of the enterprise was ambiguous, since it was registered as "La Société des Ballets Russes de Monte Carlo et Ballets de Monte Carlo."

From the beginning de Basil acted as impresario. His office in Paris at 16, rue de Gramont—previously the headquarters of Zerbazon—now became the unofficial base of the Ballets Russes, whose official address in Paris was 60, rue de la Chaussée-d'Antin. As soon as word of the new company spread in the city, dancers flocked to rue de Gramont to inquire about positions; from there they were sent to audition for Balanchine at the Théâtre Mogador, where the choreographer was staging *Orphée aux enfers*. Upon acceptance, they returned to de Basil's office to sign a contract.

The nucleus of the new company consisted of former members of the Diaghilev Ballets Russes. Serge Grigoriev was offered a contract on October 12, 1931 (on an Opéra Russe letterhead), to serve until the end of the season as "régisseur général" (a position he had held for twenty years with Diaghilev) at a salary of 4,000 francs a month. Boris Kochno was retained on November 16 for a six-month period in the capacity of "conseiller artistique" at 3,000 francs a month, and Balanchine was contracted on December 7 as "maître de ballet," to begin on January 4 for a period of four months at 10,000 francs a month.[10] (Kochno and Balanchine had already been working in these capacities since the end of that summer, before either had signed a contract.)

In spite of a contract (dated December 28) that guaranteed Nijinska unprecedented privileges, including first-class transportation, the sum of 30,000 francs, plus 10,000 francs as shareholder of the Société des Ballets Russes de Monte Carlo, in return for creating two original works for the spring season, she rejected the offer,[11] so Balanchine was the highest-salaried employee. His contract stipulated that he was to create whatever ballets and opera ballets were required; ultimately he made four new works and eighteen opera ballets. Nijinska's refusal stemmed from her plans to organize her own "Ballets Nijinska," which performed at the Opéra-Comique in Paris during May and June 1932.[12] De Basil's unusually generous offer may thus have been an attempt to eliminate a possible competitor. Massine, too, was coaxed into agreeing to create two new ballets, of which only *Jeux d'enfants* was produced.

By November 1931, most of the company had already been assembled in Paris under the direction of Balanchine. The French capital was then the dance center of Europe. There were a number of studios where celebrated dancers, many of them from the former Imperial Ballets of St. Petersburg and Moscow, conducted their classes: Olga Preobrajenskaya, Mathilda Kchessinskaya, Lubov Egorova, Alexandre Volinine. Most of the dancers who joined the post-Diaghilev Ballets Russes were the direct product of the Russian school via these émigrés established in Paris. In spite of their extreme youth, many possessed a highly polished classical technique and had already had some professional experience on the stage. Three of these youngsters were to become the pillars of the company: Tamara Toumanova (born in 1919),

Les Sylphides, Monte Carlo, 1932: Blinova, Lichine, and Toumanova with the corps de ballet.

Tatiana Riabouchinska (1917), and Irina Baronova (1919). They were joined by a number of former Diaghilev dancers, including Leon Woizikowski, Marian Ladré, Lara Obidenna, Tatiana Chamié, Eleonora Marra, Nathalie Branitska, Jean Hoyer, and others. During the first Monte Carlo season, Felia Doubrovska was engaged as a guest ballerina.

On April 12, 1932, the Ballets Russes de Monte Carlo opened, under the patronage of the Princess of Monaco, with a program consisting of *Les Sylphides, Cotillon,* and *La Concurrence.*

In Monte Carlo the repertory consisted of revivals of *Les Sylphides, Petrouchka, Swan Lake* Act II,* *Chout, Pulcinella, L'Amour sorcier,* and five new works: *Suites de*

*De Basil's company presented Act II of *Swan Lake* as it was performed in the full-length Petipa-Ivanov production. In the Diaghilev production different numbers from the rest of the ballet were incorporated in the second act; the pas de trois from the first act especially had become a standard addition. Now, when Balanchine staged it (assisted by Doubrovska, who as guest ballerina danced the lead), he dropped all the additions and restored it to the original choreography, or at least the standard choreography from the Maryinsky. This was probably the first time that the complete second act was seen in Europe. The cast included the Huntsmen, the Prince, and his friend. In the pas de deux, Odette was partnered alternately by the Prince and his friend. Odette wore a short classical tutu, while the corps de ballet was dressed in traditional knee-length tutus.

Toumanova, Lichine, and Riabouchinska rehearsing *Les Sylphides* in the studio of the Monte Carlo Theater, 1932.

8

danses, Cotillon, La Concurrence, Le Bourgeois Gentilhomme, and *Jeux d'enfants.* Balanchine's *Suites des danses* to music of Glinka had its premiere on May 5 and was performed only three times during the season; owing to budget difficulties, it was presented without scenery and danced in practice tutus. When Balanchine left, it vanished from the repertory.

News of the success of the company's first season spread throughout Europe. Ernest Ansermet, the conductor of the Orchestre de la Suisse Romande, wrote to Kochno on May 12 to explore the feasibility of appearances by the company in Geneva and Lausanne.[13] It was not difficult for de Basil to arrange a European tour, beginning in Paris at the Théâtre des Champs-Elysées.

On opening night, June 9, the auditorium was filled with diplomats, members of society, painters, musicians, writers, and critics. The company performed as if possessed: *Le Bourgeois Gentilhomme, La Concurrence,* and *Cotillon,* with Balanchine on the catwalk encouraging the dancers. The audience was ecstatic and reviews rapturous. The new Ballets Russes had conquered Paris, just as Diaghilev's company had twenty-three years earlier.

At the end of the Paris engagement, the company was to suffer its first major defection. According to Boris Kochno, following the triumph in Monte Carlo Blum and de Basil became dictatorial about their views and began to credit the success of the season to themselves. The directors' attitude led to a series of disagreements with Blum and (especially) de Basil over artistic decisions, and Balanchine and Kochno left the company in Paris. Their contracts had already expired by then. Nonetheless, both were to cooperate with de Basil in the future, Kochno sporadically from 1934 to 1937 and Balanchine in 1941. It is also possible that by then de Basil was already planning to hire Massine as ballet master and choreographer. Despite Balanchine's success with his 1932 creations, Massine was then the most famous name as choreographer and was at his prime as performer. For de Basil, Massine represented a threat. During the Monte Carlo season he had kept himself distant and had not been able to attend the premiere of his *Jeux d'enfants,* nor any of its subsequent performances in Monte Carlo or Paris. Massine was busy in London trying to organize a permanent ballet company at Covent Garden in association with Thomas Beecham. If de Basil was to follow Diaghilev's footsteps and take London by storm, he needed to distract Massine from his plans.

From Paris the company traveled to Belgium, Holland, Germany, and Switzerland in buses that were filled to capacity, with costumes stacked on the roofs.[14] Morning classes were conducted by Madame Lubov Tchernicheva at the side of the road, the dancers using cattle railings as barres—which must have presented a perplexing spectacle for those driving past on the highway!

The final engagement was in Switzerland, from November 28 through December 1, under the auspices of the Société de l'Orchestre de la Suisse Romande, conducted by Ansermet. Working with one of Diaghilev's former music directors generated great excitement among the dancers, but there was excitement of another kind as well. Kochno and Balanchine were in Paris organizing their new venture, Les

9

Reception for the company in the casino studio. Starting at third from left: Balanchine, Doubrovska, Kochno.

Ballets 33, and company gossip centered on the possibility of defections. Although those who intended to leave were secretive, it was obvious that Toumanova was the most likely threat. There were no more doubts when the role of the ballerina in *Petrouchka*—which she had monopolized until then—was passed to Riabouchinska on the last day of the Swiss engagement.

After the final performance—*Les Sylphides, Petrouchka,* and *Jeux d'enfants*—with Riabouchinska dancing in all three ballets, the company immediately returned to France for a holiday. The future now seemed more certain. Soon the preparations for a new season in Monte Carlo would be under way.

10

The Monte Carlo Theater illuminated for a gala performance.

COTILLON

Ballet in one act; music by Emmanuel Chabrier, orchestrated by Chabrier, Felix Mottl, and Vittorio Rieti; libretto by Boris Kochno; choreography by George Balanchine; set and costume design by Christian Bérard; sets executed by Prince A. Schervachidze; women's costumes executed by Madame Karinska, men's costumes by Lidvall; premiere April 12, 1932, at the Théâtre de Monte Carlo, conducted by Pierre Kolpikoff.

ORIGINAL CAST

La Toilette (The Toilette)
 Daughter of the House Tamara Toumanova
 Her Friend Nathalie Strakhova
 The First Guest David Lichine[1]

Les Présentations (The Introductions)
 Mistress of Ceremonies Valentina Blinova[2]
 Guests Mlles Blanc, Chabelska, Kirsova,
     Kervily, Marra, Morosova,
     Obidenna, Slavinska, Sonne,
     Tresahar, and Verchinina
   MM. Dolotine, Guérard, Katchourovsky,
     Ladré, Petroff, and Shabelevsky
 Master of Ceremonies Leon Woizikowski

"Le Jardin des Plaisirs" Valentina Blinova,
(The Pleasure Garden) Leon Woizikowski,
     and ensemble

Danse des Chapeaux, des Arlequins, des
Jockeys, des Espagnoles (The Dance of Hats,
Harlequins, Jockeys, and Spaniards)
    Mlles Toumanova, Strakhova,
       and Branitska;
  Kirsova, Morosova, and Tresahar

"Les Mains du Destin" Lubov Rostova and
(The Hand of Fate) Valentine Froman

"La Lanterne Magique" Mlles Toumanova,
(The Magic Lantern) Blinova, and Rostova
   MM. Froman and Lichine
     and ensemble

"Grand Rond" et Fin du Cotillon Ensemble
(Grand Rond and End of Cotillion)

Cotillon was the first ballet scheduled for rehearsal in the winter of 1931. According to Kochno, discussions had begun early that fall in Paris. Kochno had written the libretto, chosen the music with Balanchine, and commissioned the costumes and decor from Christian Bérard. This sort of close collaboration would characterize most of the company's productions.

Music For the new ballet Kochno and Balanchine chose a series of piano pieces by the late-nineteenth-century composer Emmanuel Chabrier and set the action in the period of the music. Most of the pieces used in *Cotillon*—with the exception of the "Valse romantique"—derived from Chabrier's piano suite *Dix Pièces pittoresques,* published in 1881: "Menuet pompeux," "Tourbillon," "Mauresque," "Scherzo-Valse," "Idylle," and "Danse villageoise" (now retitled "Danse rustique"). Three of these pieces—"Idylle" (which both Francis Poulenc and pianist Alfred Cortot called the real jewel of the collection), "Scherzo-Valse," and "Danse villageoise"—had been orchestrated by Chabrier for his *Suite pastorale.* Vittorio Rieti was commissioned to orchestrate "Menuet pompeux," "Tourbillon," and "Mauresque." The "Valse romantique" (the third of the *Trois valses romantiques*) had been previously orchestrated by Felix Mottl.

Action The action of *Cotillon* takes place at a ball and consists of eight scenes depicting various events and interactions among the guests. The "Menuet pompeux" begins as an overture in front of the closed curtain and continues as accompaniment to the first two scenes.

The curtain rises to display a marble room with a single line of floor-level boxes draped with red valances, all decorated in red and gold; the only furniture is a few gilt chairs. The Daughter of the House, in a lavender dress, stands on a gilt stool in the middle of the room, gazing at herself in a hand mirror while a friend helps her finish the last touches of her toilette. Through the mirror she observes the arrival of the First Guest, a man in a pink hunting-coat; she bends backwards, into his arms. He expresses his admiration for the daughter but is interrupted by the arrival of the other guests. The young girl quickly leaves the room as if intimidated by the presence of the arriving guests.

The Mistress of Ceremonies enters, wearing a romantic tutu with a black velvet bodice and an ankle-length yellow skirt appliquéd with musical notes and clefs. A baton in her hand, she introduces the guests—male guests to female guests—who are scattered around the ballroom.

As the "Tourbillon" begins, the Master of Ceremonies arrives late and in a disheveled state; he makes a careless, absentminded introduction by swooping around inside the circle formed by the guests. Clasping his hands to his head, he collapses onto a chair that is placed beneath him, then jumps up and relapses mechanically before returning to his social duties.

The Mistress and Master of Ceremonies initiate the first dance ("Mauresque"), which is repeated by the guests in a semicircle around the couple. Six couples come center stage. The Mistress and Master of Ceremonies—she is upstage (closer to the audience), baton in hand, back to the audience; he is downstage, facing her—arrange the couples in four lines with three women and three men in each line, the men facing the Master of Ceremonies, and the women, in the opposite direction, facing the Mistress of Ceremonies. They all cover their eyes with their right hand before dancing in circles and semicircles around the Mistress and Master of Ceremonies, who remain center stage, conducting the dance with their hands and supervising the steps.

To the "Scherzo-Valse," the cotillion proper begins. The guests receive party favors—hats and guitars—which provide an excuse for several dances. The dancers assume the characters of harlequins, jockeys, and Spaniards by donning the appropriate hats. First the Daughter of the House performs a "harlequin" pas de trois with her friend and the First Guest, the ladies in spangled hoods and the man with a two-pointed hat. The daughter, to the thematic repetition within the first musical subject, takes a guitar and, with both hands extended above her head, dances a variation consisting of intricate toework with little hops. The First Guest leaps from the center box as two other guests leap from the side boxes. As jockeys they gallop around the stage, leaping in and out of the boxes, and in center stage they perform a dance simulating riding movements and pass their hats to one another. Finally, the dancers don matador's hats and play guitars; as they finish, and all the guests leave the stage, two men bring in a pale blue drape to cover the center box.

From behind the drape four pairs of white-gloved hands are extended ("Idylle"). A Cavalier approaches the curtain in slow steps into arabesque with his hands against his thighs. He is about to choose a partner when a black-gloved hand appears and grabs him by the wrist. A mysterious woman comes forward, wearing a black costume appliquéd with silver stars and a silver half-moon on her head, a mask covering her eyes. The two dance as if spellbound by the mysterious atmosphere of the empty ballroom and their anonymous encounter. Sono Osato described the pas de deux:

> She lifted her leg in a slow, high developpé and then lowered it. He did the same. She repeated the motion; he did too. The languid overlapping of their legs was then changed into flat-footed steps as they faced each other, first shuffling away, their torsos arched backwards and arms touching each other's wrists, then coming towards each other as their backs flattened upright, coming together chin to chin.[3]

As the pas de deux draws to a close, the man, bewitched, does not seem to see the woman. She places her hand on his head as if to dominate the blankness of expression, and draws him out of the ballroom.

The Daughter of the House crosses the stage in two diagonals of grands jetés ("Valse romantique"). The female guests return to the ballroom and sit in a semicircle. The daughter performs a series of grandes pirouettes inside the semicircle, going from one group to the next until she arrives at the last. She sits on the floor and takes the hand of the nearest girl in hers to tell the fortune. After reading her palm, the daughter points, with an enigmatic, foreboding look, to the other side of the stage, where the mysterious woman and her partner reappear, the woman simulating the movements of a bat. Her partner runs away, frightened by the vision. The Daughter of the House, seeking a sympathetic soul, is drawn to the Mistress of Ceremonies. Their movements mirror their contrasting personalities: while the girl is direct and candid, the Mistress of Ceremonies is sophisticated and aloof and dances a variation that consists of jumps in arabesque, landing in arabesque right and left. The Daughter of the House runs in front and behind the guests resting onstage, and finding her affection unrequited, exits into a black box.

The First Guest appears, masked, holding a glass of champagne and slightly inebriated. He falls behind a screen, and when it is removed, he has vanished.

The men, puzzled by his disappearance, run around in search of their drunken friend ("Danse rustique") and leave the stage by pirouetting off the left side. As the last guests leave, the Daughter of the House walks in from the back, and in center stage, all alone, she begins a series of grandes pirouettes on pointe. The rest of the guests return and circle around her, holding hands. She continues to revolve as the curtain falls. A. V. Coton describes the final scene:

> As the coda is elaborated the guests wander off towards destinations which cannot be imagined, and as the last of them goes the Young Girl walks slowly into the centre stage[;] as the music winds into a fugue-like figure she spins a series of fouettés madder and swifter than any of the earlier movement in the work. The guests suddenly reappear, run to her, sweep into a circular formation around her as she slows her spinning, then rises on

13

to the points, and eases her movement exactly as the music elides from fugue to the final bars. The revolving circle slows and slows, precisely counterpointing her moves in an alternate direction; the visual and aural images are perfectly fused, as the final bars sigh away and the curtain gradually creeps down. . . .[4]

*Choreog-
raphy*

The action of *Cotillon* caused a great deal of puzzlement. For many critics its narrative seemed obscure; they could not identify the characters and the action in realistic terms. Coton wrote: "The guests are a convocation of other-worldly figures, and in every dance figure created there is an expectancy implied but never defined, of some eventuality whose importance to these unreal figures is immense, but completely unguessable to us, the audience."[5] It was a *ballet d'atmosphère,* full of nuances reflecting the moods of the music. It conjured up the aura of seduction of an aristocratic ballroom.

Kochno's libretto was based on a sort of action montage of interlocking dance episodes that attempted to express the various feelings portrayed by the dancers. The aim was to capture the evanescent atmosphere of emotions played one against the other. Coton wrote:

14

> The cotillion development, the solemn dances, the incident of the reading of hands, the tragic lyric of the lost couple who dance together in the absence of the other guests, the sudden confusing apparition of the Suitor, masked and drunk, imply a terroristic *motif* never directly expressed, or more than faintly suggested, by the sense content of the situation choreographically unfolded. By implication, infinities of action and contemplation exist in these shadowy figures. All the dreariness of elaborate pomp, the suave politeness, the sensuous poetry of motion suddenly revealed in irrelevancies of beautiful action, the tragedy of unrealized love, and the agony of enforced solitude, all occur simply as illuminations to the plotless phases of action, as one watches the inevitability of the unfolding of a series of attitudes and reactions—never a plot progression—towards a never revealed conclusion.[6]

It was a major step in a new aesthetic approach to choreography: bringing dance forward as the essential element of the ballet. This was a reaction particularly against the Diaghilev company's final period, when dance was often the weakest element of a production—a situation for which Kochno himself had been largely responsible. André Levinson had criticized this period for being more concerned with decor than with dancing: "The new ballet, pretentious but poor in content, naturally seeks support in the other arts. Having improved its form and tradition, having shifted its center of gravity from dance to pantomime, the new ballet . . . tried to borrow its missing significance from painting and music."[7]

Both of Kochno's libretti for 1932, *Cotillon* and *Jeux d'enfants,* lacked detailed

LEFT: "La Toilette": Toumanova, Strakhova, and Balanchine. BELOW: Lichine, Toumanova, and Strakhova. BOTTOM: Riabouchinska and corps.

ABOVE: The Jockeys: Ladré, Lichine, and Katchourovsky.
BELOW: "Hand of Fate" pas de deux: Froman and Rostova.

16

ABOVE: Toumanova and corps. BELOW: Riabouchinska,
Shabelevsky, and corps.

stories, thus allowing the choreographers to create ballets consistently set in terms of dance. While in the previous dramatic ballets both mime and dance were subordinated to the plot or to a generalized expressivity, these new libretti subjugated mime and story to dance. Kochno himself viewed *Cotillon* and *Jeux d'enfants* as a significant change: "With *Pas d'acier* in 1927, the story was so intricate that the public had to follow the long program notes to understand the action. My first attempt toward a clearer idea was *Prodigal Son* in 1929. Here I was dealing with a story that is well known. This made the action accessible to the audience in general. Afterward, I felt that my future scenarios should be based more on the visual terms of painting and dance alone." The new type of scenario created by Kochno was especially congenial to Balanchine, whose predilection for choreography independent of plot was already evident in *Apollon Musagète*.

Cotillon was significant, too, for re-establishing the importance of the female dancer, who had often been overshadowed in the later days of the Diaghilev ballet. This emphasis on the ballerina was something of a revelation in 1932. The variety of female personalities in the new company enabled the choreographer to depict and explore several different female roles. The young Toumanova especially, with her charismatic personality and technical command, served as a creative instrument for Balanchine. Her series of grandes pirouettes on pointe in *Cotillon* caused as much awe and admiration in the Paris of 1932 as Legnani's thirty-two fouettés had in the St. Petersburg of 1893.

Scenery and Costumes

Adding immeasurably to *Cotillon*'s special atmosphere were the sets and costumes by Christian Bérard. His career as a theatrical designer had begun in 1930, when he created the scenery and costumes for Lifar's *La Nuit* for a Cochran revue in London. He also contributed to Cocteau's *La Voix humaine* at the Comédie Française that same year. The success of *Cotillon* was a turning point for the young artist, who was to become one of the most influential French theatrical designers.

The set consisted of a ballroom with marble walls and a floor-level loge on each side of the stage, all ornamented in red and gold. There were several gilt chairs and stools and a four-panel folding screen, each panel decorated with medallions of gloved hands holding envelopes or tarot cards. The center box was framed by a pair of two-panel screens of painted black-and-gold lattice with medallions of horses' heads.

The women wore dresses with velvet bodices and ankle-length tulle skirts, appliquéd with barely perceptible sequins. The skirts of the Daughter of the House and her friend were studded with small stars. The skirts combined many layers of different shades of the same color as the bodice. Only the Mistress of Ceremonies wore two colors—a black bodice and a yellow skirt appliquéd with musical notes and clefs. The mysterious woman was dressed all in black with black gloves. All the other women wore elbow-length white gloves. The men wore coats of scarlet, yellow, or green with white shirts, white bow ties, and black satin breeches and black knee-socks and shoes.

The designs for the sets and costumes avoided any strict period specificity in order to enhance the abstraction of the action. Coton complimented Bérard's achievement: "We shall remember the brocaded chairs and the discreet alcoves of the ballroom, the silk coats and the knee-breeches of the men, the sea-green, lemon, cyclamen, rose, and lime of the brilliant net dresses of the women, their fans, their gloves—but we know nothing of any period or place to which they belong. As creation of atmosphere—in the absolute sense, not an atmosphere of a time or place—nothing else in Ballet compares with *Cotillon*. Decor and dress have perfectly expanded the choreographic idioms of motion, gesture, stasis, into this revelation of a ghostly assembly going about its ghostly business, away from the comprehension of men."[8]

Also contributing to the atmosphere was Kochno's sophisticated lighting design. From the time of his first exposure to ballet, lighting had seemed to him a liaison between the music and the choreography. It was he who was responsible for Diaghilev's emphasis on elaborate experimental illumination in the twenties. Until then, Diaghilev had preferred (with a few exceptions, such as *Firebird*) that ballets be lit as brightly as paintings. For *Cotillon*, Kochno hoped to create a design that would enhance the light and shadow of the music and, consequently, enhance the choreography. He used mild amber lights; but for the sake of atmosphere, to create a feeling of intimacy and isolated corners, the boxes were lit from within. Unfortunately, since the photographic techniques of the 1930s required bright lights, photographs from the period fail to capture the subtlety of the lighting effects.

Rehearsals   Rehearsals for *Cotillon* began in Paris in December 1931. When the company arrived in Monte Carlo at the start of the new year, most of the choreography had been completed, though, according to Toumanova, the episodes had not yet been assembled in their proper sequence. In fact, the first scene was the last to be staged. The final rehearsals in Monte Carlo were conducted in the theater's practice room, with Kochno, Balanchine, and Bérard supervising every detail. The photographer George Hoyningen-Huene was sent by French *Vogue* to document the work as it progressed. As in Diaghilev's company, rehearsals were generally closed to visitors. Gunsbourg especially was barred whenever possible, for he was known as a womanizer. Among the very few guests allowed were the Comtesse de Noailles, Coco Chanel, and Nora Auric. Auric, wife of composer Georges Auric, was a key personality in artistic and intellectual circles in Paris between the wars, and found financial backing for many projects. A portrait painter, she counted many famous people, including de Basil's dancers, among her subjects.

Working with Balanchine was a revelation for many of the young dancers. The choreographer demonstrated every combination in great detail and was fully responsive to the personalities of the interpreters; it was as if he had conducted a character study of each dancer before beginning rehearsals. "He had a great sensibility in perceiving the personality of the different dancers he was working with," Toumanova recalls. "Besides casting them in roles that were appropriate, he exploited their technical potentiality and individuality. It was amazing when he showed the choreography how he would become myself or Lichine or Blinova in the gestures and mannerisms he employed." Balanchine also would not hesitate to include movements that arose spontaneously from the dancers, thus making them participants in the creative process. Toumanova recalls how she would instinctively add a step or a gesture, and Balanchine would readily approve. In fact, he gave exercises in improvisation and used the results in the choreography. Toumanova describes how Balanchine asked her to look into the guest's palm for the fortune-telling scene and how he wanted to know the reason for the mysterious look on her face and her dramatic gestures. When she explained, these reactions were incorporated into the choreography. "He showed the choreography, but it was up to the dancers to comprehend the movement and to let it grow as an extension of themselves. He was always patient and tolerant with the dancers who had problems with his choreography. He would show as many times as necessary without ever getting upset or raising his voice."

Premiere and Critics

The first performance of *Cotillon* was given at a gala in honor of Prince Louis II to celebrate the national holiday of Monaco. For the occasion, Balanchine danced the First Guest, a role he had created for Lichine, who was at La Scala fulfilling a commitment to perform in Massine's *Belkis*. Lichine danced the official opening night. Riabouchinska, who arrived late in Monte Carlo after fulfilling her contract with the Chauve-Souris company, later assumed the role of the Mistress of Ceremonies, which had been created by Blinova, and made it her own. Many believe that this led to Blinova's departure from the company at the end of the season. (Riabouchinska originally had been cast as Blinova's understudy as the Child in *Jeux d'enfants*, but the role became hers after a few rehearsals.) In Monte Carlo the ballet was enthusiastically received, and in Paris, too, it was unanimously acclaimed. André Levinson found a double character in this enigmatic work:

20

> And it is in the puerile symbolism of the cotillion, in the ceremonial joke provided by the breathless Master of Ceremonies (Mr. Woidzokovsky) that these charade characters intertwine themselves in an indescribable plot of enigmatic poetry and of latent sadness. It is the same melancholy breathed by the music . . . This other Chabrier, isolated and disenchanted, who confides to the keyboard the sorrows of a failed existence . . . The double meaning of the work is personified at every turn by the sparkling Mistress of Ceremonies, Miss Riabouchinska, slender and swift like a whip in her black bodice emerging from a frou-frou of yellow tulle, and the-dreamy Miss Toumanova, who only discards her somnambula's languor to set in motion the grand rond finale with a series of vertiginous grandes pirouettes alternating with triple, quadruple and quintuple turns sur le cou de pied. Tania is not like Tamara, the young captive, the dark beauty! Every thing in this child is energy, impetus, imperious will: the splendour of her clear face, the pure line of her profile. She is a little being of great race. As soon as she touches the ground after a fantastique flight, she parts again like an arrow, sparkling and minute like a hummingbird.[9]

Cotillon was a staple of the company's repertory from its first season through the war years in South America. Even though the work was always presented with great success, it did not have the popular appeal of other ballets, such as the 1933 version of

Massine's *Le Beau Danube*. *Cotillon* had its own special audience who remained faithful to it through the thirties, but consequently it was given only a limited number of performances during any season. Its last performance in the United States was during the 1940–41 tour, when Balanchine rehearsed the original cast for the first time since his departure after the Paris season in 1932. The Tulsa Ballet, under the direction of Roman Jasinski and Moscelyne Larkin, both former members of the Ballets Russes, revived the "Hand of Fate" pas de deux for their company. When this fragment was presented during the company's engagement at Brooklyn College during the winter of 1983, it captured the imagination of the audience just as it had in the thirties. In October 1988, the Joffrey Ballet presented the first complete revival of the work since de Basil's company disbanded in 1948.

LA CONCURRENCE

Ballet in one act; music by Georges Auric; libretto by André Derain; choreography by George Balanchine; set design by André Derain, executed by Prince A. Schervachidze; costume design by André Derain, executed by Madame Karinska; curtain designed and executed by André Derain; premiere April 12, 1932, at the Théâtre de Monte Carlo, conducted by Marc-César Scotto.

21

ORIGINAL CAST

Premier Marchand (First Tailor)	Metek Borovsky	Deux Amies (Two Friends)	Valentina Blinova, Eleonora Marra
Deuxième Marchand (Second Tailor)	Yurek Shabelevsky	Le Loqueteux (The Tramp)	Leon Woizikowski
Femme du 1er Marchand (Wife of the First Tailor)	Tatiana Lipkovska	Les Jeunes Filles (The Girls)	Mlle Tamara Toumanova, Mlles Rostova, Riabouchinska, Baronova, Branitska, Strakhova, Morosova, Sonne, Slavinska, Kirsova, Tresahar
Femme du 2me Marchand (Wife of the Second Tailor)	Gala Chabelska		
Premier couple (First Couple)	Louise Lyman, Roman Jasinski	Les Voisins (The Neighbors)	Mlles Marra, Obidenna, Chamié, Blanc, Valenska MM. Hoyer, Dolotine, Lipatoff, Katcharoff, Petroff
Deuxième couple (Second Couple)	Lara Obidenna, Marian Ladré		
Leur Fille (Their Daughter)	Irina Stepanova		

La Concurrence was the second ballet scheduled for rehearsal in Monte Carlo in the spring of 1932. It was based on a scenario by André Derain, who also designed the front curtain, the scenery, and the costumes. The commissioned score was by Georges Auric and the choreography was by Balanchine. (Kochno was indirectly

ABOVE: The first two couples: Lyman, Jasinski, Ladré, and Obidenna.
BELOW: The full company in front of Derain's set.

ABOVE: Toumanova and corps in the foreground, with de Basil, Blum, Kochno, and Balanchine in the background. BELOW: Toumanova.

involved as the person responsible for the collaboration of these three artists.) It was the season's only new production in which the composer was an active participant; the other premieres were all choreographed to existing scores.

Action

La Concurrence tells the story of the rivalry of two tailors whose shops face each other on a town square. Each of them creates a variety of beautiful outfits to entice customers away from his rival. The crowd enters the shops and emerges with new finery. The plot allows the choreographer to explore how a change of clothing can alter people's behavior and stresses the psychology of make-believe.

As the ballet begins, the First Tailor opens his shop and puts his costumes on display, just as the Second Tailor is doing the same. They advance towards each other into the street, brandishing their fists, while above their shops the windows open and their wives lean out to encourage their husbands. The tailors swear at each other as they return to their shops.

Various characters make their way onto the square: two young ladies, an arrogant young couple, and an older couple with their little daughter, who is rolling a hoop. They vacillate between the two shops and are finally lured into one or the other by the tailors' enticements or by their physical persuasion. Each lady and each couple chooses a different shop.

The two ladies emerge transformed, each boasting about her new look. They quarrel, stepping on each other's toes, and finally depart in opposite directions.

The two couples and the daughter leave the shops. The daughter of the Second Couple laughs at the First Couple and sticks her tongue out at the lady, causing the affronted woman to leave the scene in a near-faint as the girl and her indulgent parents strut off haughtily.

A Tramp appears. He, too, wants to be renovated, but the tailors reject him as he is penniless. He leaves momentarily, then returns to produce a sack of money from his pocket; the tailors now fight over him until one lifts him bodily into his shop. The Tramp emerges in a checked suit, a hat, a cane, and shiny yellow shoes and walks arrogantly about the square, his gait obviously hampered by the tight fit of the shoes.

A Young Girl tiptoes in and vanishes into one of the shops. She reappears in a different costume (below-the-knee tutu) and then leaves. Two groups of girls come darting from one shop to the other. The Young Girl returns and leads some of them to one shop and the rest to the other. They emerge in new dresses (above-the-knee tutus) and begin to dance. The Young Girl performs a fouetté competition with two other girls, creating such a commotion that the neighbors lean out of their windows, annoyed by the disruption of their afternoon naps. They come out to the square, some of them in nightgowns and nightcaps, and pounce on one another. When they finally disperse, the tailors, finding themselves alone, reconcile over the handsome profits they have earned. The Young Girl watches the scene unobserved, and after the tailors return to their shops and put up the shutters, she sinks to her knees, preoccupied in dreamy contemplation, as the curtain falls.

Music

Even though Auric and Derain had both belonged to the same artistic entourage during Diaghilev's late period, *La Concurrence* marked their first collaboration. Auric's initiation as a ballet composer had occurred four years earlier with the Jean Cocteau–

Jean Börlin entertainment *Les Mariés de la Tour Eiffel* for the Ballets Suédois, which had marked the theatrical debut, and sole joint effort, of the group of composers known as "Les Six"—Auric, Germaine Tailleferre, Arthur Honegger, Darius Milhaud, Francis Poulenc, and Louis Durey (who declined to participate). Of Auric's three ballets for Diaghilev, *La Pastorale* (1925) was his first collaboration with Balanchine.

According to Auric, he and Derain worked together on the score of the ballet, first in Paris and later in Monte Carlo, to create the right feeling and style for each scene. Balanchine joined them on several occasions to familiarize himself with the music. Auric found Derain to be one of the most musical designers with whom he had ever worked. (The conductor Ernest Ansermet had remarked in a 1919 letter to Maurice de Vlaminck, "He's the first painter I've met who is musical; he has a surprising feel for music."[1])

Both designer and composer were present in Monte Carlo for Balanchine's rehearsals, and any difficulties that arose were resolved by the three collaborators. Auric never hesitated to change the score to suit the action. For *La Concurrence* he incorporated melodies from popular songs, shrieky music-box sounds, and barrel-organ effects, which suited the period and the atmosphere. André Levinson praised the score for its avoidance of excessive dissonances: "Its music belongs to the same scenic style as Diaghilev's 'Matelots,' dynamic, stimulating, strong, propitious to vigorous propulsion, without excess of dissonant tones."[2] But, when the work was presented in London the following year, Ernest Newman in the *Sunday Times* found it representative of an already dated modernistic trend from the twenties.

Choreography

Mime was essential to Derain's libretto and provided a frame for the dance passages, which eschewed the traditional form of the Petipa divertissement in favor of a more integrated style in the manner of Fokine.

Narrative was predominant in *La Concurrence,* and Balanchine devised a very spontaneous style of mime that captured a feeling of playful improvisation. Inspired by the number of talented young dancers in the company, Balanchine played the action of the adults against that of the children: while the grown-ups developed the plot—the rivalry between the two tailors—the youngsters interacted among themselves, indifferent to the commotion around them. This juxtaposition helped to diversify the action and kept the spectator's focus of attention moving from one group to the other.

The unifying element was Toumanova as the Young Girl, who moved freely between the adults and the children as a catalyst to the action.

One of Balanchine's finest achievements was the characterization of the Tramp, the memorable burlesque role created by Woizikowski. It was later passed on to Yurek Shabelevsky, who made it his own, and still later to Yurek Lazowski, who told me: "The Hobo variation had a certain jazzy influence. Do not forget that the jazz age had had a strong impact throughout Europe, and in 1932 it had not succumbed yet. The character goes from one tailor to the other in the style of Chaplin, until he is finally kicked out of the scene. When he returns he is a wealthy man, and both tailors go out of their way to measure him and to be of service. He goes into one shop and comes out with an extra-large sort of zoot suit and very small shoes. His comic movements convey the pain he undergoes, walking with one foot in and the other out. The choreography was based on funny, jazzy movements that I still found interesting in the mid-thirties when I took over the role."

Another highlight of the ballet was the fouetté competition. Members of the audience today remember how the public would roar with excitement during this sequence. These three dancers—Toumanova, Riabouchinska, and Baronova—were soon to become internationally known as the "baby ballerinas." Riabouchinska danced the role of the Young Girl at the London premiere in the summer of 1933; but after Toumanova the role was more identified with Baronova.

Scenery and Costumes

That Derain's contribution was vital to the ballet can be seen clearly from the reviews of the time, especially in France, where the music and the choreography took second place. By 1932 Derain was one of the most individualistic French painters. He had moved through fauvism and cubism, and now his main concern was the intrinsic value of each canvas as an individual expression independent of the precepts of any school. Similarly, his success as a stage designer lay in his ability to respond to each work according to its particular needs. When working for the theater, Derain tried to evoke the right atmosphere without allowing his designs to distract the audience from the characters and the action. His decor and costumes played a functional role in complementing what Brecht called the social gestus of the work: the historical and social context, the external and internal conflict. The splendor and beauty of the costumes and scenery were not allowed to become ends in themselves. He commented: "The privilege of the theatre is that of not acting by acquired conceptions . . . but by direct evocation that would not demand any effort from the spectator. . . . Painting must inspire itself by a method and it must proceed . . . by displaying and not by proving."[3]

26

For *La Concurrence* Derain designed a curtain of a soft pastel landscape with Harlequin and Pierrot leading a circus girl balancing on a horse on their way to a far-away town. The curtain rose on a backcloth representing a town whose buildings stretch vertically to the horizon. To either side of the backcloth there was a tailor's shop with costumes on display. Each shop was housed on the ground floor of a provincial-style three-story building. In the center of the scene was an arch leading into a narrow road winding its way through the town. The predominant colors were brick red and opaque shades of blue, orange, grey, and green.

As Derain had already shown in *La Boutique fantasque,* his approach was to build a flat surface without perspective. He emphasized the sharpness of the outlines to enhance a peculiarly sketchlike quality. The design was simultaneously sophisticated and childlike—a quality that perfectly matched his libretto.

Set in the late 1890s, *La Concurrence* provided an opportunity for the re-creation of splendid period costumes. Some critics pointed out that the ballet was an excellent showcase of provincial *fin-de-siècle* fashion.

Derain is remembered as a meticulous craftsman. During the dress rehearsal he examined every costume against his original sketches to be sure that Mme Karinska, who executed them, had not omitted any details. The following day, before the opening, he made an inspection visit to the dressing rooms, checking out not only the costumes but the dancers' coiffures and makeup as well. And as the oldest member of the Ballets Russes family, he became a sort of father figure to many of the young dancers, who viewed him with respect.

Premiere   Though *La Concurrence* was well received in Monte Carlo and Paris, many critics felt that it was a return to the pantomime ballet. Levinson wrote: "All this adds up to a frenzied and comical commotion, hectic, exaggerated gesturing, playful pantomime rather than ballet."[4] On July 7, 1933, *La Concurrence* was presented for the first time in London. The English press received it without enthusiasm; Ernest Newman concluded: "It is a mildly amusing little piece in a genre that represents a watering down of the last senna leaves of the modern French ballet of the weaker type: the mental strain involved in [its] making . . . could hardly have been so intense as to cause the friends of the three creators any anxiety about their health."[5]

The ballet stayed in the repertory until 1939. When the company left London in 1939, the scenery and costumes for *La Concurrence* were stored in a warehouse that was later destroyed by fire during the Blitz. Although Derain's maquettes exist in private collections, the ballet itself seems to be lost forever. Of all the theater works to which this artist contributed his beautiful and sensitive designs, only *La Boutique fantasque* is still performed today.

27

Toumanova.

JEUX D'ENFANTS

Ballet in one act; music by Georges Bizet; libretto by Boris Kochno; choreography by Léonide Massine; set design by Joan Miró, executed by Prince A. Schervachidze; costume design by Joan Miró, executed by Madame Karinska; curtain designed and executed by Joan Miró; premiere April 14, 1932, at the Théâtre de Monte Carlo, conducted by Marc-César Scotto.

ORIGINAL CAST

Les Esprits qui commandent les Jouets (The Spirits Who Govern the Toys)	Lubov Rostova, Roland Guérard
La Toupie (The Top)	Tamara Toumanova
L'Enfant (The Child)	Tatiana Riabouchinska
Les Chevaux de bois (The Rocking Horses)	MM. Shabelevsky, Hoyer, Katchourovsky, Dolotine, Katcharoff, Lipatoff, Petroff
Deux Raquettes (Two Rackets)	MM. Borovsky, Jasinski
Le Volant (The Shuttlecock)	Valentina Blinova
Les Amazons (The Amazons)	Mlles Marra, Strakhova, Obidenna, Kervily
Les Bulles de savon (The Soap Bubbles)	Mlles Tresahar, Lipkovska, Morosova, Sonne, Blanc, Chabelska, Valenska, Kirsova, Slavinska
Le Voyageur (The Traveler)	David Lichine
Les trois Sportmen (The Three Sportsmen)	MM. Woizikowski, Ladré, Guérard

Between *Ode*, his last production for Diaghilev, in 1928, and *Jeux d'enfants*, his first for de Basil, in the spring of 1932, Massine had devised choreography for the Roxy Theater in New York, La Scala in Milan, and the Cochran revues in London (where he had collaborated with Max Reinhardt on the production of *Helen!*, based on Offenbach's *La Belle Hélène*). He seems to have maintained a distance during the gestation of the new company. Probably he was offended because Blum and the Casino had rejected his proposal to reorganize the Ballets Russes after Diaghilev's death, and now he was being excluded from the company's nucleus (having been engaged only as a guest choreographer). But his distance also could have been motivated by his plan, which he pursued until late 1932, to organize a permanent company at Covent Garden with Sir Thomas Beecham.

As soon as Massine arrived in Monte Carlo in March, he began work with Kochno, who had concocted a libretto that was a variation on a theme that Massine had already treated in *La Boutique fantasque* in 1919—toys coming to life after dark.

(*Boutique* itself had been Massine's satiric version of *Die Puppenfee*, an old German ballet that Serge and Nicholas Legat had revived in St. Petersburg in 1903.) *Jeux d'enfants* was inspired by, and adapted to the structure of, Bizet's twelve-part, four-handed piano suite of 1871, in Bizet's own orchestration. But the new ballet differed significantly from *La Boutique fantasque*: in the earlier ballet the toys themselves interacted with one another; here, the story was in the hands of a human agent, the Child, who was the central figure of the action and played the dual role of spectator and participant. Like *Cotillon*, *Jeux d'enfants* did not tell a story but rather presented linked episodes, which here depicted a child's fantasy of her toys coming to life.

Action   The action of *Jeux d'enfants* follows the sequence of the twelve piano pieces by Bizet: "L'Escarpolette," "La Toupie," "La Poupée," "Les Chevaux de bois," "Le Volant," "Trompette et Tambour," "Les Bulles de savon," "Les quatre Coins," "Colin-Maillard," "Saute-Mouton," "Petit Mari, petite femme," "Le Bal."

The curtain rises to display a white disc to stage left and a shiny black cone with a scarlet tip to the right ("L'Escarpolette"—Reverie). A single, dark blue arm (that of a dancer hiding behind the disc) appears, gliding sinuously and gesticulating through the disc's center. From behind the black cone a pair of white legs appear as the bottom slides up like a window. The two figures—the Spirits who govern the toys—emerge from behind the disc and the cone, wearing white leotards (one with a blue arm), tights, and hoods. They dance the same angular steps (bending forward on one knee with the back leg stretched out)—the steps as well as the arm positions in profile to the audience—while the white disc moves up and down like a bouncing ball in slow motion.

The first toy that they bring to life is the Top ("La Toupie"—Impromptu). The Top, dressed in a vividly striped leotard and hood, walks on pointe to the center of the stage and performs a series of spins that culminate in twenty-four single and double fouettés, followed by a manège of chaîné turns around the stage, to repeat the same sequence of fouettés. She ends her variation with five unsupported pirouettes center stage.

The Child appears ("La Poupée"—Berceuse). The stage is now an enchanted world. She tiptoes in from upstage left carrying two canvases covered with childish scribbles, which the Spirits take from her and place to either side of the stage. She performs a diagonal which consists of a polka on pointe, followed by five acrobatic jumps (the first two slower). With stretched legs forward she touches the tip of her pointed toes with her hands while in mid-air. She soutenus to the left and bends forward, with her feet slightly turned in as she swings her arms with wrists bent up and looks around as if surprised by her own feat. She soutenus to the right and repeats the same; she reverses the diagonal to center stage with a double sequence of a waltz step and two pirouettes. She bends forward with arms hanging to the side, and walks upstage left like a mechanical monkey. Then she performs a diagonal of jumps with ronde versé turns combined with intricate pas de bourrée steps and finishes her variation with a pose. Finally, very proud of herself, she lies on her side downstage, her back to the audience, leaning on an elbow to watch the toys perform.

Six Wooden Rocking Horses rock sideways for her ("Les Chevaux de bois"—Scherzo). While they dance, the Child jumps, sits with legs split to the sides, jumps around the stage, and exits. After the horses leave she returns with a racket in hand and dances ("Le Volant"—Fantaisie). Two Rackets bat the Shuttlecock in the air between them. Curious, the Child gets close to a racket, but is taken aback and runs offstage in a grand jeté. The Shuttlecock is lifted by her two partners and they exit.

The Child enters and dances a short introductory variation as four huge canvases, with abstract designs nailed to them, are slid in, two to each side of the stage ("Trompette et Tambour"—Marche). Four Amazons appear from behind the canvases and fight a battle with swords and shields. The Child stands in the middle of the stage and incites them to battle, but soon she is attracted to the canvases to the right and, pretending that she is not seen by anyone, spins the different designs on them. Again, she is distracted by the fighting toys and plays with them, but whimsically runs after them to get them offstage as the four canvases disappear.

Nine Soap Bubbles float about the stage ("Les Bulles de savon"—Rondino). The Traveler enters onto a dim stage ("Les quatre Coins"—Esquisse). The Child moves to a corner to observe the Traveler, and the Spirits bring two signs, one reading "Paris" and the other, "New York," and place them to either side of the stage. The Traveler then journeys to the four corners of the world in grands jetés. The Traveler and the Child dance a tender pas de deux in which he rocks her in his arms like a doll ("Colin-Maillard"—Nocturne). They exit. Three Sportsmen do exercises to attract the Child's attention and she returns ("Saute-Mouton"—Caprice). The Child is attracted to the Tumbler as the other two leave. The jealous Top tries to separate them ("Petit Mari, petite femme"—Duo). They dance a pas de trois in which the Tumbler tries to partner the Child with one hand, the Top with the other. The spoiled Child, determined not to let him go, jumps onto his shoulder and sits there as the Top turns incessantly, still supported by the Tumbler. They exit.

The Child returns to watch the codalike finale, in which, group by group, all the toys participate, ending in a medley of movement and color ("Le Bal"—Galop) which freezes at the end of the scene. To a reprise of "L'Escarpolette," the lights dim as the Spirits enter to reclaim the life they had temporarily bestowed on the playthings. As they make their way back to the geometrical shapes onstage, the toys begin to move around like sleepwalkers. From downstage right, the Child dreamily moves across the stage to the motionless Traveler and pulls him to center stage as the cast takes its final pose. The dark blue arm reappears through the center of the white disc and gives the final command for the curtain to fall.

Choreog-
raphy

Jeux d'enfants, like *Cotillon*, was a significant development in the integration of dance and music. The prevailing trend in ballet until *Jeux d'enfants*, and especially during Diaghilev's last years, was to create dramatic ballets in which a story was translated into dance and mime terms. These works obviously centered on the narrative; music, dance, and plastic elements supported this structure. The integration of dance and expressive gesture (pantomime) especially served the development of the story. Fokine in *Les Sylphides* presented an antecedent to a new kind of ballet in which

30

there was no story to provide the structure—only a theme to give an atmosphere and locale. *Les Sylphides* was set in continuous dance terms to the musical score. Music established the structure and the mood. The choreographer's main concern was the integration of dance to music. Since he had avoided a scenario, mime had become purposeless.

Massine in *Le Soleil de nuit* of 1915 and Balanchine in *Apollon Musagète* of 1928 followed the example of Fokine in *Les Sylphides*. However, this would not become a trend until the thirties with *Cotillon, Jeux d'enfants, Les Présages, Choreartium*, etc. From the early thirties, although story ballets were standard, there was a clear trend toward the presentation of dance in purely balletic terms, without the purpose of enacting a detailed scenario. Dance became an end in itself. This was a step towards a radical transformation in ballet—that of ballet as pure art—to parallel the development of the other arts in the twentieth century. It helped to establish ballets as works of art autonomous and self-contained, with no need to borrow from other media or historical, sociological, and psychological sources. This new direction in ballet led towards the contemporary aesthetic of abstraction and non-representational art.

Jeux d'enfants was consistently set in terms of dance, rather than mime or narrative. Massine's choreography blended the classical idiom with expressive movements that depicted the personality of each character, always striving for simplicity of gesture and purity of line. He avoided presenting the toys in the traditional manner, as mechanical dolls; instead, they possessed recognizable human qualities—an aspect enhanced by Miró's use of unitards. As A. V. Coton wrote:

31

> Massine had abandoned all reference to the "unnatural" toy movement idiom of *Boutique fantasque* in composing this work. All the toys and games (toys only in a specialized balletic sense, i.e., symbols for a series of entities endowed with perfectly human attributes of movement—no toymaker ever devised such delightful conceits as the Amazons or the Athletes [Sportsmen]) danced perfectly balletic and athletic measures as against the entirely derivative movement idioms of the toys in *Boutique fantasque*.[1]

The Child's movements were appropriately childlike, with jumps in the air with both legs to the front and her hands touching her pointed toes, runs, and grimaces. Her sometimes awkward poses added a touch of whimsicality that was emphasized by her changes of mood from surprise to euphoria to aloofness. Coton described some of the other characters:

> The groupings of toys and games made entrée and characteristic patterns; the Amazons, sword-girt and with bucklers, in a series of military exercises and mock combats reminiscent of heroic groupings found on Grecian friezes and pottery; the two Rackets patterning volley and release and exchanging the partnered Shuttlecock in swung lifts backward and forward. The Soap Bubbles, a nine-part female group clad in skin-tight costuming of, respectively, lavender, lime, olive, yellow, black, crimson,

LEFT: The Spirits: Runanine and Grigorieva. BELOW: Toumanova, Rostova, and Guérard. BOTTOM: Lichine and Riabouchinska.

RIGHT: Riabouchinska,
Woizikowski, and Toumanova.
BELOW: The full company in
front of Miró's set.

orange, blue, and pink, was a superb balletic patterning of the thistledown softnesses and airiness of the movements of blown bubbles, expressed in moves on the half-point with a purely liquid flexion of the body from the ankles upward, accompanied by motions of the hands in patterns of undulation and suspension. . . . Then the Three Athletes made entry and patterned their skill as runners, acrobats, and tumblers. . . .[2]

Rehearsals Most of the dancers awaited their first encounter with Massine with a degree of fear; the former members of Diaghilev's company had spoken of the choreographer's strict discipline and his detached, inaccessible manner, for during his Diaghilev years he had been aloof, incommunicative, and an obsessive worker. But he now surprised everyone by forming a closer, more friendly working relationship with the dancers than was his wont. Though he remained somewhat distant and immersed in his work, many now attributed his previous behavior at least in part to his particular status as Diaghilev's protégé. And his extroverted new wife, Eugenia Delarova, seemed to foster the development of a more easygoing personality.

Toumanova recalls: "When I first walked into the room, I was frightened. He came in, looked at me with his expressive and beautiful eyes, and started to talk. From that moment on, he was all kindness."

For *Jeux d'enfants* Massine rehearsed each solo and ensemble separately. The company did not come together for the finale until the last rehearsals, when, to general amazement, all the dancers found their correct places without confusion. Massine had worked out on paper every detail of his interlocking patterns. (He would dedicate the last years of his life to developing his own theory of notation, which would provide him with a consistent method of working out his choreography on paper before he entered the studio. He taught his theory at the Royal Ballet School when he became teacher of choreography there in 1969.)

The rehearsal period of *Jeux d'enfants* was a pleasurable experience for the dancers. The choreography, as Riabouchinska recalls, was especially intriguing; it seemed unusual and modern next to Balanchine's more classically oriented work. She remembers how fascinated the dancers were by Massine's angular poses and movements and by his unacademic use of the torso, which avoided the straight position in favor of bending it forward and to the sides, raising the shoulders, swinging the arms. It was displayed most prominently in his choreography for the Child. Riabouchinska found most unusual the jumps when she bent forward in mid-air to touch her fingers to her pointed toes. (One must bear in mind that these young dancers had received a purely classical training in the Parisian studios of the imperial teachers, and even in their school performances they had been coached only in the imperial repertory, works such as *Esmeralda* and *Sylvia*.) She also found Balanchine's *Cotillon* unacademic because of the turned-in legs, but the basic line was still very classical in comparison to the role of the Child.

The dancers were stimulated by the presence of Kochno and Miró; the latter attended most of the rehearsals in order to study Massine's choreography while creating his designs. It had always been important for Massine to explore new direc-

34

tions in the plastic arts; and now his close collaboration with Miró allowed him to develop a better understanding of surrealism, just as his work with Picasso on *Parade* and with Georgy Yakulov on *Le Pas d'acier* had illuminated cubism and constructivism, respectively. Miró, although somewhat shy, became very much a part of the Ballets Russes group and joined the dancers during their free time to stroll or to sightsee. For Riabouchinska, Toumanova, and Lichine, it was the beginning of a long relationship with him, and for years they were to meet in and out of theaters and galleries in Barcelona, Paris, London, and New York.

Scenery and Costumes

Kochno's first-choice designer had been Alberto Giacometti, who rejected the commission. So Kochno contacted Miró, whose series of paintings and collages of 1928–29, exhibited in Paris during 1929 and 1930, he had found fascinating in their deliberate infantilism.

Since his early years in Barcelona (he was born in 1893), Miró had been a ballet enthusiast, avidly attending performances of Diaghilev's Ballets Russes in that city. In fact, it was during one such performance, at the Teatre Liceu in 1917, that Miró had first met Picasso. The dream motif in Kochno's libretto for *Jeux d'enfants* provided Miró with an appropriately surrealistic theme. The atmosphere of the ballet was enhanced by the painter's hermeticism, which emphasized the inaccessibility to adults of a child's world. The impetuous naïveté of Miró's designs was in perfect harmony with Massine's choreography and Kochno's libretto.

To set the mood, Miró designed a white front curtain with splashes of basic colors, like a child's drawing. It rose to reveal a surrealistic nursery of geometrical shapes in contrasting colors. There was a large black cone with a red tip to the left and a luminous white disc (half the size of the cone, but larger than the dancer) to the right. Against the grey blue of the backcloth, both structures gave the impression of children's paper cutouts. During the ballet, dancers brought in a white egg, four canvases with scribbles, and cylindrical signs reading "New York" and "Paris." The stage was framed by three pairs of wing-drops with alternating colors: black, white, and red on the left side and white, red, and black on the right.

Miró dressed the dancers in unitards, quite unusual for that day. The most striking costumes were those worn by the Child (a short blue dress, white socks, black toe shoes with black bows, and a large red leather bow on her head), the Top (a hood and a striped leotard of red, green, yellow, black, lavender, and white—the revolving leg was striped and the whipping leg was completely red—creating a dizzying sensation as she turned), and the Traveler (a brown "ski" outfit with a scarf).

Miró's designs were acclaimed for their originality and effectiveness. He himself always showed concern about his work in *Jeux d'enfants*. After seeing the 1934 revival in Barcelona, he wrote to Grigoriev advising him of certain details that should be checked before the ballet was presented again in Paris.[3] He was especially concerned about certain colors that had faded. As late as 1978, in a letter to Riabouchinska, he expressed his delight over a possible revival of the work in Los Angeles by the Southern California Ballet, the company of which Riabouchinska is founder and director.[4] The project, scheduled for the fall of 1979, was canceled after Massine's death in February of that year.

35

Premiere Though *Jeux d'enfants* aroused great admiration at its premiere in Monte Carlo, some of the more conservative members of the audience were shocked by its ultrasophistication. In Paris, however, the reception was stupendous. Levinson, although he disliked the unitards, praised the ballet and especially the dancers:

> Mlle Riabouchinska is the sprightly and cunning "mistress of ceremonies" for this doll revue. There is in this fair girl with her pale gold ponytail something striking, a thoroughbred elegance, a naturally proud bearing coupled with a remarkable ease in elevation, beats, and runs. . . . Mlle Toumanova seizes the opportunity to play the top, for she has an astonishing virtuosity and equilibrium for turning, grandes pirouettes in which the arms give the initial impetus and the drawing in of the leg sur le cou-de-pied prolongs it, fouettés, as they are aptly called, because one leg is the whip and the other the spinning top. Arriving unexpectedly is the Traveler, in the person of M. David Lichine, an impulsive temperament mixing imagination with technical prowess.[5]

When the ballet was presented in England at the Alhambra that summer, Ernest Newman, the music critic for the *Sunday Times*, wrote:

> We notice the same thing again in Mr. Massine's choreography to "Jeux d'enfants." One's first impression is that Bizet's charming music does not lend itself to action: . . . Yet in a very little while it becomes clear that Mr. Massine has achieved the almost impossible, by a boldness of translation that soon converts our first scepticism into willing belief. *Jeux d'enfants* is a delightful fantasy, in which action, miming, costumes and colors combine subtly to the one end. And once more we are made to realise that in Mme Baronova and Mme Riabouchinska we have two of the best young dancers of the day.[6]

The ballet marked a turning point in the career of Tatiana Riabouchinska. Her interpretation of the Child gave evidence of her unique artistry and paved the way for a series of roles so suited to her qualities that they were difficult for other dancers to inherit. It was a key work, according to Irving Deaken, "in finding and forming a new Riabouchinska, a complete balletic, modishly angular child. . . ."[7] And Arnold Haskell pointed out that "with . . . gawkish movements that must never be overstressed, [she achieved] a perfect synthesis of character."[8]

After a three-year absence from the repertory, the ballet was revived for the 1937 London season. Haskell wrote: "Today [the child prodigies] are almost grown up, but the work is still new. There is about it an extraordinary feeling of unreality; it is 'Riabouchinska in Wonderland,' with all the logic and the inevitability a dream has at the time."[9] And a critic for the *Sunday Times* wrote:

Riabouchinska [is] still unique at her child's play. Her half-awkward gambolings seemed, if anything, more inspired than ever—no easy accomplishment, this, since her technique, per se, has obviously matured. And so has that of Baronova, spinning, as the Top, to perfection. Lichine danced the Traveler with exceptional litheness and spirit. But indeed there was no episode in the whole dozen that did not exercise its remembered fascination.[10]

Jeux d'enfants was enthusiastically received on three continents and remained in the repertory until 1941. The role of the Child was always identified with Riabouchinska, although Lisa Serova danced it several times in Australia. The Top, created by Toumanova, was danced by Baronova at the London premiere, and she made the role her own; in 1938 it was passed to Alexandra Denisova. Massine revived the ballet with great success for the Teatro Colón, Buenos Aires, in 1955.

LE BOURGEOIS GENTILHOMME

Ballet in one act; music by Richard Strauss; libretto by Sobeka (Boris Kochno) after Molière; choreography by George Balanchine; set, costumes, and curtain designed by Alexandre Benois; sets executed by Prince A. Schervachidze; costumes executed by Madame Karinska; curtain executed by Georges Geerts; premiere May 3, 1932, at the Théâtre de Monte Carlo, conducted by Paul Paray.

37

ORIGINAL CAST

Cléonte	David Lichine	Branitska, Obidenna, Sonne, Tresahar
Covielle, his valet	Jasht Dolotine	
Two Gypsy tailors	Lipatoff, Katcharoff	Lucile
M. Jourdain	Marian Ladré	Nicole, her servant
M. Jourdain's retinue	Mlles Blanc, Chabelska, Lipkovska, Valenska MM. Hoyer, Guérard	

Cléonte's friends disguised as slaves
MM. Katchourovsky, Petroff, Lipatoff, Katcharoff

Ballet given by M. Jourdain in honor of the son of the Grand Turk   Mlles Valentina, Blinova, Riabouchinska,

Lucile   Tamara Toumanova
Nicole, her servant   Eleanora Marra
Turkish divertissement
I   Mlle Olga Morosova
MM. Yurek Shabelevsky, Léonide Katchourovsky
II   Mlle Natalie Strakhova
M. Metek Borovsky
III—Acrobats   Mlles Kirsova, Slavinska, Kervily, M. Roman Jasinski
Artists of the Ballet

Balanchine was immensely popular—especially with the girls, who either worshiped him or had a crush on him. With his charm and easygoing personality, he imbued every rehearsal session with spontaneity, humor, and sheer fun—a breath of fresh air compared with the strict discipline maintained by Grigoriev in accordance with the Maryinsky tradition. Grigoriev fined dancers who were late for rehearsals and performances. He enforced a strict dress code: black leotards, tights, and skirts and white socks for the women (pink tights for special rehearsals); white shirts, black tights, and white socks for the men. The women were required to wear toe shoes in class and at rehearsals. Dancers spoke softly, addressed their elders with respect, and gave full attention to the choreographer and régisseur. But when Grigoriev was not in the room, Balanchine would frequently improvise jazz tunes at the piano, to which the company would dance. Such escapades were a relief from the professional tension forced upon them at so early an age.

The last ballet created by Balanchine for the spring 1932 season was based on Molière's *Le Bourgeois Gentilhomme* (1670), as adapted by Kochno and set to music by Richard Strauss, with scenery and costumes by Alexandre Benois.

Le Bourgeois Gentilhomme is probably the masterpiece of the *comédie-ballet* genre, a form developed by Molière that consisted of song-and-dance interludes inserted between the acts of a comedy. The original work had music by Lully and choreography by Pierre Beauchamps. Molière's play had three major plot lines: the vicissitudes of the nouveau-riche Monsieur Jourdain and his family, servants, and instructors as he attempts to emulate the aristocracy; his friendship with Dorante, an unscrupulous nobleman, and Dorante's affair with the Marquise Dorimène; and the love match between Jourdain's daughter, Lucile, and Cléonte, and Cléonte's masquerade as the son of the Grand Turk to win her father's approval.

Music

Strauss's music was written in 1912 as part of a lengthy entertainment devised by Hugo von Hofmannsthal: the poet's own, heavily truncated version of Molière's play coupled with the Strauss-Hofmannsthal opera *Ariadne auf Naxos* in its original form. The venture was poorly received. With the Molière discarded and a new Prologue added in its place, *Ariadne* became a success, but a major reworking of *Le Bourgeois Gentilhomme* in 1918 proved as unsuccessful as Hofmannsthal's first version.

To preserve the best music from both versions, Strauss compiled a nine-part orchestral suite, which he introduced in 1920. It was this suite that Kochno and Balanchine used for their ballet. Although Norman del Mar, Strauss's biographer, believes the *Bourgeois Gentilhomme* orchestral suite to be one of the composer's finest works,[1] Levinson felt that the music was the ballet's main handicap; he considered it an "overly clever pastiche. . . neither old nor new, but rather modernity that has grown old."[2]

Action

Kochno's libretto for *Le Bourgeois Gentilhomme* was strictly based on the episodes between Lucile and Cléonte and was divided into nine scenes—the nine sections of the orchestral suite.

Monsieur Jourdain forbids his daughter, Lucile, to marry Cléonte because he is not of noble birth. Before the curtain, Cléonte disguises himself as the son of the

38

fabulously wealthy Grand Turk. He enters Monsieur Jourdain's house with his friends, who are disguised as his slaves. Cléonte presents himself to the master of the house; he and his friends dance for Monsieur Jourdain by way of introduction. Totally captivated by his visitors, Jourdain presents a ballet entertainment in their honor (pas de sept). Lucile enters with her servant Nicole but fails to see through Cléonte's disguise. Cléonte stages a mock Turkish ceremony to "ennoble" Monsieur Jourdain; his "slaves" form an elephant under a cloth on which Jourdain rides. A Turkish divertissement follows: a pas de trois, a pas de deux, and an acrobatic pas de quatre. Lucile attempts to flee her unwelcome suitor (pas de deux), but despite her protests her father announces their betrothal. Emboldened, Cléonte casts aside his disguise. Monsieur Jourdain good-naturedly defers to true love and offers his blessing to the happy couple.

Scenery and Costumes

Benois's sumptuous scenery and costumes were meant to suggest the splendor and elegance of the French *comédie-ballet*. Four years earlier he had designed another ballet of the same period, *Les Noces de Psyché et de l'Amour*, for Ida Rubinstein, with choreography by Nijinska; at that time his intention was to reconstruct the original designs by Bérain, the most prominent court entertainment designer for Louis XIV.

In *Le Bourgeois Gentilhomme* he attempted not to reconstruct the original designs or the style of the period but simply to evoke them. The throne room consisted of curved columns that were representative of the prevailing Louis Quatorze style, in which the simplicity of the classical line was ultimately replaced by baroque ornamentation.

The costumes were of two kinds. Those worn by the character dancers were in the pompous style of the seventeenth-century *habits de cour*: paniers embroidered in velvet and silk, with curled and powdered wigs. These designs captured the social pretensions of the foolish Monsieur Jourdain and his nouveau-riche world. The costumes for the divertissements departed from the period style to allow the dancers freedom of movement. Those worn in the acrobatic pas de quatre were anachronisms more properly at home in a modern circus routine. The Turk's costume was also more modern in concept. In the seventeenth century, local color was merely suggested by the ornaments and details on the *habit de cour*—a turban, a sash, and a long caftan would suggest a Turk, but the costume, especially below the hip, would be a contemporary *habit de cour*. Benois's design for the Turk (with the obvious exception of the ballet shoes!) was consistently Turkish.

Choreography

The action of *Le Bourgeois Gentilhomme* was propelled primarily by pantomime. The dance numbers served two functions: the solos of Lucile and Cléonte and their pas de deux expressed their personalities and emotions, while the pas de sept and the Turkish divertissement were pure entertainment. The most acclaimed pieces were Cléonte's entrance into Monsieur Jourdain's house as the Turk, the choreography for which expressed his immense vitality; the pas de sept; and the pas de deux of Lucile and Cléonte. Critics considered the pas de sept the gem of the ballet, and even today dancers remember it as one of Balanchine's most beautiful inventions. The seven dancers formed a triangle, with a lead dancer at its apex, and each of them was pro-

39

ABOVE: In front of Benois' front curtain, Cleonte (Lichine) disguises himself as the son of the Grand Turk. LEFT: Toumanova and Lichine. BELOW: "Turkish Divertissement" pas de deux: Strakhova and Borovsky.

ABOVE: "Turkish Divertissement" pas de trois: Katchourovsky, Morosova, and Shabelevsky. RIGHT: "Turkish Divertissement," the Acrobats: Slavinska, Kervily, and Kirsova, with Jasinski. BELOW: The full company in front of Benois' decor.

41

vided with a variation to show off the company's high standard of classical training. The leader of the pas de sept was first danced by Blinova, alternating with Verchinina; the role was passed to Baronova in Paris, giving her her first major opportunity of the season. Levinson had high praise for the pas de trois of the Turkish divertissement, and especially for the "ravishing" pas de sept, "with its joyous scrimmage of variations in which each soloist dismisses the preceding one with a 'get out of my way, let me in,' a pantomime that reduces to a playful game the secret rivalries of behind the scenes."[3] Pierre Michaut felt that the Turkish divertissement revealed "invention and technical skill, if not true inspiration."[4]

The ballet was admired for its flawless construction, but after the abstractions of *Cotillon* and *Jeux d'enfants,* it was considered too reminiscent of the sort of dramatic ballet that had prevailed until Diaghilev's last productions. Levinson, who had always championed the pre-eminence of dancing among all the elements of a ballet, felt that Balanchine's reliance on pantomime was often tiresome.[5] Some dancers felt that this ballet's pantomime lacked the spontaneity of *La Concurrence*—perhaps the fault of its origins in a complicated seventeenth-century play and of its creators' intention of recapturing the mood and style of Molière's comedy of manners. The mime in *Bourgeois Gentilhomme* was weighted down by the need to compensate for the loss of Molière's verbal satire. On the other hand, Derain's much lighter libretto for *La Concurrence* had allowed Balanchine to create a less calculated mime.

Premiere

42

The work was successfully performed in Monte Carlo and Paris and on tour throughout Belgium, Holland, and Germany. When the company arrived in Switzerland, though, an official announcement was made that the scenery and costumes had been destroyed in a fire and that, consequently, the work would be dropped from the repertory. According to Kochno, however, it was Strauss who was responsible for the ballet's disappearance; he felt his score was unsuitable for dance, even though he had never seen the Ballets Russes production. (Perhaps he objected to Kochno's libretto, which centered on the elements of the play that the composer found the weakest.)

Despite Strauss's objections, Balanchine remained attached to the score and created two subsequent versions; one for Denham's Ballet Russe de Monte Carlo in 1944, and another for the New York City Opera as a co-production with the New York City Ballet and its School of American Ballet in 1979. (It later entered the repertory of the New York City Ballet.) Those who have seen all three feel that the first was the most effective scenically and that its mime and dance passages were better integrated than later versions.

January 1933–
April 1934

A rehearsal of *Les Présages* in a Monte Carlo studio, attended by invited guests.

NINETEEN THIRTY-THREE was a decisive year. The success that the company had achieved in 1932 was paving its way to international recognition. New contacts had been made; Joan Miró had served as mediator between the Ballets Russes and the Teatre Liceu to arrange the company's first season in Barcelona in May,[1] and negotiations were in progress with the British impresarios B. F. Howell and Sir Oswald Stoll for future performances in London. On April 6 Howell offered de Basil a four-week season at the Lyceum Theatre beginning on May 15; Stoll, who had seen the company in Monte Carlo in 1932 and again in 1933, was proposing a season at the London Coliseum. De Basil opted for Stoll, but when the company made its London debut in July, it was not at the Coliseum but at the Alhambra Theatre. As for the United States, everything was settled: after the Paris season of 1932, a contract had been negotiated with the impresario Sol Hurok for the first American tour, to begin in December 1933.

The schedule for the first part of the year followed the same basic pattern as that of the previous year. First, there was the opera season at Monte Carlo, from January 5 to April 9. Fortunately, there was only one new production to rehearse, Verdi's *Un ballo in maschera*; thus, most of the rehearsal time could be dedicated to the new works for the spring ballet season: *Les Présages, Le Beau Danube, Beach, Scuola di ballo,* and *Rebus.*

With Balanchine gone, Massine was the appropriate choice to succeed him as ballet master and choreographer. Besides producing new works, he could revive his older ballets. In his autobiography Massine implies—misleadingly—that he then owned a fair share of the materials from Diaghilev's ballets. In reality, most of the sets, costumes, and properties were owned by the impresario E. Ray Goetz, and were in storage at Maison Bedel, a Parisian warehouse. But on January 23, 1933, through Massine's intercession, Goetz agreed to allow de Basil temporary use of the costumes and decor for fifteen ballets of the Colonel's choice.[2] In this complicated agreement, de Basil would eventually become sole proprietor of the materials pertaining to the fifteen ballets in return for his commitment to a 1933–34 American tour for which Goetz had an option until April 30, 1933. Moreover, Goetz agreed not to sell or rent any part of the Diaghilev property in his possession before April 30, 1934; de Basil would have the first option in a sale thereafter. But Goetz failed to arrange a tour to supplant Hurok's, and on November 8, 1933, he authorized Bedel to sell to de Basil and Massine all materials held in the warehouse;[3] and on August 10, 1934, de Basil bought Massine's share of the jointly owned property for 143,000 francs, to be paid in installments over a period of one year.[4]

The ballet season in Monte Carlo had begun on April 13 and had again caused a sensation, especially with the premiere of *Les Présages,* Massine's first "symphonic ballet." *Beach, Le Beau Danube,* and *Scuola di ballo* were also highly acclaimed and soon became favorites, particularly the latter two. *Rebus (Pauvrété n'est pas vice),* with libretto and choreography by Massine, music by Igor Markevitch, and scenery and costumes by Luis Cappiello, had been scheduled for May 8 but was delayed until the Paris engagement. This was its third postponement; initially it had been projected for the 1932 season. (De Basil originally wanted Picasso to design *Rebus* but, although Massine contacted the artist, nothing came of it.) As it happened, the ballet was fated never to see the light of day. De Basil had made an agreement with B. Schott Söhne,[5] owners of the music copyright through Editions Max Eschig in Paris, for the exclusive European and American rights for a period of three years; but the authorization for Britain and the United States failed. The ballet, although near completion (according to de Basil),[6] was withdrawn completely; it would have been impractical to stage a work that could be performed only on the Continent.

The company roster was impressive. Alexandra Danilova had just joined; Riabouchinska was developing further her indisputable individuality. Baronova, the company's youngest member, who had made little impact the previous year, came into the spotlight with the first important roles created for her, and assumed many of Toumanova's roles as well. Nina Verchinina's enigmatic presence was a revelation, as were Delarova's skills as a comedienne and demi-caractère dancer. The male roster was headed by Massine, who resumed his career as a performer; the experienced Woizikowski; the vital and exuberant Lichine; and the technically prodigious young André Eglevsky.

After Monte Carlo the company traveled to Barcelona for seven performances (May 13–28) at the Gran Teatre del Liceu, the sumptuous hall administered by Juan Mestres, and one of the world's leading opera houses. Barcelona had always been considered the artistic center of Spain. Its former support of Diaghilev was immediately extended to the new company, which appeared there every year until 1936, when the outbreak of the Spanish Civil War precluded further engagements. At the Liceu the dancers performed on a stage different from any other, for the proscenium boxes extended into the stage space. This architectural feature inhibited the dancers'

45

Danilova, Chamié, and Morosova on the beach terrace at Monte Carlo.

stage warm-ups, as they could be seen by the box-holders even when the front curtain was down.

For the Paris appearances the Ballets Russes was engaged by Michel Kachouk, director of the Grand Opéra Russe à Paris (the former Opéra Russe à Paris) and manager of Feodor Chaliapin.[7] Kachouk booked the company for his season of Russian opera at the Théâtre du Châtelet, in the dance sequences of *Boris Godounov, Prince Igor, The Tsar's Bride,* and *Pique Dame* and for an independent ballet season as well. Earlier in the year, plans had been made for Ansermet to conduct the Ballets Russes orchestra in Paris and London, but a two-month tour of the Soviet Union prevented him from doing so.[8] Roger Désormière was engaged instead to share the podium with Marc-César Scotto and Pierre Kolpikov.

As the summer advanced, Paris was plastered with posters announcing the appearances of Les Ballets 1933 at the Théâtre des Champs-Elysées and the Ballets Russes de Monte Carlo at the Théâtre du Châtelet. For the public the situation was rather puzzling, since many of the names associated with the new venture previously had been closely identified with the Ballets Russes. To the Parisians' delight, the rivalry was stressed by de Basil's court injunction against Balanchine for taking Toumanova from his company and against the fourteen-year-old ballerina herself for desertion. According to Toumanova, de Basil claimed that most of the 1932 repertory, especially the new ballets, had been centered on her, making her indispensable. The hearing took place on June 7—the day Les Ballets 1933 opened in Paris. When the judge asked the Colonel in what class Toumanova had traveled and he answered, "In second, like everybody else," the case was dismissed in the defendants' favor.

Les Ballets 1933 had been formed by Kochno as artistic director and Balanchine as choreographer with the aid of Vladimir Dimitriev, who had been instrumental in helping Danilova and Balanchine get out of the Soviet Union. The company had been organized around Toumanova, along with other defectors from the Monte Carlo company: Lulu Kylberg (Lubov Rostova), Tamara Tchinarova, Roman Jasinski, Yurek Shabelevsky, and others. When Tilly Losch entered the company, her husband, Edward James, became its patron, thus ending its financial vicissitudes. A Chilean copper magnate named López also helped to underwrite the new enterprise.

The repertory was very eclectic, and represented a blending of some of the most distinguished contemporary artists: André Derain and Henri Sauguet for *Fastes;* Pavel Tchelitchev for *L'Errante;* Christian Bérard for *Mozartiana;* Derain and Darius Milhaud for *Les Songes;* Emilio Terry and Nicolas Nabokov for *Les Valses de Beethoven;* and Kurt Weill, Bertolt Brecht, Caspar Neher, and Lotte Lenya for *The Seven Deadly Sins.* As the company's name indicates, it was formed to display a group of artists at a specific moment, without any intention of continuity. The result was a Parisian *succès de snobisme.* (The audience included Lincoln Kirstein, who later was instrumental in bringing Balanchine to the United States and forming the New York City Ballet.) After Paris, Les Ballets 1933 opened a short season at the Savoy Theatre in London on June 28, just before de Basil's company was to open at the Alhambra. Although it was less than a success with the general public, Les Ballets 1933 was enthusiastically received by the Bloomsbury/Sitwell set.

At the Châtelet, the Ballets Russes presented one world premiere, David Lichine's *Nocturne*. But it was Massine's *Les Présages* that provided the note of controversy and sealed the triumph of the Paris season. Sir Oswald Stoll attended every performance at the Châtelet with G. G. Reynolds, manager of the Alhambra, where the company was soon to appear; they wanted to be familiar with the dancers and repertoire. Expectations were high in London, the city that had been most supportive of Diaghilev and his company.

The London engagement opened on July 4 with *Les Sylphides*, *Les Présages*, and *Le Beau Danube*, a program that offered familiar stars (Danilova, Massine, Woizikowski) and introduced a new generation (Baronova, Riabouchinska, Verchinina, Lichine, Eglevsky). Anton Dolin, who had been a guest artist at the Châtelet, joined the company again as a danseur noble.

The company impressed London as a young and versatile ensemble in which almost every member of the corps had soloist potential. Since Diaghilev's death, London had seen various efforts at resuscitating his company, including the ballet of the Opéra Russe à Paris with Doubrovska, Nemtchinova, and Woizikowski in 1931. Although the artistry of individual dancers had been admired, none of these ventures achieved any lasting success. The Ballets Russes triumph was unexpected, and London's allegiance was immediate and lasted until the war. The three-week season was extended to four months (July 4–October 30), a success without precedent in the city's balletic history. Toumanova and a contingent of dancers from Les Ballets 1933 rejoined de Basil in September.

To end the season in grand style, the company presented the world premiere of *Choreartium*, Massine's second symphonic ballet, arousing one of the decade's most heated controversies in the music and dance worlds. In fact, the enthusiasm for Mas-

47

After a performance of *Choreartium*. Left to right: Adrianova, Psota, Petroff, Danilova, Massine, Toumanova, de Basil, Lichine, Riabouchinska, Ladré; Jasinski, Grigorieva, Borovansky.

sine's ballets was overwhelming. Agnes de Mille, then a struggling young dancer and choreographer with the Ballet Rambert, described the scene at the Alhambra:

> . . . The furor evoked by the baby ballerinas and the love commanded by Danilova were not in a class with the adulation accorded to the master of all, Léonide Massine. Seeing a Massine ballet had become one of the erotic pleasures of the London season. The expensive spectators in the stalls contented themselves with "Bravos" and gush. The devotees upstairs gave themselves unrestrainedly to screaming, jumping up and down, beating the railing, hugging one another, slathering at the mouth.[9]

After the sensational closing night at the Alhambra, the company appeared for the first time on television. Since May 2, 1932, Broadcasting House on upper Regent Street at Portland Place had been presenting "low-definition" live television. On the evening of November 3, the company's principals went to the Broadcasting House studio. In a performing area six feet wide and four deep, and under almost painfully hot lights, the dancers performed excerpts from their Alhambra repertory. According to BBC records, the program included scenes from *Jeux d'enfants*, with Riabouchinska as the Child, Baronova as the Top, and Lichine as the Traveler; from *Carnaval*, with Danilova as Columbine, Woizikowski as Harlequin, and Kirsova as Papillon; from *Petrouchka*, with Toumanova as the Ballerina, Lichine as the Blackamoor, and Woizikowski as Petrouchka; and, to conclude, the mazurka from *Le Beau Danube*, with Riabouchinska and Massine. (Due to an injury to Lichine, the Traveler was actually danced by Shabelevsky and the Blackamoor by Algeranoff.) The music was provided by a quartet from the Alhambra orchestra conducted by Efrem Kurtz.

Spirits were high after their success in London when, on December 12, the sixty-four-member ensemble set sail to New York aboard the *Lafayette*, with eighty-four backdrops and curtains, six thousand costumes, a fifty-piece orchestra, and twenty-two ballets. The tour was a venture of considerable risk. After the stock market crash, the American theatrical world was near collapse. Hurok's decision to present the company was a courageous one, especially since ballet had never been an integral part of American artistic life. After Pavlova's last visit, in 1925–26, very little had been presented: there were the Metropolitan Opera Ballet and a few sporadic performances by local groups such as the Chicago Allied Arts (organized in 1924 with Adolph Bolm as ballet master and Ruth Page as principal dancer) and Mikhail Mordkin's company (whose dancers included Vera Nemtchinova and Pierre Vladimiroff). Massine had staged some productions during his contract with the Roxy and, more importantly, his version of *Le Sacre du printemps* in Philadelphia in 1930, with Leopold Stokowski conducting the Philadelphia Orchestra and Martha Graham as the Chosen Maiden. It was a time when most of the American dance world felt that they needed to express themselves in a nonballetic idiom.

After seeing the Ballets Russes in the summer of 1932, Hurok was convinced that the time was right to reintroduce grand-scale ballet to the United States, and he took two major steps to promote the company. First, he organized an impressive sponsoring committee, headed by the Grand Duchess Marie of Russia and the banker Otto Kahn, the former chairman of the board of the Metropolitan Opera and a celebrated patron of the arts who had been responsible for the United States debut of Pavlova in 1910 and that of the Diaghilev company in 1916. Hurok also devised a sensational publicity campaign, which concentrated on three main points: the Diaghilev heritage, the company's recent European success, and, above all, the phenomenon of the three "baby ballerinas," Toumanova, Riabouchinska, and Baronova.

The "baby ballerinas" publicity campaign is legendary. Even now, after fifty years, new ballet prodigies are touted as part of the "baby ballerina" tradition and compared to de Basil's original trio. How the name came about is difficult to ascertain. It is commonly thought that the phrase was coined by the English critic Arnold Haskell during the last half of the Alhambra season, when the three dancers were reunited after Toumanova's defection to Les Ballets 1933; but whatever its origin, it was part of Hurok's well-conceived scheme to launch the company in America. Hurok strongly believed in the star system. In a telegram to de Basil dated November 12, he made clear his willingness to subsidize the appearance of Toumanova in particular.* From the first she had been a special concern; her participation was stipulated when negotiations started in the summer of 1932, before she joined Les Ballets 1933.

Although they were often referred to collectively as "the young girls" because of their extreme youth, the three ballerinas had already established themselves individually during the 1932–33 European tours. Each one's professional career predated her Ballets Russes engagements. Toumanova, a product of Preobrajenskaya, had made her debut at the age of six with Pavlova in a Red Cross benefit in 1926 and three years later was featured in *L'Eventail de Jeanne* at the Paris Opéra. Riabouchinska, a pupil of Volinine and Kchessinskaya, had danced in Paris, London, and New York with Balieff's *Chauve-Souris* revue. It was in London that Balanchine saw her in Catherine Devillier's ballet *Diana Hunts the Stag*, wearing a much-talked-about Schiaparelli costume, and he signed her for the new company. Irina Baronova, another of Preobrajenskaya's pupils, had made her professional debut opposite Doubrovska and Vilzak in Balanchine's *Orphée aux enfers* at the Théâtre Mogador in 1931. Alexandra Danilova did not join the company until the 1933 Monte Carlo season, after completing the successful London run of the musical *Waltzes from Vienna*. Balanchine reportedly had not taken her into the company in 1932 because he felt that at twenty-seven the ballerina was too old.[11] According to Massine, she was later contacted by de Basil at the choreographer's suggestion.

The Ballets Russes opened in New York at the St. James Theatre on December 22; the program consisted of *La Concurrence*, *Les Présages*, and *Le Beau Danube*. The evening had all the glitter of an opening night at the Metropolitan Opera during the thirties. The sponsoring committee turned out in force. Besides the patrons, all the

49

---

* "Is Toumanova coming? In view of tremendous publicity she has received is very valuable addition to company for our business. Will pay up to hundred dollars additional per week provided she comes."[10]

Les Matelots: Lichine, Danilova, Massine, Chamié, and Woizikowski; decor by Pruna.

royalty currently in New York was present; there were more titles in the audience than there had been at many of the European premieres. Political, financial, and social figures came in droves, as well as such key personalities in the arts as Rachmaninoff, Stokowski, Pierre Matisse, and the publisher Condé Nast.

In spite of the publicity campaign, the first-week box office receipts were unimpressive. After the splendid premiere, the most spirited public consisted of the dancers' parents, especially the mothers, who traveled with their offspring, and the company staff. Apart from New York's apathetic attitude to ballet, the repertory was not what the public expected from the heirs of Diaghilev. *Les Présages* in particular was not received as it had been in Europe, especially in London. Hurok, disconcerted, asked W. J. Henderson, the powerful music critic of the *New York Sun*, for suggestions. His advice was "more emphasis on the pre-First World War works that for the New Yorkers were representative of the Russian ballet." *Les Matelots*, *Petrouchka*, and *Carnaval* made their way back into the program. Condé Nast also helped to publicize the Ballets Russes with articles and photographs in *Vanity Fair*, including a color plate of Toumanova, Woizikowski, and Lichine in *Petrouchka*.

After the second week at the St. James, the houses improved considerably, to the point where the theater invoked a stop clause in its contract to prevent the company from leaving on tour. Hurok opted to divide the troupe into two groups. The New York forces, headed by Baronova, Riabouchinska, and Lichine, stayed at the St. James for a few weeks with a single program consisting of three favorite works: *Les Sylphides*, *Petrouchka*, and *Prince Igor*. The first, exploratory tour outside New York was undertaken by a group headed by Danilova, Toumanova, Verchinina, Delarova, Massine, and Woizikowski—with most of the repertory in tow. The company was reunited for an unforgettable season at the Auditorium Theatre in Chicago, where *Le Tricorne* was revived on February 20 with Massine as the Miller, Toumanova as his Wife, and Lichine as the Governor. The overwhelming success prompted Hurok to extend the company's stay in America through April, thus precipitating a crisis with Blum in Monte Carlo. The first United States engagement climaxed, appropriately, with the first ballet on an American theme by an international ballet company: Massine's *Union Pacific*, which had its premiere in Philadelphia at the Forrest Theatre on April 6.

LES PRÉSAGES

Choreographic symphony in four scenes; music, Tchaikovsky's Fifth Symphony in E Minor, Op. 64; libretto and choreography by Léonide Massine; set design by André Masson, executed by Prince A. Schervachidze; costume design by André Masson, executed by Madame Karinska; premiere April 13, 1933, at the Théâtre de Monte Carlo, conducted by Marc-César Scotto.

ORIGINAL CAST

First Movement

Action — Nina Verchinina

Temptation — Nathalie Branitska, Nina Tarakanova, and Roland Guérard

Movement — Mlles Berry, Chabelska, Larina, Lipkovska, Morosova, Nijinsky, Raievska, Razoumova, Tresahar, and Volkova MM. Dolotine, Eglevsky, Hoyer, Katcharoff, Lipatoff, Matouchevsky, and Psota

Second Movement

Passion — Irina Baronova; David Lichine

Fate — Leon Woizikowski

Destinies — Mlles Branitska, Delarova, Kobseva, Larina, Morosova, Obidenna, Semenova, Tresahar MM. Borovansky, Alexandroff, Ladré, Petroff

Third Movement		Fourth Movement	
Frivolity	Tatiana Riabouchinska	Passion	Irina Baronova
Variation	Mlles Berry, Branitska, Chabelska, Delarova, Kobseva, Larina, Nijinsky, Obidenna, Raievska, Razoumova, Rostova, Semenova, Sidorenko, Tchinarova, Tresahar, and Volkova	Frivolity	Tatiana Riabouchinska
		Action	Nina Verchinina
		Fate	Leon Woizikowski
		The Hero	David Lichine
		Destinies	Mlles Berry, Branitska, Chabelska, Delarova, Kobseva, Larina, Nijinsky, Obidenna, Raievska, Razoumova, Rostova, Semenova, Sidorenko, Tchinarova, Tresahar, and Volkova
			MM. Borovansky, Alexandroff, Dolotine, Eglevsky, Hoyer, Katcharoff, Ladré, Lipatoff, Matouchevsky, Petroff, and Psota

Nineteen hundred thirty-three marked the beginning of the Massine regime as well as the choreographer's most prolific year with Blum and de Basil. The management had decided to present four new works, all of which (together with three from the previous season—*Cotillon*, *La Concurrence*, and *Jeux d'enfants*) were to become staples of the repertory. The new works were scheduled to open in Monte Carlo early that summer, before the company's English debut at the Alhambra in July; de Basil and Blum hoped to take London by storm with a dazzling succession of new ballets.

Les Présages, the first new work to be presented, was Massine's setting of Tchaikovsky's Fifth Symphony. When he announced his intention of using a familiar symphony as a ballet score, Blum tried to discourage him, enlisting the support of his friend Bruno Walter, one of the world's great conductors and a man whose advice he thought Massine would take very seriously indeed. Unswayed by their arguments, Massine forged ahead. Supremely confident, he invited Walter to the final dress rehearsals; according to Massine, the maestro commented afterwards that it was a successful experiment, but hardly the basis for a method. Nonetheless, *Les Présages* immediately became a landmark in the history of modern ballet. It attracted general attention, and its impact was felt not only in the ballet world, but also—and perhaps even more forcefully—in the worlds of music and art.

Rehearsals   Preparations for the season began on January 2, when the company met in Monte Carlo after a New Year's Eve in Paris. Rehearsals for *Les Présages* began in mid-January and went on until the premiere in mid-April. With time out for lunch and dinner breaks, the sessions usually lasted from morning until about eleven at night.

Those dancers who had worked with Balanchine during the 1932 season found things very different with Massine. *Jeux d'enfants* had been only a trial run; the new works, with their distinctive styles, were even more challenging. Baronova recalls: "Massine was scientific in his approach to choreography. There was no spontaneity and humor as there had been with Balanchine. Massine came to the rehearsal studio

52

with notes, diagrams, and books, and for almost each sixteen bars of music he would have about five different choreographic interpretations or versions. He would teach them all, and then he would ask the dancers to perform them for him to choose the one he would like to keep in the ballet. It was a method of elimination. He would say do bar 2, variation 5; bar 3, variation 1; and then bar 2, variation 5; bar 3, variation 4—and so on."

Although Massine was an outstanding demi-caractère and character dancer, and had been a juvenile actor at the Maly Theatre in Moscow, most dancers who worked with him complained that he did not explain any of his characterizations. His method differed from that of most choreographers. He never offered descriptive images to help dancers interpret their roles, for he considered the movements to be self-explanatory. By his own definition, he was an intuitive artist.

According to Yurek Lazowski, who joined the company later (in 1935), Massine would demonstrate a movement or a series of movements, and the dancers would simply copy it. Baronova found this troubling: "We tried very hard to grasp what he wanted. My role was Passion, but I was only fourteen and did not know how to convey the idea of passion. I would go around the studio asking everyone how I was supposed to portray passion. I would try many ways until he would say, 'That's right,' but since I had been completely spontaneous, I did not know how to reproduce it. This approach forced us to look inside ourselves in order to explore and be able to express moods and feelings."

Delarova, Massine's wife at the time, elaborated on his working methods: "He would work out the choreography on himself at home and then, according to the music and the feel of the role, he would cast one of the dancers of the company. For example, studying the score of the waltz of Tchaikovsky's Fifth, he found it so light and airy that immediately he thought of Riabouchinska. So when he came to rehearse it, he had already written down the choreography that she was to dance. In the rehearsal studio he demonstrated every step, but he never explained much." (Massine once showed me these notebooks of his—lines of little figures arranged in patterns, like a musical score.)

Scenery and Costumes

For his designer Massine had wanted Matisse, with whom he had previously collaborated on *Le Chant du rossignol* for Diaghilev in 1920. Matisse declined, but he recommended the young French painter André Masson. *Les Présages* opened a new phase of Masson's career—an association with the theater that was to last until the 1960s.

Preliminary discussions between choreographer and painter took place in Paris during the winter of 1932. Though Masson was excited to be working with the ballet, his relationship with de Basil was stormy. In defiance of his already-signed contract, Masson protested before leaving Paris that the terms offered to him were inferior to those offered Bérard and other designers. He demanded ten thousand francs instead of the agreed-upon five thousand and, in addition, full lodgings in Monte Carlo during production.[1] De Basil refused to alter the fee but agreed to cover Masson's expenses for two weeks in March at the Hotel Bristol.[2]

53

Once he was settled in Monaco, the designer's quick temper unleashed a series of altercations both inside and outside the theater, one of which landed him in a far less agreeable abode than the Bristol—the local jail. Matisse, who lived nearby and often attended the morning rehearsals of *Les Présages*, gave evidence of his warm affection for Masson: when the tension between the designer and de Basil was at its highest, he invited Masson to go home with him to Nice, where he remained for more than two weeks, until the premiere. Masson attended the opening night in Monte Carlo and then left for Paris. As late as 1936, in Spain at the outbreak of the Civil War, he attended performances of *Les Présages* in Barcelona, and wrote to de Basil offering his help in refurbishing the decor.[3]

Les Présages, as we can now see, possessed a deep level of symbolism as well as a quality reminiscent of German expressionism. In this work Massine and Masson tried to develop an artistic concept that was very much rooted in their understanding of expressionism as the projection of the subjective tension between the individual and his environment, the tragic opposition between the subjective will and the objective rigidity of the confronting world.[4] Massine was attracted to this movement because it afforded a different mode in which to explore, in depth, the human condition.

Masson's interest in expressionism had been aroused in 1929, when he broke away from André Breton and the surrealist movement. Although his work remained largely surrealistic in character, in 1932 he had begun painting expressionistic scenes of ritual killings. During this period he felt that painting was "that in which the spaces between the figures are charged with as much energy as the figures that determine them."[5] Color, line, figure, and background were united in a dynamic whole. There are striking similarities between the color scheme of his 1933 canvas *Massacre in the Field* and the stage designs for *Les Présages*. We should keep in mind that Masson's approach to theatrical design was purely painterly.

For *Les Présages* he used an intensely violent color scheme typical of his work of that time: bright reds, greens, yellows, purples, and blues that were well suited to the lavish symbolism of the designs. Action's costume was terra-cotta; Passion's, tomato red with pink tights. Man wore a yellow vest and tights, and a yellow shirt with a red design on the chest; Fate was a batlike figure in shades of brown; Frivolity wore powder blue with light green tights. Throughout, the female corps wore purple and mauve tunics patched with black tarot symbols: spades, anchors, clubs, daggers, half-moons. All the female dancers' costumes were modeled on the classical Greek tunic —probably an effect of Masson's recently developed interest in Greek mythology. In the first two movements, the male corps wore green and mauve, and in the finale, long-sleeved coveralls with hoods, in shades of brown. For the fourth movement Lichine, as the Hero, was dressed in modern clothes—a brown T-shirt and beige pants with brown patches. The backdrop was a multicolored concatenation of comets, shooting stars, rainbows, tongues of flame, spouting hearts, and other signs of an apocalyptic vision.

Action   The theme of *Les Présages* was man's struggle against destiny, as suggested to Massine by Tchaikovsky's correspondence with his patroness, Nadezhda von Meck.

54

The work was in four scenes, one for each movement of the symphony. Each scene had a subtitle that described its content and introduced allegorical characters.

First Movement: Andante; Allegro con anima. MAN'S LIFE WITH ITS DIVERSIONS, DESIRES, AND TEMPTATIONS. The curtain rises on an empty stage lit in magenta. Action enters from the side and performs a diagonal. With both palms facing in front of her she lowers one while the other stays in the same position. She rotates the free arm in a circle around her as she turns on pointe around the stage, followed by four dancers who copy her movements. Four men enter from the other side swinging their downstage arms. As the musical theme grows, various groups make rapid entrances and exits. When the second musical theme is introduced, Eglevsky is revealed between two female dancers, and as they approach the audience he makes numerous fast turns. When the third musical theme is introduced Action makes a second entrance preceded by three couples. The first musical theme is repeated. Three female dancers enter, the first followed by the other two; the three perform a sort of gallop as a figure upstage passes transversely across the stage making slow turns. Simultaneously, five men run and leap upstage (next to the backdrop) in swift succession, hands clasped above their heads, their legs forming a triangle as they jump in a passé position. Eglevsky jumps in facing the wings and in mid-air turns his back on them. With the men leaping in the background, he begins to turn slowly, with his arms very close to his body. The second musical subject reappears and two men enter from each side surrounded by a circle of five women, and one man after the other performs a series of double tours en l'air. Facing each other, the men and women cross and uncross their arms several times above their heads. The women are lifted, their legs open in second position and their arms stretched horizontally. At this moment the third musical theme is introduced and Action makes her third entrance. She glides center stage to be partnered by Eglevsky in a short poetic duo, after which they exit. The first musical theme is reintroduced and Action makes her last entrance with the corps de ballet grouped at her side. She goes around the stage as the members of the corps separate from each other, one by one, to follow her. The corps exits, leaving Action dancing alone to the last musical phrases, finally going off backwards on pointe.

Second Movement: Andante cantabile con alcuna licenza. LOVE IN CONFLICT WITH THE BASER PASSIONS, WHICH SHATTERS THE HUMAN SOUL. THE BEAUTY OF LOVE IS IMPERILLED, BUT PREVAILS IN THE END. With the curtain remaining up, Passion and Lichine enter, Passion closer to the audience. His right arm is around her waist, with his left arm stretched forward. She holds her downstage arm in front of her, bent upward at the elbow, her other arm beneath Lichine's chin, her head resting lightly on his shoulder. They walk slowly in a diagonal (Baronova on pointe) from upstage to center stage and dance a pas de deux consisting of supported pirouettes, lifts, and interwoven bodily movements. Separating temporarily, they come back together in an affirmation of their love. When they move apart, she runs back and turns, finishing her pirouettes with her arms open wide towards him. The corps de ballet enters and dances to counterpoint around the lovers in the manner of a Greek chorus. Fate makes a dramatic entrance performing fast pirouettes, lifting his elbows like wings and stamping his heels as he goes across stage to come between the lovers. Lichine is overpowered by Fate and collapses while Baronova resists dancing with Fate, and goes to Lichine to comfort him. The second musical theme is introduced and the lovers walk offstage—Baronova following Lichine with both arms stretched out to Lichine's downstage shoulder. A pas de trois is performed and then the corps, which had momentarily left the three main characters alone, enters and dances along with Fate. The lovers reenter from opposite sides. Passion tries to entice Fate away and dances with him as the corps is grouped in a triangular pattern like a pyramid—the dancers in front on their knees, heads down resting on one hand, the dancers in back standing up with their arms stretched towards the wings in the opposite direction from the principal dancers. While Passion and Fate are performing the pas de deux, Lichine is alone and helpless downstage diagonally from Passion, Fate, and the corps. One of the most beautiful features of the pas de deux between Passion and Lichine is Passion's pirouette, in which she stretches her arms back to Fate, sideways and behind her. He catches her arms and arches her back towards him. As she rests on one point —the other leg in a passé position—Lichine springs up to fight Fate and recover his beloved, but again collapses and implores for her. Fate dances his fatal victory, exiting as the men in the corps de ballet lift the women high. Fate returns briefly to perform a macabre dance and exits. The lovers find consolation in each other and resume their pas de deux with dramatic acrobatic lifts. With the coda the corps de ballet circles around them and fades offstage slowly. The lovers leave as they came in, continuing the diagonal line in the opposite direction from their place of entry. As they exit, she walks in the air, slightly lifted by Lichine.

Third Movement: Valse; Allegro moderato. GAIETY UNTRAMMELLED, IN WHICH DESTINY FOR A TIME IS FORGOTTEN. The stage is now illuminated by a bluish light as the principal musical theme that will be identified with Frivolity is introduced. Frivolity jumps from the wings and performs a long, intricate variation of jumps that increase with batterie steps, speedy petit tours, and multiple pirouettes. With the introduction of the second musical theme an all-female corps de ballet appears as Frivolity goes off. The corps dances to counterpoint until Frivolity reenters. Now the group repeats all of her movements except for those brief moments when she poses poetically in supported arabesques against the grouped dancers. At the end of the movement Frivolity performs a circle of extremely fast chaîné turns around the stage with her elbows out, hands resting on her shoulders. Everyone exits.

Fourth Movement: Andante maestoso. THE EVIL IN MAN HAS AROUSED THE ANGRY PASSION OF WAR. AFTER FACING DANGER, THE HEROES ARE VICTORIOUS, BUT THE TRIUMPH THEY CELEBRATE IS OVER THE EVIL SPIRIT OF WAR, WHICH THEY HAVE CONQUERED. In a stage lit in magenta, Fate enters followed closely by twelve men. The Hero enters and travels around the stage in a sequence of grands jetés. He confronts Fate and his men but is overwhelmed by their power and collapses, lying downstage sideways to the audience. Fate and his men exit briefly and return with the introduction of the second musical theme. The Hero then rises and performs acrobatic leaps as Fate does a more self-contained dance; they encounter each other while preparing for battle. Action, Passion, and Frivolity cross the stage twice from left to right and come to rescue the Hero, who quickly begins to leap from right to left facing the audience. The stage darkens as it becomes crowded with the corps de ballet moving in soldier-like fashion. The lighting brightens and Action, Passion, and Frivolity along with six members of the corps are held aloft horizontally, sideways to the audience. They are carried forward, one after the other, like rockets. In stage center the corps gallops in circles that turn in different directions. To the introductory musical theme of the first movement—that of Action—the Hero enters, leaping around stage with arms raised. As the climax approaches he runs downstage, climbing upon the locked shoulders of two male dancers to stand erect, his right arm raised. Passion, Frivolity, and Action (in that order, left to right) each go on one knee facing the Hero (their backs to the audience), with one arm stretched towards him. The corps de ballet frames the stage, with arms reaching out to him.

Choreography

Characteristically for Massine, the choreography of *Les Présages* derived from a dissection of the score: every theme found its counterpart in a dancer or a group of dancers. This "choreographic counterpoint" could be so intricate that each dancer became an independent entity. In this manner the choreography became a visualization of the musical structure. One could compare the later Balanchine works and post-modern dance choreographers to Massine in this respect.

First Movement: The choreographic representation of musical themes is well exemplified in the first movement. The protagonist was Action, danced by Verchinina to the main musical theme. The arm and torso movements Massine devised for her employed the idiom of Central European modern dance as formulated by Rudolf von Laban. Through Verchinina, who had studied the principles of this school, Massine was able to incorporate Laban's ideas more poetically and effectively than most modern-dance choreographers of the time. Her classical training had given her control of her torso and arms with minimal effort and allowed her a flexibility in expression free from the rigidity and strain that Laban's students often exhibited. Massine wanted Verchinina to seem to respond instinctively to every nuance of the music.

The second musical theme was danced as a response to Action by the fifteen-year-old André Eglevsky, whose precise classical technique in pirouettes, jetés, and double tours en l'air contrasted with Verchinina's free movements. There was also an intricate pas de trois for three Temptations. The interaction of the two leading dancers with the corps was mesmerizing in its mystical association of life and gloom. Massine felt that there was a very forceful quality in the first musical subject—composed mainly of clarinets, viola, cello, and double bass—that, even though impregnated with a certain sadness, suggested to him optimism, and the idea for Action. In the second musical theme, the appearance of the bassoon with the clarinets accentuated a quality of depression and pessimism—gloom. These musical phrases inspired him to contrast both leading dancers as the juxtaposition of two aspects of life. The idea of using symbolic or abstract terms, such as Action and Passion, as names for his characters was very trendy in the expressionistic theater.

Second Movement: The languishing theme of the Andante Cantabile inspired

57

Massine to create one of the first modern romantic pas de deux. Heretofore, there had been two standard types of pas de deux: the Petipa/classical (adagio, variations, coda), which was a virtuosic vehicle for the ballerina and her partner and was usually set in the context of a divertissement; and the romantic and post-romantic/Fokine pas de deux, welded to the development of the action and in service to the story and the characterization. In *Les Présages* the pas de deux became its own raison d'être. A symbolic theme united all the movements of the ballet, but the pas de deux was self-contained and could be performed by itself. Massine's creation of a self-sufficient pas de deux was the antecedent of so many works that were later devised for the slow movements of other symphonies or concerti. It was also an antecedent of *Balustrade* (1941), in which Balanchine used the slow movement for a pas de trois.

The pas de deux proceeds until Fate intervenes. When the lovers ecstatically resume their dance, Massine gives them an extremely effective lift, very much in the acrobatic Bolshoi style, with the corps de ballet circling around them.

Third Movement: Here Tchaikovsky departed from convention and substituted a waltz for the traditional Beethovenian scherzo, creating a contrast to the emotional level of the previous movements. The principal theme is identified with the character of Frivolity and is introduced immediately, so that the movement opens with Riabouchinska alone in a dreamlike atmosphere. Her choreography increases in technical difficulty, with virtuoso steps. Except for a brief appearance of the corps de ballet alone, the movement is a solo for Riabouchinska. And at the end, a moment of grave retrospection intrudes into the lightness of the waltz with the appearance of the first theme of the first movement—Action—preparing the mood for the finale.

Fourth Movement: Bravura in style, Oriental in atmosphere—Massine felt that this music was very Eastern and Russian in tone, exotic and filled with outbursts of color and religious feeling—the fourth movement is dominated by the conflict between Man (here called the Hero) and Fate. All the figures from previous movements reappear (another Massine innovation that became a formula for subsequent choreographers). While the female corps serves as a frame for this apotheosis, the male corps suggests war, with militaristic patterns of march steps and raised arms.

The spectacular finale was a complete novelty to the West. By coincidence, it resembled the acrobatic style developed in the Soviet Union as a reaction against the expressionist and, especially, the constructivist schools. After the October Revolution, there had been a tendency to break away from the old idea of ballet as a court entertainment, and though the classics were still in the repertory, the emphasis in newer ballets was on experimentation and collaboration with the current trends in the other arts. As a result, expressionist and constructivist ideas were realized on the ballet stage. (And vice versa: the prominent theater director Vladimir Nemirovich-Danchenko produced his own version of *Swan Lake*, with Alexander Gorsky in 1920.) However, in the thirties a new, heroic type of ballet evolved, partly as a consequence of the First Congress of the Union of Soviet Writers in 1934, which encouraged the close collaboration of ballet and literature in search of the national heritage. Ballet began to borrow subjects from the classical Russian writers (as well as from Shakespeare and Lope de Vega), and a new kind of dramatic realism and temperamental style of dancing enhanced the academic tradition. Acrobatics figured largely in the portrayal of the new Soviet hero danced by such outstanding performers as Olga Lepeshinskaya and Vakhtang Chaboukiani.

Like *Jeux d'enfants*, *Les Présages* was conceived as a painting in movement. The effect of the brightly colored costumes against the backcloth was one of color in constant motion. Massine's energetic masses of dancers enhanced this idea. The choreographer has written that he drew his inspiration from the mass and volume of the ancient ruins of Selinus, Agrigento, and Paestum.[6] Groups emerged as groups or broke up before the audience even began to suspect that they had been formed. Two of Massine's favorite mass configurations were the pyramid and the snake, which decreased in height as the first dancer stood and the last knelt, or grew in the opposite direction.

There was little symmetry to most of the corps patterns. Dancers would enter, form an unpredictable group, then suddenly scatter all over the stage to form new, equally unexpected groups—and finally exit, only to re-emerge a while later. There were no empty moments, but, instead, a constant flow of movement to parallel the flow of the music. Throughout the four movements, the corps de ballet functioned like the chorus in a Greek tragedy, reacting to the leading characters and helping to create and sustain the mood.

Massine's new approach to movement was the beginning of a synthesis (which he was to develop further in *Choreartium*) of ballet and the basic principles of Central European modern dance, especially those introduced by Rudolf von Laban and his disciple, Mary Wigman. Massine's own work was evolving toward a rhythmic structure within which physical movement is sufficient to express all that is essential to dance. In *Les Présages*, he achieved a work of forceful movement and color, distorted spatial relationships (many of his group patterns looked chaotic at that time), and an ambiguously erotic and violent feeling.

The dancers' roles were milestones in their careers and were instrumental in the development of their personal styles. Like the symphonic ballet itself, Verchinina was the representative of a new dance genre. With her own eclectic style she melded the music to the choreography in unusually angular movements. In the pas de deux Baronova combined poetry and sensuality with her brilliant attack. The Andante exploited the purity of her classical line, predicting the extraordinary Aurora she was to become and the voluptuousness that was to distinguish her Queen of Shemakhan in *Le Coq d'or*. Frivolity was a vehicle for Riabouchinska's speed, lightness, elevation, and ethereal presence—qualities later used to their fullest measure by Fokine in *Le Coq d'or* and *Paganini*. In his brief but powerfully dramatic appearance as Fate, Woizikowski met the high standard of his Diaghilev performances, and Lichine as Man-Hero stamped the work with his virility, barbaric exuberance, and dramatic command.

59

LEFT: Verchinina. BELOW: Riabouchinska.
OPPOSITE ABOVE: Fourth Movement: the
Rockets. OPPOSITE BELOW: Fourth
Movement: Lichine with corps de ballet;
set by Masson.

Les Présages was the first attempt in the Western world to interpret a symphony in terms of classical dance.[7] In Russia, the avant-garde choreographer Fyodor Lopoukhov had already experimented with this idea in his controversial *Dance Symphony*, set to Beethoven's Fourth. Though Massine never saw this ballet, he might well have been exposed to Lopoukhov's principles, which the latter had defined in his book *Paths of a Ballet Master*, published in Russian in Berlin in 1925. Massine agreed with Lopoukhov that symphonic ballets should have no detailed plot, that the choreography should flow from the music, and that it should employ classical as well as demi-caractère steps along with modern movements and acrobatics.

The premiere in Monte Carlo was a triumph, as reported in the local press: "The enthusiasm of the audience was tremendous. Time after time the stars were recalled. . . . Seldom does one see such enthusiasm in the Casino Theatre. . . ."[8] It was the Paris premiere two months later that launched the "symphonic ballet" controversy that was to rage in full force for years.

In Paris, *Les Présages* achieved a total *succès de scandale* reminiscent of the old Diaghilev days. At last de Basil found his enterprise the talk of the town, with partisans from every imaginable category.

Many musicians believed that *Les Présages* was a sacrilege. They considered a symphony to be a work of art complete in itself, which required no choreographic elucidation. To them, Massine was violating the intention of the composer by using this sacrosanct form as background music. Of course, this was nothing new: Isadora Duncan had done it; but, because she was in a category all her own, experimentation was expected of her. A similar controversy was aroused, although on a much smaller scale, with *Les Sylphides* and *Carnaval*, but the works on which they were based were not as revered by musicians as the symphonies. Moreover, Massine and the Ballets Russes had by then become an institution, and his daring had a stronger impact.

Masson's designs, too, elicited many objections. In the Parisian art world, there were complaints about the lack of harmony between the backcloth and the costumes, and about the monotonous effect of a single backcloth for all four movements. Although painter-designers had previously worked closely with choreographers, the focus of their theatrical design was usually the creation of an appropriate atmosphere within a more realistic ambience. Even the surrealistic *Jeux d'enfants* stayed within the realistic boundaries of the story—a surrealistic nursery after all. Masson avoided poetry as well as realism and concentrated on pure abstract symbolism. His main concern was to capture the flow of the music through the deployment of color—the expressionistic tension that both creators had in mind—and, above all, to extend the movements of the dancers with the design of his backcloth, aiming to create visual parallels with the music.

In the dance world some felt that Massine was selling out to modern dance. Despite the criticism, for dancers, choreographers, and dance critics *Les Présages* represented a new direction, for several reasons: the abstract treatment of the music; the use of asymmetrical, almost automatic mass movement; the juxtaposition of ballet and Central European modern dance movements; the innovative pas de deux in the second section; the acrobatics, especially in the fourth section, which were quite novel for Western Europe.

A politically minded group (a minority of liberal intellectuals and artists) also voiced its objection to the militaristic feel of Massine's ballet: 1933 was a critical year in German politics, and the Hero and raised-arm motif of the fourth movement suggested a parallel to the Brown Shirts of the Nazi party.

When the ballet reached London in July, it caused a sensation and was the focus of the season. It found its most ardent advocate in Ernest Newman, the dean of British music critics:

> One could be pardoned for being sceptical, before the event, as to the possibility of anyone taking the Tchaikovski [sic] or any other symphony virtually as it stands and working out an absolutely convincing choreography to it. . . .
>
> Mr. Massine must be genuinely musical, for it is really the music of the symphony that he has translated into a ballet, and this in such a way that, incredible as it may appear to anyone who has not seen "Les Présages," the inner life of the work, as an organic piece of musical thinking, is not diminished but actually enhanced. There are points, indeed, at which none of us will henceforth be able to listen to the music in the concert room without seeing it in terms of this ballet. . . .
>
> Technically the choreography is a marvel of invention, of expressive solo movement and of the handling of groups that make the same effect upon the eye as counterpoint does upon the ear. . . . The ballet has a décor that struck one as strange at first . . . but soon justified itself to the full.[9]

The furor immediately established Massine as the most important choreographer of the moment. The box-office success was immense, and his work was highly praised as the height of the avant-garde in dance.

Les Présages remained in the repertory of the Ballets Russes de Monte Carlo until it disbanded as the Original Ballet Russe in 1948. Massine revived the ballet in 1956 for the Teatro Municipal in Rio de Janeiro. On February 17, 1989, it was revived for the Paris Opéra by Tatiana Leskova, a former member of de Basil's company who assisted Massine on the 1956 revival. Anna Kisselgoff wrote in *The New York Times* that the choreography had "a dynamic invention that stands up on its own,"[10] and that "a revelation of the production is how strongly classical and formal the choreography looks. Massine's influence over Sir Frederick Ashton (his pupil) and even George Balanchine is evident."[11]

63

LE BEAU DANUBE

Ballet in one act and two scenes; music by Johann Strauss, orchestrated by Roger Désormière; libretto and choreography by Léonide Massine; set design by Vladimir Polunine after Constantin Guys, executed by Vladimir and Elizabeth Polunine; costume design by Etienne de Beaumont; premiere April 15, 1933, at the Théâtre de Monte Carlo, conducted by Marc-César Scotto.

ORIGINAL CAST

The Father	V. Psota	The First Hand	Irina Baronova
The Mother	A. Krassnova	The Owner of the Café	J. Hoyer
The Eldest Daughter	Tatiana Riabouchinska	The Seamstresses	Mlles Verchinina, Delarova, Marra, Gueneva
The Younger Daughters	Mlles Stepanova, Slavinska	The Needlewomen	Mlles Branitska, Lipkovska
The Hussar	Léonide Massine	The Ladies of the Town	Mlles Morosova, Kirsova, Chamié, Larina
The King of the Dandies	David Lichine		
The Artist	M. Ladré	The Salesmen	MM. Dolotine, Eglevsky, Petroff, Alexandroff
The Street Dancer	Alexandra Danilova		
The Manager	J. Hoyer	The Dandies	MM. Lipatoff, Katcharoff, Matouchevsky
The Athlete	E. Borovansky		

The second novelty of the season offered a sharp contrast to the dense psychological symbolism of *Les Présages*: a new version of Massine's *Le Beau Danube*, originally staged in 1924 for Count Etienne de Beaumont's Les Soirées de Paris, a six-week season of dance at the Théâtre de la Cigale. Massine was the creative nucleus of this season, which, thanks to the Count's financial endorsement, attracted the collaboration of almost every major artistic personality in town. Although Les Soirées had a particular snob appeal, the overall artistic level was not high, even though the work of each participant was of good quality, as expected of their talent and prestige. Only a few works—*Le Beau Danube*, the Satie-Picasso *Mercure*, the Milhaud-Braque *Salade*, and the Cocteau *Romeo et Juliette*—aroused any serious interest. However, the productions in most cases lacked cohesiveness. More than anything else the works seemed to be experiments instead of well-conceived, planned ballets. It was especially difficult for Massine, who was responsible for all the choreography and did not have enough time for the careful planning he had enjoyed previously with Diaghilev. (Massine collaborated on all but the Cocteau and Tristan Tzara's *Mouchoir de Nuages*.)

Action

Scene One: A Viennese public garden in the 1860s is the scene of much gaiety and humor as a diverse group of men, women, and youths prance about in high spirits. As the curtain rises a gardener sweeps the paths. An artist makes his entrance with an easel but is ejected by the gardener. People begin to gather: young men and women, seamstresses, and a family with three daughters. The young artist returns, running after the First Hand, a little seamstress, and downstage right he begins to sketch her portrait. As the two flirt, four couples perform a waltz. Now the King of the Dandies appears and dances; two other couples join him. When he finishes dancing he catches sight of the First Hand, who is still posing for the artist. He immediately wins her away from the artist and they dance a pas de deux as an expression of their infatuation while two other couples dance in the background. The Hussar enters and joins the family, which is seated downstage left. He asks the Eldest Daughter to dance. They walk diagonally upstage right and dance a mazurka. When they finish, they stroll out of sight. Now a manager of a group of street entertainers appears to announce the arrival of the Street Dancer and the Athlete. First the Street Dancer dances alone, to be joined towards the middle of her dance by the Manager and the Athlete, who performs a weight-lifting routine. By the time their dance is ending, the other dancers (as spectators around the stage) are in a frenzy and little by little begin to dance alone or with one another.

The Hussar and the Eldest Daughter return from their walk. The Street Dancer dramatically recognizes her former lover, causing everyone to freeze in expectation. In an attempt to win him back she stages a scene of jealousy, drawing the Hussar between herself and the daughter, shocking the bourgeois family. The Eldest Daughter faints and is taken away by her indignant parents. The Street Dancer, not to be outdone by her rival, also faints and is carried by the Manager to a handy chair. The Hussar, who has remained in the middle of the stage, finds himself surrounded by the crowd, who scorn him and leave. As the first strains of *The Beautiful Blue Danube* sound he stands motionless; then, with a gesture of abandon—as if he remembered the time gone by when he loved the Street Dancer—he dramatically breaks into a waltz and begins to dance with the Street Dancer, first slowly, then with mounting exhilaration and speed. The Eldest Daughter, who has obviously slipped away from her family, comes to defy her rival. The Hussar realizes the strength of her love for him and rejects his previous lover, who accepts defeat and yields her ground. All alone, the girl and the Hussar dance a pas de deux. The girl's parents enter looking for her. They are in a rage to find her with the Hussar, but she persuades them of their love. The father is moved by the girl's despair and finally gives his approval. They all exit.

Scene Two: The crowd returns to celebrate the reconciliation. The group, which consists of ten couples, performs a quadrille. The main characters reappear to perform their coda with the corps de ballet in the background in different patterns of lines and

65

semicircles. The first to appear is the First Hand. As she exits, the King of the Dandies enters. He is followed by the Street Dancer, who is later joined by the Athlete and the King of the Dandies. This time they do not exit; the Street Dancer and the King of the Dandies go downstage right, while the Athlete goes downstage left. The First Hand enters again and performs a series of fouettés à la seconde and attitude. She joins the Athlete downstage left as the Hussar and the Eldest Daughter enter. The Hussar and girl are joined by the King of the Dandies. The lead characters come together in center stage to form a snake, each holding the person in front. The Eldest Daughter leads the group, followed by the Hussar, the Street Dancer, the King of the Dandies, the First Hand, and the Athlete. The whole line snakes around the stage and finally breaks into four horizontal lines facing the audience: the three female leads, the three male leads, the five female corps dancers, and the five male corps dancers. They all whirl in place as the curtain comes down.

Choreography

It was Massine's custom to record his ballets on film either in performance or rehearsal. (His collection, now housed at the Library and Museum of the Performing Arts in New York City, is one of the most valuable dance documents of the twentieth century.) In 1933, he studied a film of the original 1924 production, but he eliminated all the heavily dramatic scenes so the ballet could work consistently in terms of dance. The original production was in two acts: the first, narrative act ended with the resumption of the love affair of the Hussar and the Street Dancer; the second act included the reconciliation scene and the dance apotheosis, the finale. To achieve more dramatic cohesiveness, Massine rearranged the ballet into one act and two scenes. He modified some of the roles to capitalize on the technique and personalities of de Basil's dancers—especially the First Hand (Baronova), who now executed a series of fouettés en tournant, and the Eldest Daughter, which was tailored to the unique, otherworldly, ethereal personality of Riabouchinska.

66

The choreography mixed polkas, mazurkas, and marches into a string of waltzes to achieve a telling variety of mood and tempo. The episodic plot served as an excuse for this series of dances, about which A. V. Coton commented:

> Even *Boutique fantasque* is not so packed as is this work with demonstration pieces for the soloists: the mock polka of the King of the Dandies in his flirtation episode with the shopgirls, the parodied jig of the Street Dancer, the buffoon dance of the Strong Man [the Athlete] and the Impresario [Owner of the café]. For timing and precision of moving pattern, scored and danced almost to the inch in absolute stage spacing, nothing else in Ballet approaches the mazurka of the Hussar and the Daughter. Again, the waltz of the Hussar and the Street Dancer effects all its loveliness of pattern in slowly growing line and smooth elevation that innumerable other dancers in the non-balletic waltz idiom have so often indicated but never achieved.[1]

Massine was inspired when creating *Le Beau Danube* by Perrot's structure and treatment, in which the dances and the pantomime are composed as an organic dramatic unit. Massine felt that this dramatic unity was lacking in the Petipa structure, in which the flow of the action was interrupted by separating the divertissement and the pantomime passages. In the Strauss ballet, the choreographer interwove solo variations, pas de deux, and ensembles, giving to the main characters the dual function of alternately providing a center or a background to the action. The corps de ballet was treated as a collective character against the soloists; however, Massine overlooked, when necessary, the hierarchy of principals in order to give greater verisimilitude to the dramatic development. In general, his approach was more traditional than Fokine's, whose search for scenic realism fragmented the corps de ballet, breaking it down from a disciplined collective character into individual entities.

In order to enhance the dramatic development of the ballet Massine employed the device of simultaneous action as he had first done in *Les Femmes de bonne humeur* (1917). One of the best examples is the juxtaposition of the pantomime scene between the First Hand and the Artist with the opening dance of the ensemble and the appearance and dance of the King of the Dandies.

In contrast to some of Massine's earlier works all the passages were constructed in balletic dance terms: the sweeping of the Gardener, the appearance of the crowds, the skipping of the children. There are only two scenes in which mime prevails: the Street Dancer's jealousy scene and the reconciliation between the Hussar and the Eldest Daughter.

To build the climactic crescendo the choreographer devised a finale that was a variation of the coda of the traditional Petipa classical divertissement. In the traditional coda all the performers of the divertissement reappear one after the other to perform a pas, after which they all reappear with the corps de ballet and, facing the audience in horizontal lines, they repeat a pas together. The effective coda-finale in *Le Beau Danube* is described by A. V. Coton:

67

The crowd pours in, and dandies and salesmen vie with one another in displays of dancing virtuosity; the Soubrette [First Hand] dances an ecstatically joyous solo, including the spinning of thirty-two *fouettés*, with the full chorus building a counter-pattern in an undulating semicircle, as background. The Hussar bounds in and traverses the forestage in wide-arcing jumps, sweeping parabolas which extend his graceful line for the admiration of all. The Dandy and the Hussar pattern a succession of *double-tours* in counterpoint, then the Dandy spins furiously his crackling *pirouettes*, whilst the modistes and salesmen tap and stamp through their square-dance routine. As the music rises into a tearing acceleration the whole cast forms a linked chain which twists and spins up and down stage and finally eddies to a standstill. The crowd breaks off and ranks across the width of the stage, the duettists are all paired in the front line, and as the music rushes the heady Straussian peroration the men jump and turn in air, land in attitudes—a series of clockwork-action figures—the women spin single turns, inward and outward, and to this crazy pattern of speed and grace the music thumps the final bars and the curtain rushes down.[2]

69

OPPOSITE ABOVE: Riabouchinska and Lichine. OPPOSITE BELOW: Riabouchinska, Morosova, and Lichine. ABOVE: Danilova as the Street Dancer.

Le Beau Danube soon became the company's signature piece. Its sharply etched characters and the breathtaking exhilaration of its choreography placed it next to *Les Sylphides* as one of the most popular ballets in the repertory—during the 1933 Alhambra engagement, it was performed nearly every evening for four consecutive months. During the company's United States tour, many theaters demanded that *Le Beau Danube* be included in the program.

The original 1933 cast was so effective as to transcend their characters in the ballet and make them extensions of their own personalities, drawing frenzied responses from the audience. The story, though it seems not terribly gripping, was very exciting as performed by this cast. It was humorous, sentimental, dramatic. People who saw the ballet then still talk about it with great excitement, the jealousy scene particularly vivid in their minds. Even Coton says that *Le Beau Danube* and *Les Présages* were responsible for drawing audiences to the Alhambra in the summer of 1933 "who otherwise might never have been attracted to the Ballet theatre."[3]

Massine's Hussar was among his greatest interpretations. In his silver grey military uniform, he epitomized hauteur and gallantry as he made his entrance, clicked his heels to his fiancée and her parents, and threw his shako into the wings, impervious to those around him. His mazurka with Riabouchinska was the epitome of young love. And then, after the young girl fainted—

> Watch him in that moment when he stands, absolutely motionless, in the center of the stage, as, from afar, come the first strains of that waltz which, more completely than any other, conjures up the essence of old Vienna, *The Beautiful Blue Danube*. He hears it, and memory comes welling up; then, very slowly, he raises his arm until it is above his head, as the crowd pass him by in scorn, some even contemptuously snapping their fingers in his face. All about him is movement. He alone is still, yet the audience sees not the movement, nor is it conscious of what is going on. Its eyes are riveted on that still figure, and it is to be doubted that there is anyone living who could so hold an audience while practically motionless.[4]

This was perhaps the apex of Massine's performance. He sadly accepted the possible loss of his ladylove, then frantically indulged in a waltz with Danilova's Street Dancer in a vain attempt to recapture a love they both knew belonged to the past.

As the object of his affections, Riabouchinska floated in Massine's arms in a harmonious scheme of turns, arabesques, attitudes, and multiple lines of least gravitational resistance. One can see Riabouchinska's much acclaimed lightness by watching her mazurka with Massine in his film of the ballet—she gives the impression of being in the air all the time, as if she were weightless. Massine took advantage of this quality, for in the mazurka, where they hold hands most of the time, he lifts her, turns her around, throws her up in the air or sends her spinning across the stage. Her portrayal of the young girl in *Le Beau Danube* was infinitely touching, and those who saw her cannot easily forget her expression of pain and despair as she doubts the Hussar's love, or her anguished pleas to her rival, her arms extended in supplication.

The Street Dancer was Danilova's greatest creation for de Basil and, no doubt, one of her finest achievements of the 1930s. In complete contrast to Riabouchinska's shy young bourgeois girl and Baronova's spirited and coquettish First Hand, Danilova's sultry Street Dancer struck the audience afresh with each new appearance. She imparted certainty and conviction to every gesture. In her waltz with Massine, they created a vignette charged with daydream nostalgia.

Rehearsals Although most of the ballet was choreographed in Monte Carlo, rehearsals started in Paris in December right after the first European tour. According to Michel Katcharov, Massine had to persuade some of the dancers to volunteer their time, as de Basil objected to paying for such a long rehearsal period. At a divertissement presented by the company at the Gala of the Légion d'Honneur, given under the auspices of Prince Louis II of Monaco at the Casino Theatre, the dancers performed, among other numbers, three excerpts from *Le Beau Danube*: a waltz, the mazurka (with Riabouchinska and Massine), and a polka.[5] The complete ballet had its premiere in a special performance for the birthday of the Princesse de Monaco. On this occasion the Street Dancer was danced by Nina Tarakanova, not Danilova, who had missed the winter months of rehearsal and arrived in Monte Carlo just in time to begin the spring season.

Music An important element of the ballet's popularity was the music by Strauss, at a time when everyone was choosing jazzy or contemporary music for ballet scores. Massine chose the pieces and passed them on to Désormière, along with a libretto of the ballet, for orchestration. Sometimes only a few bars of a piece were used in the orchestration. The principal pieces were *Schritzen Quadrille*, *New Vienna Waltzes*, the waltz from *Die Fledermaus*, the *Tritsch, Tratsch* polka, *Vienna Chronicle*, the *Motor Quadrille*, *The Beautiful Blue Danube*, *Morning Papers*, and a piece by Josef Lanner, *Der Schondrenner*.

Scenery and Costumes The scenery and costumes were also delightful. The backcloth by Vladimir Polunine, of a high carriage with two gentlemen taking a ride in the park, evoked the romantic atmosphere of engravings by Constantin Guys. The wheels, the neck of the horse, and the tall hats of the gentlemen were rendered in sepia. Beaumont, who had designed jewelry for Cartier and sumptuous dresses for his own masquerades as a hobby, now provided the designs for the ballet costumes. Their muted color scheme emphasized sepia, russet, pearl, henna, dark green, grey, and burgundy. When other companies (especially Denham's) staged the work with new costumes and decor, it never proved as successful. Hurok decided to glamorize the costumes when the company came to the United States for the first time, and, as Danilova was to recall:

> For me they ordered a new golden yellow dress and for Massine a black uniform. Antoine, the famous French coiffeur, did special wigs for the principals, brown for me, gold for Baronova and silver for Riabouchinska.

Sad to say, these efforts did nothing for the ballet. We looked terrible. Just before the curtain Massine struck and wouldn't wear his new black costume. He appeared in the handsome grey, which made me look all the worse. My wig was impossible to fix and I lost it in the middle of my waltz on my first appearance in America! What glamour!

At the very next performance, I refused to wear my new yellow costume. Other principals followed suit and *Danube* was given as it has been conceived and became one of the most loved ballets in the repertory.[6]

*L*E BEAU DANUBE has been one of the few Massine ballets to maintain itself in the repertory. Since the 1930s and 1940s, when it was performed by de Basil's and Denham's Ballets Russes, it has been revived by various companies, including the Marquis de Cuevas's and the London Festival Ballet; it is presently in the repertory of the Joffrey Ballet.

72

BEACH

Ballet in one scene with prologue and epilogue; music by Jean Françaix; libretto by René Kerdyk; choreography by Léonide Massine; set design by Raoul Dufy, executed by Prince A. Schervachidze; costume design by Raoul Dufy and Jeanne Lanvin for the evening gowns, executed by Madame Karinska and Jeanne Lanvin; curtain design and execution by Raoul Dufy; premiere April 19, 1933, at the Théâtre de Monte Carlo, conducted by Marc-César Scotto.

ORIGINAL CAST

Nereus Kingdom

Nereus	David Lichine	Tritons	MM. Borovansky, Dolotine, Ladré,
Cupid	Tatiana Riabouchinska		Petroff
Nereids	Mlles Branitska, Delarova, Kirsova,		
	Larina, Morosova, Raievska,		
	Tarakanova, Verchinina		

Bathing Time

The bathers	Mlles Berry, Branitska, Delarova, Howard, Kirsova, Larina, Morosova, Raievska, Sorina, Tarakanova, Tresahar, Verchinina
	MM. Alexandroff, Borovansky, Dolotine, Eglevsky, Katcharoff, Ladré, Matouchevsky, Petroff
The oarsmen	Shabelevsky, Lipatoff, Psota
The astute girls	Branitska, Morosova
The languid girls	Delarova, Gueneva, Howard, Lipkovska, Marra, Verchinina

Beach Scene

The Maharajah	E. Borovansky
The Maharanée	T. Chamié
The rug vendor	J. Hoyer
The messenger boy	T. Riabouchinska
The Rose-White Maid	I. Baronova
The handsome swimmer	D. Lichine
The bathers who will fall in love with him	Delarova, Gueneva, Howard, Lipkovska, Marra, Verchinina
The sunbeams	Mlles Berry, Branitska, Delarova, Gueneva, Kirsova, Larina, Morosova, Sorina, Raievska, Tarakanova, Tresahar, Verchinina
The American sailors and the bather who is mistaken	Massine, Woizikowski, Marra
The old gentlemen and other bathers who are also mistaken	MM. Borovansky, Dolotine, Ladré, Petroff Mlles Howard, Lipkovska
Airs from the Casino	I. Baronova, D. Lichine, and T. Riabouchinska Mlles Delarova, Kirsova, Lipkovska, Marra, Morosova, Raievska, Tarakanova, Verchinina MM. Shabelevsky, Alexandroff, Borovansky, Dolotine, Eglevsky, Ladré, Petroff, Psota

Epilogue	I. Baronova, D. Lichine Mlles Branitska, Delarova, Kirsova, Larina, Morosova, Raievska, Tarakanova, Verchinina MM. Katcharoff, Hoyer, Matouchevsky

73

Massine wanted to create a ballet that would be a tribute to the principality of Monaco, which had shown such hospitality to the company. It would evoke the atmosphere of the Riviera and depict the new, jazzy generation of Cole Porter and the Fitzgeralds, a smart set devoted to vigorous physical activity and the pleasures of open-air summer life. He discussed the idea with Blum, who liked it and suggested several artists as possible collaborators; however, Massine was very authoritarian regarding every aspect of his ballets, and the final decision as to collaborators was his. He chose a team of French artists: René Kerdyk, the painter Raoul Dufy, and the composer Jean Françaix. The idea of Kerdyk's libretto was to link the paganism of Mediterranean mythology with the hedonism of modern Monte Carlo. As André Levinson has remarked, in its aesthetic approach *Beach* was an adaptation of a spectacular music-hall revue.[1] It tried to re-create the frivolous lifestyle of a contemporary resort, and its characters were all familiar Monte Carlo types: physical culture enthusiasts, millionaires, Indian rajahs, American sailors.

Music

The music had been commissioned from a twenty-year-old ex-protégé of Nadia Boulanger, Jean Françaix, who as a child prodigy had published his first composition at the age of ten; Boulanger had introduced his works in the salon of Princesse de Polignac.

Françaix used several devices to convey the atmosphere of the various scenes: for the world of Nereus, a leitmotiv for harps; for the contemporary beach scene, jazz melodies for trombone. His score showed the influence of Auric, although Françaix's freshness was in sharp contrast to Auric's more calculated style.

Action

Prologue: Nereus, the father of the water nymphs, is weary of his existence, in spite of the efforts of those lovely creatures to rouse him from his languor. Cupid releases a magic arrow that transforms him and his subjects into modern bathers at a Monte Carlo resort.

At the beach, beautiful young people play in the sand. An oarsman displays his skill; a carpet seller offers his wares and is present when a rajah passes with his splendid entourage. Nereus, in the guise of a handsome swimmer, attracts the attention of all the women, who pen notes to him and entrust them to a messenger boy for delivery. The harried messenger drops the notes, which scatter in the breeze, but he manages to collect them and disappears in haste.

The beautiful Rose-White Maid enters, arousing the jealousy of the other women as the handsome swimmer succumbs to her charms. The swimmer and the maid leave together. The messenger, unable to locate the swimmer, delivers the girls' invitations to two happy-go-lucky American sailors instead. The girls, at first reluctant, finally accept the sailors' company.

Epilogue: Twilight falls, and the casino lights appear. It is a balmy Mediterranean evening; the bathers, in evening dress, dance on the casino terrace. Nereus returns to his mythological kingdom with the Rose-White Maid, now a spirit of the sea.

Choreography

As a topical ballet, *Beach* had an antecedent in the Cocteau-Nijinska *Le Train bleu* of 1924, which had scenery by Henri Laurens and costumes by Chanel; Massine's choreography, like Nijinska's, was a stylization of sport motifs and different dance idioms within a structured balletic framework. The athletic choreography borrowed jazz movements that were in vogue and even included a short, simple, but very effective tap solo that Massine choreographed for Riabouchinska in her role as the messenger. It was most likely the first time that tap had been introduced into ballet in Europe. Massine had learned to tap while in the United States, especially during his years at the Roxy, and was able to coach Riabouchinska. The choreography also included a humorous fox-trot for Massine and Woizikowski as the American sailors, another reflection of the choreographer's Roxy experience. Only the lyrical pas de deux of Baronova and Lichine as the Rose-White Maid and the swimmer supplied a contrast to the ballet's predominantly vigorous style, though it, too, blended into the eclecticism of the overall choreographic approach.

Scenery and Costumes   As designer, no painter could have been a better choice than Raoul Dufy, who had achieved popularity with charming and witty seascapes that depicted, in a disorganized way, a naive miscellany of marine elements. He was chosen not just for his reputation as a painter but also for his importance in the world of fashion. His first attempt at theatrical design had been for the ballet *Frivolant* (1922) for the Paris Opéra, and since then, he had acquired a prestigious connection; Paul Poiret had opened a small atelier in which the painter could design textiles for his *maison de couture*. The combination of Dufy's fabrics and Poiret's dress designs was a sensational success with the habituées of Longchamp and Auteuil. Later on, Poiret persuaded Dufy to work for the firm of Bianchini-Atuyer-Terrier.

The sets for *Beach* were typical of Dufy's paintings, sharing their childlike, fish-tank quality. The painted wings gave a sense of depth and perspective to Dufy's giant aquarium.

The first backdrop, used for the prologue and epilogue, was centered on a large white shell that served as a sort of emblem; below it lay the kingdom of Nereus. There was a conglomeration of deep-sea creatures (sea horses and various other fishes), and boats and clouds ascending in a vertical line—all set against a sea-blue background. The lighting was concentrated mainly on the enormous shell, leaving the dancers only partially illuminated and accentuating the aquarium atmosphere. The second backdrop depicted fish, birds, clouds, and many kinds of boats with different flags against the same sea-blue background.

Left to right: Tarakanova, Delarova, Grigorieva, Hoyer (the Rug Vendor), Branitska, Verchinina; set by Dufy.

As for the costumes—if *La Concurrence* could be called a fashion show of the 1890s, *Beach* was a display of the summerwear for 1933. In fact, Jeanne Lanvin launched the fad of the blue dinner jacket after designing the evening gowns for the third tableau of the ballet. No wonder, when the work had its New York premiere on January 2, 1934, John Martin wrote: "*Beach* must content itself with being chic . . . it affords an opportunity for the company to reveal its collective handsomeness in scanty bathing suits, and that is perhaps sufficient. The music by Jean Françaix runs considerably to jazz and a sort of acrobatic pageantry takes the place of choreography."[2]

Premiere   In Monte Carlo the ballet had an excellent reception. Paris and London audiences found it vivacious and enjoyable, and especially liked Dufy's decor. But in New York, very few people identified with *Beach*.

According to Massine, *Beach* was never intended as more than a *pièce d'occasion*, and it remained in the repertory for only two years.

SCUOLA DI BALLO

Ballet in one act; music by Luigi Boccherini, orchestrated by Jean Françaix; libretto by Léonide Massine after Goldoni; choreography by Léonide Massine; set and costume design by Etienne de Beaumont; sets executed by Prince A. Schervachidze; costumes executed by Madame Karinska; premiere April 25, 1933, at the Théâtre de Monte Carlo, conducted by Pierre Kolpikoff.

ORIGINAL CAST

Rigadon, the professor	Leon Woizikowski	Bianca	Olga Morosova
Ridolfo, his friend	Vania Psota	Carlino	Léonide Massine
Fabrizio, an impresario	Edouard Borovansky	Philipino	Yurek Shabelevsky
Count Anselmi	André Eglevsky	Nicoletto	Marian Ladré
Rosina	Tatiana Riabouchinska	Lucrézia,	Eleonora Marra
Josephina, the favorite pupil	Irina Baronova	the mother of Rosina	
		The Notary	Jean Hoyer
Felicita, the bad pupil	Eugenia Delarova	The Carabineers	MM. Alexandroff, Katcharoff, Lipatoff, Matouchevsky

Italy was the country Massine loved the most outside his native Russia. In 1917, after a Ballets Russes season at the Teatro San Carlo in Naples, he visited for the first time the Isole dei Galli in the Gulf of Salerno. (He later purchased the islands, which

became a welcome retreat from his hectic working schedule until his death in 1979.)
From 1917 on, when he created *Les Femmes de bonne humeur*, based on a Goldoni comedy, Italian themes were a recurrent source of inspiration. Now, Massine was to choose Goldoni once again, for his next ballet.

Music   Massine had chosen music by Luigi Boccherini, orchestrated by Jean Françaix, the young composer of *Beach*. In the adaptation, according to the London *Mercury*,[1] Françaix steered a middle course between Tommasini's almost literal transcription of Scarlatti in *Les Femmes de bonne humeur* (1917) and Stravinsky's absorption of Pergolesi and others into his own idiom in *Pulcinella* (1920). Aside from the excessive use of the solo trumpet, rhythms were given bounce and verve by means of interesting block-thickening in the orchestration. (Because Boccherini's orchestration was quite simple, Françaix added extra notes to the chords as chord blocks to densen and thicken the texture orchestrally.) The various solo instruments were handled with a fine sense of tonal contrast and color gradation.

Action   *Scuola di ballo* is based on Carlo Goldoni's five-act verse play of the same name, written in 1759. It takes place in a dance school and concerns the devious efforts of Professor Rigadon to trick the impresario Fabrizio into signing a contract to sponsor a failing student, Felicita. As this plan is contrived, the viewer observes the various talents in the ballet school.

As the curtain rises after the overture, students are seen performing pirouettes and other steps in unison as the dance professor, Rigadon, walks around the studio carrying a miniature violin and a bow.

Lucrézia, an imperious stage mother, arrives with her daughter, Rosina, and urgently requests an interview with the professor, who consequently dismisses the class. Rosina is introduced to Rigadon and dances for him. He acknowledges her talent and immediately signs a contract with her mother, authorizing him to act as the girl's manager. After they depart, Ridolfo, a friend of the professor's, brings to the studio the impresario Fabrizio, who is looking for a talented dancer. Rigadon tricks the impresario into signing a contract with Felicita, the worst student in the school, making Fabrizio believe that she is so good that it would be an insult to her artistry to ask her to audition for him. Fabrizio leaves the studio taking his new discovery with him. Josephina, the school's prize student, enters with her sweetheart, Count Anselmi. They dance a passionate pas de deux in expression of their love and then leave.

Fabrizio returns to the studio with Felicita and asks her to dance for him in front of Rigadon and Ridolfo. She performs an awkward variation composed of comically faulty steps. The impresario flies into a rage realizing that he has been deceived. Rigadon and Ridolfo try in vain to calm him, but Felicita, recovered from the physical strain of her dance, employs her charms successfully. Somewhat mollified, the impresario leaves with her, to the relief of the two men. Rosina and her mother arrive for a lesson as Carlino, a fellow student, drops by. Rosina and Carlino dance a tender pas de deux.

Fabrizio returns once again to demand an audition with the other students in the

77

school in order to replace Felicita. Rosina impresses Fabrizio with a very fast variation and he wishes her to sign a contract with him. Rigadon refuses to allow this, and in the ensuing commotion Fabrizio is kicked out. However, he returns with a notary and three policemen. There is a hearing and the notary rules that the impresario must be reimbursed. Rigadon has no alternative but to comply. The ballet ends with a gay scene in which the students flirt with the notary and Fabrizio; when the two men depart with the policemen, the students dance mockingly around Rigadon and leave him alone and disconsolate in his studio.

Choreog-
raphy

This was the second time that Massine turned to Goldoni as a dramatic source: *Les Femmes de bonne humeur*, created for Diaghilev in 1917, was based on *Le donne di buon umore*. He admired Goldoni's sense of musicality and rhythm as well as the intrinsic and traditional qualities of the commedia dell'arte style, in which gesture and movement prevailed and the actors were almost puppetlike in their characterizations, a quality enhanced by the use of mime, dance, and acrobatics. Goldoni wrote the texts for more than a hundred operas, operettas (comic operas), interludes, cantatas, and serenatas, and his theatrical approach in the style of the commedia dell'arte appealed particularly to the choreographer. He was associated with such composers as Gassmann, Haydn, Vivaldi; his prolific collaboration with Galuppi lasted for about fifteen years. Many of his works were also adapted later, including those for Piccinni and Wolf-Ferrari.

78

To understand Massine's oeuvre one must take into account his involvement with the theater in Moscow, one of the leading theatrical capitals of the time, and of his love for the dramatic art. Massine attended the Moscow Theatre School as a child. While a student he participated in both ballet and opera productions at the Bolshoi Theatre and in plays at the Maly Theatre. At the Maly he was so successful that he soon established himself as a leading child actor. By his early teens he had decided on an acting career and regarded his dance training as an additional asset. At the time he left Moscow with Diaghilev, he was being considered for the role of Romeo in a forthcoming production of *Romeo and Juliet* at the Maly. In his autobiography he writes about his inclination for acting: "I thought the theater offered me a greater opportunity to express myself and to project my own personality than dancing."[2]

Massine's exposure to and interest in the commedia dell'arte may have developed during his early years in the Moscow theater. During the first two decades of the twentieth century there was a revival in Russia of the forms of the commedia dell'arte, especially with Blok and Meyerhold. By 1910 the latter had established Interlude House in St. Petersburg (in existence until 1911), where he put into practice the techniques of this genre. Since Meyerhold could not use his name—he was under contract to the Imperial Alexandrinsky Theatre—he elected to use the pseudonym Dr. Dapertutto. In conjunction with this venture, he published the theater-arts magazine *The Love for Three Oranges*, the title taken from Gozzi's tales. Soon, works of the commedia dell'arte became staples of the theater companies.

Massine found that the commedia dell'arte tradition, which had attained its literary zenith with Goldoni, was firmly in line with his own belief in "total theater."

ABOVE: Baronova, Massine, and Riabouchinska.
RIGHT: Delarova.

Commedia blended dialogue with mime, song, dance, acrobatics, and a strong visual profile. One of its most vital characteristics was spontaneity; written text and improvisation existed side by side, especially during the sixteenth and seventeenth centuries. To Massine, ballet became total theater when its drama or poetry, its music, its choreography, and its decor blended in equal degrees of importance, with no single element dominating. This is why *Parade* remained one of his favorite ballets.

In *Scuola di ballo* Massine developed the story by adroitly linking and integrating gesture and movement. Following the pattern of eighteenth-century Italian opera, dramatic conflict was carried out by expressive gesture (corresponding to the recitatives), while the dance numbers (corresponding to arias) expressed the emotional result. An unidentified critic described Massine's approach thusly: "In Massine's ballets the stylized gesture of every dancer was in equilibrium with the collective expression of gesture. His ballets were a cohesive unity of gesture and expression each achieved by the choreographer's command of pantomime and dance within the collective rhythm." This structure also enabled Massine to display the acting ability of the dancers as well as their technical virtuosity. Most of the numbers were solos and pas de deux, but he also employed the practice of a concerted finale (with all the dancers onstage) typical of eighteenth-century Neapolitan comic opera.

Massine always studied his work carefully, scrutinizing not only the choreography but all other aspects of a ballet. Riabouchinska remembers how he would come to rehearsals armed with copious notes and stacks of books. Among the books she remembers one on Italian dance figures of the eighteenth century, which he used for inspiration—probably Lambranzi's *Nuova e curiosa scuola di balli teatrali*, which first appeared in 1716 and was reprinted for the first time in 1928 in a new edition by Cyril Beaumont. Lambranzi's book consists of plates depicting dance movements, poses, and gestures of the eighteenth century, including characteristic movements of stock figures of the commedia dell'arte. Along with each plate the author had written out an appropriate musical air; there were also detailed specifications regarding costuming and general atmosphere.

In *Scuola di ballo* Massine achieved such balance in his characters that the marionette quality of commedia dell'arte fused with a humanity that prevented them from becoming caricatures. In *Scuola di ballo* every role required a strong, clearly defined personality that was projected by the steps and gestures (Massine placed great importance on the use of the hands) of each dancer into a collective whole. An unidentified critic once said: "In Massine's approach to personification there was more of the who the character is from the dance rhythm of the part and its interactions with the other characters, than from a psychological explanation of the characters. It is music and rhythm that create the ballet character (or mold a ballet character) as words do to the actor."

As in the tradition of the commedia dell'arte, where the actors were the creative forces in shaping their own parts, Massine's dancers contributed to the development of the characters they played. Massine placed his dancers in the roles that best suited them and then gave them the freedom to make the characters their own. Baronova declared: "To penetrate into Massine's roles, dancers had to work on their own and approach the parts as actors do. We had to explore the characters in order to obtain their mannerisms. For Massine, two things were of most importance: expressivity in the body and fluency of movement, both subordinated to the music. Every movement, in the mime as in the dance passages, was an extension of the previous one." Riabouchinska, too, felt that in Massine's ballets "after he gave them the basic idea, the dancers had to work on their own. They had to digest and build their interpretations as long as they were consistent with the overall approach." In other words, while Massine fixed the general style of the ballet as a point of departure for the dancers, the "trademark" of each role was established by its interpreter.

Massine has acknowledged his debt to Stanislavski as a major influence during his acting training in Moscow, when he was encouraged to look at dramatic interpretation as an extension of personal introspection. The two met in the apartment of the actress Olga Gsovska while Massine was rehearsing *Antony and Cleopatra* with her. Massine told me: "The importance of expressiveness in movement is to follow the nature of the individual feeling. Feelings cannot be imposed by the choreographer. The expression of emotion must depend on the individual nature: the fear of rape in *Le Tricorne*, the child's detachment in *Jeux d'enfants*. The choreographer uses the feeling of the interpreters within a choreographic and musical context." Stanislavski, who instructed the singers of the Bolshoi Opera in acting in 1915, stressed the unity of musical and dramatic effects. For Massine, too, the correlation between the seen and the heard was of utmost importance.

When the Ballets Russes danced Massine's ballets, the feeling of improvisation was palpable and the air of spontaneity brought each performance to special life. Each gesture seemed to be happening for the first time, with a complete naturalness and sincerity. This is one of the reasons why modern revivals of Massine's works are often deemed ineffective. In the Ballets Russes performances, every solo role was taken by a personality. In an interview for French television (at which Skibine was present), Massine was asked if his works were not performed anymore because they were démodé. His answer: "Certainly not. There are no more dancers who could perform them."[3]

Scenery and Costumes

Scuola di ballo was the first work produced and designed by Etienne de Beaumont specifically for the Ballets Russes de Monte Carlo. For the decor and costumes of this period ballet Beaumont chose as his source paintings of Tiepolo, the eighteenth-century Venetian painter—*Minuetto* in particular, according to Massine.

The decor was very simple, avoiding the elaborate conception of baroque design; it consisted of a backcloth depicting a spacious Venetian room with two arches, each with a fenced balcony at the rear and a half-moon latticework grille at the curve of the arch. An illuminated iron-and-glass lamp hung in the middle of the room. As props there were a few chairs at each side of the room.

The costumes, in various pastels, with rose and black predominating, evoked the style of the Venetian middle class of the second half of the eighteenth century. The female dancers were bewigged in period hairstyles; the male dancers wore hats.

81

Critics   *Scuola di ballo* was another example of Massine's ability to bring a detailed libretto to full balletic life. The work was premiered in Monte Carlo on April 25 and in Paris on June 13, and received a highly favorable press in both places. Only Levinson demurred, finding it inferior to *Les Femmes de bonne humeur* and *Pulcinella*, not for any lack of invention but for flaws in construction. He claimed that the dance passages were not varied enough for purposes of contrast; however, he waxed enthusiastic over the cast.[4] However, even though it was very well liked by the public and the critics and proved to be popular for several seasons, once *Femmes* was revived, *Scuola di ballo* was seldom performed again.

In London the verdict was unanimous. Ernest Newman wrote in the *Sunday Times*:

> Over all the production there is that sense of "nothing too much" that is always one of the best features of the ballet school that has arisen out of the old Italian comedy: never for a moment does the grotesquerie overshoot the mark. And once more one is astounded at Mr. Massine's genius for translating music into action. Only the musicians in the audience can fully appreciate what he does in this respect; there are a hundred subtleties in the way of capturing the very essence of a rhythm, of an accent, even of a splash of orchestral colour . . . to make them clear to the reader one would have to quote this or that bar of the music with a section from a film of the ballet.[5]

When the work was presented in New York, John Martin wrote:

> . . . *Scuola di Ballo* is the most thoroughly satisfying. It has style and taste and lusty good humor, in addition to an abundance of unexceptionally brilliant dancing. . . .
>
> There are excellent performances by Riabouchinska, whose technique has the sharpness of a diamond; by the lovely Baronova, who is all softness and daintiness of line; by Shabelevsky, who had his first opportunity to reveal himself as a brilliant dancer; by Eglevsky, with his extraordinary deliberateness of movement; and by Massine. . . . The low comedy parts were played and danced with huge gusto by Woizikovsky [*sic*], Psota and Borovansky, and on the distaff side of the roster by Eugenie Delarova, whose burlesque of bad dancing is a real piece of farce.[6]

NOCTURNE

Ballet in one act; music by Rameau, adapted by Roger Désormière; libretto by Etienne de Beaumont after Shakespeare; choreography by David Lichine; set and costume design by Etienne de Beaumont; premiere June 30, 1933, at the Théâtre du Châtelet, conducted by Efrem Kurtz.

ORIGINAL CAST

Titania	Alexandra Danilova	Puck	David Lichine
The First Betrothed Pair	Irina Baronova,	Bottom	Vania Psota
	André Eglevsky	The First Fairy	Nina Verchinina
The Second	Tatiana Riabouchinska,	Comedians, Fairies,	
Betrothed Pair	Yurek Shabelevsky	Elves, Spirits	Artists of the Ballet
Oberon	Léonide Massine		

As the second Monte Carlo season drew to an end, David Lichine felt immensely attracted to choreography. Born in 1910 in Rostov-on-Don, Lichine (David Liechtenstein) came from a musical family: his father was a composer and his sister sang with the Opéra Russe à Paris. He received his ballet training from Egorova and, especially, Nijinska, who took him with her when she was invited to choreograph for Ida Rubinstein's company. After his debut with this company in 1928, he auditioned for Diaghilev and was accepted by the Ballets Russes at the end of the 1929 Paris season, just before the impresario's death; thus, he never danced professionally for Diaghilev. He then danced for Anna Pavlova, the Opéra Russe, and for Massine in his production of *Belkis* at La Scala. He joined the Ballets Russes de Monte Carlo at the inception of the company and at that time adopted Lichine as his stage name.

For a novice, though, the possibility of choreographic experimentation with the Ballets Russes was nonexistent. Hectic rehearsal and performance schedules allowed him no time to develop his ideas, and a commission from the directorate was unlikely —the company depended on box-office receipts, so new ballets by untried young choreographers were considered too risky. Lichine was aware of the situation and asked for advice from Massine, who willingly agreed to help him.

Funding was the most important prerequisite for a new production, and through Massine, Lichine was able to obtain the unconditional sponsorship of Etienne de Beaumont, a close friend of Massine's who had always shown an interest in Lichine as a dancer. Preliminary discussions began in Monte Carlo, and as soon as the company arrived in Paris, preparations began in earnest. Even though Beaumont chose the subject and the music, he discussed the idea with Massine, who then discussed the structure of the work with Lichine. Lichine participated in these discussions because he was to choreograph the work, but all other arrangements were made by Beaumont and Massine.

The new ballet was to have a libretto by Beaumont based on Shakespeare's *A Midsummer Night's Dream*, with music by Rameau, arranged by Désormière, a friend of Beaumont's who had collaborated in his Soirées de Paris (*Le Beau Danube*) and was now chief conductor for the Paris season. Scenery and costumes were by Beaumont, inspired by the Renaissance period. The ballet was set in a forest, with one large cage onstage, where the two Athenian brides-to-be stayed during most of the ballet. Since not even photographs of this production have survived, details concerning the costumes and scenery are not available. Massine served as artistic advisor.

Music

No document has been found to establish with certainty which music by Rameau was used for *Nocturne*. However, the book *Roger Désormière et son temps*, by Denise Mayer and Pierre Souvtchinsky (Editions du Rocher, Monaco, 1966) contains a complete listing of Désormière's works, including only two orchestrations of pieces by Rameau: *Les Paladins*, first and second suites, published in 1939 and 1946, and *Acanthe et Cephise*, ballet airs arranged for wind quintet. Riabouchinska recalls that the score of *Nocturne* was played by a full orchestra, so it is safe to assume that the music was the comédie-ballet *Les Paladins*.

Action

The center of action is a forest clearing, where the divinities of the night assemble in ill humor. Four betrothed Athenians, bickering among themselves, join an already moody Oberon, king of the Elves, and Titania, queen of the Fairies.

As their followers surround the royal couple, King Oberon desperately calls for Puck, the Spirit of the Night, to bring him a love potion to soothe the dissension. Puck observes the quarreling Athenians, who appear to regret their forthcoming marriages.

Meanwhile comedians arrive to prepare an entertainment to accompany the impending ceremony. The players portray a Lion, two Lovers, and a Wall that separates them. Among them is Bottom. Puck circumvents their preparations by spreading his love potion first on the eyelids of the sleeping Titania and then on those of the seemingly ill-suited betrothed couples. He entices the comedians away. Titania awakens and sees Bottom, wearing the ass's head, and, bewitched, falls desperately in love with him. The love philter works its charm upon the two couples simultaneously, and they are reconciled.

Oberon appears, frees Titania of the charm, and the weddings take place amid great rejoicing.

Choreography

In Lichine's early works mime predominated in his attempt to make the story explicit and to help him achieve a more cohesive structure. His command of ballet as a dramatic technique progressed in successive works until it became (in *Protée*) his expressive medium.

In his development as a choreographer Lichine had Massine as his catalyst and guide—not only in Massine's direct participation in *Nocturne* but also through Lichine's involvement in Massine's own creations. Since Lichine had studied and worked with Nijinska and Balanchine as well, he must have learned from their example, too. But Riabouchinska asserts that Massine's early influence on Lichine was incontestably the most decisive: "Since we all lived together like a family, he pointed out to David things that were of interest and tried to arouse his intellectual curiosity."

In *Nocturne* Massine helped Lichine find a choreographic structure to weld the scenario to the music. Though always stern, Massine was cooperative and did not intimidate the young choreographer, who was ever attentive and considered any suggestion. Riabouchinska remembers, "David was the type that always wanted to know and discuss everything. He listened carefully to those he respected, who he knew had something to offer his artistic growth. Once he set his mind, though, no one could dissuade him!" Massine never interfered with Lichine's own ideas, and he helped him whenever necessary (no doubt frequently in the beginning) to find an appropriate answer to the choreographic questions that naturally arose.

Lichine had an advantage in his uncanny ear for music, which, according to Massine, granted him intuitive solutions to choreographic difficulties. In *Nocturne* he revealed also an innate sense of design and visual imagery, for example when Titania (Danilova) and Oberon (Massine) were carried offstage en arabesque. Lichine faced his main problem in the ensembles, where, according to the reviewer for *The Musical Times*, the "overcrowded, excessive activity was not congruous with the music or with Shakespeare's ripe and leisurely unfolding of beauty and fun."[1]

Danilova was also extremely helpful to Lichine. She dissected her role with him and was always willing to spend extra time experimenting with new ideas and movements. From their first association she was convinced he had a great deal of imagination and a genuine talent.

The ballet was only mildly successful. It was performed a few times in Paris and London and then dropped from the repertory.

CHOREARTIUM

Ballet in four scenes; music, Brahms's Fourth Symphony; choreography by Léonide Massine; sets designed by Constantin Terechkovitch and Eugène Lourié, executed by Elizabeth Polunine; costumes designed by Constantin Terechkovitch and Eugène Lourié; curtains designed and executed by Georges Annenkoff; premiere October 24, 1933, at the Alhambra Theatre, London, conducted by Efrem Kurtz.

ORIGINAL CAST

First Movement　　　Tamara Toumanova
and David Lichine

Lubov Rostova
MM. Borovansky, Ismailoff,
Katcharoff, Ladré, Lipatoff, Psota

André Eglevsky
Mlles Nina Tarakanova, Branitska, Delarova,
Lipkovska, Tresahar

Mlles Kobseva, Larina, Nijinska, Obidenna,
Raievska, Razoumova, Semenova, Tchinarova
MM. Algeranoff, Matouchevsky

Second Movement　　　Nina Verchinina

Mlles Berry, Branitska, Chabelska, Chamié,
Delarova, Kobseva, Lipkovska, Larina,
Morosova, Natova, Nijinska, Obidenna,
Raievska, Razoumova, Semenova, Sidorenko,
Tarakanova, Tchinarova, Tresahar, Volkova

Third Movement　　　Tatiana Riabouchinska
and Leon Woizikowski

Alexandra Danilova and Roman Jasinski

Mlles Delarova, Kobseva, Morosova,
Razoumova, Semenova, Tchinarova
MM. Alexandroff, Algeranoff, Hoyer,
Ismailoff, Katcharoff, Lipatoff, Matouchevsky,
Psota

Fourth Movement　　　Tamara Toumanova
David Lichine and André Eglevsky
MM. Borovansky, Ladré, Petroff, Psota

Tatiana Riabouchinska

Mlles Lubov Rostova, Branitska, Larina,
Semenova, Tresahar

Leon Woizikowski
MM. Alexandroff, Algeranoff, Ismailoff,
Katcharoff, Lipatoff, Matouchevsky

Alexandra Danilova and Nina Tarakanova
Yurek Shabelevsky

Mlles Berry, Delarova, Kobseva, Lipkovska,
Morosova, Natova, Nijinska, Obidenna,
Raievska, Razoumova, Tchinarova

86

As the successful season at the Alhambra drew to a close, London was eager to see its first Ballets Russes premiere. The pre-eminence of de Basil's company was consolidated when Captain Bruce Ottley (a well-connected London banker who was also a gifted musician and devoted balletomane) organized a strong sponsoring committee, one of whose members, Russian-born Lady Deterding, kindly offered to finance Massine's newest work, *Choreartium*,[1] set to Brahms's Fourth Symphony.

The unprecedented success of *Les Présages* had encouraged Massine to create a second symphonic ballet. With their dense, rich musical content, the symphonies of composers such as Brahms and Tchaikovsky allowed him the opportunity to explore complex movements, and the formal symphonic structure provided unity for the choreographic design. As Ernest Newman stated, "What constitutes the charm of it all [the symphonic genre, in general], for those whose minds can work along the same double lines as Massine's, is precisely the fact that the creation is all of a piece instead of being simply the succession of fragments with which most other ballets present us."[2]

Music

Massine chose Brahms because for his second symphonic ballet he wanted music that would not impose upon him specific psychological moods, as had *Les Présages*. Moreover, the contrasting musical motifs in Brahms's Fourth were less interwoven with one another, allowing him the opportunity for clearer design in an abstract ballet in which the dancers were deployed only as visual images that paralleled the music. He placed female dancers in opposition to male dancers to stress the qualities of femininity and masculinity in their movements. In *Les Présages* he had already begun to explore the use of musical phrases to juxtapose men and women, but there they had been strongly identified with specific ideas characteristic of their sexes, with Action, Passion, and Frivolity representing the feminine, Fate and the Hero identifying the masculine. In *Choreartium* he simply wanted physical movement, through the use of ballet techniques, to bring forth the feminine and masculine qualities of the dancers. As Massine states in his autobiography: "I decided to do the choreography of the ballet, which I entitled *Choreartium*, according to the instrumentation of the score, using women dancers to accentuate the delicate phrases, while the men interpreted the heavier, more robust passages. The music, with its rich orchestration and its many contrasts, lent itself admirably to this kind of interplay between masculine and feminine movements."[3]

87

Action

The following synopsis was drawn mainly from the 16mm black-and-white film of the ballet in the Massine Collection, as well as from excerpts of a 16mm black-and-white film in the Riabouchinska Collection, with Baronova and Lichine in the first movement.

Because there are no characters as such in this ballet, the names of the dancers identified with each musical theme are given instead.

First Movement: Allegro non troppo. To the opening musical theme, which is played without introduction, the first principal couple (Toumanova and Lichine) enter an empty stage. They dance to the theme as if participating in a dialogue of questions and answers conducted by the strings (represented by the woman) and the woodwinds (represented by the man). As the music grows, their pas de deux becomes more forceful; as the theme fades, they embrace and exit.

The second musical theme is composed of three musical subjects. The first is played as a modulating bridge, and a female soloist (Rostova) enters accompanied by six men. She performs a series of unsupported pirouettes, and then is partnered in supported arabesques, first singly by each of her male companions, and later by pairs. She is then lifted by her partners, carried around the stage, and finally taken offstage. As the second musical subject of this theme is played, another female soloist (Tarakanova) enters and dances with the six men from the previous entry, who have returned to the stage. The men dance in the background, creating different formations as she dances alone. The men join in a horseless chariot and exit, followed by the female lead. The third musical subject of this movement is introduced and a male soloist (Eglevsky) enters accompanied by six women. He leaps across the stage and exits as the six men return to banish the six women to the wings. With the men all alone onstage, Eglevsky leaps into the air from the upper wings and is caught mid-air by two of the men; they hold him horizontally aloft for a moment before they all scatter around the stage. The female chorus reenters and with the male chorus creates various patterns. Tarakanova and Eglevsky perform a pas de deux in the foreground; Toumanova and Lichine make a brief appearance and exit. At different points onstage, the corps de ballet forms units, each consisting of two women and one man: they create intricate formations of constantly varying patterns of supported arabesques. As the crescendo of the music anticipates the end of this musical subject, they move upstage right and form a pattern of lines—some dancers standing while others go down on one knee. As the first theme is to be reintroduced, they unfold into single lines and exit to the right.

The first theme is played and Toumanova and Lichine enter from the upper right wing to an empty stage. He lifts her several times in a diagonal—her right hand always resting on her waist and her left arm undulating with her head, with her profile to the audience when she chassés, and facing the audience when she is lifted in a left leg passé. At the end of the diagonal he puts her down and holds her outstretched right arm at waist height as she cambrés in a right leg attitude back. He performs the same introductory lift now towards the right wing, and lets go of her downstage right. As he cabrioles and performs numerous pirouettes, she arabesques and waltzes around him to center stage. From her last waltz movement she steps into a left leg attitude back to come down into a triple pirouette; without coming off pointe, she finishes in a right leg attitude front. Having finished waltzing around her, he lifts her as before. As he puts her down, she arabesques from her passé leg. The length of her left leg in arabesque passes through both his hands in a long, caressing movement as he releases her. She then turns to him and pirouettes three times with her right leg extended straight down as she revolves on the left leg. She finishes in fourth position on pointe and opens her arms to him in a majestic gesture. She runs to him; he turns his back to her as she performs a pas de chat with her back to him. The corps de ballet has already entered as this last movement is repeated.

The climax of the music is made visual in the patterns of the dancers, some static, some in motion. The entrances and exits of the dancers, and their formations, are numerous now. Three men walk onstage, each holding a woman as if she were a statue.

As the musical phrases of the first theme and the first musical subject of the second theme are interwoven, Toumanova and Rostova confront each other and, surrounded by the corps de ballet, dance partnered by Eglevsky. Eventually each is lifted by a male dancer and Eglevsky dances alone. The dancers exit. Four women enter and run across the stage in a diagonal, looking towards Toumanova, who has just been carried onstage on the shoulders of a group of men. The group runs off into the left wing—with Toumanova facing the opposite direction. A group of male dancers runs across the stage, followed by a group of female dancers. Another group of male dancers enters from the upper left wing and runs across the stage; two of these dancers carry Lichine in a Mercury-like pose on their shoulders. As they exit into the upper right wing, the remaining dancers vanish—some running backwards—into the wings. As the final chords are played, the curtain descends on an empty stage.

Second Movement: Andante moderato. The melody recalls stoic Greek songs reminiscent of antiquity. The curtain rises as the woodwind motif of the first musical theme is introduced. A linked chain of twenty women—clad in dark russet nunlike robes with a cowl-type hood—with heads bent, and holding hands, enters from the upper left wing. Their steps change rhythm at each third bar when they stop and pause for four bars to resume the serpentinelike procession around the stage to downstage center. Here the line breaks into three units and, to the pizzicato of the strings, they bourrée back. Upstage they separate into individual entities, raising their bare arms to create a continuous line with their bare legs emerging from the parted skirts of their robes. As they form a close line upstage to the opening of the string motif of the second musical theme, the soloist (Verchinina) appears, clad like her companions but in bright red. Her presence dominates the stage, with the chorus serving simply as a frame. As in *Les Présages*, Verchinina's strikingly individual qualities here inspired an unusual contrast of fluid and tensed movements rooted in a fusion of ballet and Central European modern dance technique. In the background, the chorus assembles in architectural designs resembling archways and temples. They hold their hands with the thumb, the middle and index fingers together as if performing the sign of the cross in the practice of the Orthodox Eastern Church. With arms outstretched, the soloist leaves the stage after the chorus has exited in the opposite direction from which it entered.

Third Movement: Allegro giocoso. The joyous outpouring of vitality here suggested to Massine a peasant dance, its basic traits speed and lightness. To the full orchestra the first musical theme is introduced and the principal couple, Riabouchinska and Woizikowski, enter, she sitting on his shoulder. They perform a fiery rustic dance, soon joined by six couples and two buffoonlike characters. The corps' movements, especially the men's, give a hint of Russian folk dance. A second couple,

Danilova and Jasinski, is introduced and dance together. He steps to the side and she is partnered by the men in the corps de ballet. As the music becomes more frantic the first couple exits with the corps as the second couple runs backwards in the opposite direction into the wings. When the slow passage is played, Riabouchinska appears alone and then is joined by Woizikowski. They dance a pas de deux that basically consists of intricate supported turns and lifts, contrasted with fast jetés. In a recurring lift, he holds her with raised arms above his head as she brings her knees together to her waist, and waves her legs several times left and right like a fish. They run upstage left. Facing him she performs a diagonal of repeated ronde versé turns, while he runs backwards performing pirouettes as if to avoid being caught by her. They exit and Danilova and Jasinski enter with the corps de ballet; while they dance, Riabouchinska is brought in through the downstage right wing, sitting aloft several men and facing the stage. They lift her up and down several times to center stage as the movement draws to an end. The corps de ballet and the secondary couple exit to the left; then, all alone, the main couple performs three grands jetés to the last three chords of the music and exits upstage right into the wings.

Fourth Movement: Allegro energico e passionato. As the movement opens and woodwinds and brass are played, six men dressed in black enter and make a diagonal line profiling towards the audience. At the opening of the first variation, one by one they perform double tours en l'air, the last one landing on one knee with one arm outstretched. They break apart, and the first two leading dancers from the first movement (Lichine and Eglevsky) come downstage and perform intricate footwork alternating with a series of pirouettes as the four other dancers in the background perform various configurations. The leading female dancer of the first movement (Toumanova) enters and performs an adagio, stressing arabesques and supported pirouettes with the four men of the chorus, while Lichine and Eglevsky continue to dance alone. (As Toumanova dances the adagio she is lighted by a spotlight.) Then the six men dance with her. When the adagio ends, the six men come together and with arms folded surround her. She spins a succession of double fouettés, two pirouettes in attitude back, and two pirouettes à la seconde. After the last turn, she chaînés and vanishes into the wings. Lichine and Eglevsky exit after her, performing a series of cabrioles in unison. The corps de ballet dances and as the music slows, the leading female from the third movement (Riabouchinska) enters and dances a solo of extensions and dégagés on pointe with parallel arm movements, with the four men of the chorus in the background. Her previous partner (Woizikowski) enters with four women dressed in mauve. They all pair off. The leading duo performs a pas de deux to the flute passage, consisting of supported turns, arabesques, and transverse lifts, which are copied by the four couples. The lights dim to the sound of the trombones. As the music reaches its climax, the leading couple (Riabouchinska and Woizikowski) exits. The chorus forms in patterns all over the stage and another female soloist enters, dressed in leaf green. She performs downstage a variation that consists primarily of a succession of arabesques against the corps de ballet. The stage is again brightly lit. The men retreat upstage in a horizontal line as the woman moves in diagonals copying the movements of the soloist in green. The other two leading female soloists enter, and the three women dance in front of the female corps de ballet, which is now in the background and exits in parallel lines. The soloists repeat the last step performed by the female chorus and exit into the opposite wing. The men, lined up upstage, come to the front and form an **X** formation of four diagonal squares of four men each. The first square (closest to the orchestra) performs in unison double tours en l'air, followed consecutively at each succeeding musical chord by each of the remaining groups. When the fourth and last group prepares to execute its double tours, the first square of men goes on one knee with heads bent. As the last group finishes its tours, the first group rises and in unison with the last group performs double tours. As soon as these eight dancers touch the ground, the eight from the remaining two middle groups perform the same feat; then, as these eight touch the floor, all of the sixteen perform double tours together. The sixteen men move upstage to welcome the female chorus, which enters in a serpentine formation, with raised arms, weaving a track through the men. Each man takes a woman for this final passage of supported partnering. The three leading female soloists enter and downstage perform a filigree of pointe work on a small radius. The men and women exit, each group to opposite wings. They emerge again from opposite wings and cross the stage. The dancers regroup in numerous patterns and formations, some in motion, others static. Lichine jumps onto the locked shoulders of a group of men. Another group lifts Toumanova in a left leg attitude front (both lead dancers face each other with their profiles to the audience). She raises her left arm and stretches out the right to him; he, in turn, stretches out his arm to her. Riabouchinska is lifted on the shoulder of her partner just behind and in right angle to the pyramid where Toumanova is supported. The chorus places itself, beginning upstage left, around and behind the static grouping in a serpentine formation. While the dancers in front and back of the two main characters held aloft (Toumanova and Lichine) stand up, the serpentine formation diminishes in height as it moves around them and returns to the front, upstage right, around Riabouchinska and Woizikowski. The last dancers sit on the floor to avoid blocking the audience's view of the principals.

Choreog-raphy   In *Les Présages*, Massine still felt the need to find for his choreography a strong psychological correspondence with the music; to this end he employed themes and characters that expressed definite emotions. But in *Choreartium*, he went a step further by creating a resolutely abstract ballet: no plot, theme, or characterization was imposed. This was a new approach to choreography; in previous "abstract" ballets such as Fokine's *Les Sylphides* and Balanchine's *Apollon Musagète*, although there was no literal plot there remained a traditional association with personages or milieu.

As in *Les Présages*, in *Choreartium* the choreographic patterns reflected subtleties in the instrumentation. Massine used different groups of dancers to visualize the strings, the brass, and the woodwinds. As Vera Zorina recalls, "*Choreartium* evolved completely from the score. One could see the structure of the symphony physically growing. In the first movement the leitmotif would be danced by Toumanova, while the horn section was danced by male dancers and the violin section by female dancers. In the third movement, something very airy and fast would go to Riabou-chinska, who was very light."[4]

Massine's focus of interest in *Choreartium* was mainly group construction. Freed from dramatic and narrative restrictions, he could explore the relationships between rhythmical movements through space. His experimentation with spatial values advanced the possibilities of stage placement and provided as well a new definition of atmosphere as a product of the population of space rather than of the theatrical design or the emotional content of the story or theme. He explored horizontal as well as vertical movement in an architectural approach, as in his emphasis on pyramid formations. For his massive choreographic structure of remarkable complexity he believed, as he once put it, that "the relationship with mass patterns is that those rules which apply horizontally, also apply vertically, as in architecture."

At the beginning of his career, and instigated by Diaghilev, Massine had studied many paintings, not only as a source of inspiration or for period style but in order to create in his story-ballets scenes that were realistically constructed and in which characters interacted with one another, rather than facing the observer. He felt (even though he had admired Petipa for what he was, as he had admired Racine) that in the classical academic ballet tradition, where dancers looked straight at the audience, scenes lacked credibility. (One of the great innovations of Romanticism—a practice first established by François Talma, the revolutionary French actor of the late eighteenth century—was to break away from the academic technique of the neoclassical theater, in which actors face the audience in a 180-degree arc and recite their lines to the house instead of to one another. This is one of the many theatrical advances that Romanticism bequeathed to the modern theater.) Now that Massine was experimenting with abstract ballet, he believed that it was important to find the correlation between ballet and architectural structures in order to expand the possibilities of using dancers in these structures to populate the stage. This is what motivated him to create those enormous mass constructions in motion, or dancers being held aloft vertically as statues, or horizontally. This is where his emphasis on rhythmical mass movement through space lies. He wanted the spectators to follow formations in the vertical plane as well as in the horizontal plane. As he once commented, "It required the audience to look left and right, up and down in a more total use of space."

Consequently, his vertical configurations did not consist only of static groupings in space but of moving ones as well. One example is when Lichine, standing on two dancers' shoulders in attitude, is carried across the stage into the wings, or also in the first movement when Toumanova, at the apex of a pyramid, is moved across the stage and into the wings. Tamara Tchinarova, who appeared in the original cast, points out the difference in approach between his earlier ballets and the symphonic ones: "In certain ballets, like *Les Femmes de bonne humeur*, Massine concentrated his attention in every individual movement—heads, elbows, hands. His main interest was to develop each character as an expression of personal gesture. In the symphonies, especially in the Brahms, he stressed the formation of groups. He took the dancers by the hand and led them to their positions. Once the group was constructed,

LEFT: First Movement:
Toumanova and Lichine. BELOW:
First Movement: corps de ballet.

94   ABOVE: Second Movement: Verchinina. BELOW: Second
Movement: Verchinina and ensemble.

ABOVE: Third Movement: Riabouchinska.
BELOW: Finale. This was Massine's first
use of his characteristic pyramid
construction; decor by Terechkovitch.

he was more interested in the overall effect of its composition. He treated the corps de ballet as a collective entity instead of independent units." Another important characteristic of the choreography, in addition to Massine's concentration on group formations, was the utilization of intricate and difficult hopping-step combinations contrasted with large movements.

In *Choreartium* the technique of the male dancer, who executed numerous jumps, pirouettes, and especially double tours en l'air, made an especially strong impression. It did for the male dancer what the fouettés in *Cotillon*, *La Concurrence*, and *Jeux d'enfants* had done for the female. Although the tour en l'air was traditionally employed, here its cumulative effect in the fourth movement produced a very strong impact on the audience, revitalizing the role of the male dancer.

Design

Massine's first choice as designer was Pavel Tchelitchev, with whom he had collaborated in 1928 on *Ode*. But Tchelitchev refused the commission—according to his biographer, on the grounds that he was opposed to the idea of symphonic ballets.[5] A more likely reason for his refusal was that he viewed the Ballets Russes as a rival of Les Ballets 1933, for which he had recently designed *Errante*. Instead, the sets and costumes were designed by Constantin Terechkovitch and Eugène Lourié, Russian painters who had emigrated to Paris and were very much involved with the school of Paris. Terechkovitch's highly acclaimed portraits included those of Matisse, Bonnard, Braque, Utrillo, and Riabouchinska. Lourié became better known as a set designer and art director for films in France and, later, in America. His collaboration with Jean Renoir on the 1933 film *La Règle du jeu* received high praise. The curtains for *Choreartium* were designed by Georges Annenkoff, who had been a colleague of Meyerhold's in Russia and later achieved prominence in films in France, becoming Max Ophuls's favorite art director.

96

While Masson's backcloth for *Les Présages* was almost oppressive in its overcharged, sensual atmosphere, the designers of *Choreartium* tried to recapture the coolness of an unspecified Grecian setting. The decor of the first scene was a vague landscape dominated by a rainbow. The lead female wore black and blue; in contrast, her partner was dressed all in red. The other two female soloists wore yellow (Rostova) and blue (Tarakanova). The corps de ballet wore sky blue outfits or brown robes with two-tone green scarfs. The second scene took place before a blue curtain which the lighting gradually deepened into green. The figures were clothed in somber russet robes like those of a nun, with the exception of the soloist, who wore bright red. For the third scene, the backcloth was an abstraction of yellowish beige, which heightened the white or pastel rose and blue of the costumes. The background of the last scene was an uncertain view of dark grey doorways and arches against a lighter grey background. The women of the corps were clothed in mauve, the men in black. The leading female soloists wore their costumes from the previous movements. A new soloist was introduced wearing leaf green. As in *Les Présages*, the women's costumes were modeled after classical tunics. (This ballet tunic became so popular in the early 1930s that it became known as a "symphonic costume.") This costume was appropriate to Massine's new vocabulary of large movements.

Preview   London had a preview of the ballet when a special dress rehearsal was presented on the stage of the Alhambra at midnight the night before the premiere. Osbert Sitwell introduced the proceedings to an audience that included members of London's diplomatic, financial, social, and artistic worlds: Lady Cunard, Lady Deterding, Lady Juliet Duff, Lady Diana Cooper, Somerset Maugham, Antony Tudor, Agnes de Mille, and Edith and Sacheverell Sitwell.

The participation of Osbert Sitwell was a sort of benediction on the new ballet. The Sitwells played a decisive role in London's social and intellectual life. Osbert had always supported Diaghilev—it was partly through the Sitwells that Diaghilev had been accepted by the Bloomsbury intellectuals in the twenties—and was an admirer of Massine. *Parade* and *Le Tricorne* had been particularly instrumental in converting the English intelligentsia, who had viewed Diaghilev and his company as the pastime of high society—"the old kid-glove and tiara audience of Covent Garden and Drury Lane," as Osbert dubbed it.[6]

Premiere and Critics   The premiere of *Choreartium* incited one of the most polemical discussions in the worlds of music and dance. It seemed that everyone had an opinion to air—particularly musicians, who either attacked or defended Massine vehemently. If Massine's use of a Tchaikovsky symphony had been controversial, his use of Brahms was considered by many to be blasphemy. English newspapers and journals dedicated enormous amounts of space to this issue. The chief force behind the opposition was the composer, conductor, and critic Constant Lambert, while Massine found his staunchest advocate in England's foremost music critic, the redoubtable Ernest Newman.

In the three years that followed the premiere of *Choreartium*, Newman wrote some of his most eloquent and intelligent articles on ballet in defense of Massine. These articles were often astringent, with flashes of irony and humor reminiscent of the critic's lively controversy with Bernard Shaw over Richard Strauss in the columns of *The Nation* during 1910–14.

Massine was accused of presumption in daring to attempt to interpret or translate symphonic music in terms of dance. Regarding this charge, Newman wrote:

> We are told that a ballet cannot possibly "interpret" a symphony. But what, exactly, does that mean? If it means that the musical essence of the symphony cannot be reproduced in terms of choreography, we shall all agree without argument; if some other art could say equally well what music says, there would be no necessity for music. Far from disputing the proposition that you cannot "interpret" a symphony in choreography, I go further, and say that you cannot interpret any music whatsoever in choreography. An interpretation, a translation, implies saying the same thing in other terms than the original; and it is obvious that the specific thing that music has to say can never be said in any other terms than those of music. All we can get, as between music and ballet, is correspondences, parallelisms; our gratification comes from seeing something going on on the stage that runs in harness with the sequences of shapes and moods in the music.[7]

97

Another common accusation was that since a symphony is a self-sufficient musical whole, nothing should be added to it. To this Newman responded:

> If dancing is to be restricted to music that was specifically written for dancing, I am afraid that at least half of the present ballet repertory must henceforth be banished from our sight. . . . In any case, the argument that "nothing that is complete should be or can be, added to," seems to wipe off the slate, in one fell sweep of the duster, all the great song writers from Schubert to Wolf.[8]

He went on to compare Massine's case to that of Wagner:

> If, it was said, Wagner was allowed to go on as he was doing, it would be the end of true art—just as it is now said that if the nefarious activities of Massine are not checked it will mean the ruin of both the symphony and the ballet. But Wagner quietly went on doing what he had set himself to do, and the public ranged itself on his side, let the critics foam at the mouth as they liked—another parallel with the Massine case.[9]

The controversy spread quickly over Europe, and by the time the ballet was presented in other cities, it had already become the talk of the town. With *Choreartium* Massine established himself as one of the most controversial and avant-garde artists of the time.

The American premiere of *Choreartium* was postponed until October 6, 1935, almost two years after its creation—a delay growing out of the indifferent reception America had given *Les Présages* in 1933–34. But it soon became an important feature of the company's transatlantic tours, and they frequently performed it with major national orchestras, under conductors such as Stokowski, Monteux, and Goossens, playing in the pit. The first two performances of *Choreartium* in Philadelphia, on November 12 and 15, 1935, were conducted by Stokowski, lending his approval to Massine's innovation.

While in England, critics, especially Coton and Stokes but with the exception of Newman, felt that the third movement was the least successful due to an atmosphere that was obviously reminiscent of a pastoral scene and the Russian folk dance style; they also felt that the music of the third movement was not as suitable for dance. John Martin of the *New York Times*, in his review of October 15, 1935, praised the third movement as the best, for "its great economy and charm of style." It suggested to him a "sort of bucolic Spring dance."

The ballet stayed in the repertory in South America during the war years. Massine staged a revival, differing in many choreographic passages from the original, for the Teatro Colón, Buenos Aires, in 1955, and again in 1960 for the Nervi Festival, Italy.

98

UNION PACIFIC

American ballet in one act and four scenes; music by Nicolas Nabokov, based on folk songs of the period, orchestrated in collaboration with Edward Powell; libretto by Archibald MacLeish; choreography by Léonide Massine; set design by Albert Johnson; costume design by Irene Sharaff; premiere April 6, 1934, at the Forrest Theatre, Philadelphia, conducted by Efrem Kurtz.

ORIGINAL CAST

The Surveyor of the Irish Workmen	André Eglevsky	The Mexican Girl	Tamara Toumanova
		The Mexicans	Vania Psota,
The Lady Gay	Eugenia Delarova		Edouard Borovansky
The Surveyor of the Chinese Workmen	David Lichine	The Capitalists	Edouard Borovansky, Jean Hoyer, and Vania Psota
The Barman	Léonide Massine	The Cameraman	Roland Guérard
His Assistant	Sono Osato	Irish Workmen, Chinese Workmen, Gamblers, Girls	Artists of the Ballet
The Mormon Missionary	V. Valentinov		

The idea of a ballet based on an American theme had been in Massine's mind since his first exposure to the United States through Diaghilev's Ballets Russes. According to Massine, during that company's American tour in 1916 he had been extremely impressed by a series of war-dance demonstrations given by a group of Sioux on the stage of the National Theater in Washington, D.C.—an event that prompted Massine and Ernest Ansermet (then Diaghilev's music director) to visit the Smithsonian Institution, where Ansermet investigated the musical instruments of the Indians and Massine researched tribal moon dances, nuptial ceremonies, and funeral rites. Eventually, the two men decided to create a ballet based on the story of Pocahontas. Since Bakst had a predilection for exotic themes, he was asked to design the scenery and costumes; Ansermet sent him a series of colored prints of American Indians as well as engravings of the story. For his first American ballet Massine intended to follow the concept of *Le Soleil de nuit*, avoiding a detailed scenario, and telling the story in dance sequences. As soon as the scenario was completed, he began work on the choreography, hoping to have most of it formulated before starting rehearsals upon the company's return to Europe. The ballet, which never materialized, was to have been dedicated to Mrs. Woodrow Wilson.

When the Ballets Russes de Monte Carlo arrived in the United States in December 1933, Massine told Hurok of his desire to create a ballet on an American theme. Hurok was immediately attracted to the project for its publicity potential and discussed the idea with friends and acquaintances in the arts, among them the composer Nicolas Nabokov, who had composed the music for Massine's *Ode* in 1928. Nabokov immediately thought of the poet Archibald MacLeish, who had won a Pulitzer Prize the previous year. MacLeish had already spoken to the composer about a ballet libretto he had written about the construction of the Union Pacific, the first transcontinental American railroad.[1] MacLeish's collaboration appealed to Hurok, and so did another idea of Nabokov's. Among the latter's friends was Gerald Murphy, the fashionable American expatriate based in France, who had recently arrived back in the States. Murphy owned an unusual collection of American recordings assembled by Thomas Edison at the turn of the century, some of them dating back to the 1870s. There were songs performed by Will Cassid, a noted singer of the day, as well as Chicago and New Orleans jazz and other types of black music. Nabokov suggested these to Hurok as the basis for a score.

At Hurok's instigation, Massine met with MacLeish and Murphy to listen to the recordings and discuss the project. The choreographer had already been approached by MacLeish about his scenario, but Massine had found the idea difficult to adapt to ballet. In his autobiography he explains: "I felt that the construction of a railway was not a subject for ballet. I could not envisage it at all, and when he asked me if I would do the choreography I refused, saying that subject did not appeal to me. One insuperable problem, I was sure, would be the presentation of the actual laying of the wooden sleepers and rails. I thought about this for days, mentally composing and recomposing ensemble groups, but could not find a satisfactory solution. Then, one day, I suddenly saw dancers, absolutely rigid, being carried on stage like planks. As I pictured them being laid down on the line, the scene suddenly made sense. I got very excited about the whole project, and now felt that I could make something highly original out of it."[2]

Once Massine, MacLeish, and Murphy reached agreement on the project, Nabokov suggested that a young American composer such as Copland or Thomson be asked to arrange the score, but Massine persuaded Nabokov to tackle the assignment himself.[3]

The collaborators began work when the backing for the production was guaranteed by a fund-raising committee. (The most important sources were the Barnes Foundation in Philadelphia, which had invited Nabokov to come to the United States to give a series of lectures, the Murphys, and friends of the MacLeishes.) Irene Sharaff, who had been responsible for Eva Le Gallienne's *Alice in Wonderland*, designed the costumes, while Albert Johnson, who was the scenic designer for *The Band Wagon* in 1931 and the 1934 Ziegfeld Follies, was put in charge of the scenery.

Action   The ballet is in one act and consists of an introduction and four scenes. The curtain rises to reveal a drop curtain representing a blueprint of the railroad construction plan. The surveyor of the Irish workmen dances an introductory solo. Although his

100

variation is rooted in the classical ballet vocabulary—double tours en l'air, slow pirouettes—the style of the movements is drawn from square dancing and surveying
work to establish from the beginning local color and the character. At the end of his
solo the surveyor kneels on the floor with his hands cupped at his eyes, miming a telescope and looking at the distance.

Scene One: The drop curtain rises to reveal a workers' camp at the railroad right-
of-way east of Promontory Point, where a crew of Irishmen are building the East-to-
West section of the new railroad. The rails—rigid figures in brown sacks—are carried
sideways onto the stage to be assembled. Under the supervision of the severe-looking
surveyor the crew work, pointing towards the west, swinging their arms in automatic
gestures miming the use of tap hammers and other tools of their trade. Indians appear,
hopping between the rails. The blueprint falls as the crew dance about their work.

Scene Two: In front of the blueprint drop curtain the Chinese surveyor dances an
introductory variation. The drop rises and reveals a settlement of tents where the
Chinese crew perform their tasks in constructing the West-to-East section of the line.
(Massine sharply contrasted the scenes by presenting the second crew working
towards the east.) The Chinese workers perform delicate, quick movements in an
Oriental style back and forth across the scene. The Chinese surveyor, a much gentler
personality than his Irish counterpart, is distracted by the advances of Lady Gay—a
local belle of easy virtue—who strolls out of the Big Tent, an itinerant saloon. With
great abandon she dances a solo in high heels, lifting her skirt provocatively and lur-
ing the surveyor with beckoning gestures to the tent. The surveyor dances around her
as the crew perform locomotivelike movements. She goes back into the tent and the
workers resume their chores.

Scene Three: In the Big Tent, which also serves as a dance hall and gambling den,
the Irish workmen sit at tables drinking with the girls. A Mexican girl and two
partners dance for everyone's amusement. The two men fling their sombreros on the
floor, and the girl performs a version of the jarabe tapatío, dancing skillfully on pointe
around the brim of each hat. She picks up the hats and returns them, one at a time, to
their owners. The gamblers come to the floor and dance with movements suggestive
of cardplayers. A Mormon missionary enters with a prayer book and tries with threat-
ening gestures to convert the crowd, but the barman offers him a drink and he soon
forgets his mission. The girls take over the floor and dance as Lady Gay and the Chinese surveyor arrive. The Irish workmen join the girls, followed shortly by Lady Gay,
who becomes the center of attention. The group scatters to the tables and the barman
performs an impromptu dance, first to indifference but finally to the vast amusement
of the customers. After his dance, Lady Gay and the Chinese surveyor perform a flir-
tatious dance, arousing jealousy in the Irish surveyor, who tries to come between
them. When the dance has ended, the two surveyors fight each other, soon joined by
both crews, which have taken sides in the dispute. Bottles, chairs, and tables are
employed as weapons; in the melée the tent goes dark, and the curtain falls.

Scene Four: At Promontory Point, an excited crowd gathers to celebrate the laying of the last rail. The two crews, hostile since the beginning, reconcile at the com-

101

ABOVE LEFT: The Dance Hall Girls.
ABOVE: The Irish Workers. LEFT: "The
Tent": Massine as the Barman, Osato as
his Assistant. OPPOSITE: Finale.

pletion of their task. Two engines puff in from opposite directions; high officials in top hats descend with elegantly dressed ladies. One of the officials hammers the gold spike into a laurel wreath, and the President addresses the crowd. Next to the tracks a telegraph set flashes the word DONE. Everybody dances and enjoys the drinks poured by the barman and his assistant. A photographer records the historical event in a final tableau.

Scenery and Costumes   The decor consisted of three backdrops and a drop curtain. The latter, which represented a blueprint of the construction plan for the railroad, was the only scenery used for the introductory scene. The first scene depicted a daytime workers' camp composed of barrackslike dwellings. The second scene revealed a full-moon scape with several white tents of different sizes and two electric poles. The third scene took place inside a large tent with one lamp hanging from the center. The fourth scene was a daytime variation of the second.

The costumes were based on the styles of the 1860s. The Irish crew was dressed in checked shirts, dark knickerbockers, boots, and caps. The Chinese crew wore coolie hats and other types of Oriental hats; their surveyor had fringed white buckskins

103

recalling a frontiersman's costume. Lady Gay was all in yellow with a hoop skirt, high heels, a ribboned bonnet, and long earrings. The barman wore a white apron over a tartan waistcoat and checked trousers. The missionary was dressed all in black, and the capitalists were in frock coats and top hats.

The different themes of the popular American music of the 1870s served as leit-motivs assimilated into Nabokov's own musical idiom. Through the modern orchestration one could detect such melodies as "Oh! Susanna," "Pop Goes the Weasel," and "Yankee Doodle." Massine's knowledge of American folk dance provided the basis of his choreography. The dancers, too, looked to authentic sources in building their interpretations. Lazowski reported: "The barman was jazzy. The music was more defined in its style of New Orleans, Dixieland, all in the hips. To acquire the right style, we all visited many places—especially Harlem, where we saw dances such as the jitterbug."

Choreographically, the high point of the ballet was Massine's barman solo, which earned unprecedented ovations, especially in Europe. "For my own role as the Barman," Massine explained, "I wanted to make a synthesis of various authentic American folk-dances. I was only vaguely familiar with them, and felt I must study them at the source. In New Orleans I went to the coloured quarter, and there, sitting alone in a bar, I met an old Negro, well in his eighties. When I asked him if he knew the Cake-walk, he gave me a broad grin, and said nobody had mentioned that dance for years. Then he took off his coat and performed it for me with wonderful rhythm and verve, and with the peculiar loose-limbed jerk that is the keynote of that particular dance. Back in New York I went to a night-club in Harlem, where I met a young coloured man who taught me the Strut and the Shuffle."[4]

The barman's dance started with very slow jazz movements, emphasizing the shoulders, and ended with a loose-jointed strut around the stage. He goes around the tent, uncorking imaginary bottles and serving drinks to the guests. In his tipsiness he seems to cross his eyes. Within its limited span Massine was able to incorporate a fully rounded character. Coton described the number: " . . . a witty barman who aped the flunkeyisms of all servility, guyed the drunken client, cringed before the rich one, and drew corks in an amazing convolution of steps that shivered between the techniques of *terek* and *hopak*, and that of Bill Robinson and Fred Astaire."[5] About the 1937 revival Ernest Newman commented:

> Through no fault of Massine's, *Union Pacific* is tending to become rather like a concerto, with the interest of the audience mainly concentrated on the solo performer. . . . but it cannot be denied that so prolonged a demonstration as that which followed his brilliant Bar-Tender's dance on Tuesday evening makes it a little difficult not only for the spectator but for the dancers to take up the threads of the ballet again.[6]

In contrast to the complete abstraction of *Choreartium*, *Union Pacific* was realistic. Its structure was centered on the narrative, to which the dance elements were subordinated. In *Union Pacific*, more so than in his other narrative works, Massine's aesthetic tendency was almost completely directed towards a clear transcription of the libretto. The choreographic phrases were molded to convey a dramatic idea. Only in the tent scene did dance predominate, as in *Le Beau Danube*, where a public setting induces a series of divertissements. At the end of each divertissement in the tent scene, the scene froze briefly to suggest a period photograph.

Rehearsals and Premiere
Union Pacific had a difficult birth. The company's touring schedule was hectic as never before, with constant traveling from town to town, and there was not much time for new productions to be rehearsed. Moreover, facilities were mostly inadequate: Massine had to take advantage of whatever the host theaters had to offer, and even resorted to hotel ballrooms and lobbies on occasion. Most of the *Union Pacific* rehearsals were conducted after performances, and often they lasted four hours. The dancers, though frequently exhausted, were devoted to Massine and willing to rehearse all night if necessary.

The urgency was not felt by the company alone. Nabokov had only twenty-three days to transcribe the recordings and compose and orchestrate the music. Hurok hired Eddie Powell, one of the best orchestrators in New York, to assist him.

The ballet was to have its premiere in Philadelphia on April 6. By the time the company and the collaborators met there, the situation had become even more hopeless. As Nabokov later wrote:

> There were supposed to be two orchestra rehearsals on the 4th of March [*sic*], another rehearsal on the 5th, and a general rehearsal on the morning of the 6th.
>
> By the time of the third rehearsal, nothing worked. Massine was in a frenzy and so was I. The parts were peppered with mistakes; the orchestra played like pigs; Efrem Kurtz complained that the penciled score was illegible; the dancers did not remember their steps; the group scenes did not work; the sets weren't dry and could not be hung; none of the sizes given to Johnson proved to be correct; props were falling down; the curtain was too short; the tent was too small. The costumes weren't ready or did not fit.
>
> On the 5th Massine demanded two extra rehearsals with orchestra. The Colonel and Hurok threw up their arms in despair. We worked until midnight of the 5th and still it all looked and sounded like inevitable disaster.[7]

The atmosphere was tense, and a feeling of impending catastrophe pervaded the Forrest Theatre. Only hours before its premiere, an event anticipated as the highlight of the season, the first American ballet by an international company, seemed destined to be a dead failure. During the afternoon of the sixth, the company felt as if an evil spell had been cast; none of its previous premieres had ever given rise to such chaos. Then, according to Nabokov:

In the evening at the première the unexpected happened.

The ballet started well, and after the first two numbers one could sense that it might work out after all.

I sat among the public, more dead than alive, expecting a flop. But the applause went on rising, number after number, until Massine's Barman's Dance stopped the show.[8]

The next morning the Philadelphia press reported twenty curtain calls.

Critics

Although *Union Pacific* was well received by the general public, it stirred up a lot of controversy in American artistic circles, especially in the dance community. For some it was just a well-constructed commercial piece, fodder for the Ballets Russes's publicity campaign; despite the American scenarist, the American subject, and the American tunes, it was commonly felt that the work was not American in its "method of composition," which was probably rooted in a synthesis of modes of composition based on the European balletic tradition, as introduced in the United States, and various American theatrical genres such as the music hall. At the time of the premiere of *Union Pacific*, a very strong nationalist sentiment was growing among certain members of the American dance community, especially those people involved in creating an American ballet school and company. They resented the impact of the Ballets Russes on American artistic life, and *Union Pacific* soon became their bête noire. Massine was accused of failing in his "blasphemous" attempt to create an American ballet. Lincoln Kirstein said in his "Blast at Ballet": "It was as authentically American

106

as English jazz, the average French notion of New York, or Puccini's La Fanciulla del Far [*sic*] West."[9] Obviously Massine's intention was misunderstood. The choreographer did not intend to create an "authentic" American ballet or to propose *Union Pacific* as his formula for a model of an American ballet aesthetic. His genuine and honest intention was to create a ballet inspired by an American theme (written by an American) and to integrate basic principles of American folk dance with his own artistic expression, the same concept that he had followed in *Le Tricorne*—and no one in Spain ever raised similar charges!

He was also criticized for not producing a homogeneous native feeling, as Eugene Loring or Agnes de Mille did much later. But his achievement was to present diverse ethnic groups, which was very much a part of the story, and to tell this American story à la Massine. There was also a feeling of resentment against the Russians. One critic later wrote: "It was not greeted with any particular acclaim by the critics, who seemed to think that the Russians were carrying their invasion of the United States too far."[10] Even some of the dancers felt it was no more than a *pièce d'occasion*. Still, it gave them the opportunity for outstanding performances, especially in the roles of the barman and Lady Gay. The latter role was created by Eugenia Delarova, who brought to it a piquant quality. However, it was later almost exclusively identified with Baronova, who gave remarkable performances in America and Europe. Newman found in her portrayal of Lady Gay the makings "of an exceptional player of fine-fingered comedy."[11] According to A. V. Coton, "Its interest as Ballet lay in the smaller incidentals of good dancing which illuminated the story."[12] Massine noted that one enthusiast was Marlene Dietrich, who was very much impressed with the work's theatricality. After seeing it in Los Angeles in January 1935, she rode with the ballet caravan for three nights to Santa Barbara and expressed her desire to be used (along with some of the mothers of the company) as one of the rails brought in during the first scene. She did not accompany the ballet to San Francisco but sent roses to greet every performance—especially to the handsome David Lichine, with whom she seemed quite infatuated.

When the work was presented in Paris and London, the main critical objection was that it was not more sordid. About the tent scene the critic for *Candide* commented:

> One dreams of a smoky dance hall, of a disorderly, dense, sensual, feverish atmosphere, a rough paradise where different races confront one another, and where, for a young woman, knives come in handy. Instead, we see stylized proper Broadway back drops, in front of which appear a lot of friendly people nicely dressed in the style of our grandmothers. Sure, the spectacle is pleasant, but it is the subprefecture ball.[13]

Coton also felt that "the work at its best moments was convincing melodrama of the Wild West of Custer and Cody, but totally unrelated to the struggle of those surveyors, engineers and workmen who had pitched a railroad in record time across a half-savage continent, fighting their way against hostile Indians, hunger, and—always—time."[14]

The work is important as an antecedent of Americana in ballet. Some of the dance sequences, especially that of the Irish surveyor, displayed the sort of choreographic vocabulary later used and expanded with a more coherent American folkloric style in Loring's *Billy the Kid* (1938) and de Mille's *Rodeo* (1942). According to an unidentified critic:

> In the thirties it was too early to be dogmatic about what is or is not American ballet. Massine's contribution to American ballet was that; though the conceptualization and structure of *Union Pacific* were typical of existing ones in previous works, he introduced nonetheless an emphasis in American folk character dance that along with the themes becomes an antecedent for ballets such as *Billy the Kid* and *Rodeo*.

Backstage at the Auditorium Theater, Los Angeles, after a performance of *Aurora's Wedding*:
Toumanova, Grigorieva, Charles Chaplin, Riabouchinska, de Basil, Baronova, Kochno,
Massine, Grigoriev, Paulette Goddard, and Lichine.

May 1934–
May 1935

AFTER the stupendous reception at the Alhambra the previous spring, de Basil had begun to consider the possibility of making London the official home of the Ballets Russes. Monte Carlo had been the company's cradle and generating force, but it could not give continuity to the enterprise. La Société des Bains de Mer provided sufficient funds for a spring season of about six weeks, and Hurok's contract guaranteed at least four months each year in the United States; but there remained approximately another twenty-four weeks. The solution was provided by the kind support of Baron d'Erlanger and the dedication and business acumen of Captain Bruce Ottley of Erlangers Ltd. Baron Frédéric Alfred d'Erlanger was a banker, patron of the arts, and composer, half-German but born in Paris. He was a genuine Renaissance man, having financed infant railroads in South Africa and chains of department stores in South America, and also having achieved some success as a composer—his operas *Inez Mendo* and *Tess* were produced at Covent Garden.

During the company's first London engagement, a sponsoring committee was assembled to arrange the 1934 season while the Ballets Russes appeared in the United States. This committee was headed by Bruce Ottley and included Lady Deterding; Mrs. Grenfell, wife of financier Edward Grenfell and future Lady St. Just; and Mrs. Bowen, a prominent member of society. By December 1933 Ottley had received from Geoffrey Toye, then manager of the Royal Opera House, an invitation for de Basil's company to appear there the following summer.[1] Nor by any means was this the only proposition made to the company in London. Wernher, a theatrical impresario and manager of His Majesty's Theatre, and Stoll, at the Alhambra, were equally anxious to engage the company. Doubtless, Covent Garden was the most appropriate venue, offering the Russian Ballet the glamour of a royal opera house and the possibility of future continuity. That the other offers might have been tempting, Toye suggested in a letter to Ottley:

> It is quite possible that a successful play may be put on during the next few months at His Majesty's. . . . No London manager will take off a success for the sake of a few weeks of Russian Ballet and I am sure that whatever he says now W. would not sacrifice a successful run at his theatre for Mr. de Basil. . . . It would be best for them to go to a theatre to which they can return every year. . . .[2]

The new engagement with Toye not only provided the international prestige of a world-renowned theater but had the further advantage of future collaboration with Covent Garden's resident orchestra, the London Philharmonic under the direction of Sir Thomas Beecham. The association with a ballet company capable of presenting long seasons to sold-out houses was favorable to the management of Covent Garden as well. During the past year there had been talk in the newspapers of closing the theater. Beecham's International Opera season, partly sponsored by his friend Lady Cunard, lasted only a few weeks; financially this was insufficient to support the house on a yearly schedule. In fact, there were long periods of inactivity at Covent Garden. Ballet, the other art form that rightly belonged there, had not been a permanent part of the theater's programs since Diaghilev's death.

The publicity campaign for the forthcoming season began at the beginning of the year and was brilliantly conducted by the sponsorship committee. Edwin Evans, who had recently become the music critic of the *Daily Mail*,[3] was engaged as publicist—an apt choice, as he had acquired his expertise by handling Diaghilev's public relations. However, it was decided that Evans should remain anonymous, for the Harmsworth family wanted to avoid hostile criticism from other London papers.[4]

While de Basil was in the United States, Ottley was in charge of every detail pertaining to the opening at Covent Garden. Even though he discussed every decision with the Colonel by mail or telegraph, he was the person most responsible for the success of the 1934 season. His concerns extended well beyond the business aspect. He supervised the printing of programs and the posters that were placed all over London and in the Underground, the scheduling of ballets, the rewriting of synopses, and the selection of artists' photographs to appear in every major English newspaper and magazine. He suggested to de Basil the possibility of approaching Lifar for the Covent Garden season. De Basil would consent only if Lifar became a permanent member of the company. De Basil asked Ottley to contact Woizikowski instead—he had left the company because some of his roles from the Diaghilev repertory were being monopolized by Massine. Ottley agreed and proposed Mrs. Grenfell as mediator to persuade the dancer. According to Ottley, she had a great influence over Woizikowski; but he did not accept the offer.

After the American tour ended, the company sailed from New York to France on the *Paris*, then traveled to Barcelona, where the second season at the Liceu began on May 10. Hurok's extension of the American tour had prevented the company from appearing in Monte Carlo, but since de Basil was still obliged to fulfill his engagement with the Casino, he had arranged for the ballet group that was appearing with Kachouk's Opéra Russe in Paris, under the direction of Nijinska, to take over his artistic duties with La Société des Bains de Mer. To strengthen Nijinska's group, H. Algeranoff, Tatiana Chamié, Alexandra Danilova, Roland Guérard, Roman Jasinski, Olga Kobseva, Marian Ladré, Serge Lipatoff, Tatiana Lipkovska, Nina Raievska, Galina Razoumova, Tamara Sidorenko (Grigorieva), Tamara Tchinarova, Edna Tresahar, Leon Woizikowski, and other members of the company traveled to Monte Carlo in March; Grigoriev joined the group as régisseur général, and Dorati as conductor and musical advisor. Grigoriev, in charge of the rehearsals, was assisted by the contingent of dancers from the Diaghilev company, following his usual pattern of supervising the revivals but having a group of dancers actually do the work. In the regular company this group of dancers was headed by Tchernicheva. All the revivals were presented with their original sets and costumes. For the 1934 Monte Carlo company Nijinska was in charge of her own works and for those that were not created for Diaghilev. *Variations* was designed by Annenkov, *Étude* by Bilinsky after A. Exter, *Boléro* by Gontcharova, and *Les Comédiens jaloux* by Annenkov. The repertory also included *Scuola di ballo*, *Petrouchka*, *Les Sylphides*, the Polovtsian Dances from *Prince Igor*, *Swan Lake* Act II as staged by Balanchine in 1932, and Nijinska's *Les Biches*.

Ironically, Nijinska's group had originally been organized by de Basil himself. Afraid that his company would find itself without work in between the first American

111

The 1934 Monte Carlo company: Blum, Nijinska, Tchernicheva, Dorati, and Danilova in the center.

tour and the Monte Carlo season—perhaps he doubted the chances of success in the United States—the Colonel had signed a contract with Kachouk on August 3, 1933.[5] According to this agreement, de Basil would be responsible for presenting intermittent ballet performances during the Opéra Russe season, which intended to last from November 1933 through June 1934. In addition, Massine would choreograph the opera ballets and dances. When the American venture proved triumphant, the agent Nadine Bouchonnet, acting for de Basil, improvised a ballet group with Nijinska at its head and Dolin as principal dancer.[6] Without Dolin, this group now appeared in Monaco as the Ballets Russes de Monte Carlo. Among its most prominent dancers were Ruth Chanova, Nina Youchkevitch, and Boris Kniaseff.

For Blum this unexpected arrangement presented serious problems. The new group could not participate in the official preseason galas, as the Ballets Russes had done previously. Many of the dancers popular in Monte Carlo would be absent; there were no world premieres, and no performances of some of the works dearest to the casino audiences—*Cotillon, Jeux d'enfants, Les Présages*. These complications led inexorably to the definitive breach between Blum and de Basil.

Their relationship had always been problematic. Almost from the beginning their incompatibility in temperament and artistic taste created a strain. This 1934 crisis proved to Blum that he was being excluded from the directorate of the company and placed him in an uncomfortable position with the Société des Bains de Mer, which was partly subsidizing the enterprise. The conflict was accentuated by de Basil's publicity campaign, which focused on the international aspects of the company and on de Basil himself.[7] When Miró's design for the first American souvenir program was rejected for emphasizing Monte Carlo more than the Ballets Russes, Blum protested bitterly.[8] He further resented that his name and that of Monte Carlo were not given their proper places in the programs (and in many cases omitted altogether) as had been stipulated in their original contracts of December 13, 1932, and December 15, 1933. In a letter to de Basil dated May 24, 1934,[9] Blum was indignant when he found out that the programs for the Barcelona season billed de Basil as founder and general director and that the prospectus for the London publicity campaign advertised "Ballets Russes du col. W. de Basil (de Monte Carlo)." To this Blum commented: "I do not think that the Monte Carlo Administration would accept such a wording, because it will not fail to point out to me that it is not M.W. de Basil, but the Ballets Russes, that belong to Monte Carlo." The plot to deemphasize Monte Carlo for the Covent Garden debut had again been suggested by de Basil to Ottley. In a letter to the Colonel, dated February 12, 1934,[10] Ottley agreed to drop the name Monte Carlo from the campaign. Most probably by then both men foresaw Covent Garden as the official residence of the ballet.

Matters worsened when the name Monte Carlo was again deleted, this time for the 1934 Paris engagement. In a letter to de Basil dated May 31, Blum quoted Article B of their contract:

Commencing on that day and throughout the length of this agreement, any kind of publicity undertaken by the administration of the "Ballets Russes de Monte Carlo" or its impresarios, such as press releases or advertisements, posters, billboards, programs, etc. . . . would not be able to appear in any way unless my name appears in the same type as yours, for France and Monte Carlo. In Monte Carlo both of our names should appear on the same line, whereas in Paris your name will appear on the first line and mine on the second, both in the same type. . . . Sanctions or penalties will be enforced in case of infringement of this clause.[11]

In another letter, dated June 15, Blum demanded that the programs of the Théâtre des Champs-Elysées be modified according to the contract. He was outraged that the London press, including the *Times*, was already announcing the company as "de Basil's Ballets Russes."

As a result of these disagreements, Blum decided to extricate himself from his current contract with de Basil, which was to expire in December 1934, and a new contract was drawn on August 16, to be effective until May 15, 1935. According to this new, and final, contract, Blum withdrew completely from the Ballets Russes enterprise and demanded that de Basil fulfill his commitment to the artistic responsibilities for the 1935 Monte Carlo season. Finally, the Colonel had to reimburse Blum the amount of 250,000 francs, which was paid in full, April 30, 1935.[12]

Breaking away from Monte Carlo gave de Basil added artistic independence to fulfill the needs of his two major sponsors: Covent Garden and Hurok, for both had strongly suggested the kind of repertory that they wanted to present. In a letter from Geoffrey Toye to de Basil, dated July 28, 1934,[13] Toye insists the company revive *The Good-Humoured Ladies*, *Schéhérazade*, and *Thamar* for the 1935 season and further emphasizes: ". . . it ought to be understood between us that these ballets should be prepared in time for next year's Season here." The breach with Blum did not represent a financial threat to the Colonel, for in August 1934, Erlangers Ltd.[14] had opened a loan account in de Basil's name to stabilize the finances of the company and to get it rolling smoothly between contracts. By September 10, Erlangers had credited a loan of five hundred pounds to de Basil's account at the Credit Algérien,[15] Paris, to cover salary advances for the dancers before they traveled to the United States after their summer vacation.[16]

The original company reunited to appear at the Liceu during the second week of May. With the Plaza del Teatro on the Ramblas, for centuries the theatrical district of the city, the twenty-four-hour café life, and the nonstop traffic, Barcelona was one of the company's favorite cities. The premiere of *Choreartium* and the revivals of *Carnaval*, *L'Après-midi d'un faune*, and *Le Tricorne* (which had been a favorite at the Liceu since Diaghilev first performed it there in 1924) were highly acclaimed, and the season was a great success. The revivals were coordinated and supervised by Grigoriev as régisseur général. They were staged again by a group of Diaghilev dancers—Branitska, Hoyer, Ladré, Obidenna, Chamié, and Marra—who assisted Tchernicheva and Grigoriev. Massine had complete control in reviving his own works and was instrumental in some of the revivals, notably *Firebird, Schéhérazade,* and *Aurora's Wedding.* All the Diaghilev works were revived with their original sets and costumes: *Carnaval* by Bakst, *L'Après-midi d'un faune* by Bakst, and *Le Tricorne* by Picasso.

Always preoccupied with the interpretation of his works, Massine arranged for Toumanova to study flamenco with the city's leading teacher before her Spanish debut in *Tricorne.* She recalls: "I was petrified to appear in a Spanish ballet in Spain, fearing that the audience was going to find my performance lacking in authenticity. To help me achieve a command of the style, Massine took me to Escudero's teacher, who trained me during our stay in Barcelona. Massine was kind enough to take financial responsibility for my private coaching!"

After Barcelona the company opened at the Théâtre des Champs-Elysées, the scene of its first Parisian triumphs. It was to be its last appearance in the French capital before the war. The novelties for this three-week engagement were *Choreartium, Union Pacific,* and the world premiere of Lichine's *Les Imaginaires. Choreartium* reignited the symphonic ballet controversy sparked by *Les Présages* the previous year. The anticipation generated by the American triumph helped make the season especially successful. Nonetheless, most of the company's energy was now directed towards its debut at the Royal Opera House at Covent Garden.

One of the company's major concerns at the moment was Baronova's health. She had injured herself during a performance at the end of the American tour and was not dancing. Ottley was afraid she would be unable to dance the opening night at Covent Garden. As usual, the publicity campaign was centered on the stars, and the opening program for Covent Garden had already been chosen, each work considered a vehicle for presenting the stars: Act II of *Swan Lake* for Danilova; *Le Tricorne* for Massine and Toumanova; and *Les Présages* for Verchinina, Baronova, Riabouchinska, and Lichine. Baronova was so identified with her role that there was no one to replace her in this work, and to reschedule a new ballet would present a problem in finding a way to introduce all the other dancers. In addition, *Les Présages* was the most popular work from the previous season. With swift diplomacy Ottley advised de Basil to consider the possibility of including in his repertory *The Haunted Ballroom,* a ballet recently created by the Sadler's Wells company, with music by Toye and choreography by Ninette de Valois.[17] Hostilities had surfaced by now between the supporters of both companies. Besides the animosities to be expected between any two rival companies based in the same city (especially when one of them is foreign), it seems that de Valois's group had also negotiated to perform at Covent Garden that season, with the hope of becoming a permanent feature there.[18] Later on, there were plans for both groups to participate in a benefit gala to raise financial support for Nijinsky. In the spring Lord Keynes had contacted Ottley regarding the project on behalf of the Camargo Society and the Nijinsky Foundation, of which Karsavina was chairman.[19] The program was to consist of one full ballet, *Petrouchka,* to be performed by the Ballets Russes in honor of Nijinsky, with Stravinsky conducting; and a divertissement featuring guest appearances by Argentinita, Spessivtseva, Lopokova, Nikitina, Mar-

114

kova, Nijinska, Kyra Nijinsky, Escudero, Dolin, Lifar, and Chaliapin.[20] Even though important members of society were part of the organizing committee—the Duke of Portland, the Countess of Oxford, Lady Ottoline Morrell—the project did not materialize.[21]

After a lengthy preparation period and a series of tentative dates, the opening of the Ballets Russes at Covent Garden finally took place on June 19. It was an extraordinary event, comparable to the Diaghilev company's London debut at Covent Garden in 1911. From now until 1939 the Ballets Russes was a permanent feature of the Royal Opera House's seasons and an integral aspect of London artistic life.

The opening program included Bizet's *Scènes bohémiennes* as the overture and Act II of *Swan Lake*, both conducted by Beecham; *Le Tricorne*, conducted by Dorati; and *Les Présages*, conducted by Kurtz. The evening ended with a fifteen-minute ovation.

Those who attended that first night must have been surprised to find ashtrays neatly affixed to their seats; for the first time, smoking was permitted in London's home of opera. If at the beginning people were reluctant to smoke, they soon charged the atmosphere with tobacco fumes. The next morning, newspaper headlines proclaimed: FIRST NIGHT OF BALLET AND SMOKING AT COVENT GARDEN.

The first gala performance to be held at Covent Garden since the First World War took place on July 17. As in former times, the auditorium was beautifully decorated with garlands of roses. The boxes were crowded with brilliantly bejeweled royalty, and there was an equally glittering contingent of society figures and artists. Four ballets were presented: *Les Sylphides*, *Les Présages*, *La Boutique fantasque*, and the Polovtsian Dances from *Prince Igor*. After the performance a dinner party took place on the stage. At the ends of two long tables sat the four prima ballerinas, presiding in traditional Russian dress. The bridges in the center were raised to form a platform where impromptu dance entertainment was given. When the divertissement ended, the bridges were lowered and the stage became a ballroom for the three hundred guests.

Though there were no world premieres, two works were new to London: *Union Pacific* (July 6) and *Les Imaginaires* (July 31). But of greater interest were the revivals of *Le Tricorne* (June 19), Fokine's *L'Oiseau de feu* (June 25), *La Boutique fantasque* (July 16), and Massine's *Contes russes* (August 7). The season was such a success that it was extended until August 11, causing the arrangements to install a new ventilation system that summer to be postponed, eventually necessitating the addition of extra work shifts so that it would be completed in time for the opening of the opera season. It was the first time that Covent Garden remained open as late as mid-August. The last performance was sold out, and rows of people stood behind the circles. Many in the gallery had waited over twenty-four hours in a queue that extended along Floral Street around the back of the Opera House.

After a successful opera and ballet season, the future of the theater seemed more stable. New projects for its modernization began. The famous foyer was enlarged, refurbished, and fitted with two new bars. The dressing rooms were repainted and a

115

ABOVE: *La Boutique fantasque*: Danilova and Massine; decor by Derain. BELOW: *L'Oiseau de feu*:
Grigorieva, Petroff, and company; decor by Gontcharova.

number of them were fitted with new showers, and the stage was equipped with the theater's largest cyclorama to date.

The contract with Covent Garden for 1935 guaranteed a twelve-week season with a four-week option clause.

𝒯HE second American tour started with the inauguration of the Palacio de Bellas Artes in Mexico City on September 25. After that came the company's first Canadian tour and its second tour of the United States: seasons in the most important cities and a series of exhausting and seemingly endless one-night stands. Four revivals were presented during this tour: *Aurora's Wedding* (Philadelphia, November 12), *Le Soleil de nuit* (Philadelphia, February 15), *Les Femmes de bonne humeur* (Philadelphia, February 16), and *Schéhérazade* (February 16). Except for *Soleil*

ABOVE: *Les Femmes de bonne humeur*: Morosova. RIGHT: *Le Soleil de Nuit*: Baronova and Massine; costumes by Larionov.

de nuit, Massine's first work for Diaghilev, these ballets held a special place in the repertory, for they had become audience favorites and marked a new stage in the artistic development of the company.

Of the four revivals, *Aurora's Wedding*, especially, afforded the dancers the opportunity to achieve a higher command of Petipa's style and not confine themselves to the schools of post-Petipa choreographers—a limitation that had seriously affected the level of dancing in Diaghilev's company. Kochno recalls: "It took a long time to train Diaghilev's dancers for *The Sleeping Princess* in 1921. They had been completely molded—almost deformed—especially by Massine. De Basil's company presented Petipa's work in the grand manner." Most of de Basil's dancers, with the exception of Diaghilev's, were very young and had been trained by the imperial ballerinas and from the beginning had been exposed to Petipa-style classicism through Act II of *Swan Lake. Aurora's Wedding* was a further step in the refinement of a style they already possessed.

Aurora's Wedding as presented by de Basil's company consisted of the following items:

1. Prelude.
2. Polonaise.
3. The dance of the Seven Ladies and their partners (the pas de sept from Act I, scene i), followed by the Lilac Fairy variation; the Finger variation, usually danced by one of the company's alternate Auroras; and other fairies' variations from the first act of the ballet.
4. Scene and dance of the Duchesses, Act II.
5. Farandole, Act II.
6. Florestan and His Sisters.
7. Little Red Riding Hood.
8. Blue Bird pas de deux.
9. The Porcelain Princesses (pas de trois for two women and one man, to the Danse Chinoise from *The Nutcracker*).
10. The Three Ivans (choreographed by Nijinska).
11. Grand pas de deux.
12. Mazurka.

In the pas de sept Aurora would be partnered by one of the company's leading male dancers who was not dancing the Blue Bird that night (usually Massine or Lichine). After the pas de sept, Aurora would leave the stage until her entrance for the adagio. The number of variations that followed changed over time. When the ballet was first revived during the American tour, no variations were included; later on there were as many as six, and never less than three. The Grand Pas de Deux consisted of the adagio and the Sugar Plum variation. There was no male variation or coda.

Aurora's revival was the collective effort of the group of Diaghilev dancers who usually assisted Tchernicheva and Grigoriev in the revivals, as usual directed and supervised by the ballet mistress and régisseur. Toumanova remembers Branitska working with her in the pas de sept, and Riabouchinska only recalls Tchernicheva teaching her the Blue Bird pas de deux and Grigoriev supervising the production with his book of notes. The costumes, besides Bakst's, included some from Benois's *Le Pavillon d'Armide* and Gontcharova's designs for Aurora's appliquéd tutu and for the divertissement of the Porcelain Princesses. Bakst's third act backdrop was used.

As for the other two revivals, *Les Femmes de bonne humeur* was Massine's first work and the finest in the commedia dell'arte school. *Schéhérazade*, besides being a significant work of Diaghilev's Fokine period, was a vehicle for reintroducing the artistry of Lubov Tchernicheva; later, the role of Zobéide was passed to Tamara Grigorieva, who also offered a memorable and beautiful portrayal.

Towards the end of the American tour, two premieres were presented: Massine's *Jardin public*, to music of Dukelsky, and Massine's restaging of Balanchine's 1929 ballet *Le Bal*, to music of Rieti, with a libretto by Kochno and enormously striking decor by Giorgio de Chirico.

119

Schéhérazade: Grigorieva.

LES IMAGINAIRES

Ballet in one act and two scenes; music by Georges Auric; libretto by Etienne de Beaumont and David Lichine; choreography by David Lichine; set and costume design by Etienne de Beaumont; costumes executed by Madame Karinska; premiere June 11, 1934, at the Théâtre des Champs-Elysées, conducted by Efrem Kurtz.

ORIGINAL CAST

The Circle	Tatiana Riabouchinska	The Spirit of the Sponge	Vania Psota
The Polygon	Leon Woizikowski	The Sponge	Narcisse Matouchevsky
The Triangle	David Lichine	*The Comet	Tamara Toumanova
The Spirit of the Chalk	Lubov Rostova	Points and Letters	Artists of the Ballet
The Chalk	Vera Nelidova		

* This part was added for the London premiere.

120   The spring–summer dance season in Paris was rich in international events. At the Théâtre des Champs-Elysées the Ballets Russes was preceded by Ida Rubinstein's company. The Paris Opéra was preparing the first performances of Lifar's *La Vie de Polichinelle,* and there was to be a busy schedule of dance recitals by Argentinita, Uday Shankar, and others. De Basil's company presented three novelties: *Choreartium* on May 30, *Union Pacific* on June 4, and the world premiere of Lichine's *Les Imaginaires* on June 11.

The ballet was financed by Count Etienne de Beaumont, who also provided the idea, scenery, and costumes. Lichine wrote the scenario.

Action   The libretto, an attempt to poeticize Euclid, concerns the adventures of a Circle, a Triangle, and a Polygon, a sort of Janus with one face à la Pierrot and the other like that of a blackamoor. The Polygon becomes jealous of the love affair between the Circle and the Triangle and asks the Sponge to erase his rival from the blackboard, upon whose surface all these creatures dwell. After the elimination of the Triangle, the Circle finds consolation by asking the Chalk and its spirit to re-create her beloved. When the Triangle is brought back to life, the Polygon disfigures the Circle in a fit of rage, provoking madness and general panic among the algebraic (symbols or letters) and geometric characters. The blackboard, unable to withstand this chaos any longer, collapses.

In concept the work was more characteristic of the twenties than the thirties. The plot derived from an attempt at symbolism in the personification of inanimate objects. The treatment was reminiscent of constructivist productions: the sets served as props and provided various levels of action for the dancers. The choreographer employed objects and constructions such as the hand with the chalk and the cloth that erased all the figures at the end. Still, what ultimately sealed the ballet's fate were the incongruities in the libretto and the contradiction between content and form. If Lichine's intention was to dehumanize his characters by portraying them as geometrical symbols by which human nature cannot be depicted, he contradicted himself by imbuing them with the most exalted human feelings of love and jealousy. It was inappropriate for these inanimate objects to enact passionate emotions. If in symbolism the idea—where the tangible represents the intangible—is to remain infinitely associated with the image, that image has to be irrevocably expressive of such an idea. If the image contradicts the idea, there is no symbolic discourse.

Music   Auric produced an undistinguished score. Emile Vuillermoz, writing in *Excelsior,* felt that another composer should have been commissioned for this score, one who would not have taken his job so seriously. He added:

> In fact, [Auric's] music belongs to the category of the "imaginaries." It is not, honestly speaking, of real existence. It is composed of whims, doubts, vague aspirations and unaccomplished efforts. It remains in the limbo of hesitant and uncertain inspiration that does not achieve an objective creation. Incapable to state itself, it anxiously compensates by employing various contradicting . . . techniques and formulas, and the show ends before the irresolute musician makes a decision.[1]

Choreog-raphy   Lichine's choreography could not resolve the paradoxes of the scenario. Indeed, it enhanced the incompatibility between method and intention, if there was any. According to Riabouchinska, Lichine was so eager to develop his choreographic talents that he struggled to use any idea offered to him. At this early stage, his powers of discrimination were undeveloped, and *Les Imaginaires* found him lacking the intellectual resources to deal with the intrinsic problems in the scenario.

With no one to advise him, Tchinarova recalls, Lichine felt his way intuitively and would frequently change his mind from one day to the next. According to one review, he employed devices from other ballets that gave the work the character of pastiche.[2] Tchinarova felt that the last tableau in particular was similar in approach to the last tableau of *Jeux d'enfants.* One of Lichine's characteristic touches was the virtuosity of the choreography, his feeling for original groupings. He had not yet developed a cohesive personal style and as a result employed asymmetrical groupings (spontaneous, disorganized à la Massine in the symphonies) in very symmetrical patterns. He would use anything. After the Paris failure, Lichine added a new part—the Comet, for Toumanova—for the London premiere. To accommodate her (and her expectant public), Lichine even gave her a series of fouettés.

The *Daily Telegraph* reported: "Triangle and Circle perform dances effective and

121

ABOVE: Lichine with corps de ballet. BELOW:
Riabouchinska, Lichine, and Toumanova.

122

characteristic enough, if not strikingly original. The best scenes are those in which a comic element is introduced by Chalk, a white-face highbrow, and Sponge, twin-sister to Humpty-Dumpty. These, in spite of their conflicting duties, appear to have discovered a modus vivendi; the one enjoying creation as much as the other delights in annihilation."[3]

Some of the devices were naive and unimaginative. When the Sponge erased the Triangle, it did so with a black cloth; when the Triangle was to be revived, an immense white hand with chalk was brought to the middle of the stage (some French critics suggested that only the Vaseline was missing!), and at the end the black cloth covered the scene and erased it all.

Scenery and Costumes

The best element in Beaumont's work was the background of geometrical forms that allowed for more than one level of action. The scenery consisted of two back-cloths. The first, a light grey, had an uneven dark grey blackboard painted on it, with a silver backcloth behind the cutouts. The blackboard had two geometrical forms cut out at slightly different heights, through which the dancers appeared. For the London premiere new sets were commissioned from Lesley Blanch and Frieda Harris, who followed Beaumont's original concept, although the shapes on the blackboard were different.

For the costumes Beaumont resorted to an evocation of medieval and Italian buffoonery, with a touch of Martian. The Polygon, in black, white, and grey, resembled a double-faced Prince of Fools. The Triangle was dressed all in white with a Dantesque wig. The Circle, in pink, red, and green, wore a variation of a classical tutu, with circles around her breasts and a cap covering her hair. The Chalk looked like a Columbine in white and blue, and the Spirit of the Chalk evoked a troubadour's chatelaine.

Premiere

The Parisian elite that gathered at the Théâtre des Champs-Elysées to see and to be seen included the Count and Countess de Beaumont, Misia Sert, Cocteau, Chagall, Auric, and Jean-Louis Vaudoyer.

Critics

In Paris the press dismissed the work as a failure. Emile Vuillermoz, writing in *Excelsior,* found a contradiction in the title, as imaginary numbers in math do not correspond to geometric figures. However, he gave the most detailed and sympathetic critique of the work:

> This theme, a bit unexpected, offers amusing choreographic possibilities. The evolutions of angles and curves and the play of descriptive geometry in the space could provide inspiration of infinite richness to an experienced choreographer. David Lichine has created some ingenious movements and some pleasant details, but has not taken from his subject all that we could have expected.[4]

123

JARDIN PUBLIC

Ballet in one act; music by Vladimir Dukelsky; libretto by Vladimir Dukelsky and Léonide Massine based on a fragment of *The Counterfeiters* by André Gide; choreography by Léonide Massine; set and costume design by Jean Lurçat (second version by Alice Halicka); premiere March 8, 1935, at the Auditorium Theatre, Chicago, conducted by Antal Dorati.

ORIGINAL CAST

The Statue	Roman Jasinski	The Poor Couple	Tamara Toumanova and Léonide Massine
The Sweepers	MM. Alexandroff, Bousloff, Hoyer, Ismailoff, Platoff, Tovaroff	The Rich Couple	Alexandra Danilova and Paul Petroff
The Leading Nurse	Olga Morosova	Pas de Six	Alexandra Danilova, Tamara Toumanova, Léonide Massine, Yurek Shabelevsky, Paul Petroff, and Serge Ismailoff
The Nurses	Mlles Chabelska, Chamié, Nelidova, Obidenna, Osato, Razoumova, Serova, Tchinarova, and Volkova		
The Old Runner	Marian Ladré	The Old Couple	Paulina Strogova and Serge Bousloff
The Schoolboys	MM. Belsky, Katcharoff, Kosloff, Lipatoff, and Matouchevsky	The Vision	Vera Zorina and Roman Jasinski
The Poet	Yurek Shabelevsky	The Military Orchestra	MM. Belsky, Katcharoff, Kosloff, Lipatoff, and Matouchevsky
The Workmen	MM. Alexandroff, Bousloff, Hoyer, Guérard, Lazowski, Platoff, Psota, and Tovaroff		
The One Who Commits Suicide	Serge Ismailoff	The Woman Renting the Chairs	Eugenia Delarova

When the Ballets Russes arrived in the United States in the fall of 1934, Massine renewed his contact with Vladimir Dukelsky, who was then residing in New York City. Dukelsky was a young Russian composer who first emerged onto the classical music scene in 1925 with the ballet music for Diaghilev's *Zéphire et Flore,* with choreography by Massine. Along with Poulenc, Auric, and Rieti, he was one of the four pianists at the London premiere of *Les Noces.* By the late twenties he had embarked on a successful career as a composer of light music; with his name altered to Vernon Duke (at Gershwin's suggestion), he achieved prominence composing scores for films and musical comedy: *Ziegfeld Follies* (1935), *Goldwyn Follies* (1938), *Cabin in the Sky* (1940).

During Massine's stay in New York, Dukelsky approached him with a passage from André Gide's novel *Les Faux-monnayeurs* (*The Counterfeiters*) as a potential subject for a ballet.[1] This excerpt, concerning a public park where various unrelated characters meet, found Massine's approval. The next step was to obtain permission from Gide, who not only consented but suggested the title *Jardin public* and agreed to forfeit his royalties in America. De Basil consented to the project on the condition that outside funding be provided. To this end Estrella Elizaga, international socialite and personal friend of Dukelsky, was retained. She provided the necessary money through a fund-raising committee that she organized.

Action   Gide asked that the pertinent passage from his novel be included in its entirety with the program notes, but because of its length it was replaced by a scenario by Dukelsky and Massine:

> The scene is a public park. It is early morning and still dark. Then a statue of Laocoön is seen and from a door in the pedestal a drummer emerges to beat the tattoo which indicates the opening of the park.
>
> The sweepers enter to prepare the park for its daily quota of visitors. At sunrise, the first of these to appear are the nurses with their charges. After them trails an old roué, who selects the prettiest for his attentions. The nurses scatter, and the park is filled with a group of chattering, quarreling schoolboys. A poet follows them, making a leisurely visit to ruminate on the absurdities of civilization, and to make his daily communion with nature. In contrast to him are the rugged and uncouth workers who come to eat their meagre lunch.
>
> A man bent on suicide enters, but the passers-by distract him, till he finally disappears in disgust. Two pairs of lovers next attract us—a poor couple who cannot go elsewhere for their pathetic confidences, then a bored divorcée and her fashionable young man who express themselves in a rhumba à la Ritz. A pas de six follows, engaging the two couples, the suicide and the poet. The suicide tries to persuade the wealthy couple to kill themselves, but they indignantly refuse. He then has an argument with the poet on life and death, and finally shoots himself. Next an old couple appear, to recall the days of their youth in this very park; seated on a bench they re-live in a vision the melancholy waltz of their courtship. . . .
>
> The day is over, and the church clock chimes seven, recalling the characters to their homes, and to reality. As she leaves, the old lady drops her handbag, and it is snatched by the poor lover, who empties the money from it, and wantonly destroys a faded daguerrotype which [the old lady] has been admiring during her reverie on the bench. The arrival of a shabby military band heralds the approaching gaiety of the park by night, and now it is fully illuminated, and a poor chair-vendor circulates among imaginary citizens, hawking her wares in vain and expressing her annoyance at the bad rhythm of the musicians.

125

Throngs begin to gather. The pretty nurse is pursued by the old roué, the schoolboys romp about interfering with many, and the workers, together with the poor couple, menace the wealthy lovers, who in turn become hostile to the poor couple. Everyone joins in the workers' growing protest. Meanwhile the poor couple return the stolen handbag to the old lady, spurning the reward which she offers. The workers pursue and drive out the wealthy couple, then return to pay homage to the poor lovers.

The statue of Laocoön is illuminated, the drummer beats the park's closing tattoo, and the poet who has been observing this life eagerly is thrilled by the spectacle.[2]

Choreog-raphy

The choreography of *Jardin public* included few passages of pure dancing, stressing instead statuesque effects and poses. Although the work was conceived in realistic terms, Massine introduced symbolic touches such as the drummer, who functions as a Greek chorus. The choreographic and interpretative highlights were the dance of the Poor Couple performed by Toumanova and Massine, the pas de six in the style of an opera sextet, the miming of the suicide scene by Platoff, the comic scene of Delarova's chair vendor, and the finale. Of Delarova, Arnold Haskell commented in the *Daily Telegraph* (July 24, 1935): "[She] is given full scope for her vigorous comedy scene. She has created a character that can be placed beside Massine's barman."

Music

Dukelsky's score, with its distorted jazz idioms, was conspicuously a product of the twenties. As such it was severely taken to task by Newman:

> The music . . . is like a belated ghost from the generation 1920–1930 or thereabouts; one feels, indeed, that it is just the sort of thing Diaghileff would have imagined to be truly representative of modern music in his last days. Dukelsky, apparently, still thinks we are likely to be impressed by a profusion of discords without any distinction or continuity of ideas to justify them. The absurdity of this method of making discord the mezza voce, as it were, of your composition is that you have nothing in reserve for an emotional fortissimo; Dukelsky has tortured and twisted the basic musical speech so thoroughly for nothing more exciting than a dance of Nurses or of Schoolboys that no extra sophisticating of it is left him for the music of the Suicide.[3]

Similarly, Lambert noted that "Dukelsky's score is a disappointment after his earlier theatre work. 'Zephyr and Flora,' in spite of its rather costive harmonic and orchestral style, was one of the most attractive of the neo-classical Diaghileff ballets and had an agreeable melodic freshness."[4]

Rehearsals and Premiere

Like *Union Pacific*, *Jardin public* was created and produced under near-catastrophic conditions. The company was committed to bookings all over the country, and under the strain of constant rehearsals, performances, and travel, the new

ABOVE: Toumanova and Massine as the Poor
Couple. BELOW: corps de ballet; set by Lurçat.

ballet was allotted whatever time and space could be spared. Luckily, an intensive rehearsal period was scheduled in the basement grill of the Hotel Piccadilly on West Forty-fifth Street, New York, at the end of the coast-to-coast tour. At the time Jean Lurçat, the French artist world famous for his tapestry designs, was commissioned to do the scenery and costumes. Lurçat created a somber decor of a park composed of silhouettes of people and trees in shades of purple.

The ballet had its premiere in Chicago on March 8, 1935, but the reception was not enthusiastic. It was no more successful in New York on March 21, or in Barcelona, while in London, on July 23, the reception was downright disastrous.

Critics

Although the ballet was a failure, some of its passages manifested Massine's masterful craftsmanship and his deftness of characterization. Fragments of the ballet have survived on film, and the scene of the poor lovers (danced by Toumanova and Massine) is a particular case in point. The problem lay, no doubt, in the attempt to transpose faithfully from one medium to another.

Massine's episodic treatment of contrasting moods lacked any unifying factor other than the space where the action takes place. As Constant Lambert wrote: "The scenario . . . reminds one of the type of book so popular nowadays in which the only unifying element is the fact that all the characters happen to have taken the same train to Brighton or happen to be on the same sinking ship."[5] By contrast, in Gide's text, besides the park as a unifying element, there was the feeling of social alienation that enhanced the impersonal drama of all these characters. All of them together created a sort of collective character that became a representation of the human condition. This, of course, was not achieved in the ballet, and Massine's flat characters became too defined and strong onstage.

128

The question was not, as Lambert claimed, that the ballet "contains too many episodes which cannot be made clear plastically" or that "not even Massine can make this literary or cinematic episode choreographically clear." Rather, it was that the choreographer's approach did not capture the essence of the novel. The work would have been more effectively conceived by attempting a poetic rather than a realistic evocation. It is easy to understand why Kochno, after seeing the work in London (as Baronova recalls), remarked that the whole conception was erroneous. Still, Ernest Newman believed that, despite a disturbing mixture of episodes, Massine had created a

> superb final tableau, in which not only is the eye delighted by the skilled grouping, but the mind feels that all the separate strands of the preceding scenes are now combined into a massive yet lucid contrapuntal whole. Once more one admires the fertility of Massine's imagination, but at the same time wonders a little doubtfully whether the ballet will be able to maintain itself in spite of the music.[6]

Other versions

Despite the failure of *Jardin public,* Massine was fond of this work. He was particularly drawn to its social content, and he never doubted his artistic achievement in many of its episodes—especially that of the poor lovers, which, he has said, served as a point of departure for his *Nobilissima Visione* (1938), in which he was to incorporate the movements, and even the costume style, that he had devised for Toumanova and himself. Today, viewing photographs of Massine and Toumanova in *Jardin public* and Massine and Nini Theilade in *Nobilissima Visione,* one could easily mistake them as belonging to the same ballet.

After the London season, Massine contacted Dukelsky to rework the score for a new, revised version to be presented during the spring 1936 season in New York, with new scenery and costumes by Alice Halicka, a Polish artist based in Paris, who later made other contributions to the theater, including scenery and costumes for Balanchine's *Le Baiser de la fée* for the Paris Opéra in 1947. At George Gershwin's instigation, Dukelsky asked Joseph Schillinger for help in improving the orchestration. A version with minor changes in score, choreography, and costumes was presented in New York on April 19, and when the company sailed back to Europe on the S.S. *Paris,* the composer went along to make still further adjustments before the ballet was reintroduced at Covent Garden on June 29, 1936. In spite of all this, the work was received with indifference in London.

In *Jardin public* Massine attempted to create a ballet of social awareness. However, he was criticized, especially in the United States, for presenting a superficial work that, while indicating the economic situation of the Depression, failed to offer a solution or elaborate on the theme. Four decades later, he commented: "*Jardin public* happened at the wrong time. Its concept would have been more appreciated after Ionesco had made his appearance on the theatrical scene." Certainly *Jardin public* is a precursor of World War II ballets with social themes, such as *Miracle in the Gorbals* (1944) and Roland Petit's *Les Rendezvous* (1945), whose stories focused on the lower stratum of society and depicted the decay of the social order and the human condition.

129

The Russian ballerinas at a recent party in their honour included MLLE. LISA SEROVA and MLLE. VERA ZORINA (left and centre). They are with MR. C. BARRAND and MR. "BUNNY" TATTERSALL (right)

MRS. BRUCE OTTLEY, COLONEL W. DE BASIL, and LADY GALWAY at the party for Colonel de Basil's Russian Ballet.

MLLE. TATIANA RIABOUCHINSKA, one of the prima ballerinas, is a juvenile blonde. She is with MR. BORIS KOCHNO, author of the libretto for "Les Cent Baisers."

MME. BRONISLAVA NIJINSKA, sister of Nijinsky, is responsible for the choreography of "Les Cent Baisers." She is with BARON FRÉDÉRIC D'ERLANGER, who wrote the music, and MLLE. IRINA BARONOVA, who dances the Princess (right)

M. SHABELEVSKY, MLLE. DORA LAVROVA, M. BOROVANSKY, M. R. JASINSKY, MLLE. ANNA VOLKOVA, M. ALEXIS KOSLOFF, and MLLE. ALNASSOVA are here seen (from left to right) round the table.

MME. TCHERNICHEVA (shown on our facing page in costume for "Scheherazade") and M. DAVID LICHINE, the famous dancer who is the Prince in "Les Cent Baisers."

BALLERINAS IN "MUFTI."

June 1935–May 1936

By 1935 the Russian Ballet had achieved a more stable existence. London had been established as its operating center, and when the company moved into Covent Garden in the summer, there was, as there had been in Monte Carlo in 1933, the feeling of being home. The house subscription system was extended to cover an annual three-month ballet season.

The company opened at the Royal Opera House on June 11, after the close of Sir Thomas Beecham's successful International Grand Opera season.

The Ballets Russes participated in the production of *Prince Igor* (June 13, 15, and 17) during the regular opera season. The outstanding cast included Elisabeth Rethberg, Karin Branzell, Charles Kullman, Paul Schoeffler, Alexander Kipnis, and Herbert Janssen—all singing in German! (Multilingual productions were standard until the fifties. In 1950, when Victoria de los Angeles made her sensational Covent Garden debut in *La Bohème*, she sang Mimi in the original Italian, while the Royal Opera company sang in English.)

The program for opening night consisted of *La Boutique fantasque*, with Danilova and Massine as the can-can dancers; *Les Présages*, with Verchinina, Baronova, Riabouchinska, and Lichine; and the company's first English performance of *Aurora's Wedding*, with Toumanova and Petroff as the Princess and Prince, and Riabouchinska and Guérard as Florine and the Blue Bird.

The Edinburgh *Evening News* reported: "The return of the Russian Ballet to Covent Garden tonight is causing a more pronounced flutter in the world of theatre and art than the opening of the most brilliant international opera season could provoke."[1]

Aurora's Wedding became a popular vehicle with which to present the company's favorite artists and demonstrate their command of the classical style. Toumanova and Baronova excelled in their interpretations of Aurora; each brought to the character the individual qualities that made them such distinctive ballerinas. So contrasting and personal were their interpretations that, according to Lazowski, each "dominated the stage in such a way that one felt as if the ballet had become a different work through her presence, so overwhelming were their stage personalities. One could watch either one over and over again throughout the years. There was no point of contact in the two portrayals. Each added her own touches, Toumanova technically and Baronova stylistically. Every gesture, every nuance, every step had a different flavor. Tamara was regal, detached, enigmatic. Irina was courtly but, above all, the essence of womanhood."[2] Audiences had their preferences—especially the gallery, which contained vociferous rival factions. Nevertheless, one thing is clear: according to the reviews, eyewitnesses, and the incomplete 16mm films that recorded their performances, both were incomparable. Danilova also danced Aurora,

Aurora's Wedding: Danilova and Lichine with the full company; set and costumes by Bakst.

though infrequently. In Australia and during the 1940–41 American tour, Denisova shared the part; when the company settled in South America, the role was taken over by Nana Gollner, and, later still, Tatiana Stepanova. Besides Petroff, Dolin and Lichine danced Prince Charming from time to time.

The role of Princess Florine in the Blue Bird pas de deux became so identified with Riabouchinska that she had a virtual monopoly on it. Characteristically, she made it so much her own that it was difficult for other dancers to inherit it. Although she was not a purely classical dancer (her hybrid style placed her in a category apart), she brought to the role a magical quality that made her interpretation unforgettable. According to most descriptions she projected an unusual quality, a supernatural aura combined with a very warm and human element that set her apart from her environment and other dancers, a quality that made her particularly successful in a variety of roles—fairy-tale or romantic heroines, young girls or supernatural creatures. Denby later commented: " . . . in the Bluebird she is a sparkling Princess with a wonderful blue bird of her own. . . . She creates a magic world around her; a very rare dancer indeed."[3] During this first season in London, her interpretation was compared to Markova's. Haskell wrote: "Where I find that Riabouchinska excels is in her artistry. . . . She removes this dance far from the schoolroom, suggests flight to an unusual degree and has made of it something very much her own."[4] Much later, in Australia (1939–40) and the United States (1940–41) Geneviève Moulin alternated in the role. As her Blue Bird, Riabouchinska had Lichine, Jasinski, Guérard, or, surprisingly, Massine. Dolin and Lifar also danced the part during the Australian tours. In Riabouchinska's opinion Guérard was perhaps the most technically accomplished, although the others surpassed him in stage presence. The partnership of Riabouchinska and Lichine had a magnetism that electrified audiences. Their number always stopped the show.

Besides *Aurora's Wedding*, there were revivals new to London: *Schéhérazade* (June 19), *Les Femmes de bonne humeur* (August 6), *Thamar* (August 16), and *Le Spectre de la rose* (August 23). *Schéhérazade* and *Thamar* were vehicles for Tchernicheva's return to the London stage. Even though Fokine did not like her as Zobeïde (he wrote in *Memoirs of a Ballet Master*: "Lubov Tchernicheva, described by some critics as a wonderful interpreter of this role, added so much 'tragedy' to it that for me it destroyed the whole originality and charm of the part"),[5] her acting and her stage presence impressed critics and colleagues, who admired her in both roles. Newman praised her highly in *Thamar*, and Gordon Anthony, who captured her noble beauty in his photographs, wrote of her breathtaking performance as "a sensual, homicidal queen of nymphomaniacs" in this role.[6] Massine, Danilova, Morosova, Grigorieva, and Tchinarova danced *Les Femmes de bonne humeur*, while *Le Spectre de la rose* was interpreted by Baronova and Petroff.

The only works new to the English public were *Jardin public* and Massine's version of *Le Bal*, with the de Chirico decor designed for the Balanchine/Diaghilev production in 1929. *Le Bal* was as unsuccessful in London as it had been in the United States. Ernest Newman wrote in the *Sunday Times* of June 23 that "the music by Rieti

133

Le Spectre de la rose: Lichine and Riabouchinska.

134

is one of the worst specimens that have come down to us of a bad genre in a bad epoch. Its emptiness and boring ugliness have evidently posed Mr. Massine with some of the most difficult problems he has ever had to face; and it can not be pretended that he has solved all of them. But one's first feeling of indifference or repulsion gradually give way to a detached interest in some of the lines and combinations of lines projected in this curiously acrobatic choreography." Nijinska's *Les Cent Baisers* was the season's only world premiere.

The company's reception was so overwhelming that on August 22, two days before the last performance, the Colonel gave a party to show his appreciation of the British public's support. Needless to say, Ottley was instrumental in organizing this event. The affair, called "Grand Rout and Cabaret Entertainment," was held at the Royal Opera House with the participation of the London Philharmonic Orchestra under the direction of Beecham, who conducted a series of Viennese waltzes. Though many celebrities from the world of finance, society, and art were present (Kchessinskaya and the Grand Duke André, Lady Cunard, the Paul Robesons), entry to the party cost only six shillings to accommodate devotees from the amphitheater and gallery.

The high note on which the season ended was marred by the death of Nijinska's son, Leon, in early September. The entire family was involved in a car accident while traveling from Deauville to Paris. Nijinska's other child, Irina, was severely injured, but the choreographer and her husband escaped relatively unharmed.

When the Ballets Russes opened at the Metropolitan Opera House on October 9, New Yorkers for the first time were able to appreciate the company to the full. Manhattan had always presented a problem to Hurok because of the lack of a suitable venue. With the newly remodeled Metropolitan at his disposal, he could provide the company not only with a spacious stage and ample facilities but with a theater of the standards of Covent Garden, the Teatre Liceu, and the Salle Garnier in Monte Carlo. Even though the company's previous New York engagements, especially opening nights, had been attended by gala audiences, it was not until this season that the Ballets Russes attracted the full regalia of New York society. The famous Diamond Horseshoe, a tier of thirty-five boxes belonging to the "crème de la crème," included a constellation of Vanderbilts, Astors, and Morgans.

The precarious financial situation that the Met had been experiencing since the Crash of 1929 was alleviated by the subleasing of the theater to Hurok. The increased use of the auditorium would help the Metropolitan Opera Association to meet the expenses of the house. In fact, on October 12 of the previous year, a plan to merge the Philharmonic-Symphony Society with the Met had been proposed to cure these

The company arrives in New York.

Massine and his wife, Delarova, with their dog Smokey.

financial ills. But nothing had materialized owing to the negative reactions of then guest conductor Bruno Walter and, above all, Toscanini.[7]

Their third American tour established the Ballets Russes as an institution in the United States. The propagation of ballet as an art form and as a commercial proposition was one of Hurok's most magnificent undertakings, though local ballet ventures, still cradlebound, resented the so-called Russian invasion. In Agnes de Mille's words: "Hurok imported de Basil's Ballet Russe de Monte Carlo and the craze that was to endure seventeen years and sweep everything else to corners."[8] But had it not been for the Ballets Russes, the general American consciousness of ballet would not have developed so rapidly. Hurok's publicity campaign, along with the cross-country tours, were so masterfully arranged that the Russian Ballet was the most popular expression of entertainment available on a grand scale throughout the country after cinema and radio. These expeditions, with their taxing one-night stands, were probably Hurok's most extraordinary achievement. *Time* magazine reported in a 1936 article:

> Ballet had suddenly become a rage not only in Manhattan but in 100 other U.S. cities visited by the Monte Carlo dancers since last October. The fever began in earnest last season when the company toured 20,000 miles. . . . It played to capacity audiences . . . [in] houses in Little Rock, Ark., El Paso, Tex., Portland, Me. In Brockton, Mass., a leading citizen was impressed because the ballet's appearance there was one of the rare occasions when he had known his townsfolk to turn out in formal evening clothes.[9]

The company and orchestra traveled in eleven Pullman cars, with a special train for scenery and costumes. The repertory was staggered so that as three ballets were playing in one town, another three were being readied at the next, and so on, up to five consecutive programs. The company performed in all sorts of places, from school auditoriums to professionally equipped theaters.

The strain on the artists at times was overwhelming. Only the enjoyment and satisfaction they received from their work carried them through. It is possible that this great physical effort contributed to the abbreviation of many careers. The dancers started at a very early age and were never given the opportunity to conserve their vitality and strength. The declining standards of these artists in later years, and in some cases their early retirement from the ballet, were probably due to strained health and nerves. Many of them were worn out by the time they were twenty-five. Their regular schedule consisted of an average of three hundred performances a year, with three ballets a night—six on Wednesdays and Saturdays.

Apart from New York, Chicago, Los Angeles, and San Francisco, the tours,

137

Danilova, Massine, and Baronova in a Russian divertissement
devised for a backstage party.

which lasted over six months, were tedious. Although the dancers were traveling throughout the country, they never had the opportunity to become exposed to American life and culture. Their existence was confined to trains, post-performance rehearsals of new works to comply with the American demand for novelty, and, of course, performances. Haskell described it:

> Otherwise the story of these tours is one of deadly monotony; lack of sleep, tasteless food, inane interviews and creative frustration. One rarely realized in which town one was appearing and in any case it made not the slightest difference. Only the warming charm of Sol Hurok and his masterly organization and the comfort and warmth of railway stations and hotels made the whole thing possible and, but for a cancelled or late performance through snow or flood, the ballet was like a circus; arrived on time, gave its show and departed.[10]

Under these circumstances dancers found diversion in the internal conflicts of the organization, gossip, card playing, and personal melodrama. There were professional rivalries, romances, and even suicide threats. An amusing story concerns a married dancer-choreographer who was having an affair with a dancer. His wife, whom all knew to be going through a crisis, left a note, during intermission, on the dressing table of another dancer, saying that she was going to jump off a bridge. When her colleague read the note, she tried immediately to track her down by asking in the theater where there was a bridge. To her dismay, she was informed that New York City had more than one. The company mobilized itself into a posse of taxis to search for the desperate victim. As the search party returned to the hotel, she was discovered in the lobby.

In the big cities of New York, Chicago, Los Angeles, and San Francisco, life was more exciting, and there were glamorous parties to attend. Besides the good theaters and comfortable conditions, it had become usual for the company to perform with the leading symphony orchestras conducted by the most prestigious conductors—Stokowski and Ormandy in Philadelphia, Goossens in Cincinnati, Monteux in San Francisco. The dancers enjoyed Los Angeles for its climate and Hollywood for its thirties glamour. In New York the work schedule was even more demanding, but to compensate there was the nightlife of Harlem and Greenwich Village and the other special attractions of the city.

On April 16 the Ballets Russes returned to New York and opened a second two-week engagement at the Metropolitan Opera House.

Nijinska's *Les Noces* had its first American performance on April 20, led magnificently by Grigorieva. The score had first been heard in the United States in a League of Composers concert on February 14, 1926. Under the same auspices, the first *Les Noces*, a version choreographed by Elizabeth Andersen-Ivantzova, had been staged at the Metropolitan in May 1929. For the Ballets Russes performance the singers, the four pianists, and the conductor, Eugene Fuerst, were provided by The Art of Musical

Russia, a corporation that presented programs of Russian music. John Martin wrote in the *New York Times* that "the de Basil Ballet Russe should be given a rising vote of thanks by the entire dance community, for here is assuredly one of the great works of our time."[11] But W. J. Henderson, the venerable music critic of the New York *Sun*, wrote: "But when all was done, there remained only the impression of vocal howlings, monotonous in rhythm and tonality, instrumental poundings, insistent to the point of brutality, and a final accomplishment of nothing more than the construction of a rude exterior without inner content."[12]

Unfortunately, the very need for singers and four pianists made the work a difficult one to present, and after New York it was dropped.

When the U.S. tour ended, the company traveled to Europe to open its Barcelona season at the Liceu on May 20.

LES CENT BAISERS

Ballet in one act; music by Baron Frédéric d'Erlanger; libretto by Boris Kochno, after the fairy tale by Hans Christian Andersen; choreographed by Bronislava Nijinska; set and costume design by Jean Hugo; sets executed by Prince A. Schervachidze; costumes executed by Madame Karinska; premiere July 18, 1935, at Covent Garden, London, conducted by Antal Dorati.

139

ORIGINAL CAST

The Princess	Irina Baronova	The Gardener	Roman Jasinski
The King	Edouard Borovansky	The Birdcatcher	Yurek Lazowski
The Prince	David Lichine	The Swineherd	Vania Psota
The Maids of Honor	Verchinina, Zorina,		

Grigorieva, Morosova, Tresahar, Serova, Dimina, Nelidova, Osato, Razoumova, Tchinarova, and Volkova

Les Cent Baisers was a milestone in the artistic development of the three-year-old company—it marked the return of Boris Kochno to its counsel and the renewal of his and Nijinska's affiliation with de Basil. Kochno had been greatly responsible for the creative success of 1932, and since he was very much in contact with Parisian artistic circles, his advice could be instrumental in furthering the company's development. The Ballets Russes, now almost exclusively a touring company, was very much isolated from new creative directions and needed Kochno's advice to provide it with new ideas. Although Massine, the person mainly responsible for the artistic direction of the company, had introduced symphonic ballets, he could not, because of his absorption in that genre, diversify the repertory. New ballets were needed for 1935, but Massine was able to produce only one new work, *Jardin public* (he was at present planning his 1936 ballet *Symphonie fantastique*). Since it was imperative to present a world premiere for the Covent Garden season, Massine suggested that de Basil persuade Kochno to devise and take charge of a new production. Kochno agreed and conceived the idea of *Les Cent Baisers,* adapted the libretto, from Hans Christian Andersen's tale "The Swineherd and the Princess," and, according to Kochno, it was he who suggested Bronislava Nijinska as choreographer and Jean Hugo as scenery and costume designer. It had already been decided that d'Erlanger was to finance the production and compose the score.

Nijinska's association was also important. She was the only important Diaghilev choreographer still not represented in the repertory and her choreography could expand the stylistic range of the dancers.

Though *Les Cent Baisers* was Nijinska's first (and only) creation for de Basil's Ballets Russes, it was by no means her first association with the company: she had already been in charge of the mixed second company formed in the spring of 1934 to fulfill the annual engagement in Monte Carlo while the main company toured in the United States.

The first production conference took place in the spring in Paris with Nijinska, Kochno, de Basil, d'Erlanger, and Sevastianov present. Nijinska's desire to create the Princess's choreography on Danilova, with whom she had worked happily (during the 1934 Monte Carlo season), prompted a disagreement with d'Erlanger, who favored Baronova and to whom, in fact, he was dedicating the score. The baron made it clear that his financial support for the project depended on Baronova's involvement. According to Baronova, Nijinska agreed to accept her on a trial basis.

Action — The curtain rises on a meadow before the gate of a castle, where maids of honor in rigid poses form two diamond formations, one to each side of the stage. The Princess enters through the gate and they all dance, awaiting the arrival of her suitor, a neighboring prince. He arrives with a retinue consisting of a gardener and a birdcatcher, each bearing a gift: the gardener a rose, and the birdcatcher a caged bird. Each dances a variation with steps and movements characteristic of their occupations before they present the gifts to the curious Princess. When she discovers the contents of the cases she is terribly disappointed, not realizing that the gifts—the rose of happiness and the bird of song—possess special qualities. She mocks the Prince for his poor gifts and disdainfully retires to the castle with her companions.

The Prince sends his retinue away and, alone, dances a variation expressive of his sorrow. Suddenly, he hears strange music. A swineherd approaches, making the melody by scraping the inside of a bowl with a spoon. The Prince wonders if the music would charm the Princess and attempts to buy the instrument from the swineherd. He refuses the money but accepts in exchange the Prince's velvet jacket and

140

feathered hat, and then leaves. The Prince, disguised in the swineherd's outfit, begins to play the bowl and spoon outside the castle. The maids hear the unusual sounds and peer over the castle's wall; fascinated by the music, they come out to dance. The Princess has also heard the music and comes through the gate dancing a variation as the Prince hides behind a tree. She is delighted by the instrument and covets it, but the Prince demands a hundred kisses as payment. The Princess is horrified that she must kiss a man of such low estate but her desire is such that she complies. The maids of honor form a semicircle around the couple to keep the Princess from being observed by anyone at the castle. The kissing scene serves as the basis for a pas de deux consisting of imaginative supported turns and lifts that alternate with the kisses. The King emerges from the castle and is enraged by the sight of his daughter kissing a swineherd. He sends them all back to the castle, where in the confusion the door is shut in the face of the Princess, the last to enter. All alone, she prostrates herself before the doors as the Prince reveals his real identity. As night falls, the Prince, now disillusioned with the Princess, retrieves the discarded gifts, bids her farewell, and departs sorrowfully.

Music   D'Erlanger's music was acclaimed for being melodious, skillfully scored, and well suited to the development of the story. The score was composed under Kochno's guidance in order to fit the music to his detailed libretto. As a result, it was very descriptive and provided opportunities for the choreography in terms of ensembles, solo variations, and the pas de deux. A flute figure anticipates the arrival of the Prince; an oboe solo accompanies the piping of the swineherd, and the drums mark the closing of the gate. The main musical parts were the opening scherzo, which comprised the first scene of the Princess and her maids of honor, and the Grand Valse, which included the arrival of the swineherd and lasted through the closing scene. However, the tuneful Lamento and dance of the Prince was the public's favorite.

The anonymous critic of the *Times* of London commented that it followed on the Tchaikovsky tradition "with a quotation from *The Swan Lake* to signify the Prince Magician's disconsolation" and added that it contained "plenty of episodic material to match the resourceful choreography of Mlle Nijinska."[1] Ernest Newman of the *Sunday Times* and Edwin Evans of the *Daily Mail* agreed that the music was effective and well suited for the purposes of the ballet.[2]

Rehearsals   Rehearsals for *Les Cent Baisers* began at the Chenies Street drill hall (behind the Dow Street police station), where Diaghilev's *Sleeping Princess* had been rehearsed in 1921. Nijinska's severe discipline was established from the start, and the dancers immediately felt that she had arbitrary likes and dislikes. Her sarcasm more than once reduced some of the dancers to tears, but her eccentric personality fascinated them all. Baronova offered a wonderful description: "She smoked continuously with a cigarette holder, wore trousers and incredibly white kid gloves because she disliked touching a sweaty body. She employed grand gestures that at times looked a little disproportionate to her petite figure. She sometimes moved in ways that were characteristic of the Girl in Blue in *Les Biches*."

The other dancers involved in the production were excited to be working with Nijinska. Nonetheless, they felt that the choreographer's demands and difficult personality at times became overwhelming. As Vasilieva explained: "Sometimes she would call for a full rehearsal at the end of a three-ballet program, because she was not satisfied with some of the details in that evening's rendition of the work, and she would not allow anyone on demi-pointe. One time it happened after we had matinée and evening performances."[3]

Most people thought she resembled her brother. She had Mongol features, with pale blue eyes, which were always watery; and when she spoke, the saliva dried up in the corners of her mouth. Apart from some ill-applied lipstick, she never wore any makeup.

The first days of rehearsals were nervous ones for the management. But as choreographer and ballerina worked together, a very special communication and understanding developed between them. When the trial period was over, all the artistic collaborators began to work in haste to get the production ready.

Nijinska's method of choreographing seemed to follow a middle course between that of Massine and that of Balanchine. As Baronova described it: "The ideas were clear from the very beginning; and even though there was obviously a prearranged structure, once she was in the studio she involved the dancers in the creative process. There was not much experimentation, as [there had been] with Massine. Her choreography seemed to flow spontaneously. Even when she was improvising, she always projected the conviction that she knew her ultimate goals, for she was precise and direct in her explanations."

142

The fact that she demonstrated every movement made things easier for the dancers. "It was easy to work with her because one was able to copy every step," Vasilieva recounts. "She showed everything the way she wanted it. She would even demonstrate the male dancers' tours en l'air and grandes pirouettes."

Choreog-
raphy

The choreography of *Les Cent Baisers* had a hybrid quality that places the work in a category by itself. Although it is considered one of Nijinska's most classical compositions, the academic steps were often distorted. For instance, a pas de chat would begin with the right foot when it was supposed to start with the left. The arm movements, according to Baronova, "were not academic but stylized and exotic. They possessed a sort of Oriental or Eastern feeling, with the wrists bent back a little, but always elegant and expressive." She also employed virtuoso combinations, with a predominance of multiple turns, fouettés, chaîné turns, and jumps. In one of Baronova's variations she had to enter through a gate already executing a series of difficult turns on the diagonal, all the way to the opposite corner.

Nijinska's use of the corps de ballet followed the classical tradition insofar as its deployment was characterized by symmetrical formations, and it served as a background to the action, bringing the main characters into relief, interacting with them and sustaining the mood. However, Nijinska's treatment of the ensembles had a peculiarity that occurred in most of her works, clearly seen in the two that have survived, *Les Noces* and *Les Biches*. She had a predilection for grouping the dancers in

ABOVE: Baronova as the Princess. BELOW: Baronova and Petroff as
the Princess and Prince.

frozen clusters, from which they would detach themselves singly or in small numbers to resume motion. This device was employed cyclically as the work progressed, so there was a constant transition from rigidity to action, which gave the corps de ballet at times a quality of being an entity all its own, independent and oblivious of the action. In this respect, Nijinska's work was closer to the classical tradition than was that of most modern choreographers of her time. The others had basically treated the ensembles as an organic part of the action, either as a background chorus responding to the action or simultaneously as part of the action to give credibility to the development of the story. The approaches, until then, of choreographers such as Fokine, Massine, and Balanchine (with the exception of Fokine's abstract ballet *Les Sylphides*) had a common denominator: soloists and ensembles (especially in the prevailing story ballets) were part of an active, integrated whole. They reacted to and shared at all times the same problem and, consequently, the same space. Nijinska, on the contrary, would detach the rigid ensembles from the narrative as if they were autonomous and inhabited a space (or sub-space) of their own within the general scenic space. In her polarization of the space, she seemed to be expanding the spatial limitations of the stage: a space within a space.

In this respect, the treatment of the all-female corps de ballet in *Les Cent Baisers* was reminiscent of the group arrangements in *Les Noces* and *Les Biches*, especially in the rigidly posing dancers that eventually begin to move. One can see the continuity of Nijinska's usage of the corps in Levinson's description of her ensembles in *Etude* of 1931 as " . . . whole panels of high-relief sculpture that detach themselves from the wall."[4] And thirteen years later, Edwin Denby described her use of the corps de ballet in *Chopin Concerto* of 1944:

> The structure of the piece—like that of much of Mme Nijinska's work—is based on a formal contrast: in the background rigid impersonal groups or clusters of dancers, that seem to have the weight of statues. In the foreground, rapid arrowy flights performed by individual soloists. One appreciates their flashes of lightness and freedom because of the weight they seem to rise over, as if the constraint of the group were the springboard for the soloist's release.[5]

Both descriptions apply to *Les Cent Baisers* as well.

Nijinska's use of the corps de ballet was very much in the tradition of the chorus of the Russian opera; it was a protagonist with a role of its own.

If Massine was the dramatist and Balanchine the poet, Nijinska's work might plausibly be viewed as an attempt to unite these separate tendencies. Her command of the theater was very subtle, especially in her choreographic approach to Kochno's adaptation, where humor plays an important role in the development of the characters, deriving mostly from the interplay of sophistication, the expression of feeling, and the assumed identities.[6] The irony in the libretto is very tantalizing. But of course, the choice of the story was appropriately theatrical as a comment on contrived appearances. The Prince brings to the Princess magical gifts, which she rejects, unaware of their true value. Later on, he wins her love when he is disguised as a swineherd.

Scenery
and
Costumes

Jean Hugo was a particularly good choice as designer. Basically a romantic, he had established his reputation as production designer of the dramas of his great-grandfather, Victor. His baroque imagination also allowed him to make occasional excursions into surrealism: he designed the costumes and masks for *Les Mariés de la Tour Eiffel* for the Ballets Suédois in 1921 and *Romeo et Juliette* for Count de Beaumont's Soirées de Paris in 1924 (both were Cocteau projects). In another medium, he served as art director of Dreyer's film *La Passion de Jeanne d'Arc* in 1928. A member of the Diaghilev circle and a close friend of Misia Sert, he had a studio in the Palais Royal that was a gathering place of the Parisian intelligentsia and the *haut monde* of the twenties.

When Kochno asked Hugo to collaborate on the new ballet, the designer was reluctant. He had left the theater by the end of 1928 and by 1929 he was already established at Mas de Fourque, the family property in Lunel in southern France that he had inherited from his grandmother,[7] and his residence until his death in 1984. Kochno was as persuasive as ever. For further discussions he and d'Erlanger visited Hugo at his home. The librettist had been working closely on the musical score with d'Erlanger, whose first venture this was as a ballet composer; he needed the expert guidance of Kochno, especially in regard to the structure of the dance forms. De Basil joined them at Hugo's home while en route to Paris from Barcelona. The meeting must have been successful, because immediately afterwards the designer began work on *Les Cent Baisers*: "The following Sunday, in the square of Lunel, the florist had arranged a stand consisting of long bands of three-colored flowers: violet, pomegranate, and orange. After that Monday, I started to design the costume maquettes following this harmony or discordance of colors, adding lemon yellow, mauve, dusty rose, and sky blue."[8]

When the maquettes were finished, they were sent to Mme Karinska's atelier in Paris, where the costumes were to be constructed. Bérard offered to supervise the execution to save Hugo unnecessary trips to Paris.

When the designer arrived in London for the *répétition générale*, Kochno took him directly to the theater. Visiting the company's wardrobe, he was pleased with the fine execution of his designs. On the other hand, he felt that his decor looked sinister in the theater's morning light: "a haunted chateau in the forest of lost paths."[9] He decided to modify the decor, and right on the stage he painted pigeons and nests in the archways.

Hugo's sets and costumes and Kochno's lighting designs created the proper romantic atmosphere for *Les Cent Baisers*. The scenery featured a castle in a forest, with a forbidding gate outside which the action takes place. The women's costumes were knee-length tutus in the Elizabethan style; and while the corps was dressed in various shades, the Princess wore all black. The men's costumes derived from Elizabethan style. All the costumes, and the decor, were reminiscent of harshly colored turn-of-the-century fairy-tale illustrations. Still, some critics felt that Hugo's work

145

was conventional and dull. Even Nijinska apparently would have preferred a more modern approach.[10]

There were twenty-two curtain calls on opening night and great interest in the ballet as representative of a new phase in Nijinska's career. To many it was an amplification of the dance idioms already presented in *Les Biches*. Arnold Haskell, reviewer for the *Daily Telegraph*, wrote: " . . . La Nijinska, using some of the most complex movements in the repertory of Classicism, has succeeded in creating a romantic fairy tale in a manner that is highly personal, and so sure is her touch that virtuosity is never used for its own sake, but to develop the story."[11] And Constant Lambert wrote in the *Sunday Referee*: "One does not know which to admire most, the virtuosity of the solo dancers, the construction of the ensembles, or the easy transition from dance to mime and back again."[12]

The role of the Princess gave Baronova an opportunity to show her skill as an actress. She successfully imparted an emotional quality to a series of incredibly complicated technical feats. Haskell added: "Baronova surmounts difficulties greater than in Aurora, but so easy is her attack that it is by her poetry and the quality of her acting that she holds one."[13]

Riabouchinska, who understudied the part of the Princess, later commented: "Nijinska created the role especially for Irina. Every gesture, every combination exploited Irina's personality, feeling for movement and technique. Though I danced it, I never felt it was mine. Baronova gave meaning to Nijinska's choreography."

Since 1933 Baronova had been exposed to a large range of ballets, including Act II of *Swan Lake*, which she first danced (at the age of fourteen) with Dolin at the Alhambra Theatre. Later, she developed rapidly into the type of modern classical ballerina who possessed, besides her fine technique, a flexible style and versatility as an actress. Working with Nijinska was a turning point in her artistic growth. Before, she had never had the opportunity for careful dissection of her roles. Nijinska's approach, which differed drastically from Massine's, gave the sixteen-year-old Baronova the self-awareness she needed to probe into herself and bring forth her full potential. In 1936, when Nijinska was restaging *Les Noces* in the upstairs studio at the Met, Baronova asked to be part of the corps de ballet to gain more exposure to a totally different style.

The role of the Prince was created by Lichine, one of the small group of dancers in the company who had previously worked with Nijinska in the Opéra Russe à Paris and the ballet company of Ida Rubinstein. Lichine's portrayal was both patrician and impish. Perhaps the highest tribute to his characterization was the sense of despair that engulfed the audience at his departure.

Les Cent Baisers, after a two-year absence, returned to the repertory during the London season of 1937. About the revival in New York the same year, John Martin wrote:

As individual in style as Fokine's work, this is a ballet that wears exceedingly well. Its choreography is witty, ingeniously characterized for every one of the story's personages and merciless upon the dancers. . . . Here is a work that makes full use of the brilliance which distinguishes the ballet style of dancing and shows once more what a thorough mistress of its secrets Mme Nijinska is.[14]

During the 1936 Australian tour, Nina Youskevitch and Tamara Tchinarova both danced the role of the Princess. When Baronova left the company in 1939, it was taken by Toumanova and Denisova (the latter had already danced it the previous year during the same tour). On only a few hours' notice, Riabouchinska had taught Denisova the part in the dining room of her Sydney apartment. The work was a success right up to its final performances, on the 1940–41 U.S. tour, when Baronova resumed her original role and was again acclaimed.

Grace Robert commented five years after it was last seen in the United States that it "seems to be one of the last really effective works by Bronislava Nijinska. Short and to the point, it tells an old story with a modern and worldly twist. . . . It takes on the properties of an authentic, though slight, work of art."[15]

Massine rehearsing *Symphonie fantastique* on the roof of the Teatre Liceu, Barcelona.

June 1936- April 1937

WHEN the Ballets Russes arrived in Barcelona during the second week of May, Spain was in a state of political turmoil, owing to the election in February of the Popular Front. The cause of the Spanish Republic was popularly supported by artists, intellectuals, and leftist workers, and the atmosphere was enlivened by the many foreigners who, morally and ideologically compelled to offer their services, had crossed the Pyrenees to form the International Brigades.

Life in Barcelona, although exhilarating, was not easy. The political tension had produced many strikes, including a general walkout of waiters, which made restaurant service unobtainable. Public activities were nonexistent, except for the ballet performances, which were attended nightly by members of both political parties and by old friends of the Ballets Russes, such as Miró and Masson. So successful was the company that the initially scheduled nine performances at the Liceu were extended to fourteen.

By the time the company left Barcelona, the political situation had deteriorated even further. Toumanova recalls: "We were told to go to the train station individually, because it was safer to avoid the formation of groups on the streets. We carried our luggage ourselves—the taxis had stopped working. As we walked down the Ramblas, shooting started in a nearby neighborhood. We practically ran to the station. Once there, the confusion was incredible. Multitudes of people were trying to board the train. Members of the company were scattered all over. Our code to identify one another when lost was whistling the musical leitmotif of *Schéhérazade*. Every time we heard the tune, we would scream 'Su-da, su-da' (Come here!). The trip was a nightmare. There were so many people that only the very old and mothers with small children were seated.''

The artistic and social life of London in 1936 provided a dramatic contrast. The Second International Exhibition of Surrealism was on view in the new Burlington Art Gallery. The opera season at Covent Garden marked the triumphant British debut of Kirsten Flagstad in *Tristan und Isolde*, and the ballet season, during the summer, was followed by the continuation of Beecham's famous Sunday afternoon programs, now at Covent Garden, in the fall. The BBC was to begin its series of afternoon and evening television programs in November, six of them to be conducted by Toscanini. In addition, the Dresden State Opera was to visit Covent Garden, and on November 6 Strauss was to conduct his *Ariadne auf Naxos*.

Following Beecham's Grand Opera at Covent Garden, audiences were to witness the confrontation of two international ballet companies: the already familiar Ballets Russes of de Basil and the newly created Ballets de Monte Carlo, with René Blum as artistic director and Fokine as ballet master and choreographer.

The Ballets de Monte Carlo had been created by Blum after he and de Basil had separated in 1935 and was organized around the nucleus of the Ballet du Théâtre National de Lithuanie, which had been based since 1930 at the National Opera Theatre in Kaunas. De Basil had arranged for this company to fulfill his obligations at the Monte Carlo Casino during the winter 1935 season. It appeared there from January 15 through 31. The company included Vera Nemtchinova and Oboukhov as leading dancers, Nicolas Zverev as ballet master, and Gofmekler as conductor. The repertory consisted of the full-length *Swan Lake*, *Coppelia*, *Raymonda*, and *Giselle*, as well as *Carnaval*, Balanchine's *Aubade* as choreographed for Nemtchinova in 1930 for the Nemtchinova-Dolin company, and *Bolero*. *La Fille mal gardée* was an alternate in the program. The repertory also included *Les Fiançailles*, *Islamey* (music by Balakireff), and *Un Divertissement*. For the London season, Hélène Kirsova, Maria Ruanova, Kouznetsova, Eglevsky, Panaiev, and Woizikowski joined the company. (Woizikowski had left de Basil in 1934 as the result of disagreements with Massine over the role of the Miller in *Le Tricorne*, which Massine monopolized. Upon his departure he formed his own company, which included Blinova, Tarakanova, Raievska, Froman, Eglevsky, and Youskevitch. This company visited Paris and London during 1935 and 1936 and was the showcase for two works choreographed by Woizikowski: *Port Said* [music by K. Konstantinov] and *L'Amour sorcier*.) Blum's first choice for choreographer had been Balanchine. In November 1935 Blum wrote to him in New York, inviting him to come to Monte Carlo and take charge of the company as he had done in 1932.[1] Balanchine's immediate response was that he could not accept any proposition until the summer of 1936, owing to a prior commitment with the Metropolitan Opera.[2]

Blum learned, in February 1936, that Fokine had arrived in Paris from Milan, where he had been invited by La Scala to create a new ballet, *The Love for Three Oranges*. He called on Fokine, inviting him to Monte Carlo to supervise revivals of

Grigoriev.

Lichine and Riabouchinska.

Petrouchka, Carnaval, and *Schéhérazade.* Initially, Fokine was hired for a month, but as the working relationship developed, he was retained as company choreographer.

For English audiences, the summer of 1936 was a period of unparalleled enthusiasm for ballet. A ticket line for those seats not sold by subscription began to form at Covent Garden forty-eight hours before the opening-night performance of de Basil's company. The opening-night program on June 15 began with *Aurora's Wedding,* with Baronova and Petroff, Riabouchinska and Lichine, and Grigorieva as the Lilac Fairy, and continued with *Choreartium,* with Toumanova, Verchinina, and Lichine, and *La Boutique fantasque* with Danilova and Massine. Blum's company, which opened at the Alhambra on July 7, gave Londoners another opportunity to see many outstanding dancers, some of whom had already appeared at the Alhambra as members of the Lithuanian company in February 1935. Nemtchinova especially was admired. Toumanova, who as a child had seen Nemtchinova's Salle Pleyel concerts with Dolin, believed her to be one of the finest dancers of her generation, possessing an impeccable technique, a seductive stage presence, and a refined style.

The war between the companies was vigorously waged even by taxi drivers, a few of whom refused categorically to take anyone to the Alhambra. For them the Ballets Russes, after three years of appearances, was London's home company.

London had gone ballet mad. In spite of the fact that it was high summer, and house parties had begun to go to Ascot, the most fashionable people stayed in town to attend performances, crowding the theaters night after night. There were also two ballet exhibitions: one, of eighty-five costume and scenery designs by Alexandre Benois, at the Storran Gallery during June and July; the other, a collection of paintings of the Ballets Russes by Robin Darwin, in July, at MM. Agnews'. The unprecedented popularity of ballet was stimulated further by the publication of many books on the subject. In the summer of 1936 alone, four volumes appeared: *The Birth of Ballets Russes* by Prince Peter Lieven; *Footnotes to Ballet*, compiled by Caryl Brahms; and *Prelude to Ballet* and *A Balletomane's Scrapbook* by Arnold Haskell. The rage for ballet cut across all age groups; and starting that June, special school matinees for children were arranged, featuring appropriate programs, with all seats for de Basil's company at half price.

The highlights of the Ballets de Monte Carlo season were the new Fokine works: *L'Epreuve d'amour* (music from Effisio Catte's *Der Rekrut*), *Les Elements* (Bach), *Don Juan* (Gluck), and *Les Elfes* (Mendelssohn), none of which had been seen in London. Two new productions, *Le Pavillon* and *Symphonie fantastique*, were given by the Ballets Russes, and a gala performance took place on July 14. This very special event also marked the return to the stage of two important figures from previous generations, Mathilda Kchessinskaya and Lydia Sokolova. The program that evening consisted of *Aurora's Wedding*, *Les Présages* (presented in practice clothes and with no scenery), *Danses slaves et tziganes*, and *Le Beau Danube*.

Danses slaves et tziganes, originally arranged by Nijinska as a ballet interlude in Dargomïzhsky's *Rusalka* for the Opéra Russe à Paris in 1931, was a piece she had

Riabouchinska being fitted for her *Pavillon* costume by Karinska, as the designer, Cecil Beaton, looks on.

The company at Covent Garden, with guest artist Mathilda Kchessinskaya (in white, at the center of the group).

already revived for de Basil's company during the United States tour. On this occasion the work was staged with the 1909 Korovine decor for Diaghilev's *Le Festin*, and the dances were rearranged by the choreographer to suit the needs of the guest artists. The divertissement, which originally included three items, now consisted of four: the "Danse slave," performed by Danilova; an interpolated Russian dance to music of Liadov for Sokolova; the "Danse boyard," performed by Kchessinskaya; and the "Danse tzigane," led by Lichine and Shabelevsky. Sokolova's last performance had been in *Le Sacre du printemps* seven years earlier on the same stage. But the real sensation of the evening was the return of La Kchessinskaya after many years of retirement; her last London appearance had been in 1911 with Diaghilev. (Preobrajenskaya, Kchessinskaya's lifelong rival, had declined de Basil's invitation to participate in the event.)

The "Danse boyard" was an appropriate choice for the nearly sixty-five-year-old ballerina. It was a dance of style that displayed her continued command of her art. She repeated the number in response to the audience's ecstatic stomping and shouting.

The enormous success of de Basil's Ballets Russes in Europe and America prompted E. J. Tait of J. C. Williamson Management to arrange the company's first tour to Australia and New Zealand. In 1927 Massine had negotiated with Tait and Williamson to take the Diaghilev company to Australia, but they had felt that "the time [was] not yet ripe for a season of this nature."[3] Now, since de Basil had a three-year contract with Hurok and had arranged as well for the company's first Berlin season (Scala Theatre) in October, de Basil had to put together a second company to

153

The second company visits a tribe of
indigenous Australians.

fulfill the Australian engagement. Arnold Haskell described the haste with which the second company was organized: "The new company had been formed in a hurry; conceived six weeks before sailing, finally decided upon three weeks before sailing, and completed almost upon the station platform. (Some important documents were actually completed at the Gare de Lyon, two of the chief executives nearly missing their train.)"[4] Matters were further complicated by a dispute between Massine and de Basil, which began as the Covent Garden season drew to a close. Massine did not want the new company to perform his ballets in Australia, where he would not be on hand to supervise. He brought his case before Justice Bucknill in London, hoping to obtain a restraining order. When it became apparent that the petition would not be granted before the new company left England, however, he rehearsed the company himself, assisted by de Basil's principal dancers,[5] for he wished his ballets to be shown to Australian audiences in authentic form.

The sixty-two-member second company, with a repertory of twenty-one ballets, sailed at the beginning of September on the S.S. *Moldavia*, arriving in Adelaide in early October. Woizikowski, who had rejoined de Basil during the last week at Covent Garden, was now ballet master and leading male dancer; Jan Hoyer was régisseur; and the leading ballerinas were Valentina Blinova and Hélène Kirsova. Soloists included Tamara Tchinarova, Nina Youskevitch, Nina Raievska, Roland Guérard, Igor Youskevitch, Mira Dimina, and Thadée Slavinsky. Jascha Horenstein and Ivan Clayton were in charge of the orchestra. Arnold Haskell accompanied the second company to Australia in order to help popularize and interpret ballet, as he had done during de Basil's first American tour.

The company's opening night in Adelaide on October 13 at the Theatre Royal coincided with the city's centenary. For the Australians the Ballets Russes was a revelation, introducing them to works by Balanchine and Massine, as well as to some by Fokine never previously performed there. One result of the tours by Pavlova and by the Dandré-Levitoff Russian Ballet headed by Spessivtseva and Vilzak in 1934 was that Fokine had become a familiar name to the Australians: *Les Sylphides* was in the repertory of the only Australian ballet company in existence, founded in 1934 by Louise Lightfoot and Mischa Burlakov. Although strictly amateur, this company lasted until the end of the Second World War, performing Fokine's masterpiece and other works that originated with the Pavlova company.

In Adelaide the Ballets Russes offered *Les Sylphides*, *Le Spectre de la rose*, *Schéhérazade*, *La Boutique fantasque*, *Carnaval*, *Le Beau Danube*, *Swan Lake* Act II, *Prince Igor*, *L'Après-midi d'un faune*, and *Aurora's Wedding*. The next engagement, in Melbourne, began October 31; the new works presented there were *Petrouchka*, *Scuola di ballo*, *Firebird*, *L'Amour sorcier*, *Cotillon*, *Contes russes*, *Les Cent Baisers*, *Thamar*, *Port Said*, and *Soleil de nuit*. The season created a furor, the final performance climaxing with a fifteen-minute ovation.

The hot and humid Melbourne summer made the arduous schedule nearly unbearable. However, the fatigue of the principals gave the soloists opportunities to

155

L'Après-midi d'un faune: LEFT: Grigorieva and Lichine. RIGHT: Lichine with Razoumova, Osato, and Obidenna.

alternate with them in almost all the leading roles, and members of the corps got to dance solo parts. One night, at the beginning of the Blue Bird pas de deux, Kirsova collapsed onstage and had to be carried off by Guérard. Golovina immediately took her place and the performance continued.

The company duplicated its success in Sydney and New Zealand, then returned to Australia for short seasons in Brisbane, Sydney, Melbourne, and Adelaide. The original schedule of sixteen weeks was extended to forty-two.

But the tour did not go as smoothly as it may have seemed to outsiders. There were constant threats of strikes because the company had split into two factions, one backing Woizikowski, the other Hoyer. The troupe had been accompanied to Australia by de Basil's legal advisor, Lidji, who represented the company, and by Philippov, a personal friend of de Basil's, representing the Colonel himself. Lidji and Philippov disagreed over the management of the company, and each claimed to be de Basil's true representative; nonetheless, despite this internal conflict, it was Tait and J. C. Williamson Management who were really in charge. But when artistic differences arose between Hoyer and Woizikowski, and the dancers, motivated by personal preference and the hope of getting coveted roles, took sides, Tait, who could control the management dispute, could do nothing. Tchinarova recalls that in Brisbane there were two régisseurs and two managements, one headed by Lidji and the other by Philippov.[6] Later, however, Lidji went off to confer with de Basil in the United States, and Hoyer resigned as régisseur.

Two dancers married while in the Antipodes: Slavinsky married the comedienne Marie Doran, and Kirsova became the wife of the Danish consul, Erik Fischer. She later opened a school in Sydney that was instrumental in the development of ballet in Australia. A sad note was the death from leukemia of Mira Dimina on November 22.

The company's tour achieved in Australia what Diaghilev had brought about in England: it helped the public to understand the art of ballet and encouraged the formation of an indigenous school, which spawned future companies. Later visits inspired a reassessment and a more critical attitude.

While the second company was conquering Australia, the main troupe had its first triumphant season, October 1–15, 1936, at the Scala Theatre in Berlin. (Toumanova did not participate, preferring to stay in Marienbad with her parents.) For the German public it was a resurrection of the classical ballet, which had been neglected in favor of modern dance.

In Berlin, the company was acclaimed by the local critics, as well as by reviewers from other major German cities. The *Hamburger Anzeiger* of October 9 referred to it as the most important artistic manifestation in Europe and America. At the Scala, the Ballets Russes presented only three programs. The first consisted of *Aurora's Wedding* with Baronova and Petroff (pas de deux), Riabouchinska and Lichine (Blue Bird); *Schéhérazade* with Tchernicheva and Shabelevsky; *Le Beau Danube* with Danilova, Riabouchinska, Massine, and Lichine; *Swan Lake* with Danilova; and *La Boutique fantasque* led by Danilova and Massine. The last program presented *Le Pavillon* with Danilova, Riabouchinska, and Lichine, *Firebird* with Danilova, and *Prince*

Igor. (Baronova appeared only in the first program due to surgery that kept her from participating during the October engagement at the Met; she was able to resume dancing at the beginning of the U.S. tour in November.)

Joseph Lewitan, editor of the German dance journal *Der Tanz*, wrote in an article for the December issue of *Dancing Times* that the company performed to capacity houses. The furor that the season created was undoubtedly a turning point for classical dance in Germany.

The main company sailed for New York, where they began their season at the Metropolitan Opera House on October 29. Massine's *Symphonie fantastique* was the highlight of the opening night.

Following fifteen performances at the Met, the company boarded its private train for its fourth tour of the United States and Canada. Three works from the Diaghilev repertory were revived for the first time: Massine's *Cimarosiana* on November 4, Fokine's *Cléopâtre* on November 10, and his *Les Papillons* on December 27. The tour comprised one hundred fifty performances.

As the tour drew to a close, the ballet returned to the Met on April 9 for a five-day engagement.

Before the company left the United States, preliminary discussions were held by de Basil, Hurok, and modern dancers Charles Weidman and Doris Humphrey about the possibility of creating a ballet based on James Thurber cartoons for the next American tour. Irving Kolodin, then a music critic at the *Sun*, and on friendly terms

157

The company in the United States.

with all parties, including Hurok, remembered that after the company left he met regularly, in the role of mediator between de Basil and Weidman and Humphrey, with the impresario and the artists, but nothing materialized.[7]

As the tour ended, the Ballets Russes had proved an indisputable commercial success. On May 2, the United Press announced that the company had stepped into "the million dollar industry class" and added: "In three American seasons the de Basil ballet has amassed well over $2,000,000—a figure made all the more remarkable by the fact that the last ballet to swing about the nation, the Diaghileff ballet, ended with a net loss of $350,000." They reiterated that the "sudden popularity of the ballet in the United States is the latest phenomenon of the entertainment world."

The company appeared at the Maggio Musicale in Florence, from May 5 to 19, after leaving the United States.

Danilova at Henry Clifford's villa in Florence.

SYMPHONIE FANTASTIQUE

Choreographic symphony in five scenes; music, *Symphonie fantastique* by Hector Berlioz; libretto by Hector Berlioz; choreography by Léonide Massine; set design by Christian Bérard, executed by Prince A. Schervachidze; costume design by Christian Bérard; costumes for the second, third, and fourth movements executed by Madame Karinska, for the first and fifth movements executed by Madame Larose; premiere July 24, 1936, at Covent Garden, London, conducted by Efrem Kurtz.

ORIGINAL CAST

First Movement

The Young Musician	Léonide Massine
The Beloved	Tamara Toumanova
Gaiety	Alexandra Danilova, Yurek Lazowski, Mlles Nelidova, Serova, and Volkova
Melancholy	MM. Jasinski, Zoritch, and Ozoline
Reverie	Tatiana Riabouchinska, Mlles Abricossova, Branitska, Grigorieva, Marra, Razoumova, Strakhova, Tchinarova, and Zorina
Passion	MM. Borovansky, Bousloff, Guérard, Ismailoff, Katcharoff, Ladré, Matouchevsky, Petroff, and Rostoff

Second Movement—The Ball

The Guests	Mlles Chabelska, Leontieva, Lipkovska, Osato, Radova, Razoumova, Strakhova, and Tchinarova MM. Alexandroff, Alonso, Borovansky, Hoyer, Ismailoff, Katcharoff, Kosloff, Ladré, Lipatoff, Matouchevsky, Rostoff, and Zeglovsky
The Beloved	Tamara Toumanova
The Young Musician	Léonide Massine

Third Movement

The Old Shepherd	Marc Platoff
The Young Shepherd	George Zoritch
The Young Musician	Léonide Massine
The Beloved	Tamara Toumanova
The Deer	Alexis Kosloff
The Picnic	Mlles Verchinina, Branitska, Grigorieva, and Lvova
The Children	Tatiana Riabouchinska, Mlles Abricossova, Dimina, and Serova
The Winds	MM. Petroff, Guérard, and Bousloff

Fourth Movement

The Young Musician	Léonide Massine
The Jailer	Yurek Shabelevsky
The Judges	MM. Alexandroff, Bousloff, Guérard, Hoyer, Katcharoff, Ladré, Lazowski, Lipatoff, Matouchevsky, and Ozoline
The Executioners	MM. Borovansky, Ismailoff, Rostoff, and Zeglovsky
The Crowd	Mlles Marra, Chamié, Grossen, Korsinska, Krasnova, Lvova, Michel, Roussova, and Youchkevitch MM. Alonso and Kosloff

Fifth Movement

The Monsters	MM. Jasinski, Petroff, and Zoritch
The Witches	Alexandra Danilova, Tatiana Riabouchinska, Tamara Toumanova, Nina Verchinina, and Vera Zorina
The Ghosts	Mlles Adrianova, Roussova, Serova, Strakhova, and Volkova
The Vampires	Mlles Lipkovska, Nelidova, Radova, Tchinarova, and Tresahar
The Spectres	Mlles Abricossova, Branitska, Gollner, Grigorieva, Osato, Rostova, and Youchkevitch
The Furies	Mlles Chabelska, Chamié, Delarova, Guérard, Korsinska, Krassnova, Lvova, Marra, and Michel
The Devils	MM. Alonso, Borovansky, Katcharoff, Kosloff, Ladré, Lazowski, Lipatoff, and Matouchevsky
The Monks	MM. Platoff, Alexandroff, Bousloff, Guérard, Hoyer, Ismailoff, Ozoline, Rostoff, and Zeglovsky

The success of *Choreartium* encouraged Massine to plan another symphonic ballet, this time to Berlioz's *Symphonie fantastique*. In his memoirs, Antal Dorati suggests that he had recommended Berlioz's work since the composer himself had provided a program, which made it more appropriate for dance.[1] But a letter from Ansermet to Massine makes clear that the choreographer had considered using the *Symphonie fantastique* as early as January 1933, probably in lieu of Tchaikovsky's Fifth, and Dorati did not join the company until November 1933—though he probably did influence Massine's final decision. In his letter Ansermet also expressed his opinion of Massine's symphonic experiments: "The idea of which M. de Basil spoke to me of using Florent Schmitt or the Fantastic Symphony continues to frighten me. In general, I think it would be better to drop the idea of creating ballets to already composed music, which is always deformed by choreographers."[2]

Although Massine planned the ballet in 1934, the actual work did not begin until the next year, soon after Kochno renewed his association with de Basil. The first rehearsals took place in late spring 1936 in London, with Kochno as unofficial artistic collaborator and lighting designer and Bérard as designer.

The *Symphonie fantastique* was a logical choice for Massine's third symphonic ballet. In *Les Présages* he fully explored the possibilities of a psychological and philosophical ballet, while in *Choreartium* he emphasized abstract movement and atmosphere. Now, in *Symphonie fantastique*, these two approaches could be fused within the framework of a story.

Berlioz's detailed program, distributed to the audience at the symphony's first performances, consisted of five episodes (one per movement) depicting the hallucinations of a young musician who attempts suicide by an overdose of opium but succeeds only in achieving a state of semiconsciousness. The music and story expressed the composer's anguished love for the actress Henrietta Smithson. The libretto's extreme romantic symbolism presented the world as a metaphor for the tormented human soul. Berlioz's emotional extremes were well suited to Massine's neoexpressionistic contrasts of action and tempo, which concentrated on feelings of horror and despair.

In Massine's words, the Berlioz score offered him "all the emotional resources that music can supply and a synopsis that could be developed in terms of dance." He followed the episodic structure of the music, but each movement was treated as an independent tableau. Only the characters of the Musician and the Beloved appear in all five movements and, along with the musical idée fixe, provide a sense of continuity. Massine based his ballet on the revised program written by Berlioz in 1855. (In the first program, written by the composer for the premiere of the symphony, only the last two movements had depicted the opium dream.)

Action

First Movement: Reveries. The curtain rises on a room where the Musician is spotlighted sitting at a table. In a gesture of despair he takes a dose of opium in a cup. As he is thrown into a state of hallucination, the walls seem to open and the scene lightens to reveal a fantastic landscape dominated by a Sphinx-like figure with open wings. Groups of dancers appear as a succession of visions, allegorical representations of the different phases of the Musician's delirium: gaiety, melancholy, reverie, and passion. Pervading these visions are glimpses of his Beloved, who makes her first appearance gliding in on pointe when the musical idée fixe is played. This musical motif accompanies her every entrance throughout the ballet. Each time she appears he tries to reach her, but fails. At last, he seizes the Beloved. He lifts her amidst other figures but she escapes, leaving him in complete solitude.

Second Movement: The Ball. The curtain rises on an empty Renaissance ballroom somberly lit by giant blackamoors holding candelabra aloft between the arches of the background. As the mutterings of the cellos, basses, and harps increase, the lighting brightens, and when the melody of the waltz begins, the stage is taken by thirteen whirling couples; the men dressed in black and the women in white tulle dresses. The Musician arrives and searches for his Beloved but realizes that all the women resemble her. She arrives finally, seeming to float among the guests. He pursues and again seizes her. Ecstatically he dances with her but she vanishes once more. Alone once more, he joins the feverish waltzing of the other couples.

Third Movement: In the Country. In a classical Roman *campagna* the Musician tastes the happiness of nature and pastoral life. As the scene opens an old shepherd plays his pipe (to the sound of the English horn in the orchestra) and is answered by a young shepherd (the oboe). The Musician enters and contemplates a dreamlike sun-bleached plain with ruins. Women, young maidens, and children come upon the scene for a picnic, while a deer plays among the ruins. The Musician sits on a broken column and the picnickers dance. As the cellos and basses play the musical idée fixe, the Beloved, suspended by wires, flies above the scene to haunt the Musician. A storm arises and upon a darkened stage, the Winds, creatures with wings, make a sudden appearance. Peace returns. The young shepherd is attracted by a shepherdess with hair to her waist, and they join in a serene dance as expression of their love. The group of women and children return to their homes. The old shepherd plays his pipe (again to the English horn), but there is no answer from the young shepherd, for he has gone with the girl. As the orchestra plays the final cadence the Musician stands up and gazes into the horizon.

Fourth Movement: March to the Scaffold. In a prison courtyard a group of Daumier-like men and women enter upon the scene gossiping about the murder of the Beloved by the Musician during a fit of jealousy. The Musician is brought in by a grotesque jailer. They are followed by four executioners in red and ten judges in tall hats and long black robes, reading their large law books. The judges perform jerky little jumps that emphasize the caricature in their portrayal. The Musician is threatened by the judges, who, with marionettelike movements, point into the books as if condemning his crime. As the crowd berates him, the executioners lift and turn the Musician as if torturing him: first, on an imaginary rack, and then, on an imaginary wheel. As he is lifted on their shoulders the vision of the Beloved appears again, but he hangs his head in shame. The procession halts as he is beheaded at the moment that the vision disappears and the musical idée fixe abruptly ends.

Fifth Movement: Dream of a Witches' Sabbath. A dark cavern, where the witches prepare to celebrate the Musician's funeral rites, is invaded by monsters, crawling like an army of ants. In the midst of a satanic debauch reminiscent of Brueghel and Bosch, the Beloved appears as the chief of all these diabolical creatures. Her musical motif has now become grotesque. To the tolling of bells, somber monks bring the writhing body of the Musician. The creatures dance around him and when the Dies Irae is heard they perform a parody of Christian rituals with monks imitating walking crosses. For a moment the creatures disperse and the music becomes low; accompanied by the sound of violins, violas, cellos, double basses, and bassoons, the Beloved makes an impressive exit executing a series of fouettés with her long hair waving loose around her. The creatures return and the Beloved, with a smile on her face, leads the ballet to a diabolical, triumphant conclusion.

Scenery and Costumes

The duality of shadow and light was a dominant aspect of the mise en scène, and it was enhanced throughout the production by Kochno's elaborate lighting design. To accentuate the dichotomy between real-life characters and those in the dream world, Bérard resorted to a juxtaposition of styles in costuming: while the Musician and the Beloved were dressed in costumes of the Romantic period, Berlioz's own time, the visions were clothed in an eclectic, allegorical style based on classical tunics. Only in the waltz did the other dancers' costumes replicate those of the Musician and the Beloved, for the waltz was used to project the Musician's inner turmoil.

For the costumes in the first, fourth, and fifth movements, Bérard resorted to dramatic combinations of red, green, white, and black, while pastel colors prevailed in the pastoral scene.

162

For the first scene, Bérard designed a bare room with only a table and chair. When the dream sequence begins the walls seem to give way to an unspecified and rather timeless wasteland, dominated by the statue of a Sphinx with open wings. The second scene takes place in a Renaissance ballroom bounded by two tiers of crimson arches opening into a deep blue night. Between the arches very large blackamoors hold lighted candelabra aloft. With the introduction of the cellos, basses, and harp, there is a gradual intensification of the lighting, reaching its brightest point when the waltz begins and the dancers appear onstage. The pastoral scene takes place in a Roman *campagna* of muted colors with broken columns and a backcloth depicting a ruined aqueduct. For the fourth tableau, Bérard designed a cavernous prison courtyard lugubriously lighted through the iron bars. The fifth movement took place in a grim cavern.

Choreography

Choreographically, Massine employed techniques that he had explored in his first two symphonic ballets, especially mass configurations based on simultaneous vertical and horizontal triangular formations. A group of dancers would create a pyramid, with the Musician standing on the diagonal gazing at it. So not only did the pyramid itself present a vertical triangular formation but the position of the Musician in relation to the pyramid created a horizontal triangular formation. There were many variations of this principle.

One of Massine's purposes in creating these constructions was to achieve the illusion of three-dimensional movement through space as these various masses moved. For Massine, energy was equivalent to mass; consequently, the architecture of the scene (the population of the space) generated an energy that created a physical tension that drew expressivity from the interpreter. This expressivity was (as a result of that moment) dramatic and plastically adequate to the specific scenic and musical mood and choreographic feeling.

Following the musical structure, Massine utilized sharply syncopated rhythms, along with a contrapuntal choreographic structure that gave each dancer a different phrase of movement within the same musical phrase. This is clearest in the scene at the Ball, where the febrile waltzing of the couples, each doing different steps, not only created a juxtaposition of ecstasy and vertigo but expressed the inner turmoil of the protagonist. In the waltz, more so than in any other scene, Massine's choreography produced the illusion that the music was being created by the movements of the dancers. The scene had a strong theatrical impact. The women in romantic white tulle dresses and black shoes and the men in black evening dress whirling around Bérard's blood-red ballroom, all enhanced by Kochno's somber lighting, created an illusionistic effect.

The leitmotiv as a device to convey recurrent ideas was used by Massine following Berlioz's symbolism. It was always danced by the Beloved. There was no choreographic leitmotiv for the Beloved—she simply appeared whenever the musical idée fixe was played.

Symphonie fantastique was a demonstration of Massine's theatrical genius. As Kochno once said: "To study Massine's ballets one must approach him not only as a choreographer but as a metteur en scène." The fourth and fifth scenes were extraordinary in their dramatic effect. In the fourth, the Musician's suffering was vividly conveyed without the use of stage props. At the end of the scene the guillotine falls, giving the impression that he has been beheaded. The entrance of the judges in small allegro beats, moving as marionettes, was an effective satire on justice. In the fifth scene, the appearance of four crosses at the corners of the stage, each composed of two monks standing back to back, the one in front raising his arms straight above his head, and the one in back extending them to the sides, testified to Massine's masterful use of his dancers to create plastic images.

Symphonie fantastique was one of the most emotionally demanding and time-consuming ballets Massine created for de Basil's company. Dancers devoted most of their free time to extra rehearsals, especially during weekends. Ernest Newman, after watching a rehearsal of *Symphonie fantastique* the day before the premiere, wrote to his wife, Vera:

> They all looked worn out this morning. Riabouchinska looked like a wraith with galloping consumption, and was coughing all the time and Baronova is sick. How they stand this life is a mystery to me. Ballet dancing must be a hard life. They have two more rehearsals and the performance tomorrow. How any girl can take up ballet dancing as a career is beyond my comprehension. And what skinny creatures they mostly are. They remind me of

163

164

ABOVE LEFT:
"Reveries": Massine
and Toumanova. ABOVE
RIGHT: "Pastorale":
Verchinina. RIGHT: First
Movement: Massine's
pyramid construction,
with Toumanova as the
Beloved and Massine as
the Musician. OPPOSITE
ABOVE LEFT: Third
Movement: Zoritch and
Verchinina in front of
Bérard's decor.

OPPOSITE ABOVE
RIGHT: "Prison":
Massine and
Toumanova. OPPOSITE
BELOW: "Witches'
Sabbath": Toumanova.

worker bees who work like niggers to make money for goodness knows who—for they don't—they get precious little out of it for themselves.[3]

The production itself was so intricate that Covent Garden stagehands told a reporter for the *Evening News* that it gave them as much work as any other ten ballets put together.[4]

On opening night the dance community was represented in force by Karsavina, Sokolova, Marie Rambert, Lopokova, and Dolin. During the pause after the second movement Toumanova's costume for the flying scene could not be found. According to Toumanova's mother, Bérard and Mme Karinska were hysterical, but Mme Toumanova, wasting no time, improvised a tulle costume on her daughter. It was exactly the idea Bérard had imagined for the flying ghost, and from that day on, the real costume was replaced by Mme Toumanova's creation, which she improvised at every performance.

Critics

As was expected, the new work stirred up much controversy. Nevertheless, even those who were not partisan to the symphonic ballet genre acclaimed Massine's achievement. *Symphonie fantastique* had such an impact that many critics felt they could not do it justice after seeing it only once. As a whole, it was praised for the cohesiveness of each tableau and for the dramatization of the libretto in terms of dance. Ernest Newman gave it the highest accolade when he wrote: "One feels, indeed, that had Berlioz had a choreographer like Massine ready to his hand it would have been in some such form as this that he would have planned to have his work presented."[5] Yet he also felt that at times the music simply overpowered the dance: "Having to tell the whole story to a concert audience in music pure and simple, [Berlioz] naturally turned an incomparable gift for orchestral description on the business of suggesting the atmosphere of the scene to the eye through the ear; and now and then he has done his own part of the job so thoroughly that nothing that the choreographer can put before the eye can be anything but the faintest shadow of what Berlioz makes us visualize, so to speak, through the ear."[6]

The critics almost unanimously judged the third scene a masterpiece. Even Constant Lambert, Massine's antagonist on the issue of symphonic ballets, wrote: "It was surprising to discover how successfully the pastoral scene 'came off,' for on paper one would have said it was an impossible task. . . . Bérard, of course, is more static than dynamic, and Massine more classical than romantic, so when both are treating the most serene and classical music in the symphony we get a closer fusion of three minds than we get elsewhere in this ballet."[7] Lambert must be referring here specifically to the choreography of the third movement, and especially to that of the pas de deux between the shepherd and shepherdess, which was its main dance feature. The pas de deux was neoclassical in style and choreographically it stressed slow, serene movements, long arabesques, slow lifts, turns and dégagés. Grace Robert, writing about it in retrospect ten years later, said that in 1946 it had seemed to her to be "faintly reminiscent of Balanchine."[8] It was also classical in its mood, in Massine's attempt to re-create a feeling for antiquity, and especially in the style. It was classical à la Massine.

Newman wrote of the third scene: "The result has been as convincing a demonstration of [Massine's] genius as he has ever given us, an idyll of the first order, with a new miming and a new translation of music into terms of dance. So skillfully and imaginatively has it all been done that there is soon an end of our first fears of an intrusive realism when we catch sight of the deer in the background; even this animal is woven harmoniously into the general texture of the idyll."[9]

In *Symphonie fantastique* Massine had one of his greatest roles. As the young romantic musician, who is both protagonist and narrator of the action, he gave proof once again of his extraordinary acting abilities. His subtle interpretation was dominated by his economy of movement and expression. Attempting to convey Berlioz's candid exposition of his emotional life, Massine tried to make visible in his performance the romantic qualities of the music, not by means of exaggerated facial expressions but by the intensity of his performance, which allowed him to dominate the stage even while remaining practically motionless. This power was felt by all who worked with him. Toumanova recalls, "When dancing with him, one was under the spell of his presence, and he demanded from others complete immersion to match his own force and dynamism as a performer. He was like a volcano that swept everyone along, making all of us reach unpredictable heights of emotion."

The role of the Beloved was pivotal in Toumanova's career. Hitherto she had created diverse roles in which she had manifested her technical brilliance and charismatic stage presence. Most had been choreographed by Balanchine, who exploited her physique and personality. But only Massine gave her roles that demanded more depth in dramatic interpretations, in such revivals as *Le Tricorne* and the 1935 *Jardin public*. In *Symphonie fantastique* she appeared through the first four movements as the ideal romantic heroine, dramatic and poetic, a part that suited her enigmatic personality as well as her looks. Anatole Chujoy, the reviewer for *Dance*, wrote: "Her performance of the Beloved is one of understanding, self-restraint, fine dramatic, if slightly enigmatic, acting and, of course, peerless technical execution."[10] With her pale face framed by dark hair, she glided among the ghostly figures as the ever-unattainable ideal of beauty and perfection. In contrast, the fifth movement found her metamorphosed into a satanic creature. As Grace Robert put it, "Detached and beautiful through four movements, she was changed in the fifth into a fury whose like has not been seen on the stage since the grand manner passed away."[11]

When *Symphonie fantastique* was presented at Covent Garden in the summer of 1937, the role of the Beloved was danced by Baronova, and a few changes had taken place in the production. The fifth scene had a new backcloth depicting a snowy landscape with a church, to allow better visibility of the groupings, and a new dress had been designed for the heroine, both additions by Bérard.

During the war years the ballet survived in the repertory in South America; it was presented after the war during the last European season before the company disbanded. After almost ten years without the supervision of the choreographer or the participation of members of the original cast, this monumental work had lost, if not choreography, then surely style and mood. However, Pierre Michaut, commenting

167

on the Paris revival in 1947, praised it as a great work and acclaimed Massine's originality and craftsmanship in arranging the mass configurations. In 1948, Massine staged a successful revival for the Teatro Colón, Buenos Aires, with the help of the 16mm film of the original production, now in the Dance Collection of the New York Public Library at the Museum and Library of the Performing Arts, Lincoln Center; and the fifties saw two important revivals, one for the Royal Danish Ballet, the other for the Paris Opéra Ballet.

LE PAVILLON

Ballet in one act; music by Alexander Borodin, orchestrated by Antal Dorati; libretto by Boris Kochno; choreography by David Lichine; set design by Cecil Beaton, executed by Prince A. Schervachidze; costume design by Cecil Beaton, executed by Madame Karinska; premiere August 11, 1936, at Covent Garden, London, conducted by Antal Dorati.

ORIGINAL CAST

The Young Lady	Irina Baronova	The Spirits of the Garden	Mlles Tamara
The Chief Spirit	Tatiana Riabouchinska		Grigorieva, Lubov Rostova, Adrianova,
The Poet	David Lichine		Dimina, Golovina, Leontieva, Nelidova,
			Osato, Razoumova, Serova, Strakhova,
			Tchinarova, Tresahar, Volkova

When the company arrived in London in early June from Barcelona, Lichine began work on a ballet tentatively called *Esquisse de Musique,* based on the *Four Seasons* by Aleksandr Glazunov. The ballet was abandoned and instead de Basil asked Kochno, who had arrived in London with Bérard at about this time as unofficial artistic collaborator on *Symphonie fantastique,* to devise a libretto for Lichine. This was to mark Lichine's first successful attempt at choreography since his failure with *Les Imaginaires* in 1934. His previous works, although unsuccessful, had not been a financial loss for de Basil, for they had been completely underwritten by Count Etienne de Beaumont. Although all new productions are a risk, having Kochno in charge of the new ballet provided a safeguard for the success of the new work. By now Kochno was one of the most knowledgeable and esteemed personalities in ballet and was greatly admired for his impeccable taste and special intuition in bringing together the right collaborators. His presence almost assured the management (de Basil) of a significant work, if not a big hit. The new ballet, *Le Pavillon*, was to have scenery and costumes by Cecil Beaton, and music by Borodin arranged by Antal Dorati. Beaton's name was also a drawing card, for he was an up-and-coming figure in smart circles.

Kochno's libretto was set in the late Romantic period. The idea served as a pretext for a ballet that concentrated on dance patterns instead of telling a detailed story through mime.

Action A poet awaits a maiden at night in a garden pavilion. The spirits of the garden appear, led by their queen, and haunt the place; they entice the poet away. When the maiden arrives, she is deeply grieved to discover that the poet has broken his promise, and she dances a melancholy solo. The poet returns and as evidence of their love for each other they dance a pas de deux. The spirits return and vainly try to lure the poet away again. As day breaks, the powerless spirits vanish.

Music The music for this ballet was chosen by Kochno and Dorati. They wanted to use lesser-known pieces by Alexander Borodin, and decided on chamber and piano works to be orchestrated by Dorati. The ballet score included pieces from the string quartets, no. 1 in A major and no. 2 in D major, and the *Petite Suite*.

Choreography Kochno's guidance contributed greatly to Lichine's growth as a choreographer. Lichine had had neither an artistic education in the tradition of the Imperial Ballet nor the support and tutelage that Diaghilev had offered his protégés; he belonged to a new generation of choreographers who developed by perseverance and discovered their personal style through a long process of trial and error. In addition, opportunities for young choreographers were few, since companies survived from hand to mouth and could not afford to gamble financially by taking chances with unproven talent. Lichine had been more fortunate than most in finding encouragement and support from Beaumont and Massine.

Lichine and Kochno exchanged ideas about all aspects of *Le Pavillon*, including lighting and the style of the late Romantic period, enabling Lichine to achieve a more cohesive structure and development than in his two previous attempts. But Kochno was also careful not to impose his own views. When working with young choreographers (Lichine, Roland Petit, Jean Babilée, Janine Charrat, and, at the beginning, Balanchine), he explains, he would "discuss the idea, the music, the period, and the structure, but afterwards I would leave them all to themselves for them to explore their own creativity and personality. We would exchange opinions with the different artistic collaborators in order to achieve a homogenous work, but I never imposed myself and attended rehearsals only when invited."

Baronova felt that although *Le Pavillon* was a step forward for Lichine, "at the time, David was still full of undisciplined ideas and was not ready to be seriously guided by Kochno, who was the only real professional in the group [of people involved in the rehearsals of *Le Pavillon*]. As far as the cast was concerned, we were in our teens, and at the beginning we could not take him seriously as a choreographer." Riabouchinska, too, felt that Kochno was important in guiding Lichine in many

169

respects, but she thought the story lacked the well-structured action that was probably what Lichine needed at the time: "Don't forget that this was only his third ballet, and he did not yet have the command to easily move the patterns of the ensembles." The best parts of the ballet, she felt, were the variations for the soloists and a very effective pas de deux for himself and Baronova, which Riabouchinska remembers as being "very gentle, very romantic."

Baronova recalls: "He devised a touching pas de deux with myself in which he projected much tenderness. David had a streak of romanticism that was not evident in his character but that came forth in his ballets. The gentleness and tolerance that was always present in his later choreography was envisioned in this pas de deux."

Baronova, Riabouchinska, and Lichine.

As Riabouchinska stated, the highlights of the ballet were the pas de deux and the variations, especially Lichine's own. According to Ernest Newman, "The episodes in which he himself dances are somehow not quite in the same key as the rest of the ballet—it is as if a violin virtuoso, writing a concerto for himself, had put all he knew of subtlety and bravura into his solo passages, while relying, for the rest, on the safe conventions of concerto composition, but Lichine's part exploits his individual style as dancer and mime. He was admirably seconded by Riabouchinska and Baronova."[1]

Scenery and Costumes

For a long time de Basil had hoped to interest British artists in collaborating with his company. Cecil Beaton was a close friend of Kochno and had recently designed his first ballet, *Apparitions*, to choreography by Ashton, for the Vic-Wells. His romantic designs had been admired for their simplicity and taste, and Beaton also provided snob value because of his social connections. (Baronova has called him "a talented dilettante, more interested in society than anything else.")

According to the *Evening Standard*, the set of *Le Pavillon* was "rather reminiscent of those lanterns once fashionable for illuminating suburban entrance halls,"[2] but the company called it *le pissoir* for its resemblance to those on the boulevard Haussmann. The romantic-style costumes, in cool shades of blue, were not what Beaton had planned. As he explains in his book *Ballet*:

> In a setting of hydrangea blues, I designed the dancers' dresses on a basis of underskirts in many shades of clear blue. Over these they were to wear gauze skirts, wings and flowers in all the brightest colours imaginable, but when Kochno saw the half-finished dresses hanging in the wardrobe, a positive riot of blue, he was enchanted with the effect, and said that they must be left as they were. Being new to the business and uncertain of my own judgement, I foolishly said, "yes," and the final result on the stage was just blue upon blue upon blue.[3]

After opening night, Beaton proposed to alter the costumes to fit his original conception, but de Basil refused to allow any further changes, prompting Beaton to develop a new strategy:

> I went to my friend Karinska and said, "You know how I planned this. I will pay for any alterations myself, but will you help me carry them out?" She agreed, and immediately got to work on the brilliant birdwings, flowers and overskirts. When they were ready she surreptitiously removed the costumes from the dressing rooms, completed the alterations, and returned them only ten minutes before the ballet was due to start. I enjoyed watching the consternation among the corps de ballet when they saw their new costumes. . . . De Basil was also in the audience that evening, and when he saw the transformation his fury knew no bounds. He became white with rage—even whiter than usual. I was sent for; the Rus-

171

Ottley, Riabouchinska, and de Basil on the set of *Le Pavillon*.

172

sian stage manager intimated to me on the way to the office that scandal—
the Russian word which means every kind of appalling "to-do"—had,
well, truly broken loose.[4]

Although the changes made Beaton happy, Ernest Newman felt that "the new costumes, which somehow or other kept bringing up before me visions of Christmas
crackers, are not an improvement on the old."[5]

Critics   In this ballet Lichine tried to recapture the feeling of the romantic style. The
Times of London commented that the style derived from a "romantic view purely
classical." The review praised Lichine's slow, pacing solo at the beginning, which culminated in a series of grandes pirouettes à la seconde; Baronova's solo, which
exploited her "lovely arabesque and her special gift of suggesting a dreamy wistful-
ness"; the poetic adagio between Lichine and Baronova, which was followed by and

contrasted with the "flamboyant duet" with Riabouchinska as he attempts to capture her. The *Times* held that the weakest choreography was that for the corps de ballet, which reminded "one uncomfortably of the most stereotyped *ensemble* work of Petipa or Coralli; of those gallops and brilliant *codas* which showed off team work in pirouettes, and *bravura entrechats*."[6]

In the *Daily Telegraph* Haskell complimented Lichine's ability to exploit the best qualities of his cast, showing "Baronova's long line, her rare poise and poetical feeling" and Riabouchinska's "lightness and rapidity." He saluted the duo danced by Grigorieva and Rostova as the two leading spirits and singled out Razoumova, Tchinarova, and Volkova as "fine examples of the Russian school and the backbone of most of the works in the repertory."[7]

When the ballet was presented in New York, John Martin of the *New York Times* wrote that the most interesting moments were found in the pas de deux originally created by Baronova (Danilova, who had understudied the part but did not dance it in London until the third performance, took over the role of the young lady in the New York premiere). He felt that the handling of the ensemble was "stiff rather than formal."[8]

That the ballet wore exceedingly well for numerous seasons validated Haskell's observation that "all the mistakes are on the good side, and the young choreographer is protected throughout by his great musical sensibility."[9]

Newman also commented favorably on Lichine's musicality, pointing out that Borodin's music was not always effective and remarking that Lichine's "music sense had enabled him to make the most of whatever opportunities are offered him."[10]

173

The ballet was last performed by the company during the 1939–40 Australian tour, with Toumanova dancing the part originally created by Baronova and Leskova alternating with Riabouchinska as Chief of the Spirits.

Battle of the Ballets—

COL. W. de BASIL, Ballet Head, Now Has to Compete With a New Russian Ballet Troupe Founded by Leonide Massine.

RINGSIDE VIEW of the Battle of the Ballets Russes Is Caricatured by Alex Gard, Himself a Russian and a Balletomane, at the Right. Dancers Baronova and Riabouchinska Are de Basil's Seconds While Toumanova and Danilova Hold the Sponges for Massine.

TATIANA RIABOUCHINSKA, Ballerina of Ethereal Lightness, Remains With the de Basil Group Although Other Dancers Have Gone Over to the Massine Company.

IRINA BARONOVA, Shown at the Left in Her Costume as "The Top" in the Ballet "Children's Games" Will Continue to Dance in Colonel de Basil's Ballets Russes for a Sixth Season. She's the Youngest of the Company's Ballerine.

DAVID LICHINE Becomes the Leading Male Dancer in the de Basil Group Now That Leonide Massine Has Started His Own Company. The World Famous Michel Fokine Becomes Chief Choreographer for the de Basil Troupe.

When Col. W. de Basil (short and Frenchified for Col. Wassili Gregorievitch Voskresensky) general director of the Ballets Russes, and Leonide Massine, premier danseur and choreographer, couldn't agree on Massine's billing, they started something. It's become a ... Russian revolution—an artistic and social war.

Now there are two companies to vie with each other for artistic, commercial and social success. Massine resigned from de Basil's company and started his own troupe, now in rehearsal in Monte Carlo. The de Basil company just concluded its fifth American season and they, too, will just be resting and rehearsing on the shores of the Mediterranean.

Both groups are planning new ballets as ammunition on the artistic front of this unique battle; both groups have experienced men to handle their booking as bullets on the commercial side; and both groups have lined up imposing arrays of socially prominent patrons as power in the social sector.

Backing of such artistic endeavors as the Ballets Russes has long been an outlet for social ambitions and both the old and new companies are recruiting willing patrons. The de Basil company has Prince Serge Obolensky as its art director and it is more than likely that his relative by marriage, Vincent Astor, will be active behind the scenes of that ballet

in New York Society

GENERAL MANAGER of the New Ballets Russes Is Someone Who Used to Present the Company. Next Season Gallo Will Manage de Corps.

TAMARA TOUMANOVA Gave Up Her Recent Hollywood Residence to Join Massine's Troupe. The Success in Motion Pictures of Vera Zorina, Who Danced With the Ballets This Year Has Turned the Eyes of the Young Ballerinas Toward California.

ARTISTIC DIRECTOR of the New Ballets Russes Is the Title Now Borne by Leonide Massine, Whose Dancing Companions Will Include Serge Lifar and Nini Theilade. The Costume and Fierce Expression Are From His Role in "Scheherazade."

ALEXANDRA DANILOVA Completed Her Tour With the de Basil Troupe Just in Time to Report for Rehearsals in Monte Carlo with the New Rival Organisation.

enterprise. Mrs. Bror G. Dahlberg and Frank Crowninshield are reported to have invested heavily and Savely Sorine, artist and stage designer, and Vernon Duke (Vladimir Dukelsky) composer, will give of their artistic talents as well as lend their names to the social roster of de Basil's supporters.

On the other side, those financially interested are Julius Fleischmann, Mrs. Otto Kahn, Sergei Denham, Anna... of Marlboro, Chauncey McCormick, Mrs. E. G. Chadwick, Mrs. Charles B. Goodspeed, Mrs. Paul More, Mme. Helena Rubinstein, Frederick Dwight, Harold F. McCormick and Leonard Hanna. With such personages in the audiences, the show should be as interesting on one side of the footlights as the other.

After some preliminary skirmishes in Europe, the two ballet companies will bring their contest for fame and fortune to this country where each group will open its season at the Metropolitan Opera House in October—the de Basil ballet going to bat first. Then will come a six months transcontinental conflict as the two groups follow each other around the key cities performing some of the same, and some different dances, in their bid for public preference.

May 1937-
May 1938

I T WAS not long before difficulties arose between de Basil and Massine over the artistic direction of the company. Massine's 1936 injunction petition had been a sign of the deterioration of their relationship. Frustrated in his desire to be appointed artistic director, Massine sought to organize a company of his own, over which he would have complete artistic control. Financial support was offered by Julius Fleischmann, a Cincinnati industrialist and ballet enthusiast who had followed the company throughout its American and European tours.

In the spring of 1937, during the company's United States tour, Massine began conferring with a group of potential American patrons. Rumors abounded, but details remained elusive. John Martin in the *New York Times* mentioned the possibility of an international company to be based at the Metropolitan Opera House that would bring together Massine, Balanchine, and Lifar as choreographers. In any event, nothing could be settled definitively until the next year. Massine's contract with the Colonel, due to expire on September 15, was extended to January 1938, because de Basil's contract with Hurok still had a season to run in the fall and winter of 1937–38, and the star choreographer was very much a part of that agreement. Aware of Massine's plans, de Basil hired Fokine, whose contract with the year-old Ballets de Monte Carlo was to expire in June 1937, for a period of two years beginning at Covent Garden in June 1937.

Fokine's departure opened the way for the reorganization of Blum's company. The new troupe was to be sponsored by World Art, Inc. (a name taken from Diaghilev's *Mir Jskusstva*), with Hurok as American manager, Fleischmann as president of the board of directors, and Serge Denham as vice-president, with headquarters in Monte Carlo, and plans to tour in Europe and the United States. In the meantime, de Basil's company was being incorporated in the United States and abroad, with the Colonel as founder-director, Prince Serge Obolensky as artistic director, and Fokine as choreographer, and an artistic committee that included the painter Savely Sorine, former *Vanity Fair* editor Frank Crowninshield, and Vernon Duke. The roster of dancers included Tchernicheva, Baronova, Riabouchinska, Verchinina, Grigorieva, Morosova, Lichine, Shabelevsky, Jasinski, Petroff, and Lazowski, with Grigoriev as régisseur and Dorati as conductor.

Since the dancers' contracts were negotiated on a seasonal basis and all had different expiration dates, Massine's faction was trying to persuade those whose contracts expired sometime in late 1937 or spring 1938 to join the new Ballet Russe de Monte Carlo for the spring season of 1938. Dancers who chose to join Massine included Toumanova, Danilova, Markova, Rostova, Theilade, Tarakanova, Krassovska, Lifar, Zoritch, and Guérard. Efrem Kurtz was conductor.

All this was taking place during the fall and winter of 1937–38. According to the *New York Times* (November 20, 1937), the Ballets de Monte Carlo was sold on November 19 by Blum to World Art, Inc., for $30,000, plus a reimbursement to Blum for $10,800 for creating three new ballets. The purchase was to be effective as of February 1, 1938.

Thanks to the impending split, the atmosphere in the company was extremely tense. Massine and de Basil were not on speaking terms, and the dancers themselves had all taken sides. De Basil, Grigoriev, and Sevastianov were wary of Massine and Hurok's attempts to persuade dancers to leave with him. According to Lazowski, "For months we lived in a state of friction. One day there was an official announcement on the billboard at Covent Garden prohibiting everyone from being in the wings when Massine danced. The copyright lawsuit had not yet been settled, and Léonide Fedorovitch did not want anyone to study his roles."

Massine's imminent departure was the main impetus behind the copyright lawsuit he brought against the de Basil company in the summer of 1937 in London. Massine wanted to establish his sole ownership of the copyrights of all of his ballets in the company's repertory, while de Basil sought an injunction to restrain Massine from making such a claim. From the beginning of their affiliation, Massine's ballets had been responsible in great part for the artistic success and development of the Ballets Russes. De Basil could not do without the works that had stamped the company's style.

The ballets in question fell into three groups. The first, and largest, group comprised eight works devised before June 1, 1932; the second six had been devised between January 1, 1932, and August 10, 1934; and the third group of three had been created since August 10, 1934.

Massine and de Basil had had no written agreement until November 1932. This document specified that Massine was to render his services as ballet master, choreographer, and chief dancer. In the capacity of choreographer he was to produce the new ballets necessary for the season, arrange dances for the opera season, and hold himself at the disposal of the director. The arrangement continued until August 10, 1934, when the parties entered into a new agreement. It stated that "The director desires to engage the services of the artist, and the artist has agreed to give his services to the director (*a*) as a choreographer, (*b*) as a 'collaborateur artistique' and *maître de ballet*, and (*c*) as a dancer." And went on: "The artist shall compose and arrange such dances and ballets as may be suitable to and may be required by the director for the purposes of the Ballets Russes throughout the period of this engagement, and will be responsible for the entire choreography of such ballets and dances."[1] The 1934 contract added the title of collaborateur artistique and specified that Massine's contract with de Basil was exclusive and that the choreographer could not participate in or provide his services to any production of ballets, films, plays, or any other kind of entertainment without the written consent of de Basil.

On February 23, 1938, the case was decided. The Lord Justice Greer ruled that of the eight ballets in the first group, four would go to the plaintiff, Massine, and four to the defendant, de Basil. The other nine in the next two groups would go to the defendant. The judge explained that there was an implied term in the contract stating that the producer was entitled to the benefits of that for which he had paid, whether or not the payee was an independent contractor.

In the meantime, throughout the spring of 1937 de Basil had been announcing future productions in order to intimidate his competitors. Fokine was to stage a revival of his 1914 *Le Coq d'or*, the company's first *Giselle*, and a version of *Adventures of Arlequin*, which he had staged in November 1922 with the Fokine Ballet at Mark's Strand in New York, and with another group, under his direction, at New York's Lewisohn Stadium in 1934. Laurent Novikov, with whom the company took classes in Chicago, was to revive the two-act *Don Quixote* he had staged for Pavlova, and Frederick Ashton was tentatively scheduled to create *Ariane*, a ballet to music by the young American composer Newell Chase, the husband of Verchinina; later it was announced that he would instead devise a new version of Lord Berners's *The Triumph of Neptune*. Vania Psota, who was to become the company's choreographer during the South American years, was to produce his first ballet, *Village Holiday*, to music of Dvořák. Lichine had been commissioned to do *Francesca da Rimini*. (By now Massine's plans to create a fourth symphonic ballet, to Mozart's Symphony no. 40 in G minor, had been abandoned.) The list of tentative works was unrealistic, and only two materialized, *Le Coq d'or* and *Francesca da Rimini*.

To celebrate the coronation of George VI, Covent Garden was the site of a historic opera and ballet season in 1937, which included the first visits of the Paris Opéra and the Opéra-Comique. The Royal Opera presented two cycles of the *Ring*, one with Frida Leider and the other with Kirsten Flagstad, conducted by Furtwängler, and Beecham conducted a series of *Tristans* with Flagstad and Melchior. The Ballets Russes participated in the new productions of *Prince Igor*, conducted by Eugene Goossens, and Gluck's *Orphée et Euridice*, conducted by Fritz Reiner, with

177

Riabouchinska and Lichine in Italy. Their travels inspired his ballet
Francesca da Rimini.

choreography by Lichine. In this version of the opera, first seen in London in 1920, most of the choral music was sung offstage, while the action was mimed by the dancers. The last scene, set to music from other Gluck operas, was pure dance. The cast included Danilova, Baronova, Riabouchinska, Morosova, and Grigorieva. *Orphée et Euridice* was presented on a double bill with *Le Beau Danube* in the presence of Queen Mary and her entourage. As one critic put it, "Only the Russian dancers could rise to the delicious effrontery of giving us Johann Strauss on top of Gluck."[2]

Before the ballet season began, balletomanes had a rare opportunity to observe the dancers at work on television. Two rehearsals were broadcast on June 28, with commentaries by Arnold Haskell, who described the rehearsal process and explained the ballet technicalities. By mid-1937 the quality of television transmission had improved considerably. The previous year the broadcast studio had been transferred to Alexandra Palace on Muswell Hill, where the world's first regular high-definition system had been adopted. It was from here that the Ballets Russes was seen in Lichine's pas de deux from *Orphée et Euridice*, danced by Baronova and Zoritch; two pas de trois from *Cimarosiana*, danced by Grigorieva, Rostova, and Zoritch, and Danilova, Jasinski, and Petroff; and variations, the Blue Bird pas de deux, and the grand pas de deux from *Aurora's Wedding*. De Basil attended the televised rehearsals, which were conducted by Grigoriev and Vladimiroff. During the season, on September 24, Riabouchinska and Petroff performed *Le Spectre de la rose* for television. According to *Radio Times*, they arrived at the studio an hour later than scheduled, almost when they were due on the air. The misunderstanding did not prevent them from making up and getting into their costumes in minutes so that the program could start on time.

Boasting both Fokine and Massine, who had not worked together since Diaghilev's time, the Russian ballet season promised to be a spectacular one. The company opened on July 1 with *Cimarosiana* (which had not been seen in London since 1928),

La Boutique fantasque, and *Aurora's Wedding*, which was presented against a Bakst backcloth for a different scene of the ballet instead of with the familiar grand stair-case. Felia Doubrovska joined the company for a few performances during the season and made her debut with de Basil on July 14 in the Blue Bird pas de deux with Lichine and an outstanding Danilova as Aurora.

According to the reviews, the company was at its peak. Critics noted the technical and stylistic progress of solo dancers, as well as a new precision, neatness, and certainty in the corps de ballet. Janet Flanner wrote in *The New Yorker*: "At Covent Garden, the de Basil Ballets Russes opened as, and still are, a triumph. Even at the old Châtelet in Paris, when Diaghilev was alive, we never saw a first night at which both spectators and dancers were more brilliantly ebullient; at which floral tributes were more florid . . . and at which a pandemonium of applause seemed more suitable."[3]

Besides its professional obligations, the company had a strenuous social agenda. It was frequently entertained at the Savoy Grill or in private homes, and there were

179

The company rehearsing *Orphée* at the Alexandra Palace, London. Standing: Baronova, Zoritch, and Lichine.

important galas and benefits. In July, for example, the stars performed in aid of the Vic-Wells Ballet at Dorchester's Completion Fund Party, the occasion for a glittering gathering of stage and society luminaries.

In August the company went on vacation, to resume performances in September. This arrangement was the result of the new sublease of the Royal Opera House by Covent Garden Musical Productions, Ltd. This association, formed under the chairmanship of Captain Bruce Ottley, took control of the theater from September to the end of February, thus allowing the ballet season to be extended.

On September 7, the company returned to Covent Garden for a five-week engagement before leaving for its annual six-month tour of North America. The schedule included seven revivals of Fokine works from his Diaghilev period: *Petrouchka*, *Prince Igor*, *Les Sylphides*, *Le Spectre de la rose*, *Les Papillons*, *Cléopâtre*, and *Schéhérazade*. Although some of these ballets had already been staged for the company by Grigoriev, Fokine was able to devote special attention to atmosphere and interpretation. The choreographer's insistence on thoroughly rehearsing all of his ballets was received with much enthusiasm by the dancers but created a lot of extra work for them: Riabouchinska recalls that she had to relearn her role in *Spectre*, since her portrayal, though technically beyond reproach, was not satisfactory to Fokine.

Two works by David Lichine were also in progress, *Le Lion amoureux* and a revised version of *Les Dieux Mendiants*, first choreographed by Balanchine for Diaghilev. Altogether the program for the five weeks included twenty-two ballets. Besides those already mentioned, there were Lichine's *Francesca da Rimini*, Petipa's *Aurora's Wedding* and *Swan Lake* Act II, Nijinska's *Danses slaves et tziganes* and *Les Cent Baisers*, and Nijinsky's *L'Après-midi d'un faune*.

In all, the London season saw 123 performances and four world premieres: *Francesca da Rimini*, *Le Coq d'or*, *Le Lion amoureux*, and *Les Dieux Mendiants*. The coronation season ended at midnight on October 9 after what was virtually a gala performance. Tribute was paid to de Basil for his achievement in ballet: Ottley, on behalf of the subscribers, presented the Colonel with an eighteenth-century gold cockerel as a souvenir of the new work. On stage, the entire company was surrounded with bouquets and wreaths. The houselights were turned on, and the audience rose to its feet, cheering and applauding. After the national anthem was sung, and the fire curtain lowered, the vociferous gallery could still be heard backstage.

The phenomenal success of the season broke all records. As the *Times* reported, "Some of the enthusiasts there had made their first appearance in Floral Street as early as Thursday, and just before midnight on Friday the gallery queue for the last performance already numbered nearly 400 people."[4] According to *The Observer*, by Saturday morning it had grown to five hundred, and that evening the gallery was filled with "a double tier of enthusiasts. In other words, the gallery was full as L.C.C. regulations allow—and then perhaps a little bit fuller."[5]

The fifth American season of the de Basil Ballet Russe opened at the Metropolitan Opera House in New York on October 22. Although the Met had become the home of the Ballets Russes since 1935, its availability during the late fall was limited by the opera season. The present ten-day engagement included the four works that

Cléopâtre, costumes by Sonia Delaunay.
LEFT: Shabelevsky and Tchernicheva.
BELOW: Petroff and Riabouchinska.

LEFT: Baronova and Danilova on the *Queen Mary* boat train, leaving Waterloo Station, London. RIGHT: Jasinski, Riabouchinska, Danilova, and Osato at the Normandie Village Hotel on Sunset Boulevard.

182

had been introduced at Covent Garden as well as sixteen popular items from the repertory. Then, after a single performance at the Brooklyn Academy of Music on November 1, the company embarked on a coast-to-coast tour of the United States and Canada. On January 30, in Oakland, Massine departed, a moment long foreseen that nonetheless left the company in a state of shock.

In February the company appeared in Vancouver, B.C., where two young, talented dancers were recruited: Patricia Meyers and Rosemary Doveson, who were Russianized as Alexandra Denisova and Natasha Sobinova. As Denisova remembers: "We went to [attempt to] audition several times during de Basil's engagement, the last one in British Columbia. Finally, on closing night we got into our practice outfits and went backstage. It was madness all around us because the scenery was being torn down. There we found David Lichine, who consented to take a look at us. In a corner of the stage he asked us to do a few steps and then asked our teacher, June Roper, if we had a place to go. She willingly offered her studio. By the time we got to the school it was two o'clock in the morning. The Colonel, Riabouchinska, Shabelevsky, and I think Baronova, and other principals, came along with Lichine. We danced until the wee hours of the morning. Next thing we knew, we were in the lobby of a Vancouver hotel, where our parents signed the contracts. I didn't want to join the company [because] I was only fifteen and had never been away from home. [She was not forced to go but was encouraged to take advantage of the opportunity.] Two days later we joined them in Portland. The rest of the American tour was very difficult for us. Everything was done in Russian or French, and we spoke only English. We felt very much left out."

After Vancouver, the company made a few stops on the way back east, giving a final performance at the Westchester County Center on March 11. The splendor of *Le Coq d'or* had impressed Condé Nast, who published in the March issue of *Vogue* a beautiful color plate by Bruehl of Fokine's ballet with Baronova, Riabouchinska, Grigorieva, and Algeranoff—apparently the only photographic record of the work in color.

The company's return to Europe began with what was to be its last appearance at the Scala Theatre in Berlin, April 1–15. The season was again a great success. The ballet performed to capacity houses and Goebbels proposed to de Basil that he move his company into the Deutsches Theatre free of charge for an extended season right after the Scala appearance, an offer that de Basil declined. In the April issue of the dance journal *Der Tanz* there appeared a six-page illustrated article called "Triumph der Ballettkunst" ("The Triumph of Ballet") by Karl Pfauter.

In transit, before they reached Berlin, Kurtz, Danilova, Guérard, Rostova, Platoff, and Zoritch, among others, defected from the company to join Massine in Monte Carlo. Toumanova also joined the new Ballet Russe de Monte Carlo after taking a year off from performing, at the end of the usual one-year contract, to visit with her parents in Los Angeles. She returned to the stage in the spring of 1938 when she joined the new company.

At the Scala, *Le Coq d'or* established itself as the season favorite. In spite of the political turmoil in Germany at the time, the reception in Berlin was without precedent. The leaders of the Third Reich were among the enthusiasts who attended the theater nightly. (Fokine, the only member of the company asked to visit Hermann Göring's box after the first performance of *Le Coq d'or*, refused; Göring later congratulated the cast backstage.) It was during this season that the beautiful action photographs were taken by the German photographer K. Weidenbaum. His photographs of *Le Coq d'or* received particular attention.

Baronova, reminiscing about the 1938 Berlin season, recalled: "The Reichstag's members came backstage to invite us for supper. We first naively refused, but soon we realized that it was an order, and we were asked to bring our passports. Even though they were very correct and polite, a great tension permeated the atmosphere, especially when we were on the streets where Jewish shops were vandalized [although Lichine was possibly the only Jewish member of the company]. When we returned to the hotel, they would check our passports, see us in and click their heels." The few times that Hitler came to the theater, the first two rows were occupied with S.S. members. He sat in the third row with his entourage, and the next two rows behind him were also for S.S. members.

After Berlin, the company appeared for the first time in Copenhagen, at the Royal Opera House, also with great success. The Danish monarch attended the first performance—*Les Cent Baisers*, with a Dane, Paul Petroff, as the Prince.

183

FRANCESCA DA RIMINI

Ballet in two scenes; music, Francesca da Rimini Fantasy by Tchaikovsky; libretto by David Lichine and Henry Clifford; choreography by David Lichine; set design by Oliver Messel, executed by Prince A. Schervachidze; costume design by Oliver Messel, executed by Madame Karinska; premiere July 15, 1937, at Covent Garden, London, conducted by Antal Dorati.

ORIGINAL CAST

Francesca	Lubov Tchernicheva	Dwarves	Alonso, Dzikovsky, Katcharoff, Kosloff
Gianciotto Malatesta, Francesca's husband	Mark Platoff	Francesca's Ladies	Grigorieva, Rostova, Chabelska, Chamié, Lipkovska, Novikova, Obidenna, Orlova, Tresahar
Paolo, Malatesta's younger brother	Paul Petroff	Visions	
Chiara, Francesca's nurse	Eleonora Marra	Angelic Apparition	Tatiana Riabouchinska
Girolamo, Malatesta's spy	Edouard Borovansky	Guinevere	Alexandra Danilova
		Lancelot	Roman Jasinski
Domenico, Paolo's friend	Yurek Lazowski	Chorus	Adrianova, Abricossova, Leontieva, Nelidova, Razoumova, Serova, Volkova
Signors of Rimini	Alexandroff, Algeranoff, Belsky, Bousloff, Ismailoff, Lavroff, Lipatoff, Matouchevsky, Rostoff, Runanine, Sobichevsky, Vlassoff, Wust, Zeglovsky	Musicians	Kosmovska, Lvova, Osato, Radova, Strakhova
		Soldiers, servants, and townspeople	

184

The first novelty of the 1937 London season was Lichine's *Francesca da Rimini*. Nourished in the tradition of dance-drama as practiced by Fokine and Massine, Lichine in his fourth ballet turned to music dramatization. Since 1935, Lichine and Riabouchinska had been spending their holidays outside Florence at the villa of Henry Clifford, a curator of paintings at the Philadelphia Museum, and the young choreographer became fascinated by Italian Renaissance art.[1] A visit to Rimini in 1936 left Lichine deeply affected by the medieval atmosphere of the Malatesta castle, where Francesca had lived and died in the thirteenth century, and inspired him to create a ballet based on her story. Clifford, whose knowledge of Italian art was exemplary, encouraged the choreographer and even offered him financial assistance. (It was rumored that an anonymous admirer of Tchernicheva sponsored the ballet, and although Riabouchinska has affirmed that Clifford was mainly responsible, she does not dismiss the possibility that someone else might have contributed as well.)

The tragic tale of Francesca and her lover, her brother-in-law Paolo Malatesta, was immortalized by Dante in the Fifth Canto of his *Inferno*, and it was on this that Tchaikovsky based his orchestral fantasy.

Fokine had created a version for a benefit for war orphans, November 28, 1915, at the Maryinsky Theatre. This work followed the structure of Dante's Canto and began in Hell, where Francesca tells her story. In order to transfer the action from Hell to Malatesta's castle and then back to Hell, Fokine employed a flashback device, using special lighting on different sections of the stage. The role of Francesca was danced by Lubov Egorova and that of Paolo by Pierre Vladimiroff. Lichine probably learned about Fokine's version from Vladimiroff, who, with his wife Doubrovska, accompanied the choreographer and Riabouchinska to Rimini.

Although Lichine structured his ballet around the three parts of Tchaikovsky's work, he did not follow the program provided by the composer. Instead, Clifford wrote a dramatic scenario in two scenes: the first part of the score served as the first scene of the ballet, while the second and third parts were used for the second scene. Oliver Messel, who had just designed George Cukor's 1936 film of *Romeo and Juliet*, was commissioned to do the scenery and costumes for the ballet.

Action   As the curtain rises, a revolting-looking Malatesta holds court in his council room. Four dwarves frolic around him as the courtiers discuss the marriage by proxy of Malatesta with Francesca, the daughter of the Lord of Ravenna—an alliance arranged to end the wars between Rimini and Ravenna. The courtiers fear that Francesca might reject her deformed husband when she finally meets him. Francesca arrives with her nurse, Chiara, Malatesta's younger brother, Paolo, and Girolamo, Malatesta's spy. The latter whispers in his master's ear that Paolo and Francesca have fallen in love during the journey from Ravenna. To appease her husband, Francesca kneels before him, but can hardly conceal her horror when she looks at him closely. Malatesta, in a fury, approaches Francesca, as the horrified Chiara extends a crucifix before her lady. Girolamo pushes the nurse aside, and Malatesta roughly carries Francesca out of the room. The handsome Paolo tries to follow them, but the soldiers block his way. In the commotion the courtiers dance around the room. Unexpectedly, Francesca returns in flight. Paolo attempts to flee with her, but the cruel Girolamo prevents their escape.

The second scene takes place in Francesca's room. Francesca is alone, sitting on her sofa with her hair loose, as she nervously awaits her beloved. Paolo arrives and they embrace. They sit on the sofa to read the love story of Lancelot and Guinevere when an angel appears, dances around them, and finally takes the book away from them. Other celestial creatures appear with trumpets and lyres and unveil two figures: a vision representing Lancelot and Guinevere. The figures dance a pas de deux portraying their passionate and tragic love. Paolo and Francesca embrace and kiss ecstatically. They all dance, Francesca, center stage left, and Paolo, center stage right. They come together, but dramatically reject each other as if overwhelmed by guilt. Paolo dances with virile steps consisting mainly of turns and double tours en l'air while Francesca, turning around dramatically with her arms on her head, stretches them out to him, and then turns away. They come together finally as the supernatural creatures vanish.

Trumpets herald the arrival of Malatesta. Francesca pleads with Paolo to hide in the terrace outside the window. The doors are slammed as Malatesta stands with drawn sword in the company of his faithful dwarves, who immediately begin to search the room. Paolo is found and the two brothers fight. In despair, Francesca follows them around the room as the courtiers begin to crowd the scene. At last, Paolo is slain. Francesca agonizedly crawls to him and holds his dead body tenderly in her arms. Then, standing up, she defiantly bares her breast and flings herself on Malatesta's sword. As she dies beside her lover, the curtain falls.

Choreography *Francesca da Rimini* consisted primarily of mime rather than dance. Only a few passages, such as the vision of angels and the apparition of Guinevere and Lancelot, employed straight dance, and even these were not purely classical. The mime passages were in a naturalistic, personal style rather than conventional ballet mime. Like Fokine, Lichine sought to blend mime and dance into one undifferentiated entity.

In order to achieve historical accuracy, Lichine studied Renaissance art, particularly sculpture. Doubrovska remembered how, while they were traveling together in Italy, Lichine would carefully study the poses of the figures in paintings and sculptures. But he did not simply copy the poses. As he explained in an interview: "When I see a statue, I look at it for a long time and mentally make my own statue, with not only one pose, but a whole series, which is in effect as though the statue had come to life and was performing a series of dance steps. . . . But simply to use another artist's poses—no!"[2] The most important influences were the works of Duccio, Luca della Robbia, and Giotto; all works about which Henry Clifford could offer expert advice.

The dense orchestration at the beginning of the first scene, with its rushing scales suggesting the infernal winds of the second circle of Hell, inspired Lichine to devise a scene of such force that it startled the audience. It depicted the decadent early Renaissance atmosphere of lust and corruption typified by Gian Ciotto (Gian the Lame) Malatesta and his descendants (one of whom, Sigismondo Malatesta [1417–68], married many times, killed two of his wives, impregnated his daughter, attempted to sodomize his son, and ravished the corpse of a German lady who preferred death to the surrender of her honor[3]). The court scene was extremely well conceived, with courtiers and dwarves milling about in frenzied excitement. The first part of the second scene depicted the vision and affirmation of the lovers' passion. In the finale, the frightened courtiers witnessed the brothers' duel and the death of Francesca; it made a violent climax to the crescendo of the music. The critic for the *Times* stated: "The opening and closing scenes, danced to the whirlwind music, have been given a nightmare horror that removes them from the real world even of the Renaissance into Limbo."[4]

Scenery and Costumes Messel's costumes and scenery arbitrarily moved the period of action from the thirteenth century to the fifteenth, a choice indicative of the designer's predilection

ABOVE: Danilova and Jasinski.
ABOVE RIGHT: Gianciotto
(Platoff) kills Paolo (Petroff).
RIGHT: Francesca is slain by
Gianciotto (Platoff).

for the preciousness of that period. He based his designs for the ballet on Carpaccio and Botticelli.

The first scene occurs in the council room of Malatesta's palace. In the background are three windows with a view of the Italian countryside. Upstage right, on a dais, is the canopied throne. The scene is grimly lighted.

The second and third scenes take place in Francesca's chamber. In the background a window leads out to a terrace. Upstage right, Francesca's bed is beneath an arched portico; there is a sofa in front of the bed. Upstage left is a closed, arched door studded with iron nails.

The costumes were fashioned after those of the late fourteenth and early fifteenth centuries. The women wore dresses with close-fitting bodices and long, tight sleeves; on their heads they wore short wimples. The men wore tights and short, close-fitting jackets; some also wore capes.

Critics   *Francesca da Rimini* marked Lichine as a choreographer of great potential, destined for future prominence. Arnold Haskell wrote the day after the premiere: "With this work the young artist gains his choreographic spurs. The immediate impression is that this is magnificent theatre throughout, ranging from powerful and exciting melodrama to true tragedy."[5]

About the work's theatrical power Grace Robert commented: "The vivid violence with which *Francesca da Rimini* progressed left the audience dazed. One felt a sense of shock as though it were a personal experience through which one had somehow passed physically uninjured but mentally numb."[6] And, indeed, watching the silent film of the ballet, one is struck by its sheer theatricality.[7]

Francesca da Rimini provided dramatically challenging roles for Tchernicheva, Petroff, and Platoff. Tchernicheva played her role in the grand manner. The reviewer for the *Times* described her as "a Baldovinetti portrait come to life. . . . [She] moves with an unmatched beauty of movement through the alternating scenes of horror and romance, and by the contrast of her serenity increases their dramatic effect."[8] Her love scenes with Paolo were both tender and touched with passion and fervor, undoubtedly infused with her very real love for Petroff. Haskell's review added: "The focal point is the tragedienne, Tchernicheva. With what skill she develops her character, showing fear, tenderness and the final heroic gesture of baring her breast for the deathblow. This culminating murder is a magnificent piece of choreographic production."[9] When she is pierced by her husband's sword, the audience always gasped.

Besides a poetic portrayal of Paolo by Petroff and a menacing Gianciotto by Platoff, the secondary roles were well developed. Among them were Borovansky's Girolamo, the spy who brings down the first curtain with a vicious seizure of power; Marra's protective nurse; and Riabouchinska's sensitive Angelic Vision. The vision pas de deux, danced by Danilova and Jasinski, was controversial for its invention and eroticism. Messel's costume for Guinevere, simulating a nude body with a long, dark wig à la Lady Godiva, added to the controversy. (Since Danilova was dark, she wore a dark wig; when Moulin danced the part, she wore a blond wig.) A reviewer for the

188

Morning Post wrote: "According to the Inferno, Paolo and Francesca were reading a romantic chronicle; in the ballet, to judge by the apparition conjured up, they were reading an erotic and lurid feuilleton in the popular Press of the period. Whoever dreamed of such a Guinevere and Lancelot at the court of King Arthur?"[10]

LE COQ D'OR

Ballet in three scenes, with prologue and epilogue; music from *Le Coq d'or* by Rimsky-Korsakov, adapted by Nicolas Tcherepnin; libretto by Fokine, after Bielsky's libretto from Pushkin's poem; choreography by Michel Fokine; set design by Natalia Gontcharova, executed by Prince A. Schervachidze; costume design by Natalia Gontcharova, executed by Madame Karinska; curtain designed and executed by Natalia Gontcharova; premiere September 23, 1937, at Covent Garden, London, conducted by Efrem Kurtz.

ORIGINAL CAST

The Golden Cockerel	Tatiana Riabouchinska
The Queen of Shemakhan	Irina Baronova
King Dodon	Marc Platoff
Dodon's Sons	
Prince Guidon	Yurek Lazowski
Prince Aphron	Serge Ismailoff
Amelpha, Dodon's nurse	Tatiana Chamié
Polkan, Commander-in-chief	Edouard Borovansky
The Astrologer	H. Algeranoff
Boyars	MM. Alexandroff, Belsky, Bousloff, Dzikovsky, Guérard, Ladré, Lavroff, Matouchevsky, Rostoff, Runanine, Vlassoff, Zeglovsky
Peasant Women	Mlles Chabelska, Novikova, Orlova, Radova
Russian Dancers	Mlles Kosmovska, Lipkovska, Nelidova, Obidenna, Razoumova, Roussova, Serova, Tresahar
Cooks	Mlles Volkova, Leontieva
Messengers	MM. Lazovsky, Ismailoff
Youths	MM. Katcharoff, Kosloff, Lavroff, Lipatoff, Sobichevsky, Wust
Visions	Roman Jasinski, Paul Petroff, Tamara Grigorieva, Sono Osato, Olga Morosova, Lubov Rostova
Warriors	Mlles Abricossova, Lvova, Obidenna, Roussova
Oriental Dancers	Mlles Adrianova, Chabelska, Kosmovska, Kouznetsova, Leontieva, Nelidova, Orlova, Radova, Razoumova, Serova, Tresahar, Volkova

Diaghilev's production of Rimsky-Korsakov's opera *Le Coq d'or*, with choreography by Fokine and a double cast of singers and dancers, had aroused considerable controversy when it was first presented at the Paris Opéra in 1914. Although it was an artistic triumph, strenuous opposition from the Rimsky-Korsakov family forced Diaghilev to drop it from the repertory. The composer's widow and his son Andrei brought a case based on the Musical and Literary Convention (a product of the Bern Convention on copyrights) that existed between France and Russia, arguing that the division of the action from the singing departed from the composer's original intention.[1] Nevertheless, Diaghilev's version subsequently was presented at the Drury Lane in London, since no such agreement existed between Russia and Great Britain. In 1918, after the war, the Metropolitan Opera produced a revival of *Le Coq d'or*: an opera-ballet version with choreography by Adolph Bolm, who had played King Dodon for Diaghilev in London.

When Fokine joined de Basil's company in the spring of 1937, he and the Colonel discussed the idea of a revival of *Le Coq d'or* as a co-production with Beecham's Covent Garden Opera. But Fokine soon decided that he preferred to mount a condensed, straight-dance version of *Le Coq*. To this end, Nicolas Tcherepnin, who had been a pupil of Rimsky-Korsakov, adapted and arranged the score, after Dorati had made substantial cuts in the opera, into an all-instrumental version; the three acts of the opera were reduced to three scenes plus a prologue and an epilogue, all connected by musical passages from the opera that sustained the mood and served to unify the development of the action; they also provided the leitmotivs of the Golden Cockerel and the Queen of Shemakhan. In the opera, each character has its own musical theme —the Cockerel's is an allegro, the Queen lento, the Astrologer moderato, and the King moderato. Some musical motifs were identified with certain instruments, such as the Cockerel's with trumpets and the King's with cello and basses. Fokine devised a scenario based on the opera libretto V. I. Bielsky had made from Pushkin's poem. Kurtz's only involvement with the music was his conducting chores on opening night.

Prologue: The curtain opens to the sound of trumpets introducing the musical theme of the Golden Cockerel. A bird of fabulous golden plumage appears, spotlighted downstage left, on her knees, head bent down and wings outstretched to either side, before a night-scene drop depicting a walled town with onion-dome turrets in the distance. An Astrologer enters and catches the bird with his cloak; when he takes it out from the folds of the cloak, it has been miraculously transformed into a gold-painted wooden bird of normal size. The Astrologer looks at the sky through a telescope and as the orchestra plays the musical theme of the Queen of Shemakhan, the daughter of the air, he becomes enchanted with his vision of her (which we do not see) and initiates an elaborate ruse to win her for his own. With magical gestures he passes his hands over the bird, wraps it in his cloak, and sets out for the court of King Dodon.

(This is the only time during the ballet when the Queen does not appear when her leitmotiv is played. In Fokine's memoirs he said that he intended to have her

190

Action

appear in the sky during the Prologue, but that de Basil would not allow it. Lazowski hints that the Colonel was afraid of the danger to Baronova.)

Scene One: At court, the lazy, fat old King Dodon is holding a war council with his sons, Prince Guidon and Prince Aphron, his advisors, and his commander-in-chief, Polkan. They are undecided about their course of action. Prince Guidon, placing his helmet center stage, dances a variation in support of peace and art. The variation is rooted in Russian fold steps, stressing pirouettes and tours en l'air. After his dance, his supporters lift Guidon up and down as his rival, Prince Aphron, takes the floor, sword and shield in hand, to perform a variation glorifying war. His dance combines warlike movements with folk steps, jumps, pirouettes, and tours en l'air. The two princes confront each other and Aphron overpowers Guidon. At this crucial moment the Astrologer arrives and diverts everyone's attention. He kneels in front of the King and bows, and with mystical gestures produces the golden bird. He tells the King of its magical power: it will crow to warn him of the approach of the enemy. The King is skeptical, but to get a better look at the bird, he and his boyars come closer and encircle it. Abruptly all step back, astonished by the sight of a human-size fabulous bird that rises from the ground in front of their eyes. Riabouchinska, squatting on her pointes, knees off the floor, arms outstretched to the side like wings, slowly rises, beaking on both of her shoulders. She steps over and around on her fourth position on pointe, still beaking on her shoulders, and kneels halfway down and stretches up several times, now beaking on the boyars. She flutters her wings and advances kicking to the front and then to the sides, scaring everyone away. Simulating crowing with her lips, she squats and then rises, repeatedly, makes rapid promenades in attitude back, begins an incessant cycle of quick pirouettes and chaîné turns around the stage, and finally darts back to where she had originally first appeared and stands erect, profile to the audience, elbows back and one leg in a turn-in passé position, motionless. Polkan advises the mesmerized King not to accept the strange gift, but Dodon is completely taken by it. The King offers jewels to the Astrologer, who refuses them and instead exacts a promise from the monarch that is to be honored sometime in the future. The Cockerel is lifted high in the air, and is carried out as if on a perch. With the bird guarding his kingdom, Dodon dismisses everyone and gets ready to eat and sleep. The women, led by his nurse, Amelpha, prepare the King's table and bed and entertain him with peasant dances. After dinner, the King is put to bed. The lights dim and everyone falls asleep, but the Golden Cockerel flashes in in grands jetés and dances to warn the King of danger. Hearing the bird, the King's men rush in, and the monarch calls for his two sons and their respective armies and sends them off to war. He dismisses everyone and goes back to sleep. The stage darkens completely except for the King's bed. As Dodon is seen gesturing as if in the throes of a nightmare, the Queen of Shemakhan makes a brief appearance on a huge water lily spotlighted in blue. The Golden Cockerel leaps in again and dances to warn the King of more danger. The bird makes such a commotion that the King's men appear once again and try to decipher its message. They remind the King of his duty to go to war. Polkan assembles the army, and Dodon's huge horse is brought onto the stage as the

191

King puts on his armor. With the aid of his assistants and a ladder, the King clumsily saddles and mounts the horse and departs with his troops as the women bid him farewell, waving handkerchiefs.

Scene Two: Dodon arrives with his men at a battlefield enveloped in fog, to discover that his sons' rivalry has ended in the destruction of their armies and in their stabbing each other to death. The King is overcome by grief. Soon he and his men are spellbound by the vision of a fantastic tent that rises from the ground. The monarch orders his men to fire on it, but suddenly, as if it had been nothing more than a hallucination, they are submerged in darkness. When they decide to retreat, the tent appears in front of them. Inside are the Queen of Shemakhan, reclining on cushions, and her exotic retinue. Dazed, some of the soldiers run away and Polkan, also affected, tries in vain to persuade the King to leave. The Queen emerges from the tent, stretching out her arms, and performs a solo to the music of the "Hymn to the Sun." Seductively she moves with the stylized, symbolic hand and arm gestures, called mudra, used in Hindu religious ceremonies and dancing, while performing a most difficult dance featuring intricate pas de bourrées, piqué to the side developing into arabesque and ronde versé, finishing in multiple pirouettes. The King asks who she is; she answers and invites him into the tent. Her attendants entertain them while Dodon tries to make love to her. She then dances a pas de trois with two attendants; she is handed a tambourine and performs another long variation for the King, after which she entices Dodon to dance for her. He removes his crown and puts it aside with the scepter and orb. She ties a kerchief around his head in the style of a peasant girl, and watches as he prances and capers around until he falls exhausted to the floor, having made a fool of himself. He asks her to marry him and offers her his kingdom; she accepts, and after being handed the scepter and the orb, dances another variation. Everyone surrounds the Queen and joins her in a grand finale. The crowd lifts her in their midst to an imaginary throne, where she appears to sit holding the scepter and orb as the curtain falls.

Scene Three: Dodon's people eagerly assemble outside his palace after messengers arrive announcing the King's arrival with his new bride. The crowd forms lines, holding handkerchiefs and banners. First, a section of the monarch's army enters, followed by the contingent of dancers in the Queen's bridal party. The people are filled with excitement by the dancers and fascinated by the sight of all the exotic creatures dressed in brightly colored or golden costumes: blackamoors; monsters with horns or with one eye in the middle of the forehead; men with heads of dogs and tails of monkeys; dwarves; giants; all bearing precious jewels. Finally, the royal chariot arrives, with the Queen and Dodon, followed by the rest of the army. The King introduces his bride and she dances for the people, still holding the scepter and orb. The Astrologer enters and, entranced by the presence of the Queen, claims her as his reward. In vain Dodon tries to dissuade him and finally, losing his temper, hits the Astrologer with the scepter, killing him, and provoking the Queen to laughter. The lights dim. Dodon approaches the Queen, but disdainfully she refuses him. The Golden Cockerel appears and beaks the King on the head until he falls, dead. The Queen laughs and dances offstage while the people mourn their dead king. The scene is frozen; the

Astrologer stands up, mimes to the audience that all was illusion save for himself and the Queen, and departs. The Golden Cockerel enters to its musical theme and dances and hovers among the motionless figures. As it crows and whirls its wings in fourth position on pointe downstage left, where it had first appeared, the night-scene drop with the town in the distance falls before it, and then the curtain.

Scenery and Costumes

This was to be de Basil's most costly production so far, with three changes of scene and one hundred fifty costumes. Natalia Gontcharova re-created her curtain and other design from the original 1914 production; however, the 1937 version was more elaborate, especially the second scene.

The first scene opened on a yellow wall with a gate in the middle and a tower to each side of the gate. Depicted on the wall were animals in fighting position, flowers, and bushes. Above the wall, and open to the sky, could be seen the distant dome turrets and buildings of the town. Before the wall and to each side were huge trees—one green, the other cinnamon—with enormous flowers. Upstage left was a four-poster bed, and downstage left a throne with a smaller throne to each side. On the floor was a reddish carpet. Scene Two took place in front of and inside a tent of green silk adorned with flower and leaf patterns. The drawn curtains of the tent revealed an exotic interior with furnishings and cushions. The third scene took place outside the palace in a square containing two large pavilions with turrets. The walls of the larger pavilion, stage right, were decorated with patterns of huge flowers and had tiny windows; the pavilion gates were open and a carpet was spread at the entrance.

The costumes were based on the originals, although some had to be modified to accommodate the new choreography; for example, the Queen now wore a very short overskirt rather than the narrow, knee-length overskirt worn by Karsavina in 1914. The costumes of the King's court were inspired by Russian peasant dress and those of the Queen's by traditional Eastern dress. The Queen wore a crown, with long braids to her waist. Under her overskirt she wore baggy trousers of crimson trimmed with gold. The Astrologer was dressed in a dark blue cloak appliquéd with stars and crescent moons, and wore a conical hat. The most striking costume was the Cockerel's: a leotard and cap of real gold thread, and a comb, wings (which hid the arms), and tail of gold-painted leather.

The Cockerel's costume was completely new, for in 1914 the character had been represented by a prop, a gilded artificial bird perched on a swinging rope. New costumes were also added for the arrival of the Queen's entourage at Dodon's court.

Rehearsals

Owing to the size of the production, rehearsals were held at the Chenies Street drill hall, where Diaghilev's *Sleeping Princess* had been rehearsed in 1921. According to Fokine, *Le Coq* was the first ballet that he had choreographed in its entirety before the first rehearsal. However, whenever he came to work on any new ballet he always had the scene precomposed in his head and knew from the very beginning what he wanted. It seemed to his dancers that he never left anything to improvisation. He did not depend on notes. However, some of the dancers vaguely recall that during the rehearsals of *Le Coq* Fokine occasionally checked some sort of notes.

Fokine used all sorts of devices to obtain specific movement qualities from the dancers. As Riabouchinska, who danced the title role, recounts: "After rehearsals, M.

193

Fokine would stay in the studio and make me jump over a series of chairs that he had placed in a circle. He would sit there and scrutinize me, making suggestions about my grand jeté, my arm movements to convey the idea of a cockerel's wings, my head movements and facial expressions. At first there was a chair for each jump, but after I had mastered the series of grands jetés for my entrance, he would start adding an extra chair for each jump, up to three. It was killing, but only then was I able to acquire the speed, coordination, and the expression his character demanded.

"M. Fokine was very particular about every detail of his choreography. I recall one day when Grigoriev had to hold him back in the wings, as he intended to grab Shabelevsky from the stage when Yura had changed a step in *Schéhérazade*."

Olga Morosova, who later played the role of the Queen, remembers having to execute a series of bourrées using the stylized, symbolic arm movements of Indian dance, holding a glassful of water in each hand. The exercise was repeated until almost no water was spilled.

Premiere

194

The opening night audience included the royal family, accompanied by the Duchess of Gloucester; King Carol of Rumania; Alphonse XIII, ex-king of Spain and patron of Diaghilev; Arabian sheiks and other exotic rulers in colorful traditional dress; Cecil Beaton, Tamara Karsavina, Lydia Sokolova, Victor Dandré, and Michel Larionov. The program opened with *Swan Lake* Act II, with Danilova and Petroff.

When the first intermission curtain fell, the cast of *Le Coq d'or* was already onstage, made up and bewigged, waiting for the costumes to arrive from Mme Karinska's atelier. As a last resort, de Basil had called the fire department and arranged for ambulances to pick up the costumes and take them to the theater. The intermission dragged on for fifty minutes. When the costumes finally arrived, some were found to be unfinished and had to be pinned together. The Cockerel's costume included long, cumbersome leggings that rendered impossible the execution of certain movements. As the overture began, Karinska was onstage cutting the leggings and making adjustments with pins so that Riabouchinska could dance. Throughout the performance Karinska and Mme Larose, the wardrobe mistress, remained on the alert in the wings to repin when necessary.

When the curtain opened after the prologue, which took place in front of a dark drop, the lighting failed momentarily. Suddenly the stage was brilliantly illuminated, and thunderous applause greeted Gontcharova's opulent polychromatic decor and costumes. Her vivid depiction of ancient Russia in red, rose, gold, brown, yellow, green, and blue was breathtaking. The ballet was brightly lit in order to bring out the colors and patterns. Only when the Queen appeared was the scene veiled by a silky blue light, which enhanced the mood. The ballet impressed its audience as the most magnificent spectacle since the war, a return to the early works of Diaghilev, romantic in its exoticism, color, emotion, fantasy, and legend.

There were endless curtain calls for the dancers, the choreographer, the designer, and the conductor, and Fokine's performers applauded him warmly.

The program for the evening closed with Massine's *Cimarosiana*, originally produced by Diaghilev in 1924.

ABOVE: The Astrologer (Algeranoff) on the road to the court of King Dodon;
curtain by Gontcharova. BELOW: The Astrologer arrives at court.

LEFT: Platoff as King Dodon, Algeranoff as the Astrologer, and Riabouchinska as the Golden Cockerel. BELOW: Riabouchinska in one of her striking grands jetés. BOTTOM: Riabouchinska perched on the hands of the boyars.

ABOVE: The Queen of Shemakhan (Baronova) appears to King Dodon (Platoff) in a dream. BELOW: The Queen with her entourage.

Critics   *Le Coq d'or* was the big hit of the season. Critics praised it as a work of art and greeted the dancers' interpretations with high acclaim. Ernest Newman wrote in the *Sunday Times*: "Riabouchinska's Golden Cockerel was a creation on her part as well as on Fokine's and Gontcharova's. Baronova's Queen is manifestly going to be one of the outstanding figures of ballet. Platoff was richly humorous as the doddering King Dodon; and there was fine characterization in Algeranoff's astrologer."[2] Haskell, in the *Daily Telegraph*, said: "Riabouchinska as the Cockerel has a role that no one could fill more convincingly. It has lightness and brightness; how fine the mimed indication of the crowing! Baronova's Queen is a brilliantly conceived character study as well as a dazzling piece of technical dancing, again presented with the simplicity that is the keynote of the Russian art itself."[3]

On the other side of the Atlantic, John Martin wrote after *Le Coq*'s premiere in New York on October 23, 1937:

> Irina Baronova . . . overtops herself as the Queen. She has a new depth and inner assurance that allow her greater freedom of mood than she has ever had before, and her Queen is not just an attractive little girl dancing well, but a fascinating and sparkling character. Tatiana Riabouchinska brings her crisp style and virtuosity to the role of the Cockerel and plays it with a superior detachment that belongs by rights to the only other creature in the piece who travels naturally on its points.[4]

198   There was a great deal of discussion over the adaptation of the opera. Some critics felt that the words were necessary to convey certain narrative passages. Others believed that dancers depicted the characters more convincingly than singers. Newman said:

> You cannot do this sort of thing, of course, without the original suffering to some extent. . . . But on the whole the thing pans out astonishingly well. We miss, needless to say, a great deal of fun of the satire when we are deprived of the words; but in its place we get a quantity of fun that is quite as good in its way. The second act in particular has virtues that more than compensate us for the conversion of the opera into a ballet. One is never quite able to believe in the Queen of Shemakhan in the opera.[5]

Irving Kolodin wrote in the *New York Sun*:

> Pundits may fulminate at his effrontery in applying a ruthless scissor to Rimsky-Korsakov's opera, but it was not apparent that the worth of the composer's achievement had been diminished. Since Rimsky-Korsakov himself arranged a liberal portion of the score for concert performance, it is clear that he did not consider the voices essential to the effect of the music.[6]

Fokine, in an open letter to the *Times* in London, explained that the music itself was sufficiently narrative in character to support the balletic interpretation, and added: "I have altered the intentions of the composer much less than the composer himself altered those of the poet."[7] Dancers who had not been directly exposed to Diaghilev but were familiar with other of Fokine's works in the repertory did not feel there was a lack of dancing.

Although the work was generally well received, it was found to be overly static by some viewers who had become used to the emphasis on pure dance. Arnold Haskell, whose sensibilities had been developed under Diaghilev, was more understanding of Fokine's approach: "The layman may possibly find that there is not enough dancing. . . . The whole thing is dancing but, to use the opera parallel, there is recitative dancing and aria dancing."[8]

The action moved swiftly between the episodes of mime and dance. In the first scene mime predominated. However, the second was almost completely danced through. The third blended both equally. In the prologue and the epilogue, the Astrologer as narrator addressed himself to the audience. This device of having a middle person interposed between the characters of the story and the audience enhanced the sense of irony of the satire.

The choreography, with the exception of the role of the Golden Cockerel, was rooted in two styles: Russian folk for Dodon's court, and Eastern-Hindu style for the Queen of Shemakhan and her people. The balletic highlights were provided by the Golden Cockerel and the Queen, the only roles danced on pointe. The Cockerel's steps were performed in turn-in position, with the exception of some pirouettes and rapid promenades in attitude back. Pointes were used even when the bird rose and fell in a squatting position and in a series of single tours en l'air around the stage. The role stressed jumps that according to Grace Robert were made more effective by Riabouchinska's "unbelievable grands jetés." In his memoirs Fokine said that she "was just born for the title role."

The choreography for the Queen was an attempt to convey the Oriental atmosphere through balletic technique. It was one of Fokine's most intricate virtuoso parts and its continuity in the second scene made it more exhausting. Even when not dancing the Queen was rarely off her pointes. It was a beautiful personification of mood with gestures that were characteristic of a moon-breasted sculpture from Belur. The softness of the arms and the supple use of the torso made the choreography appear easier. About Baronova's opening solo Grace Robert stated that it "was performed with a deceptive ease and simplicity that made light of its formidable technical difficulties."[9]

John Martin, after Fokine's death in 1942, categorized *Le Coq d'or* as one of the ten masterpieces of Fokine's seventy creations, along with *Les Sylphides*, *Petrouchka*, *Prince Igor*, *Le Spectre de la rose*, *Carnaval*, *Schéhérazade*, *Firebird*, *Don Juan*, and *Paganini*.[10]

In the seasons that followed, the work was a triumph wherever it was performed. At the Metropolitan Opera two extra performances had to be scheduled for the first week of de Basil's fall 1937 engagement.[11] The ballet stayed in the repertory until the final performance of the company in Spain in 1948.

In 1976, the London Festival Ballet restaged *Le Coq d'or* under the direction of Nicholas Beriozoff, with scenery and costumes by André Delfau after Gontcharova. Unfortunately, this revival was not authentic. Beriozoff, who was never a member of de Basil's company, was not able to re-create Fokine's work. His version had a different libretto, different choreography, and a new musical arrangement and adaptation of the opera by Geoffrey Corbett. For some of the critics and the de Basil dancers who saw this revival, it bore little resemblance to the 1937 original. The following changes were noted by Peter Williams, reviewer for *Dance and Dancers*, who had seen the 1937 version:[12] The Queen appears in the prologue when her musical theme is played. The second scene begins with a battle between the Princes' armies and the Queen's fantasylike troop. The death of Dodon's sons is depicted, but they do not kill each other. The "Hymn to the Sun" is first played to provide the theme for a pas de deux with the Queen and King, then it is repeated later in the scene for her solo. At the end, the Astrologer is rejuvenated and leaves in loving union with the Queen.

LES DIEUX MENDIANTS

200

Ballet in one act; music by Handel, arranged by Sir Thomas Beecham; based upon a pastorale by Sobeka (Boris Kochno); choreographed by David Lichine; set design by Léon Bakst (from *Daphnis et Chloé*); costume design by Juan Gris (from *Les Tentations de la bergère*); premiere September 17, 1937, at Covent Garden, London, conducted by Sir Thomas Beecham.

ORIGINAL CAST

The Serving Maid	Alexandra Danilova	Ladies	Mlles Abricossova, Lvova, Novikova, Osato, Radova, Roussova
Divinities			
The Shepherd	Yurek Shabelevsky	Noblemen	MM. Belsky, Bousloff, Ismailoff, Rostoff, Runanine, Zeglovsky
Two Ladies	Tamara Grigorieva, Lubov Rostova	Servants	MM. Dzikovsky, Kosloff, Sobichevsky, Wust
A Nobleman	Paul Petroff		

Diaghilev originally produced *Les Dieux Mendiants* on a moment's notice, when he realized that there were not enough world premieres for his 1928 London season. Balanchine devised the choreography in a few days; the decor consisted of the first and third scenes of Bakst's *Daphnis et Chloé*, and the costumes were those that Juan Gris designed for *Les Tentations de la bergère*. The ballet, in two scenes, had a libretto by Boris Kochno (using the pseudonym Sobeka) and was set to a hodgepodge of music by Handel arranged by Sir Thomas Beecham: one selection each from *Rodrigo*, *Il Pastor Fido*, *Teseo*, *Admeto*; four selections from *Alcina*, and airs from the opus 6 concerti grossi, including the "Hornpipe" movement from no. 7.[1]

On February 21, 1936, the Sadler's Wells Ballet presented Ninette de Valois's *The Gods Go a-Begging*, to a slightly altered libretto, the same music, with scenery and costumes by Hugh Stevenson. (In de Valois's version, the Serving Maid is attended by two assistant maids; there are six black lackeys instead of four, and when the Shepherd and the Serving Maid are expelled by the Noblemen, the stage dims and Mercury enters to reveal them as Divinities.)

The next year it was Colonel de Basil's turn. Beecham's 1937 coronation opera season at Covent Garden was a stirring success, and de Basil was afraid to follow at its heels with a fall season that offered London only two premieres: Lichine's *Le Lion amoureux* and Fokine's drastically revised *Le Coq d'or*. Although the company had revived *Cimarosiana*, *Cléopâtre*, and *Les Papillons* during the summer, the Colonel wanted still more new works for the fall, and decided to mount a new version of *Les Dieux Mendiants* choreographed by Lichine.

It was a most appropriate choice for the emergency. Diaghilev's production had been a popular success in London nine years earlier; the scenery and costumes were stored in de Basil's London warehouse; and Danilova, who had created the leading role, was available to re-create it. The ballet would also ensure the participation of Sir Thomas, who was partial to Handel—and especially to Handel as rearranged by Beecham.

201

Action
    Lichine's ballet faithfully adhered to Kochno's libretto:

Scene One: Introduction (*moderato maestoso*) and *allegro*. Preparations are in progress for a "Fête champêtre"; a humble Serving Maid and numerous black lackeys enter with food and proceed to prepare a feast in a woodland clearing. Various Noblemen and their ladies arrive.

Scene Two: Menuet (*grazioso*). A Shepherd who has lost his way strays into the company, where the ladies seek to captivate him and try to entice him into the lively movement of the "fête."

Scene Three: Hornpipe (*allegro*). Dance of the Shepherd.

Scene Four: Musette (*moderato*). Suddenly the Shepherd catches sight of the humble Serving Maid who, having finished preparations for the feast, conceals herself from the Noblemen.

Scene Five: Ensemble (*presto*).

Scene Six: Larghetto (*andantino*). Moved by tender feelings for the Maid, the Shepherd joins her. The company partakes of the feast and afterward strays into the woods.

Scene Seven: Tamborino (*allegro*). The black lackeys now execute a droll measure with great agility.

Scene Eight: Gavotte (*andantino grazioso*). The returning Noblemen are indignant when they observe the love scene between the Shepherd and the Serving Maid. (In Lichine's version, the Noblemen do not become indignant, nor do they try to punish the Shepherd and Serving Maid; rather, they merely make fun of the humble couple.)

Scene Nine: Dramatico (*andante*). The moment arrives when the Shepherd and the humble Serving Maid doff their rags and reveal themselves as Divinities.

Scene Ten: Bourrée (*allegro*). Finale and apotheosis.

Choreography

As Lichine himself has admitted, "It was really more a fabrication than an inspiration."[2] According to Danilova, he followed whatever guidelines she could provide, especially regarding the correlation between musical passages and her role, which he wedded to his own choreographic design. The role of the Serving Maid was the only one danced on pointe.

It was not Lichine's intention to reconstruct Balanchine's choreography. He tried to create the choreography from scratch, adhering faithfully to the correlation between action and music as indicated by Kochno and Beecham. However, he was pressed for time and therefore suggested to Danilova that, whenever possible, she make use of any memories she had of her part in the Balanchine production. As a result, the action, music, and overall style closely followed the original production. The critic for the *Times* commented that Lichine's version "did not depart widely in style from the old; everything else was retained from the original production, including even Mme Danilova, who danced the serving maid and became a veritable goddess at the end."[3]

202

Besides the choreography, two aspects differed from the original: Lichine toned down the indignation of the Noblemen when they found the Shepherd and the Serving Maid in love; and he relied only minimally on mime, trying to create a period dance suite instead of concentrating on the narrative. The critic for *The Observer* commented:

> Lichine's version, which is almost a dance suite, could do with a bit more drama; it would probably be better if he followed the scenario more closely in making the noblemen "indignant at the love passage" between shepherd and shepherdess. Without this the denouement is rather weak. Yet it is an extremely pleasant, harmonious work, technically exacting but not too exacting for Shabelevsky, who dances his long, difficult *pas seul* with his characteristically neat vigour. There is also Danilova to be mentioned, the one performer to-night who not only danced admirably but who gave her dancing a meaning and an air.[4]

Critics

Despite the conditions under which the ballet was produced—only four days for rehearsals—it further revealed the capacity Lichine had demonstrated in *Francesca da Rimini* for handling complex and inventive group patterns. The critic for the *Times* called Lichine's choreography "excellent, deft, and light on the ground," and

ABOVE: Shabelevsky as the Shepherd. RIGHT: Riabouchinska and Jasinski.

concluded that "the total effect of this heterogeneously assembled ballet is enchanting." "Only in the Gavotte," he commented, "does his invention seem forced. The misfit was possibly emphasized by the rather slow pace adopted by the conductor, especially in the reprise."[5]

A. V. Coton felt that the work was not an appropriate one for Lichine's approach: "His concern is with strong action, novel scenario, and melodrama; a dancer turned choreographer will almost always be inventive in the genre in which he best dances."[6] To Coton the pas de trois for the lord and ladies and the pas de deux were the choreographic highlights. Shabelevsky's role was a "hot-paced demonstration piece," but the dancer made it convincing through his astounding good looks and refined manner.

According to *The Observer*, de Valois's recent version was the more dramatic work, and Coton felt that it was better constructed.

But Lichine kept improving on his version, which stayed in the repertory for two years. When Danilova left the company in early 1938, Riabouchinska took over the role of the Serving Maid. Jasinski alternated with Shabelevsky as the Shepherd.

LE LION AMOUREUX

204

Ballet in one act; music by Karol Rathaus; libretto by David Lichine and Henry Clifford, based on La Fontaine's fable; choreography by David Lichine; set and costume design by Pierre Roy; sets executed by Prince A. Schervachidze; costumes executed by Madame Karinska; premiere October 6, 1937, at Covent Garden, London, conducted by Antal Dorati.

ORIGINAL CAST

The Master of Ceremony	Waldemar Wust	The Wig Maker	Marian Ladré
The Painter	Edouard Borovansky	The Queen	Alice Nikitina
The Flower Girl	Tatiana Riabouchinska	The Lion	David Lichine
The Flautist	Yurek Lazowski		Artists of the Ballet

For the second half of the 1937 Covent Garden engagement, de Basil announced new versions of two Diaghilev works: *Les Dieux Mendiants*, to be choreographed by Lichine, and *Le Triomphe de Neptune*, to be choreographed by Frederick Ashton. When arrangements for the latter fell through, de Basil decided that Lichine should create a completely new ballet to take its place and proposed *Le Lion amou-*

ABOVE: Nikitina and Lichine. BELOW: Lichine and
corps de ballet.

reux, based on a fable by La Fontaine.[1] The Polish composer Karol Rathaus agreed to write the music, and Pierre Roy (best remembered for his many *Vogue* covers) set to work on the decor. Lord Rothermere, the British newspaper magnate, was approached to finance the production.

Lord Rothermere had been one of Diaghilev's last patrons, inspired by his relationships with the dancers Hélène Komarova and Alice Nikitina. At the present time he was much involved in international politics as an advocate of the reunification of Hungary and as an unofficial liaison with Hitler.[2] Nikitina, popular in London, was invited to star in the new ballet as a guest artist. After Diaghilev's death she had appeared in Cochran's revues of the early thirties, and in the London season of Les Ballets 1933. When de Basil asked her to join the cast, she was in Milan being coached by Luisa Tetrazzini for her operatic debut as Gilda in *Rigoletto*, which took place in Palermo in 1938.

Action

Le Lion amoureux was based on La Fontaine's fable of the same name. In a room at court the Queen is having her portrait painted. Besides the painter, several characters (a Master of Ceremony, a Flower Girl, a Flautist, and a Wig Maker) are part of the scene and interact and dance with one another. When the portrait is finished they examine it and dance in great celebration. A lion breaks into the scene, creating a big commotion and frightening the courtiers away. Some of the Queen's servants try, unsuccessfully, to capture it. However, when the lion sees the portrait of the Queen, he falls in love with her. The Queen dances, and seduces him; love-struck, he is easily chained. The courtiers celebrate the occasion as the lion turns out to be a young suitor in disguise. The "lion" and the Queen lead the whole court in a grand finale.

206

Music

Rathaus had been a student of Franz Schreker in Vienna and Berlin and settled in London in 1934. During his stay in Berlin his teacher regarded him as a great hope for contemporary music. From 1940 until his death in 1954 he was a professor of composition at Queens College in New York. This was his second balletic venture. He had written one previous ballet, *Der letzte Pierrot*, produced in Berlin in 1927. According to the *Times*, the music for *Le Lion amoureux* was "mixed in style, now conventional and now 'modernistic.' But the composer at least knows how to write good tunes for dancing. Was it a coincidence that when the painter set to work on the Queen's portrait the music became reminiscent of *Tosca?*"[3]

Scenery and Costumes

Roy's design consisted of a court room opening on a garden with a balustrade in the background and the upper halves of three arches suspended from the theater ceiling. The costumes were in the style of Louis XIV. Although all the women wore short tutus, the Queen was dressed in a short chiffon skirt. Lichine had a realistic lion wig and clawlike gloves.

The decor and costumes by Pierre Roy were described in the *Times* as "mildly surrealistic, or to be blunt, rather silly, though the colouring is agreeable." Besides his many covers for *Vogue*, Roy is probably best remembered as the designer of Janine Charrat's version of *Jeu de cartes* for the Ballets des Champs-Elysées in 1945.

Choreog-
raphy

From the beginning the work seemed ill-fated. Riabouchinska recalls how unhappy Lichine was to have to invent a ballet so quickly, especially since he had never before worked with Nikitina. *Le Lion* was not a success. It was confusing and not even the program notes helped to elucidate the story. Coton commented that the "first third of the action was occupied with a series of episodic encounters between the Master of Ceremony, the Portrait Painter, a Flower Girl, a Wig Maker and a Flautist, the validity of any one of these figures (except the Portraitist) in the action was never made clear by either the scenario or dancing sequences."[4] The writer of the "Sitter Out" complained that the program never made it clear that the lion was a young man in disguise.[5] According to Haskell, in the finale the cast "seem to mock the public."[6] Probably, since the dénouement was not clear, it seemed to the audience that the dancers had been performing a farce. Its best choreography was Lichine's solo as the lion. He entered leaping backwards, and his movements, according to Coton, were "vaguely allied to the traditional action of lions—much ferocious displaying of teeth, cracking of jaws and luxurious rollings around the scene."[7] Lichine tried to take advantage of Nikitina's line and beautiful arabesque, and the *Times* noted that despite the weakness of her choreography, "she danced with the piquant elegance that has always marked her performances."[8] Riabouchinska and Lazowski were better provided for in their little solos.

Critics

The ballet was dropped from the repertory after the fourth performance. It received one favorable review—from Haskell, writing in the *Daily Telegraph*: "This ballet is the first work to be seen at Covent Garden for a long time in which all the elements have been planned together and the first under these conditions attempted by Lichine."[9] Haskell was forgetting Lichine's second ballet, *Les Imaginaires*.

207

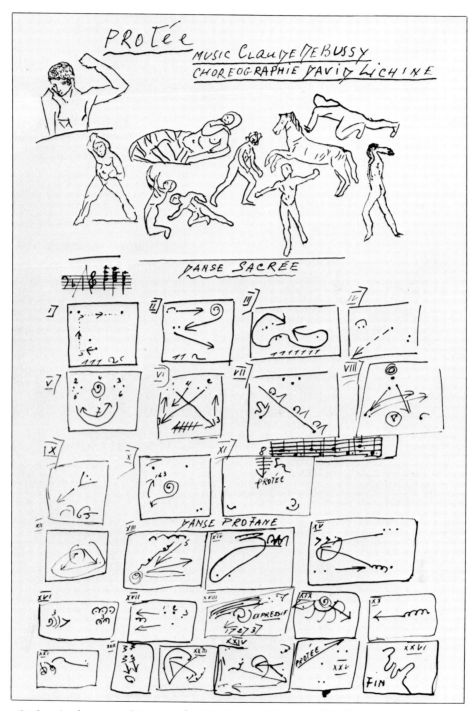

Lichine's choreographic notes for *Protée*, reproduced in *The Home*, an Australian periodical, December 1938.

June 1938–May 1939

THROUGHOUT the first months of 1938 the press in both London and New York devoted considerable attention to the fate of the two rival Ballets Russes companies. The Battle of the Ballets became an artistic and social war that involved some of the most prominent artists and personalities of the time.

In March an announcement was made by the *New York Times* of the unexpected attempt to merge both factions. The new organization, under a merger agreement instigated by Sol Hurok, was to consist of de Basil's company and the newly formed Massine–Blum Ballet Russe de Monte Carlo and was to retain the name Ballet Russe de Monte Carlo. Although Hurok was now only interested in managing Massine's new company, he wanted to acquire the best elements of de Basil—that is, a famous roster and a popular repertory, but without de Basil as general director. An agreement was actually signed on April 15, at the office of Perkins, Malone and Washburn in New York. According to the *New York Times*,[1] the proposed company would have Julius Fleischmann, former president of World Art, Inc., as president, with Serge Denham as vice-president and director, René Blum as co-director, Massine as head of the artistic council, and Prince Serge Obolensky as secretary. The board of governors included Fleischmann, Denham, de Basil, Mrs. E. Gerry Chadwick, Chauncey McCormick, Henry Clifford, Mrs. Otto H. Kahn, Mrs. Cameron Clark, Boris Sergievsky, Baron de Gunzburg, Watson Washburn, and Leonard Hanna. Sol Hurok was in charge of the American tour and would also take part in the direction of the company's annual London season at Covent Garden. The company was to include eighty dancers, fourteen of them principals; three conductors, with Efrem Kurtz as music director; and a repertory of one hundred and ten productions.

In the *New York Times* de Basil was mentioned only as a member of the board of governors. But Bruce Ottley's announcement in the London *Times* a few days earlier had assigned him a larger role:

> The new company, which is to be known as United Art Incorporated, is to have a strong board of directors under the presidency of Mr. Fleischmann, an American business man. The management will be shared by Colonel de Basil and M. Denham with M. Massine as artistic director. M. René Blum, brother of the late Prime Minister of France, who has also been working in America with World Art, will be managing director during the company's annual visit to the Casino Theatre at Monte Carlo. Apart from the Monte Carlo season the company's tours will be in charge of Mr. S. Hurok.[2]

Soon, however, the efforts to assemble what Hurok envisioned as "the finest ballet company that . . . ever existed"[3] were abandoned. The merger agreement was signed by proxy in New York after de Basil had left for Germany. The coming-to-terms continued while de Basil's group played Berlin and Copenhagen, and Massine's played Monte Carlo; both companies were to meet in Paris on June 1 to reorganize and proceed to London for their first season together. However, even before Paris, problems arose concerning the roles and the power of different individuals, especially Hurok, Denham, de Basil, and Massine. De Basil was horrified to discover that according to the new agreement, which he had not signed personally (since he had already left New York for Berlin), he had relinquished his rights to produce Massine's *Symphonie fantastique*, *La Boutique fantasque*, *Le Tricorne*, and Fokine's *Le Coq d'or*. Since de Basil was not fluent in English, he claimed it was the fault of the translator for failing to make the terms of the agreement clear to him, and that he would never in his right mind have agreed to such a thing. (He had just emerged from a lawsuit against Massine over the rights to three of the ballets named, among others, and Fokine's work was his latest and greatest success.) He accused Universal Art of plotting in New York to get him out of the picture. This is probably why the *New York Times* and the London *Times* were so at odds in describing his position in the new company. Aggravating the situation were the increasing disagreements among the artists about who was dancing which roles and when, especially in those ballets that appeared in both repertories. Both factions threatened to withdraw, and the serious complications began.

In June, the *Times* announced a new lawsuit, by which Universal Art sought to restrain de Basil from producing the four ballets: *Le Coq d'or*, *Symphonie fantastique*, *La Boutique fantasque*, and *Le Tricorne*.[4] The American corporation justified this action with the agreement signed in April, whereby the Colonel had relinquished his rights to those ballets to the plaintiffs. On June 8, de Basil wrote a letter repudiating the contract with the assertion that if he had known what it contained he would not have allowed it to be signed on his behalf by a proxy.

In the end, de Basil was forced to sacrifice his position in order to save the company. When de Basil and his London committee realized that the situation was serious, he was advised to resign temporarily in order to preserve the company as an entity from Universal Art. The company was renamed Educational Ballets, Ltd., but now with Victor Dandré as chairman and director, Sevastianov as managing director, Grigoriev as assistant manager, and Fokine as chief choreographer. Baron d'Erlanger was the main financial backer of the new company, while Dandré's role was largely decorative. In an affidavit de Basil agreed that the proposed productions at Covent Garden were under the control of Educational Ballets, Ltd., and that the ballets owned by him had been sold to that company in October 1937. De Basil then proposed to bring a counterclaim for rescinding his agreement with Universal Art, Inc.; but the judge claimed that since Educational Ballets, Ltd., was not under de Basil's control and de Basil had nothing to do with the new season at Covent Garden, the judge could not bring Universal Art's injunction to prevent it from performing the ballets in question.[5] This was a shock to Hurok, who knew how de Basil felt about being the only man in power, and he never suspected the Colonel would step down under the circumstances. If this was a preconceived scheme from the very beginning, it failed. And so, de Basil's name did not appear on any advance notices for the forthcoming engagement.

211

Baron d'Erlanger and Riabouchinska at Covent Garden.

Y MAY, de Basil had completed all the contractual arrangements with C. A. Barrand, secretary and business manager of Covent Garden, and had secured the required three-month immigration permits for the company and its personnel.[6] This task had to be accomplished yearly and was not easy, considering that the majority of the company were stateless and thus held Nansen passports. Among those traveling to England with the company were Vera Nemtchinova, Pierre Vladimiroff (who, as in 1937, was to teach company class) and Felia Doubrovska, Prince Schervachidze, and the young Hungarian conductor Georg Solti. (Doubrovska, who had been a guest artist during the 1937 Covent Garden season, did not dance for the company in 1938 and was this time merely accompanying her husband.) Although they went to London under contract, Natalia Gontcharova, Giorgio de Chirico, and André Derain did not travel with the company. With the exception of Sevastianov and Baronova, who had arrived earlier in England from Berlin, the company was supposed to leave Paris for London on June 1. But legal complications that arose in London between de Basil and Universal Art, Inc. (formerly World Art) delayed the company's arrival until June 18, two days before opening night, leaving only one day for (intensive) rehearsals on the stage.

By now, anticipation for the new season was running high, fueled by newspaper headlines such as COVENT GARDEN'S MYSTERY SEASON OF RUSSIAN BALLET BY A NAMELESS COMPANY.[7] As usual, opening night found a distinguished audience assembled in wholehearted support of the company. The Russian ballet season had always been an occasion for London to present a display of summer fashion, and this season was no exception: the Royal Opera House was blazing with flowered dresses with bright, splashy patterns, life-size animal prints, feathers, wings and birds as headdresses, as well as umbrellalike cloaks.

The performance began twenty-five minutes late. The reviewer for the *Birmingham Post* wrote: "Yet apparently [*Le Coq d'or*] was the cause of considerable perturbation behind the scenes last night, and certainly it gave the occasion for tremendous gossip in the foyers during the first interval. The question was whether it could be performed at all, for, with a crowning touch of grotesquerie, *Le Coq d'or* had been taken to court."[8] It was not known until the last minute whether *Le Coq d'or* was going to be presented, although it was programed. That evening, the scenery was ready, the dancers were all impatiently waiting onstage as Covent Garden's lawyers, the company's lawyers, and other authorities gave the okay for the curtain to go up. The complications and the arguments, even until that very moment, were endless. Considering the last-minute difficulties the company faced, one wonders that opening night happened at all. Discussions had lasted the entire day, with talks continuing onstage even as the scenery was being put into place. When the curtain finally went up, the first applause came from backstage. Members of the audience, sensing its significance, joined in.

The evening's program consisted of *Les Sylphides* with Nemtchinova, Riabouchinska, Volkova, and Jasinski; *Le Coq d'or* with Riabouchinska and Baronova and two new dancers, Rostoff and Kosmovska; and *Aurora's Wedding* with the fairies' variations danced by Tresahar, Volkova, Razoumova, and Leontieva.

Although the soloists gave commendable performances, the corps de ballet was criticized for its lack of unanimity, particularly in *Les Sylphides*. Arnold Haskell wrote: "The first night was a misfortune; highly strung dancers (and public) kept waiting by a display of stupidity and ill manners from some one or other in authority. The magic of a first night had gone beyond recall, and Baronova, a great Baronova, and Riabouchinska as individuals alone saved the occasion and distinguished it by their brilliance."[9]

In the midst of this crisis, both ballerinas impressed critics and audience alike with a new depth in characterization and a fluency of movement that made their interpretations more memorable than ever. And as the season progressed, performances in general reached surprisingly high standards of style and discipline. No doubt the careless quality of the corps during the first performances was a result of the fact that until the first week of July, new dancers were still joining the company and were struggling to learn the choreography as they went onstage. In many cases, they were learning their parts for the next ballet during intermission. Unfortunately, Fokine had been involved in a car accident near Boulogne the week before the opening night in London and had to remain in France to give testimony in court about the incident, and therefore could not be in London for rehearsals.[10]

The year-long Fokine–de Basil association proved beneficial for both dancers and choreographer. Since leaving Diaghilev in 1914, Fokine had not had the opportunity to work steadily with a full-size professional company. He was now able to create new works, as well as to restage a number of his previous ballets under his strict supervision. Since his departure, most of these works had been deformed technically and stylistically by ballet masters and dancers alike. In reviving his ballets, Fokine's concern with detail, according to Riabouchinska, bordered on obsession: "Not only was he concerned about the steps, but about the slightest position of the arms and head, as well as facial expression." This attention to details of choreography, dramatic structure, and period style was evident in the 1938 revivals. When *Petrouchka* was presented on June 30, Francis Toye commented, "There seemed to emerge details, new or half forgotten, that lent exceptional vividness and point to certain details of the choreography,"[11] and the reviewer for the *Observer* felt the performance had "a rare assurance and a general smoothness that delighted."[12]

All of Fokine's revivals were highly praised. *Les Sylphides* was particularly cited for its dreamlike quality; according to the *Times* critic, the dancers' arms had the "roundness which has too often been lost in recent performances of the ballet."[13] Baronova has discussed the difference between the version danced before Fokine came to work with the company and the one enhanced by his supervision:

Basically choreographically, Grigoriev had revived the work correctly; nevertheless, the choreographer emphasized his authentic interpre-

213

Petrouchka: Yurek Lazowski.

tation and above all arms. The tendency before Fokine rehearsed us was to exaggerate the arm movements in a pseudo-*Swan Lake* style. The first time that he took us in a rehearsal he was scandalized and yelled that we were supposed to be sylphs and not swans and consequently that elbows did not bend down like the wings of a bird. He explained that it was just a tender soft quivering as if the arms were breathing. Another example was the male variation with mannerisms such as bringing his hand on the knee and stroking it down to the toe, something that Fokine rejected as not his, demanding instead a poetic *port de bras* forward. By the time we danced these roles, they had accumulated a lot of affectations that came from different interpreters during the gap between when Fokine left Diaghilev and when he came to us. Until he came to the company people didn't give a real thought of what the whole thing was all about. It took its creator to make clear to us that it was a conversation among the sylphs and all the little creatures that were perched somewhere out there in the forest. All the gestures have to be expressive of the searching for them, of the talking to them, responding, listening to their whispering. Tatiana's Prelude in every movement was a conversation. Now she is in this corner, now in the other, or she has heard something and rushes back as if moved by the breeze. Today the work presents the same problems that it presented to us before Fokine came. Unfortunately, it has become a boring curtain raiser. Dancers

do not know what it is all about and it seems as if every gesture was a pose
à la Taglioni. It has no atmosphere, just a classroom exercise. Stylistically
as well as technically it is a very difficult ballet. For every relevé one had
to slide and travel to project the sensation of constant moving and float-
ing, like willow trees moved by the air.

Riabouchinska, commenting on her by now legendary interpretation of the Prelude,
said: "There are details, which according to Fokine are key for the work's poetic
effect and which are systematically ignored. One of them is at the end of the Prelude.
That moment when one rushes upstage, back to the audience and arms raised to the
forest, dancers immediately bourrée in a semicircle to face the audience, and then,
facing straight to the audience, they continue to bourrée to center stage where they
finally take their last pose. In this passage Fokine demanded not to turn to the audience, but instead, to bourrée backwards—in a cambré position—from upstage to
center stage, with arms softly coming to the side as one ecstatically looked into the
stars. Then, almost by accident, by surprise, to turn to take the last pose before rushing off. Balanchine knew and understood Fokine, for when he staged and coached us
in *Les Sylphides* in 1932 he would also emphasize this passage."

As during the previous year, the outstanding feature of summer theatrical life in
London was the appearance of two major ballet companies. On July 12 the Massine–
Blum Ballet Russe de Monte Carlo opened at Drury Lane, presenting three new Massine works: *Gaîté Parisienne*, *Seventh Symphony*, and *Nobilissima Visione*. Educational
Ballets (the new de Basil company minus de Basil) presented *Cendrillon*, choreographed by Fokine; *Protée*, choreographed by Lichine; but *La Nymphe endormie*, with
choreography by Fokine and designs by Derain, to the music of Couperin, did not see
the light.

In spite of the novelties introduced by both companies, the highlights of the
season were Fokine's ballets, some of which were in both repertories. As Haskell
noted: "Fokine, the creator of modern Russian ballet, is the outstanding figure of the
present season, both sides of Bow Street. His works form the bulk of every repertory.
No man can always be inspired, but even at his least inspired his work has an academic perfection that gives satisfaction and is an invaluable lesson to dancers."[14]

The confrontation of the two Russian ballet companies was resented by many of
their admirers, who were disheartened at not having one nucleus that would include
such artists as Fokine, Massine, Baronova, Danilova, Riabouchinska, Toumanova, and
Lichine. Many people sincerely felt that the personal interests and personality conflicts that had caused the schism were also contributing to the artistic disintegration
of the Russian ballet. Ninette de Valois commented: "It is possible to regret the formation of a second company, leading to a divided attention. Such a step might
enlarge but not necessarily strengthen the hold on the market economically, and it
has added the danger of possibly weakening the direction and the artistic aims in the
relation to the whole."[15] Balletomanes would visit both theaters every evening in
order to see their favorite dancers in their famous roles; during intermissions they

215

would exchange seats (and critiques), gliding across the foyer that was Bow Street. The Battle of the Ballets captured the attention not only of English newspapers and journals but of the *New York Times*, the Cairo *Sphinx*, the Bombay *Illustrated Weekly of India*, the Johannesburg *Star*, the Buenos Aires *La Nación*, and many others.

During the Educational Ballets' season the company visited the BBC studios in Alexandra Palace three times. On July 3 a rehearsal of *Protée* was televised featuring Lichine, Osato, Adrianova, Denisova, Lerina, and Sobinova, with Solti conducting. On the tenth, the company performed *Aurora's Wedding*, featuring Nemtchinova, Riabouchinska, Volkova, Petroff, Lichine, and Jasinski; on August 7, a memorable performance of *Les Sylphides* was led by Nemtchinova, Riabouchinska, Leontieva, and Petroff, followed by a talk by Fokine.

Throughout the season, rumors circulated that the company would either tour the United States, this time under the management of Fortune Gallo, or go to Australia. The tour had become of great concern to many dancers. More and more there was talk of war and it seemed obvious by then, after Hitler had annexed Austria and claimed the Sudetenland, that no one could prevent Germany from engulfing eastern Europe. Under the threats of war, the non-Russian and non-European dancers preferred to be away from the Continent, with access to their families in the United States, Canada, Cuba, or Argentina. However, the majority of the company's members feared for the safety of their families who might be stranded in Europe.

After the cancellation of a United States tour, the company sailed on the *Maloja* for Australia on August 21.[16] Among the cities visited en route were Port Said and Bombay, the latter being of special interest as the home of the world-renowned Hindu dancer Menaka, who performed with her troupe for the Russian artists.

The arrival in Australia of the Covent Garden Russian Ballet (as the Educational

Sevastianov, Lichine, Dolin, and Riabouchinska.

Members of the company sightseeing in New Zealand.

Ballets was named especially for the tour) was the most decisive event in the dance
history of the continent. It placed Melbourne and Sydney, along with London,
Monte Carlo, and New York, among the great ballet centers. For the first time a
troupe of international repute was to remain in the country for a period of several
months, encouraging the growing appreciation of ballet, the seeds of which had been
planted by the earlier visits of a variety of individual dancers and troupes. Credit
must also be given to the journalistic skills of Arnold Haskell, who was accompanying
the company once again. Now Australia and New Zealand could be exposed to the
artistry of some of the world's greatest dancers, as well as an extensive repertory that
included works by Petipa, Fokine, Massine, Nijinska, and Balanchine. The most
important feature was the presence of Fokine in his only visit to the continent.
Lichine's *Prodigal Son* had its world premiere in Sydney, and in addition to the many
Australian premieres, Dolin's *Bolero*, a solo, was also given.

In Australia and New Zealand, the company enjoyed a more restful schedule
than it had had during the American tours: ten weeks in Melbourne, nine in Sydney,
two in Adelaide, and seven in New Zealand. This gave the ensemble the opportunity
to present longer seasons in every city and to enjoy proper facilities for practice and
rehearsal.[17]

The tour was a triumph. It had opened in Melbourne at His Majesty's Theatre
with *Les Sylphides, Cendrillon,* and *Aurora's Wedding* on September 28. (This was the
same day Hitler invited Britain, France, and Italy to the meeting that culminated in

217

218

ABOVE: Dolin and Riabouchinska in the "Bluebird" pas de deux, in Melbourne.
RIGHT: Baronova as the Swan Queen.

the Munich Pact. This settlement delayed the war for eleven months but was considered by Harold Nicolson, a prominent member of British Parliament, to be a betrayal of the Czechs and a surrender to the Third Reich.[18] Churchill's feelings were of an "unmitigated defeat.") For opening night the theater was decorated with an exact copy of the floral arrangement at the top of the main staircase at Covent Garden—it had been packed in ice and sent to Australia as a tribute to the company. (It was rumored that Baron d'Erlanger had paid for it.) The tour closed with a memorable midnight farewell performance at Sydney's Theatre Royal on April 27. The performance was given by only Baronova, Riabouchinska, Dolin, and Lichine, supported by a few soloists, without a corps de ballet. The program consisted of solos and pas de deux from *Les Sylphides*; *L'Après-midi d'un faune* as a solo for Lichine; Dolin's *Bolero*; *Swan Lake* Act II with Baronova and Dolin; *Jeux d'enfants* with Riabouchinska and Lichine; and *Aurora's Wedding*. Eight members of the company chose to defect to Australia: Kira Abricossova, Raissa Kousnetzova, Tamara Tchinarova (where she later met and married the actor Peter Finch), Edouard Borovansky, Serge Bousloff, Valery Shaievsky, Edouard Sobichevsky, and Valentin Zeglovsky. Borovansky was later to found the Borovansky Ballet, which provided the genesis for the Australian Ballet. On their way to London, Baronova, Riabouchinska, Dolin, and Lichine, aided by other members of the company, gave two recitals at McKinley High School Auditorium in Honolulu. For these divertissement performances, Dorati conducted the Honolulu Symphony Orchestra.

219

PROTÉE

Ballet in one act; music, *Danse sacrée et Danse profane* by Claude Debussy; libretto by David Lichine and Henry Clifford; choreography by David Lichine; set design by Giorgio de Chirico, executed by Prince A. Schervachidze; costume design by Giorgio de Chirico, executed by Madame Karinska; premiere July 5, 1938, at Covent Garden, London, conducted by Antal Dorati.

ORIGINAL CAST

| Protée | David Lichine | The Maidens | Anna Adrianova, Alexandra Denisova, Sono Osato, Lisa Serova, Natasha Sobinova |

After his collaboration with Lichine in *Francesca da Rimini* and *Le Lion amoureux*, Henry Clifford and his wife, Esther, maintained a closer rapport with the choreographer and other dancers. At the Cliffords' villa in Florence one sunny afternoon

Lichine got the idea for *Protée*. The residence was surrounded by a cypress garden and had a swimming pool with shell-shaped fountains. Magnificent statues encircled the pool and garden, imparting a classical atmosphere. A group of friends, which included Riabouchinska, Baronova, and Sevastianov, leisurely gathered around the pool; Lichine, who had just dived into the pool, emerged and, jokingly personifying Proteus, walked around the garden improvising steps and classical poses and then dove back into the water. What had started as a jest soon developed into the schema of a ballet. Lichine and Clifford developed a scenario intended as an intimate piece that would serve as the basis for a choreographic essay rooted in Greek classicism. The libretto revolved around five nymphs who come to a temple on the seashore to evoke Proteus.

Music The choice of music narrowed to Debussy. He was one of Lichine's favorite composers; moreover, his preference for ancient musical modes, clearly manifested in his piano preludes *Danseuses de Delphes* and in his orchestration of Satie's *Trois Gymno-pédies*, made him ideal. After a period of musical research with Clifford, Lichine decided on *Danse sacrée et Danse profane* of 1904, for chromatic harp and strings. Not only did the music capture the atmosphere, it fit the two-part scenario.

Action The ballet is divided into two scenes, the first danced to the *Danse sacrée*.

As the curtain rises, the strings open before the theme of the solo harp is introduced. Five nymphs appear by the seashore to evoke, ritualistically, the appearance of Proteus. In prayerlike attitude each dances in turn to the harp solo as the others dance in accompaniment, weaving in and out with languid steps. From the bottom of the sea two horses emerge, facing the audience, drawing a chariot carrying Proteus, one arm resting on his head.

Danse profane: Proteus steps between two pillars center stage and descends several stone steps onto the stage. As he dances his introductory solo, the horses return to the ocean. The nymphs dance around him, and he takes turns partnering each one. Each nymph takes advantage of her duo with Proteus to implore him to reveal her destiny. He finally evades the nymphs, dons a pair of antlers that he finds by the temple, runs across the stage, and dives into the waves. The five nymphs form an imploring group by the shore, praying for his return.

Scenery and Costumes As designer, Lichine, following Clifford's suggestion, chose de Chirico because he had always shown a predilection for antiquity. De Chirico accepted the commission and in June, after the designs had been finished, traveled to London to meet with his collaborators and to supervise the reproduction of his maquettes. The decor featured a temple by the sea. The stage wings depict portions of classical constructions and, across upstage back and in a semicircle, an ocean edged with high waves. In the middle, and next to the waves, were two columns linked on top by a pointed structure, with a piece of crimson drape hanging in between. On the horizon a distant temple appears to stage left; to the right, a barely visible village on a hilltop. The scene is dominated by gold, silver, slate blue, and white.

Proteus wore a sleeveless leotard, the front in silver and the back a dark flesh color, appliquéd and with epaulettes of slate blue, white, and brown leather simulat-

220

ing the patterns of waves; and white, ochre, and brown in the back. One nymph wore a sleeveless white silk dress with smocking at the waist of a short-kilted skirt bound with three bars of Petersham ribbon; the neck and shoulder straps were in gold braid; on the chest was a mysterious cup-and-ball pattern in silver grey satin outlined in gold braid. Another was dressed in beige crepe with extended epaulettes of white and sand leather appliqué creating a wave pattern; an undulant band of similar leather was appliquéd down the front and down the spine. A third, sleeveless dress had a lemon yellow crepe basque ending in a flare, and a primrose-colored crepe skirt, cut high to reveal the left thigh; the chest and back were appliquéd with stylized palm fronds of brown kid; pleated mushroom-colored drapery hung across the right shoulder, on which there was a stiffened knot of white and brown material. Another sleeveless dress consisted of a Cambridge blue crepe bodice with a square neck bordered in stitched white kid; three vertical bands of a similar kid went down the chest; a panel of pleated aquamarine material fell from the left shoulder to the waist with two padded mushroom-colored pieces of material falling across the right shoulder from the left; the flared skirt was of a cream-colored crepe worn over a dove grey underskirt and appliquéd with typical Chiricoesque volutes in sand color. The last dress was an exact replica of this one, but emphasized green, pink, and blue. Each nymph wore a wig made of ribbons.

The mise en scène and costumes harmonized with the sensuousness and simplicity of Debussy's music and Lichine's choreography. As in de Chirico's other stage designs for ballet and opera (*Le Bal* in 1929, *Pulcinella* in 1930, *Les Bacchantes* in 1937, *I Puritani* in 1938, and *Bacchus and Ariane*, also in 1938), the emphasis was on broad, simple, and vigorous forms. His ever-present motif of classical ruins also appeared in *Protée*, and his main achievement here was the creation of a mood that enhanced the dreamlike effect.

Choreography

Choreographically Lichine borrowed from Greek bas-relief the angular arms and legs in profile, though no attempt was made at actual historical reconstruction. Even though the ballet tried to recapture or suggest an archaic atmosphere of ancient Hellenic dance, it was consistently danced in ballet terms. Its structure was rooted in ensembles, solos, and pas de deux. As opposed to what Fokine and Nijinsky had done in *Narcisse, Daphnis et Chloé*, and *L'Après-midi d'un faune*, which were danced barefoot or in sandals, Lichine employed strict classical pointe technique. In contrast to the rigidity of *L'Après-midi d'un faune*, *Protée* was set in constant movement.

Lichine employed only six dancers, each in the capacity of soloist and all interacting by dancing with and opposite one another. This did not give the impression of a spectacle aimed at theatrical presentation, but rather of a spontaneous communication in terms of dance among the characters. One of its attractions was the feeling it produced—as if a voyeur had caught sight of an intimate gathering of a god with his nymphs.

Except for the angularity of the movements, the poses in profile, and the rounded, clenched fists facing in, the choreography made use of classical technique that stressed purity of line and plasticity of movement.

221

A rare sequence of performance photographs featuring Adrianova, Denisova, Osato, Serova, Sobinova, and Dolin; set by de Chirico.

Critics   The ballet was very well received. The critic for *Mercury* called it "a perfect miniature, with no stylistic incongruities, aesthetically satisfying within its restricted limits and a very sympathetic interpretation of Debussy's music . . . it is a 'spectacle' pure and simple, not in the sense that *Schéhérazade* is a spectacle for the uninitiated, but a spectacle for connoisseurs: and as such, it is perfect."[1] Arnold Haskell, writing in *The Bystander* on July 13, felt that "[for] the first time Lichine seems to have seen a work clearly as a whole and not to have intruded his tendency for theatrical flamboyance." Francis Toye found the work charming and complimented Lichine for contriving "a delightful entrance for himself, with his two horses rising realistically from the sea, and one of the most effective leaping exits seen on the stage since Nijinsky vanished at the end of *Spectre de la Rose*."[2] He thought Lichine was admirable as Protée, and of the cast he said: "Headed by Sono Osato and Anna Adrianova they gave a performance which, for unanimity, grace and accurate poise could scarcely have been bettered. It was a triumph for five young dancers. . . ."[3]

Now that Lichine was establishing himself as a choreographer, he realized the need to mold his own dancers. In *Protée* he resorted to young, less important members of the company who lately had attracted attention in their performances in small solos: Adrianova, Osato, and Serova. To these three Lichine added the two promising fifteen-year-old Canadian discoveries, Denisova and Sobinova. (None of the female members of the cast were Russians; Adrianova and Osato were Americans and Serova was English.)

The role of Proteus was later danced by Dolin and Jasinski. The work remained in the repertory until 1941, when it was presented during the American tour.

CENDRILLON

Ballet in three scenes; music by Baron Frédéric d'Erlanger; choreography by Michel Fokine; set design by Natalia Gontcharova, executed by Prince A. Schervachidze; costumes designed by Natalia Gontcharova, executed by Madame Karinska; premiere July 19, 1938, at Covent Garden, London, conducted by Antal Dorati.

ORIGINAL CAST

Cinderella	Tatiana Riabouchinska	The Prince	David Lichine
The Two Ugly Sisters	Marian Ladré,	The Lord of the Mountain	Yurek Lazowski
	H. Algeranoff	The Lord of the Vale	Roman Jasinski
The Good Fairy	Tamara Grigorieva	The Chamberlain	Dimitri Rostoff
The Cat	Raissa Kouznetsova	A Fair Peasant Girl	Anna Volkova

A Dark Peasant Girl	Sono Osato	Lords and Ladies	Mlles Abricossova,
Heralds	Mlles Chabelska, Kosmovska,	of the Court	Novikova, Obidenna,
	Orlova, Tresahar		Razoumova, Roussova, Tchinarova
Retinue of the Fairy	Mlles Adrianova,		MM. Belsky, Borovansky, Runanine,
	Denisova, Leontieva, Lerina,		Shaievsky, Vlassoff, Zeglovsky
	Nelidova, Osato, Serova,	Peasants	Mlles Adrianova, Denisova,
	Sobinova, Volkova, Wassilieva		Leontieva, Lerina, Lvova, Nelidova,
	MM. Alexandroff, Andahazy, Bousloff,		Serova, Sobinova, Wassilieva
	Ismailoff		MM. Alexandroff, Alonso, Andahazy,
Denizens of Fairyland	MM. Alonso,		Bousloff, Dzikovsky, Ismailoff, Kosloff,
	Dzikovsky, Kosloff, Lipatoff,		Lipatoff, Matouchak, Sobichevsky
	Matouchak, Sobichevsky		

When the merger plans between de Basil and Massine fell through, de Basil felt that it was necessary to announce an important production for the forthcoming London summer season, when the Massine–Blum Ballet Russe de Monte Carlo would also be appearing in London. The subject chosen was Perrault's story of Cinderella. There would be a new score by Baron Frédéric d'Erlanger, who was also to finance the ballet; Fokine was to devise the choreography, and Gontcharova was commissioned to design the scenery and costumes.

Rehearsals began in April in Berlin's Scala Theatre, resumed in Paris after the Copenhagen engagement, and were concluded at Covent Garden.

Several previous ballets had been based on the tale of Cinderella, the most important being Petipa's 1893 version, with undistinguished music by Baron Fittinghof-Schell, in which Pierina Legnani had introduced the famous thirty-two fouettés. (Fokine's 1938 version, of course, predated the Prokofiev score, which was first produced in 1945 at the Bolshoi.)

Falling as it did midway through the crisis of the first split season, the evening of *Cendrillon*'s premiere provided much-needed festivity. There was a party for celebrity guests and the company in the foyer of Covent Garden before the performance. That evening's program was dedicated as a Michel Fokine Festival and opened with *Les Sylphides*, with Baronova, Riabouchinska, Leontieva, and Petroff; followed with *Cendrillon*; and continued with *Le Spectre de la rose*, with Baronova and Petroff, and *Prince Igor*, led by Grigorieva, Nelidova, and Shabelevsky. After the performance d'Erlanger gave a dinner-ball for the cast and friends of the company.

Action *Cendrillon*, like *Coq d'or*, was performed in one act and three scenes.

Scene One: Towards the end of the Prelude the curtain goes up and the Prince's Chamberlain delivers the invitation for the ball to the two Ugly Sisters; they take it to Cinderella in the kitchen and taunt her because she is not invited. Cinderella's cat emerges from underneath the table and plays as the two sisters dance to a humoresque, putting on their corsets and making Cinderella help them to dress. When they are ready to go, the two practice their curtsies and leave; Cinderella closes the door

225

behind them and stays alone, disconsolate, with her faithful cat. She now dances a variation, holding a hand mirror. A storm breaks and in the midst of terrifying lightning three knocks are heard at the door. Cinderella opens it to find an old lady enveloped in a grey cloak and hood. She invites the stranger to sit by the fire. When the storm dies down, the guest discards her cloak to reveal herself as the alluring Good Fairy, with wand in hand and conical hat. She dances and then brings in her retinue, who carry Cinderella's ballgown and slippers (she has heretofore appeared in character shoes matching the color of her dress). The fairies dance and help her to dress as she repeatedly stands up, then sits on the bench, astonished by her own transformation: when her pointe shoes are put on, she runs forward on pointe as if it is a feat of magic. The Denizens of Fairyland, Cinderella's escort, enter and support her in arabesques and turns, then lift her up in the air as she looks around in amazement. They put her back on the floor and the Good Fairy tries to lead her outside by the hand, but she resists as if frightened by the unexpected; soon she is overwhelmed by excitement and runs out the door. The scene immediately darkens, and torches appear to illuminate an enchanted moonlit landscape with a huge pumpkin, stage left. Cinderella dances and, in grande écarte, is passed from one to the other of her escorts. As they all dance, the pumpkin divides at the command of the Good Fairy, and a carriage drawn by winged white horses appears from within, on a second level, against a thunderous blue-black sky, giving the impression that the coach is suspended in air. Cinderella is lifted by her feet to reach the second level in order to enter her carriage and, once she is inside, it flies off followed by the Good Fairy's retinue, also on the second level, as if gliding across the sky. A drop depicting the carriage's flight is lowered and the orchestra plays the interlude to describe the journey to the ball.

Scene Two: The curtain goes up on the ballroom, where the courtiers are performing their dance. Four heralds with trumpets enter through a curtain and announce the arrival of the Prince. The curtain is drawn as the Prince descends a spiral staircase. He greets the guests and performs a variation, which he interrupts to salute several ladies and then resumes. The atmosphere changes to one of mystery when the Good Fairy arrives, wand in hand, as Cinderella's horses are seen through a colonnade terrace in a second level of the ballroom. The guests are agog with curiosity when Cinderella arrives sitting on her heels, lifted up in the air by two footmen; her cat, also lifted by two footmen, is brought in close behind. Cinderella dances and the Prince is entranced. He asks her to dance and they perform a pas de deux. When the pas de deux is over, the Denizens of Fairyland dance in the background and Cinderella dances another variation. The Lord of the Mountain and the Lord of the Vale each perform a dance and then everyone joins in a general dance. The clock strikes midnight; in her flight Cinderella loses the slipper that her cat had untied just before her departure. The Prince tries to follow her but is stopped by the cat, who searches for the slipper; she returns with it in her mouth and gives it to him. Cinderella has already departed in her carriage and the Prince presses the shoe to his heart. The curtain falls and the second interlude is played.

Scene Three: To the last phrase of the interlude, the curtain goes up on the castle square. The Chamberlain, in the presence of the Prince, is conducting the shoe-fitting trial. The Ugly Sisters attempt the impossible but end up on the floor, looking ridiculous. Cinderella has just arrived and anxiously looks the people over. She breaks through the cordon of guards and rushes to the Chamberlain, imploring to be included. Although the Chamberlain refuses because of her poor and shabby appearance, the Prince intervenes and conducts the test himself. The Prince holds her by one hand raised above her head and, while on pointe on one foot, her leg dégagés several times front to meet the extension of the Prince's arm, and then poses in penché arabesque, until finally she allows him to fit the shoe, leading to a pas de deux. Everyone rejoices in a general dance. Cinderella and the Prince exit and the villagers and peasants perform a dance. When they return (she is already in royal robes), the Prince and Cinderella are held aloft in profile, center stage, wearing long trains stretching out behind them. The Good Fairy is also held aloft, behind and facing them, as she places the crowns on their heads. The apotheosis leads to a symmetrical grand finale, which ends with all the main characters lining up facing the audience, with the corps behind them. To the last chord of the music they all finish and pose in attitude front. Curtain.

Choreography In his adaptation of the fairy tale, Fokine adhered as closely as possible to the original Perrault story. The only major changes were the introduction of Cinderella's cat, which accompanies her to the ball to untie her ballet shoe, making its loss plausible, and using men *en travesti* for the parts of the Ugly Sisters. The detailed plot required a great deal of pantomime, but the dance sequences were not used merely as divertissements in the manner of Petipa. Rather, Fokine believed in a fusing of mime with expressive dancing that aided the advancement of the action. Pointes were first introduced in the ballet by the Good Fairy and were worn by Cinderella from the moment she comes under the Good Fairy's spell. All the fairies danced on pointe. The choreography of the second scene was traditional in approach; Fokine opted here for the formality of ballet classicism. The variations employed classical academic enchaînements, including a series of cabrioles battues for the Prince, and the pas de deux was based on the traditional adagio technique. However, what saved Cinderella's variations and the pas de deux in this scene from a constricted classicism so atypical of Fokine was Riabouchinska's superimposition of the choreographer's emotional sensibility, which coincided with the character and story development. The scene varied from the classical structure insofar as the variations and the pas de deux were not in sequence; instead they were designed to further the plot.

Choreographically, the highlights in the first scene were Cinderella's variation with the mirror, which served as an internal monologue; the scene of the two stepsisters, played by male dancers *en travesti*, preparing themselves to go to the ball, which provided a touch of burlesque, especially when they try on corsets in front of the mirrors and practice their curtsies; and the Good Fairy's variation. The second scene's high points were the courtiers' dance as the curtain goes up, and the variations and pas de deux of Cinderella and the Prince. The third scene offered the fitting of the shoe and pas de deux as the choreographic climax of the ballet.

227

LEFT: The invitation to the ball; Algeranoff and Ladré as the Ugly Sisters. BELOW: Grigorieva as the Good Fairy. BOTTOM: Cinderella (Riabouchinska) and her Cat (Kouznetsova).

ABOVE: Cinderella's coach departs for the ball. RIGHT: Cinderella (Riabouchinska) and the Prince (Lichine).

*Scenery
and
Costumes*

Gontcharova transported the story from its conventional eighteenth-century setting to the Middle Ages. The color scheme employed more subtle shades than the unrelentingly brilliant ones she had used in *Le Coq d'or*. The Good Fairy's dress was of a bright pink-over-white tulle with appliqués of silver flowers; the Prince's suit was mauve and amethyst satin embroidered in silver. Cinderella had three costumes: a pale, dove grey dress, which was a stylization of rags—plain, below the knee, with uneven length; a ball gown of pink tulle; and, for the grand finale, an underdress of royal blue brocade with silver trimming and a full-length polonaise of opal blue taffeta with appliquéd silver leaves.

The first scene shows half the exterior of a gabled house with clothes hanging in a garden. The center stage depicts the kitchen with a low, sloping, beamed ceiling and wooden floors; the only furnishings are a bench and a table covered with a cloth. At stage left there is a wall with a door. The following scene takes place on a two-level stage. It is a lilac-moonlight landscape with a huge pumpkin to the left, on the ground level, which splits open to reveal the golden carriage with white, winged horses on the higher level as if suspended in the sky. The peach-tinted ballroom has a second-level gothic-colonnaded terrace open to a crescent moon sky. It is brightly illuminated except for the moment when Cinderella arrives. The third scene takes place in the castle square with the castle wall and turret depicted. Gontcharova designed two front curtains: one shows Cinderella's broom and slippers and the Prince's coat of arms, and the other shows the distant carriage in flight through the sky. Newman complimented the designer's work as "that combination of extravagant fantasy and good taste of which the Russians seem to have the secret."[1] Richard Buckle, however, writing in the new magazine *Ballet*, did not like the designer's conception, commenting that "Gontcharova, a naive designer admirable in *Coq d'or* and *Ygrouchka*, where naiveté is required, when faced with the courtly splendours of a formal scene, becomes as unbridled as a housewife with a passion for royalty."[2]

Music

D'Erlanger's music lacked point and definition, but Ernest Newman and Francis Toye felt it fulfilled its purpose well.

D'Erlanger based his score strictly on the development of the action. The first scene was preceded by a prelude and the second and third by interludes that allowed for the change of scenery. The two interludes depicted the carriage's flight to and from the palace. The action was clearly expressed in the music: the thundering of the storm, the knocks on Cinderella's door, the trumpets to announce the arrival of the Prince, the clock striking midnight. Ernest Newman felt that it went "accommodatingly with the story and the action yet never attracting special attention to itself, and above all, never raising any of those plaguey problems of psychological characterisation that seem to upset some people so much when they are confronted with them in ballet."[3] Edwin Evans in the *Daily Mail* commented that it "sometimes recalls Baron d'Erlanger's earlier fairy tale ballet,"[4] although this was less apparent in the waltz tempo which is used for the pas de deux in the second scene and the dance of the villagers and peasants in the third. However, the critic of the *Times* found the score for *Les Cent Baisers* more successful.[5] Although all the London critics agreed that it was pleasant and melodious, and that it served its purpose, Francis Toye, writing for the *Daily Telegraph*, commented that "it could gain in fact from a few more touches of brilliance and hardness, because a greater variety of colour would thereby be achieved."[6]

Critics   While certain critics praised Fokine's approach, others considered the ballet to be static and slow-moving by contemporary standards. Ernest Newman wrote: "The production is intellectually one and indivisible down even to the drop curtain. . . . The term ballet, however, has changed its meaning a good deal in recent years; and perhaps the proper term for much of *Cendrillon* would be pantomime in the good sense of the term."[7]

Although choreographically the ballet did not attempt to present any new approach, Fokine's treatment of the story received high compliments. Francis Toye felt that the choreographer had "provided some unusually deft touches of which one, the refusal of Cinderella to let anybody but the Prince himself try on the slipper, was exceptionally charming and successful," and another, the idea to "treat the two ugly sisters like dames. . . . "[8] Newman stated that "by a daring stroke of genius which we cannot sufficiently admire, Fokine has enlarged the appeal of Cinderella by endowing her with Dick Whittington's cat, in the present instance an engaging little animal, charmingly played by Raissa Kouznetsova."[9]

One of the sustaining features of the ballet was Riabouchinska's portrayal of Cinderella. Fokine very much enjoyed working with her. In *Cendrillon*, he gave her a mime dance role with both pathos and comedy. Her delicate blond beauty was the quintessence of fairy-tale heroine. Newman acclaimed the entire cast: "Riabouchinska, with a part to play that gives her the fullest opportunity to devote her art to the exploitation of her own personality, is a delicious Cinderella. Lichine is a true Prince Charming, and Grigorieva the best of good fairies. The two Ugly Step-Sisters, Messrs. Ladré and Algeranoff, show us, as the Russian ballet always does, that farce is most effective when it stops just short of the limit of whole-hoggery."[10]

On July 15, 1939, the sixteen-year-old Denisova danced her first Cinderella. According to Beryl de Zoete, the critic for the *Daily Telegraph*, "It was beautifully danced, but one realized for the first time how much the charm of the part has hitherto depended on the fanciful and touching interpretation of Riabouchinska."[11]

Indeed, so distinctive was Riabouchinska's personality that the roles she created were impossible for other dancers to interpret adequately. It was not a question of technique, but of stage presence. In 1936 Deaken wrote: "She gives to all her roles an aura that can only be called a Riabouchinska aura. Let any other dancer appear in any one of her roles and it becomes simply a dance done by someone wearing Riabouchinska's costume . . . is so distinctly and individually hers that a role in her hands becomes hers and hers alone."[12] Arnold Haskell wrote at the end of the 1938 Covent Garden season: "Her dancing gives one the impression that it is not assumed for our entertainment in a theatre but that it is a natural part of her being, spontaneous and unforced. . . . Her performance in *Cinderella* is a thing of rare beauty, not only when she dances but when she is sitting in the coach on her way to the ball."[13]

231

Riabouchinska's performances in 1938 began to reflect her exposure to Fokine, which marked a turning point in her career. Critics noticed in her a new depth in characterization and technical accomplishment. At the end of the season Haskell stated that she "proved herself the dancer of the London season."[14]

When the ballet was presented in the United States in 1940, it was well received by the press. Walter Terry wrote that it was "a gorgeous picture-book pageant illustrated in kaleidoscopic colors."[15] Grace Robert, writing about it in 1947, regretted that, then, it was only performed in the matinées, felt that it "recalled pages from an illuminated manuscript," and hoped for a revival.[16] The ballet was never presented after the 1940–41 United States tour.

THE PRODIGAL SON

Ballet in one act and three scenes; music by Serge Prokofiev; libretto by Boris Kochno; choreography by David Lichine; set and costume design by Georges Rouault; sets executed by Prince A. Schervachidze; costumes executed by Vera Soudeikina (Stravinsky); premiere December 30, 1938, at the Theatre Royal, Sydney, conducted by Antal Dorati.

232

ORIGINAL CAST

The Siren	Tamara Grigorieva	The Companions	Boris Belsky and Valery Shaievsky
The Son	Anton Dolin		
The Father	Dimitri Rostoff	The Beggar	Alberto Alonso
The Sisters	Tamara Tchinarova and Kira Abricossova		Corps de Ballet

When a new work was needed, it had become customary for de Basil to revive one of the many Diaghilev ballets for which the company possessed the decor and costumes. With luck, sometimes the original choreography could be staged by its creator, as was the case in Massine's *Midnight Sun*, *Les Femmes de bonne humeur*, *Le Tricorne*, and Nijinska's *Les Noces*. Grigoriev, with the assistance of old members of the Diaghilev company, especially his wife, Tchernicheva, and notebooks in which he had recorded the choreography, had originally revived mainly Fokine's works, such as *Petrouchka*, *Carnaval*, and *Schéhérazade*, and also Petipa's *Aurora's Wedding*. In 1932, it was Balanchine who was in charge of staging Fokine's *Les Sylphides*, and *Swan Lake* Act II. New choreography had to be provided for Balanchine's *Le Bal* and *The Gods Go a-Begging*. This practice was by no means new: Diaghilev had frequently commissioned new choreography for some of his previous creations, such as *Le Sacre du printemps* and *Le Chant du rossignol*. Now, for the forthcoming season, the choice turned to *Le Fils prodigue*, with new choreography by Lichine. It was faster and less expensive to redo Balanchine's old work than to produce a new one, especially under the pressure of touring. Since they already had the original costumes and scenery, music, and libretto, they could not go wrong.

Le Fils prodigue (*The Prodigal Son*) was originally presented by Diaghilev's Ballets Russes at the Théâtre Sarah-Bernhardt in Paris on May 21, 1929. The libretto, by Boris Kochno, was based on an adaptation of the parable in the Gospel of Luke. The score was commissioned from Prokofiev, scenery and costumes were by Rouault, and the choreography was by Balanchine. The cast was headed by Doubrovska as the Siren and Lifar as the Son. The ballet was last performed during Diaghilev's 1929 London season. It was not until 1950 that Balanchine staged a modified version for the New York City Ballet. In 1977 he made a new change by dropping the dance of the Companions. When the American Ballet Theatre revived the work in 1980, this passage was reinserted.

Action

Kochno's ten-episode libretto was divided into three scenes. In Lichine's version the first scene introduces the Son, all alone, sitting on a bench outside the house and thinking of a way to obtain parental permission to leave home. He dances a variation expressing his energy and zest for life. His sisters come out of the house and try to dissuade him. The Father also comes out and in a dance the Son asks to be released to enjoy the pleasures of life. The older man becomes upset and forbids him to go. After the Father has reentered the house, followed by the two Sisters, the Son's two Companions arrive. The three dance and go out into the world.

The second scene depicts the inside of the tent where all the revellers are gathered. The Son and the Companions arrive, and he arrogantly introduces himself by shaking hands. He then dances alone and with the others. The Siren arrives seated on a platter, lifted above the heads of the four men who carry her. Her arms, extended to the sides, are holding on to a hoop, and her train, draped around the border of the platter, hangs partway to the floor behind her. She is brought around behind the table to be placed on its center. The Son climbs on the table in fascination and approaches her. Very aloof, she looks at him provocatively and then stands up and steps down onto a bench and onto the floor. In center stage, she dances a variation with the hoop, stepping in and out of it on pointe and repeatedly falling to her knees. The Son joins her, and both dance stepping in and out of the hoop. He joins the crowd to allow his friends to dance with her also. They carry her to the stage right of the table, where she is given a goblet of wine. Standing on the table, she falls, her body rigid, over the revellers, who are seated on the table in profile to the audience, and she is passed from one pair of raised hands to the next, so that she gives the impression of rolling over their arms. She is received at the other end of the table by the Son, who takes her to the center of the stage for their pas de deux. As they dance, she first seduces and then sadistically rejects him.

233

The pas de deux consists of intertwining movements and was characterized by a cold distance that gave the feeling of calculation rather than erotic spontaneity to the seduction.

After the pas de deux she is lifted like a fish, with her legs open to the side, on top of a pyramid of men on the table, while the Son, at stage level, extends his arm and yearns to possess her.

The striking drinking scene that follows is an example of Lichine's inventive use of groupings. The Siren, raised by the revellers as the apex of the pyramid, is given a jar of wine; she pours it down a pipeline of hands into the mouth of the Son, who is seated at its base on the floor. About this scene Baronova remarked, "David had a wonderful imagination for an image or a line in the composition of a group. He was like a painter or sculptor who knew how to make a visual impression."

The Son becomes drunk and the revellers dance dizzily around him, while the Siren bourrées around him in a circle, still pouring wine. When he is completely inebriated, she dances, rejoicing in her triumph and entertaining the revellers with a lascivious dance, drawing them into the orgiastic climax. The Son is tossed in the air and his money rolls about the stage as the revellers strip him. One of the Companions carries the Siren to the table and ravishes her; then, one by one, first the Companions, then the revellers, couple with her in quick succession, to create a scene of compulsive debauchery. When the Son recovers, he finds himself almost naked, and alone in the cavernous setting. He dances a solo which is a lament of grief and repentance.

The third scene depicts his return to the patriarchal home. Exhausted and ashamed, he collapses outside the house. His sisters see him and go to his aid. When the Father comes out he appears upset, but at the sight of the repentant Son dragging himself towards him, he stretches out his arms, bends down and picks him up and carries him inside as the curtain falls.

234

Scenery and Costumes

A previous libretto and mise en scène restricted Lichine, but his choreographic approach and utilization of props were distinctively personal.

In both productions, the long table, reminiscent of the Last Supper, devised by Kochno, is the center of the action. In Balanchine's version the table is used for multiple purposes. In the first scene it appears upside down as the fence; then in the second scene the revellers turn it right side up to fulfill its purpose as a table. In the stripping scene it is set vertically as a pillar and then it is turned upside down to become the ship. In the last scene, it becomes the fence again. Although the table is an integral part of the choreographic design, Balanchine did not resort to it much as a second level of action, though he uses it as such for the drinking scene when the Siren is lifted and pours the wine into the Son's mouth as he is moving across the length of the table. Lichine, instead, only used it as a table in the second scene; and from the very beginning of this scene, when the revellers are introduced, it is utilized as a second level of action.

Lichine's use of the table provided the added dimension of a theater within a theater, bringing out the mysteries of the performance as a religious service in which the individuality of the spectator merges into some sublime vision of the inner world.

It became the sacrificial altar of the performance. This heightened the function of the stage and the role of the theater as temple.

There were minor differences in costuming: the Siren's headpiece was shorter, the revellers, like the Siren, had their legs crisscrossed with stripes, and the Son's outfits were modified. He did not wear the cloak, and his costume consisted of a deep blue sleeveless bodice with white shorts. He wore a white turban.

The main divergences, however, were in the artistic intentions of the choreographers.

Choreography

Balanchine's method of representation was objective-realistic; and his intention was to present a stylized interpretation of reality.

Lichine's approach was subjective-naturalistic; he tried to reveal life through the parable by making the audience experience the events as actual facts and provoking an emotional reaction. This was a prevailing tendency in the theater in the thirties, reflecting the influence of Artaud and the Theater of Cruelty.

The Prodigal Son was the first ballet in which Lichine was solely responsible for the artistic input. Until this time, he had always had collaborators—de Beaumont, Kochno, Clifford—who were part of the creative process, and their direct influence was vital. For the *Prodigal Son* Lichine had nobody: he was given the libretto, the music, and an existing design production without anyone to assist him. His main concern was to adapt the story on his own creative terms. Baronova has commented: "Lichine's choreographic talent began to show itself fully in *Le Fils prodigue*. One could perceive his maturity from the moment that he started to rehearse. When he came to the studio he had definite ideas of what he wanted, yet always allowed himself to be spontaneous. By then he had more command of rehearsals and exerted a stronger influence on the dancers. He would manipulate them emotionally either by perplexing them or by making uncomfortable remarks, out of which he would get the kind of movement or emotion he needed. It was a contradictory way of stimulating the dancers and making them feel good in order to obtain a specific mood. This approach was already evident before, but in *Le Fils prodigue* it was more subtle and effective."

The style and eroticism of *The Prodigal Son* were new elements in the de Basil repertory, with great impact upon the company. Baronova commented: "Its style was totally different. Erotic? Yes. Yet with taste and no vulgarity. The purpose of the eroticism was not to shock; it had a definite function in the interpretation of the story. It was definitely done with *gout raffiné!* I don't think that David would have ever done anything vulgar—daring, yes; vulgar, no. The certain aspects of his life that were rough never came on stage. That's why it was acceptable without being a scandal. To me it was a relief from the *Sylphides* and *Swan Lakes* and being pure and queen-like. I found the role of the Siren most exciting."

One aspect that gave balance to the work was the fusion of drama, humor, and tenderness. Lichine created humorous passages that were almost naive and amusing, such as the bewilderment of the Son after the wine affects him. Yet, as one reviewer noted, these did not detract from the drama: "There were touches of comedy here

235

Clockwise from upper left: Dolin
and Baronova; Baronova, wearing
a false nose, as the Siren; the
Siren (Osato) pours wine down
a pipeline of revelers' hands, into
the mouth of the Prodigal Son
(Lichine); Dolin.

and there, but he presented them deftly and swiftly, so that they gave spice to the role without spoiling the dramatic sweep of the story."[1]

There is an intrinsic quality of the grotesque in Kochno's conception of the revellers. However, this element is stressed more by Balanchine, especially in his lost 1929 version. Balanchine saw the revellers as caricatures and to that end made their movements mechanical—as in the marching and the flapping of their elbows. This deformation, enhanced by the costumes, emphasizes the inhuman distancing between them and the Son. Even the Companions turn to mockery and the grotesque. According to Agnes de Mille, they were depicted sticking out their tongues, thumbing their noses, and pulling their ears with jerky movements.[2] Dolin remembered that some of their contortions provoked laughter in the audience.[3] The dimension of cruelty in the revellers also permeates the portrayal of Balanchine's Siren: she is not a woman, but a stylization of a temptress. She is a symbol.

In contrast, Lichine's grotesquerie is slight, inasmuch as it is part of the revellers' characterization but not what characterizes them. Above all, their movements are endowed with humanity. What is grotesque is their physical appearance, which emphasizes the alienation between the Son and these creatures of the underworld. Lichine's Companions are a couple of rascals, and his Siren is a voluptuous woman, a seductress. At the beginning she is distant, calculating, but provocative, and she ends like a carnivorous bird (an unscrupulous nymphomaniac) who excites and then incites the men to ravish her.

These are not the only differences in treatment between Balanchine and Lichine. In the Lichine version there is no medallion, and the Siren does not steal anything from the Son—once she gets him drunk, she initiates her orgy with the other men.

Balanchine's Son is pathological; Lichine's is a rogue who disobeys his Father and learns a good lesson in how to deal with certain elements. Balanchine's Father is reluctant to forgive; it is the Son who works his way into his arms, and even then it is a while before the embrace is returned. Lichine's Father is disapproving at first, but as soon as he sees his Son crawling to him, he bends down and very tenderly lifts him up.

Baronova adds: "The touching scene between the Son and the Father, the way he [Lichine] imagined their relationship and forgiveness provided equilibrium to the emotional content. There was enormous heart in it." Baronova felt that even though some of the scenes in the tent were rough and erotic, they were balanced by the tenderness between the Father and the Son, and the family togetherness, at the end.

Riabouchinska, too, stresses Lichine's emphasis on human emotion: "In Lichine's works one could always find a feeling of human compassion, warmth and tenderheartedness that at least I did not find in any other choreographer with the exception of Fokine. In Pavillon one could find it in the pas de deux, in Lion amoureux when the lion falls in love with the queen and is easily chained and in the Prodigal Son between the father and son."

The role of the Son was first danced by Anton Dolin, since Lichine had injured

237

himself dancing *Protée* at Covent Garden. Because of his injury he choreographed the part on Dolin, which led to noticeable differences in interpretation when he finally took over the role himself. An Australian critic noted:

> Dolin made the Prodigal Son a bouncing, impudent fellow, who showed off and stood out in whatever company he happened to be. He treated his old father with thinly disguised derision, and the roystering band was only a sort of decorative frieze behind his impassioned solo dancing. Lichine, on the other hand, entered last night more sympathetically and naturally into the general picture. The patriarch's denunciation seemed really to terrify him, and the banqueters were his companions rather than a group of scoundrels simulating wonder and respect. This adventurer of Lichine's was a merry, likable fellow. His downfall resulted from excessive geniality rather than from arrogance and pride.[4]

Critics

The first dancers to alternate in the role of the Siren were Grigorieva, who danced the opening in Australia; Baronova, who opened with it in London; and Osato, who danced the opening in New York. From the very beginning the three alternated in the role. Baronova thought the character was so unusual that every time she performed it, she made up with a false nose to give added strength to her appearance. Arnold Haskell wrote in the *Bystander*: "Baronova's dancing was beyond criticism. She alone could have carried out these difficulties without a trace of hesitation. . . . "[5]

238

In *The Dancing Times* Haskell wrote: "Tamara Grigorieva as the Temptress becomes a star in her own right with an extremely sensitive creation. Always musical and obviously deeply intelligent . . . she is not the conventional oriental vamp, but a figure symbolical of temptations."[6]

About Osato, John Martin of the *New York Times* wrote: "Her exotic beauty and her grasp of the mood and manner of the choreographer make her completely and delightfully right."[7]

The ballet was well received in Australia, England, and the United States. Irving Kolodin wrote following the New York premiere:

> If there was any doubt, after "Graduation Ball," that David Lichine is the choreographic find of recent ballet seasons here, it was resolved with last night's first performance of "Prodigal Son". . .
>
> That theatrical sense which was always a strong element in Lichine's personal performance continued to assert itself in this work. . . . There is much meat in the solos of this episode, but Lichine's use of the background figures, the roisterers and the hangers-on in the sin den, is constantly fresh, unexpected and ingenious.[8]

John Martin wrote:

> It proves more clearly than any other one thing the fact of his originality, for having taken over a work whose structure so inevitably involved somebody else's creation, he has transformed it entirely into his own vein.[9]

The production remained in the repertory until the company disbanded in 1948. In 1946, when it was again presented in New York, Irving Kolodin called it "one of the few contemporary works . . . [which] may unblushingly be called a masterpiece."[10] The work was taken to Europe when the company returned after the war, and was very well received again in London, and for the first time in Paris. It was revived in 1977 by Jasinski for the Dallas Ballet and in 1985 for his Tulsa Ballet Theatre.

239

Verchinina and Toumanova.

June 1939–September 1940

THE COMPANY began rehearsals in London on June 12 at a studio on Tottenham Court Road, since Covent Garden was still occupied by the Opera Company, and did not move to the theater until June 17. The repertory for the forthcoming season was extensive: besides works cherished by Londoners, there was to be the British premiere of Lichine's *Prodigal Son* and the world premiere of Fokine's *Paganini*. There was also mention in the press of a third premiere, Lichine's *Songe chorégraphique*, to music of Debussy, but this never came to pass.[1]

In contrast to the Australian sojourn, so detached from the conflict in Europe, the company now found itself in the midst of political crisis. In June there was a mention in the press that Hitler possessed a life-size painting of Riabouchinska in his Berlin apartment.[2] Speculation abounded. Did she pose for the portrait? Who could the artist have been? Or was it simply made from a photograph and bought by Hitler in a Berlin gallery? Four decades later, Riabouchinska remarked: "We all received floral tributes from the German leaders, especially Göring and Goebbels, who also visited us backstage; but Hitler never did so."

For the 1939 season, the company was billed, as in the Australian tour, as Covent Garden Russian Ballet presented by Educational Ballets, Ltd. The season opened on June 19 with *Carnaval*, *The Prodigal Son*, *Protée*, and *Aurora's Wedding*. The scheduling of *Carnaval* rather than *Les Sylphides* was criticized by Arnold Haskell, who felt that "*Carnaval* even brilliantly danced is not for an opening night."[3] Richard Buckle disagreed, asserting that "it is perhaps the ideal ballet with which to open a season."[4] Nonetheless, both agreed in their acclaim of Riabouchinska. Haskell wrote: "Riabouchinska's Columbine I could not wish different; it is true porcelain, but it throws the other performances out of gear. When Columbine is thistle-down, what of *Papillon?*" And Buckle wrote, "Riabouchinska as Columbine was fragile and perfect. She always provokes in me hackneyed but sincere comparisons with Dresden china."

In *Aurora's Wedding* the stars of the company had an ideal vehicle to display their style and virtuosity. Buckle wrote: "Baronova's serene perfection as Aurora is now a matter of course. In the *pas de deux* with Petroff and in her tinkling variation she is perfect enough to send electric currents through the atmosphere."

Most of Haskell's attention throughout the season was focused on Lichine. As he wrote, in anticipation, for the June issue of *Dancing Times*: "The future hope of a very fine company seems undoubtedly to lie with David Lichine. . . . Lichine's long disablement has given him the time to study and to watch dancing, it has turned him into a very excellent critic, and it has toned down his youthful impetuosity. . . . The Australian tour has brought out the fact beyond a doubt that the future is his."[5]

By this time Lichine was coming into his own as a choreographer. The previous

242

Baronova as Princess Aurora.

year he and Riabouchinska (who had been a couple for several years now) had begun to work closely with some of the youngest dancers, to mold them to the choreographer's needs, especially the young Canadian recruits, Denisova and Sobinova, who were beginning to develop rapidly. While Sobinova was a very individual, lyrical dancer, Denisova had shown promise as a classical ballerina. About her first London *Aurora*, at age sixteen, Haskell commented, "She was beautifully simple and amazingly dignified. This was the sketch of something big to come."[6] The tutelage given by Lichine and Riabouchinska was very instrumental in their artistic growth.

Throughout the six-week engagement balletomanes turned out in force. On June 29, King George and Queen Elizabeth visited Covent Garden in their first evening out since their return from a trip to Canada and the United States.[7]

It was during this season that Verchinina, who had been in the United States for a year, made a glorious comeback. Besides dancing Chiarina in *Carnaval*, the company revived for her the three symphonic ballets, and London saw her for what would be the last time in *Les Présages*, *Choreartium*, and *Symphonie fantastique*. New talent had also been discovered in the Parisian studios by Dandré and Tchernicheva before the season started: Tatiana Leskova, Geneviève Moulin, Nina Popova, Tatiana Becheneva, and Oleg and Vassia Tupine.

Despite the company's artistic success, the future of its directorship was a concern to many. Haskell wrote: "The Russians today are a democracy, a collection of individuals whose aim it is to exploit their individuality."[8] "Ballet, unlike nations, does not thrive under a democracy. It demands an individual to enforce his taste and knowledge...."[9] "... I have seen enough, however, to realize that the Russian Ballet must put its house in order, and that quickly."[10]

A week before the season ended, Sevastianov resigned when he learned of the possible reappointment of de Basil. According to a spokesman, his departure was due to the troupe's inability "to accept all his views in regard to the direction and control of the company."[11] Sevastianov's decision also necessitated the resignation of his prima ballerina wife, Baronova. There were rumors of his intention to found with her a small company that would include Benois as artistic director and Nijinska as choreographer.[12] (However, Baronova does not recall ever discussing the project.)

As a solution to the crisis, the critic from the *Observer* (who signed his column H.G.) felt that "A single directing personality seems the obvious move in the right direction. Colonel de Basil ... seems the obvious choice!"[13] On August 13, the *Observer* announced: "In the last few days, the situation has completely changed. That very remarkable man, Colonel de Basil ... has been recalled to direct operations. He is to have complete artistic control of the company that was recently at Covent Garden. His title will be 'general director.'"[14]

The farewell performance of the season included *Swan Lake*, *Paganini*, *Protée*, and *Aurora's Wedding*. The applause was deafening, and the stage was banked with bouquets of flowers, while the dancers were crowned with laurel wreaths. The *Observer* described it as "one of the most remarkable scenes that the century-old theatre at Covent Garden has ever witnessed."[15] A few days earlier, it had been announced that Baronova would be leaving the company, and that night, after innumerable curtain calls, and after the fire curtain had been lowered, the audience started to shout her name as a last tribute. Then "Lichine appeared in the auditorium and explained that the mechanic had already gone away and it was impossible to get the curtain up. The applause continued, and in the end Madame Baronova herself appeared in the stalls and made a short speech of thanks."[16]

The departure of Baronova was a blow to the company that had nurtured her development into a classical ballerina of extraordinary depth and brilliance. Her creations were going to suffer, as well as those roles that had become closely identified with her: Aurora, the Swan Queen, Firebird. But if the Ballets Russes was to suffer an irreplaceable loss, Baronova was to find herself at the peak of her career, only twenty years old, without a company to frame her memorable interpretations. Now, at the suggestion of her husband, Baronova went to Hollywood, where she would make her film debut in 1939 in MGM's *Florian*, in which she had a dancing-acting part portraying a ballerina. The film, directed by Edwin L. Marin, starred Robert Young.

In August the dancers scattered all over Europe for their vacation, after which the company was to open a three-week engagement in Berlin at the Scala Theatre at the beginning of September. Lichine's new ballet, *Perpetuum Mobile* (later to be called *Graduation Ball*), was tentatively scheduled to have its premiere there.[17] The company was booked to sail for Australia on October 7.

The Scala engagement was of great concern to some members of the company, especially those who were Jewish. According to Baronova, Sevastianov, fearing for the safety of these dancers, asked for personal assurances from Goebbels, who in turn guaranteed that as far as he was concerned, all of the Ballets Russes personnel were non-Jewish.[18]

Owing to the increasing international tension, the Berlin season was optimistically postponed for a week. Then, on August 23, the Soviet-German non-aggression pact was signed. On September 3 war broke out.

By August 30 most of the dancers had assembled in Paris to leave for Berlin; 16, rue de Gramont now became the company's headquarters. De Basil was back from Sospel on the French-Italian border, where he and his wife, Olga Morosova, had lived since his resignation as director in 1938. He was in charge of arrangements to leave for Australia, while Vova (Vsevolod) Grigoriev, Serge Grigoriev's son, the company's secretary, hoped to succeed in getting the music scores that had already been sent to Berlin out of Germany via Italy.

In Paris the Russian dancers, including those stranded there from Denham's Ballet Russe, were gathered in solidarity. De Basil spared no effort to get them all out of Europe, and through Lifar's connections, particularly with the playwright Jean Giraudoux, who recently had been appointed the French Minister of Information, de Basil arranged for the dancers who had complied with draft regulations to be released.[19] According to Kathrine Sorley Walker, Lifar suggested "that they should create a combined company with Franco-British backing,"[20] a very unrealistic proposition at a moment when both countries were at war with Germany. After six weeks of vicissitudes, the group stranded in Paris traveled to London. Other company members had already left Europe via England for the United States and Canada. Lichine and Ria-bouchinska, who had been spending their holidays in Switzerland and Monte Carlo, took a roundabout route through Italy to get a ship to America.

For those in London, the gloomy days seemed endless. According to Leskova, the ship and day of departure for Australia were kept secret, and the dancers met at a Lyons Corner House every evening until the information was revealed. Finally, on November 18, they sailed from Tilbury. The voyage, made under the threat of mines and torpedoes, lasted six weeks. From the United States, the *Mariposa* sailed with Toumanova, Riabouchinska, Denisova, Orlova, Lichine, Dorati, Ismailoff, and others. It also carried a great number of survivors from the H.M.S. *Athenia*, a British liner that was the first passenger ship sunk at the beginning of the war; it had been torpedoed by the Germans off the Hebrides. By coincidence, both ships arrived on December 26 at their Australian destination.

245

L'Après-midi d'un faune: Serge Lifar.

The company opened in Australia under the new name of Original Ballet Russe. They had been obliged to drop the name Covent Garden Russian Ballet before leaving London, for the connection with this theater was now severed. A glamorous opening night took place on December 30 at the Theatre Royal in Sydney. Even though Baronova and Dolin, members of the previous tour, were missing, it was the most complete Ballets Russes company ever to visit Australia. Besides the familiar names from previous tours, this engagement marked the debut of Nemtchinova, Toumanova, Verchinina, Morosova, Lifar, Panaiev, and Skibine.

The program consisted of *Les Sylphides* with Riabouchinska, Volkova, Stepanova, and Lifar; *Paganini* with the original cast except for Denisova in Baronova's role; and *Aurora's Wedding* with Toumanova-Petroff and Riabouchinska-Jasinski. At the final curtain, the female dancers were banked with bouquets of flowers, while the males were crowned with laurel wreaths. De Basil, on his first visit to Australia, addressed the audience, and E. J. Tait, chairman of J. C. Williamson, Ltd., Australia's well-known theatrical management company, made a welcoming speech. Afterwards there was a party onstage for two hundred guests.

The company's third Australian tour found a keen critical appreciation of dance and extremely enthusiastic critics and balletomanes. Nemtchinova, although no

246

Nemtchinova as the Swan Queen.

longer the dancer she had been years earlier, was much admired in *Swan Lake*, *Petrouchka*, *Firebird*, and *Coppélia*. Toumanova was praised for her technique and regal bearing. She was now dancing for the first time Baronova's roles in *Les Présages*, *Les Cent Baisers*, and *Le Pavillon*. Verchinina was a revelation in the symphonic ballets, and Morosova made her debut in *Les Femmes de bonne humeur*. Lifar's repertory consisted of the Blue Bird pas de deux, *Swan Lake*, *Les Sylphides*, *Le Spectre de la rose*, and his own *Icare*. The premiere of this work, on February 18, got a mixed reception from the critics; nevertheless, there were twenty-five curtain calls. It later became one of Jasinski's most acclaimed roles. Lifar also rearranged Massine's *Le Beau Danube*, now entitled *Le Danube Bleu*. (According to Riabouchinska, "Where Massine had us entering from the right, Lifar had us do it from the left.") The cast included Lichine as the Hussar, Morosova as the Street Dancer, Lazowski as the King of the Dandies, Volkova as the Second Hand, and Riabouchinska in her original role. On February 23, Lifar staged the seven-minute *Pavane*, which was Massine's old *Las Meninas* with new choreography by Lifar, music by Fauré, and the original costumes by José María Sert. Lifar left Sydney on March 1.

On March 1, *Graduation Ball* had its premiere. According to Edward Pask, after the company's last evening performance on the twelfth, there was a special midnight benefit for the Polish War Victims' Relief. The novelties presented for the benefit were a Japanese dance by Algeranoff, the *Don Quixote* pas de deux with Toumanova and Petroff, and Verchinina's *Étude Chorégraphique*, her first ballet for the company, to music by Handel.

The opening performance in Melbourne on March 14 received over thirty curtain calls. After a tour of several Australian cities, the Ballets Russes returned to Sydney on July 13; by this time three Australians had joined the company: Phyllida Cooper (Lydia Couprina), Valerie Tweedie (Irina Lavrova), and Allison Lee (Helene Lineva); these three remained in Australia when the company departed for the United States. At the Theatre Royal on July 25, Verchinina premiered another work, *Étude*, set to Bach's Aria, Arioso, and Sarabande, arranged by Dorati. The designs had been announced as by Laudon-Saint Hill, but instead the all-female cast wore mauve, buff, and blue leotards; there was no decor. The work, in Verchinina's own modern idiom, was led by the choreographer. In *Enter the Colonies Dancing*, Edward Pask states that the ballet met with mixed feelings, and quotes the following unidentified review:

247

> Though not lacking in beauty, *Étude* is austerely cold, built on severe classical lines. The dancers are all women. As an exhibition of classical dancing, it has considerable merit; its emotional content is negligible. Mlle Verchinina has used Bach's music and sought to interpret it in terms of ballet, mainly by artistic groupings and graceful movement. There is no story, no drama, no heart-throb. . . .[21]

On July 29, Igor Schwezoff's *La Lutte éternelle*, to Schumann's *Études symphoniques*, was presented in Sydney, led by Skibine, Verchinina, Toumanova, Svetlova,

Coppélia: Toumanova (left, in rehearsal) and Riabouchinska.

248

and Osato. On August 12, a two-act *Coppélia* was staged by Anatole Oboukhov after Petipa. It was a natural choice to add to the repertory, since Oboukhov had brought his music score to Australia and knew the work of the Maryinsky Theatre, and de Basil owned Anna Pavlova's decor for the first act. For the second act the decor was rented locally, and the costumes were all designed by Sviatoslav Toumine and constructed by Mme Larose.[22]

Australia had last seen *Coppélia* with Adeline Genée and Alexandre Volinine during their 1913 visit with members of the Imperial Russian Ballet. De Basil's production presented three Swanildas: Riabouchinska, Toumanova, and Nemtchinova.

The company toured Australia; however, the tour to New Zealand was canceled. In order to help more dancers flee Europe, and not knowing how many would finally arrive in Australia, the company allowed for a total of eighty-four. Unquestionably, this added burden was the reason behind the reduction of wages and the financial impossibility of doing more touring. The last performance, as on the previous trip, was a special midnight performance in Sydney on September 19.

During the Australian season, a series of benefit performances was presented to raise funds for the Allies.

PAGANINI

Ballet in one act and three scenes; music, Rhapsody on a Theme of Paganini by Serge Rachmaninoff; libretto by Serge Rachmaninoff and Michel Fokine; choreography by Michel Fokine; set design by Serge Soudeikine, executed by Oreste Allegri; costume design by Serge Soudeikine, executed by Vera Soudeikine; premiere June 30, 1939, at Covent Garden, London, conducted by Antal Dorati.

ORIGINAL CAST

Paganini	Dimitri Rostoff
The Divine Genius	Irina Baronova
A Florentine Beauty	Tatiana Riabouchinska
Guile	Tamara Grigorieva
A Florentine Youth	Paul Petroff
Scandal	Yurek Lazowski
Gossip	Alberto Alonso
Envy	Tatiana Leskova, Vanda Grossen
Satan	Borislav Runanine
The Evil Spirits	Mlles Obidenna, Roussova MM. Irman, Ladré, Matouchak
The Ghosts	Mlles Denisova, Leontieva, Serova, Sobinova
The Phantoms	MM. Alexandroff, Hoyer, Ignatoff, Nicolaieff, Vlassoff
Paganini's Rivals	MM. Algeranoff, Belsky
Their Sponsors	MM. Dzikovsky, Ristic, Tupine, Unguer
The Florentine Maids	Mlles Lvova, Nelidova, Osato, Roy, Strakhova, Volkova
The Florentine Youths	MM. Andahazy, Belsky, Dzikovsky, Ismailoff, Ristic, Tupine
The Divine Spirits	Mlles Denisova, Leontieva, Lerina, Lvova, Moulin, Nelidova, Razoumova, Roy, Sanina, Serova, Sobinova, Strakhova, Tresahar, Volkova, Wassilieva, Wolska
Paganini's Doubles	MM. Algeranoff, Alonso, Andahazy, Belsky, Dzikovsky, Ismailoff, Lazovsky, Ristic, Unguer
Piano Solo	Eric Harrison

Fokine had long wanted to do a ballet with Serge Rachmaninoff. The first discussions of a possible collaboration took place in 1937, when Fokine and his wife visited the composer at his home in Senar, Switzerland. According to the choreographer's memoirs,[1] it was Rachmaninoff who suggested a ballet based on the life of Niccolò Paganini, the great romantic virtuoso violinist (said to have made a pact with the devil), and proposed that they use an already existing score, his Rhapsody on a Theme of Paganini. Fokine began studying the life of Paganini and found himself identifying with several aspects of it, notably imitation and plagiarism by his contemporaries, and adverse criticism.

Fokine was not the first to use Paganini as the basis for a ballet. Balanchine had already done so in his 1934 *Transcendence*, to a libretto by Lincoln Kirstein and music by Liszt, arranged by George Antheil. Then, in 1938, the newly organized Denham Ballet Russe de Monte Carlo announced that Balanchine would create another ballet about Paganini, to music of Tommasini, but it was Ashton who was finally commissioned. According to David Vaughan, "By the time Ashton was ready to start work on it, during the summer of 1939, Fokine was preparing his own *Paganini*, to the Rachmaninov Rhapsody, and that may have been a factor in the decision to change the story of *Le Diable s'amuse*."[2]

Action

Scene One: In the shadows of a concert hall, Paganini appears, walking slowly towards the audience. He bows to it, breaks two strings of his violin (according to the legend he did this to transpose the music into another key), and begins to play as his music is rendered by the piano solo. On a lower level, various allegorical figures appear from among a cardboard audience—Scandal, Gossip, and Envy—and whisper to the audience. The figures perform macabre dances, yearning for the musician. A mysterious pair of hands emerges from behind Paganini and guides the violinist's movements; soon, behind and above Paganini, appears a goat-headed Satan, to whom the hands belong. Veiled spirits, as the dead rising from the grave, surround the musician; Guile detaches herself from them and dances in a frenzy around Paganini. She jumps back and forth from Paganini's platform to the lower stage level, where the simulated audience is located, and is lifted several times by Gossip and Scandal. In the forefront the vision of two look-alike rivals appears, each with two music critic

250

Sponsors who, with mechanical movements, write their critiques. This vision disappears. The nightmarish scene reaches its climax as all the Evil Spirits dance around Paganini and his shadow is projected around and against the semicircular pillared hall. The allegorical figures leap off the platform into darkness. All alone, Paganini bows to the audience and the curtain falls.

Scene Two: Village youths are dancing in a serene Florentine square on a hilltop, when the Florentine Beauty appears with a basket of flowers. She runs playfully, escaping the lover who pursues her. Together they dance a pas de deux in which their subtle emotions are expressed by their running and hiding, swift lifts and supported pirouettes. As the pas de deux ends, she sits on his knee. Paganini enters and his presence frightens the crowd. He takes a guitar from one of the young men and begins to play. The music affects the Florentine Beauty, who runs around seeking refuge with her friends and dropping her straw hat. Entranced, she is unable to resist the compulsion to dance; as if possessed, she abandons herself to the music and with increasing frenzy, bends, whirls, and circles around the violinist until she drops exhausted at his feet. Then, as if hypnotized, she stands up, dances, and with her arms hanging to the side, looks at him from the cambré position, and bourrées offstage behind him.

Scene Three: Alone in his study, Paganini tries to compose but finds no inspiration. The Divine Genius glides across the stage and takes him by the arm to center stage, where he attempts to guide his hands. A group of Divine Spirits in delicate chains form the background as the Divine Genius dances to inspire him. They exit and he returns alone to his work. From behind him a double jumps out playing a violin. To Paganini's surprise one double after the other jump in and fill the stage. The Evil Spirits from the first scene reappear to torment him. He fights them back with his bow, and the stage is plunged into darkness. When the lights come back on he is lying on a couch; in the background a staircase leads to heaven. The Divine Genius enters with her Spirits and drives away the Spirits of Evil. She dances and calls to Paganini's soul and leads him up the stairs to heaven. With Paganini following, she arabesques, ascending the stairs, and points the way as the curtain falls.

The Fokine-Rachmaninoff libretto evoked the legend rather than the real circumstances of the violinist's life. It was carefully related to the musical score, for which the composer had written a new ending. The scenery and costumes were commissioned from Serge Soudeikine, making this the first company creation based on the collaboration of three Russian artists. (*Balustrade* was to be the second and last.)

Scenery and Costumes

For the first scene Soudeikine designed a semicircular domed concert hall surrounded by columns. There were two levels of action. The stage level had two rows of cardboard spectators with their backs to the audience; above was a sixty-by-fifty-foot platform, the concert stage where Paganini was to appear. Greys and blues dominated the scene, although some of the costumes contrasted with the somber coloring: the two characters of Envy were dressed in green, Scandal in red, and Guile in mauve with a purple wig. The Evil Spirits wore black tights with skeletons painted on them; the Sponsors wore eighteenth-century outfits with white curly wigs; and Gossip appeared with an effective four-faced mask.

In contrast, the second scene depicted in pastels a daytime square on a hilltop. The women wore dresses with tight bodices with V necks, tight long sleeves loose at the shoulders, and high-waisted pleated skirts. Each wore a different toque. The men wore tights and shirts with long draping at the elbows. All the costumes were in pastel shades of blue, green, violet, and purple. The Florentine Beauty wore a pink dress with a pink straw hat and was the only character in this scene to dance on pointe.

The third tableau consisted of a grim room with a worktable; above a wall in the back appear the turrets of city buildings. When the stage is somberly brightened for the death scene, it reveals gothic ruins and a staircase with its top covered by the clouds; the Divine Genius and Spirits are attired in white dresses with hoods and wings.

In *Paganini* Fokine made clever use of theatrical techniques expressive of a romantic-expressionistic sensibility. Some of the technical effects caused problems in performance: lighting the violins with green light from the inside; using black light to make the white dresses of the Divine Spirits appear phosphorescent in the third scene. The first scene employed inventive lighting effects to create a macabre, grotesque atmosphere. Paganini was famous for his sensational entrances, and in the ballet he seemed to float forward in the dim light like some demoniacal spirit taking mortal shape before the audience. The spirits impersonating Guile, Envy, Gossip, and Satan

251

in the form of a goat appeared and disappeared in the darkness by means of spotlights.

The lyrical, pastoral scene was in contrast brightly lit. The diabolism of the violinist was underscored by the effect his presence had on the simple village people.

The third scene was a return to the macabre. While Paganini lies on his deathbed, the forces of good and evil encounter each other. Caricatures of the artist play transparent violins illuminated from the inside. The all-white winged, hooded dresses worn by the Divine Spirits were lighted by the use of black light. Cochran, who had already employed *lumière noire* in a 1936 revue, advised the choreographer of its possibilities. The effect was astounding.

Rehearsals   The company started rehearsing as soon as it arrived in Australia. After working with Fokine on two new ballets and a number of revivals, the dancers had acquired a sense of his style, and in spite of his ironic sense of humor and bad temper, the work advanced smoothly. Baronova, who created the role of the Divine Genius, recalled that "details had been worked out by the time Fokine came to the rehearsal, and he explained to the dancers the psychological symbolism [allegorical symbolism] of the characters." Yet he also indulged in spontaneous creativity. As he had told Arnold Haskell in an interview a few years earlier, "Once the score has become a part of me images are formed, which I occasionally fix in little drawings. That is the general plan, but the fantasy comes during rehearsals."[3]

Fokine's method of working differed from one dancer to another, showing his concern for each individual personality. Dimitri Rostoff, whose memorable performance in the basically mime role of Paganini was highly acclaimed, recalls that the choreographer gave him the basic movements and development of the character, but allowed him complete freedom of interpretation. Rostoff later recalled: "The fact that Paganini was an acting part throughout the whole ballet gave the character a certain detachment. In other words, the superiority of his being was enhanced by the lack of mobility in the same dimension as the other characters. I was first disappointed when I was told that it was a straight miming role, but when I understood its difficulties I found it to be a challenge."

As the work progressed, the dancers became more and more impressed with the ballet's complexity. No previous production had been as intricately staged. The ballet was choreographed in sequence with the entire company present at all times, a method Riabouchinska enjoyed:

> We were all there throughout the rehearsals, and the ballet unfolded wondrously before our eyes. Every scene was systematically taken from the beginning until it was entirely staged. After that, all the rehearsals were runthroughs. The intensity was always there. I do not recall Fokine ever taking anyone separately or coaching me alone in my variation. It would have made no sense. The high point of my role was not its technical difficulty, although it was very technical, but the intensity of the emotions that could be conveyed only when I was interacting with other dancers.

In every rehearsal we were completely immersed in the drama, and it was as draining as a performance. In my variation, I had to fall to the floor, and with my knee on the floor I had to renversé, turning on that knee. At the dress rehearsal at Covent Garden I avoided going on my knee because after months of rehearsals it was sore and infected, and I wanted to take it easy in preparation for the opening. From the first box, where he always sat, Fokine screamed, "If you do not go all the way I will stop the performance!"

And he would have done it. According to Baronova, once, in London, he pulled Nemtchinova off the stage during a performance when she was not executing the right choreography in *Les Sylphides*. Also in London, during a rehearsal of *Prince Igor*, a discussion about the tempo arose between Beecham and Fokine. At that evening's performance Beecham took his own tempo, and the choreographer started to clap from his box the tempo he desired, causing the conductor to exit. Fokine stepped to the podium and instructed the orchestra "from number twelve, please."

Sevastianov and Dandré, after attending a rehearsal of *Paganini* in Melbourne, found it extremely effective without costumes or scenery. They suggested to Fokine the possibility of presenting the work in practice clothes and with no decor, but the choreographer opposed this idea, feeling that the ballet would lose much of its symbolism.

Premiere   The premiere of *Paganini* on June 30 was the highlight of the Covent Garden season. Along with *Carnaval* and *Coq d'or*, the work was presented to celebrate Fokine's jubilee—the fiftieth anniversary of his theatrical debut. Although *Paganini* aroused mixed feelings, the anonymous critic of the *Times* hailed it as a "striking creation."[4] Beryl de Zoete wrote in the *Daily Telegraph* that "the ballet was received with the utmost enthusiasm, and indeed it is a remarkable demonstration of Fokine's great mastery."[5] Arnold Haskell recognized Fokine's craftsmanship but disliked the ballet's super-romanticism, which he felt to be banal and démodé. Above all, he found Soudeikine's work hideous.[6] Nevertheless, he added: "In all justice I must record in no uncertain terms that it was not only a success, but the success of years. An enthusiastic audience lapped it up, skulls, skeletons, angels, demons and even the box of chocolates background, which was treated to a round of applause on its own."

Choreog-   The first scene was mimed, with the exception of the role of Guile (Grigorieva),
raphy   which was highly technical. There was an emphasis on lifts and floor movements—the dancers constantly rose and fell, as if on springboards, as they jumped back and forth from the floor to the platform, thereby heightening the tension.

The second episode was more consistently set in terms of dance. There were ensembles danced by the villagers and a lyrical pas de deux between the Florentine Beauty (Riabouchinska) and a friend (Petroff). The pas de deux consisted mainly of lifts and supported pirouettes, made difficult, as Riabouchinska remembers, by a basket of flowers she held with both hands. The climactic moment of the ballet was her variation when Paganini appears in the square. She dances to his music, then drops,

LEFT: Paganini (Rostoff) in the concert hall, guided by the Devil. BELOW: Paganini and the Florentine Beauty (Riabouchinska).

255

ABOVE: Paganini confronts his imitators.
RIGHT: Baronova as the Divine Genius.

exhausted, to the floor. She then stands, possessed, dances and follows him offstage, bourrees backwards with her arms down, looking at him from a cambré position.

Riabouchinska's Florentine Beauty is considered to be one of her greatest achievements. Beryl de Zoete, the critic for the *Daily Telegraph*, wrote:

> Riabouchinska's dance in this variation, when, irresistibly drawn by Paganini's guitar, she whirls and circles round him, half falling and recovering, and finally dropping prostrate at his feet, is among her greatest triumphs. . . . The melody and lightness of her bending and fleeting body are indescribable. Surely Fokine, knowing that only in dance could the prodigious music of Paganini be adumbrated, has here chosen Riabouchinska for its medium.[7]

Arnold Haskell wrote:

> Riabouchinska excelled in one of the best conceived roles of her career. How convincingly she can now act! Her mime is as part of her dancing, infinitely musical and spontaneous.[8]

Grace Robert described this dance as

> one of the most brilliant solos ever devised by Fokine. . . . It was performed with coruscant speed by Tatiana Riabouchinska. At first a lovely Tanagra-like figure glowing with happiness, she became a maddened creature demoniacally possessed. This must be one of the most hectically paced solos in the history of ballet. It is difficult to imagine who could have replaced Riabouchinska in this part.[9]

The third scene combined mime and dance. The choreography of the Divine Spirits was mainly based on bourrées, arabesques, and attitudes in lines or small circles. The Divine Genius (Baronova) was a highly technical role, stressing multiple pirouettes that were made more difficult by the distraction of the black light. Unfortunately, the role itself did not offer great possibilities for characterization. Haskell wrote: "Baronova did well with a role that even she could not illuminate."[10] When Baronova left the company, the role was passed on to Denisova, and Baronova did not reassume it when she rejoined de Basil for the 1940–41 United States tour.

Critics   Fokine's ballet was highly acclaimed in Australia and proved to be one of the company's most successful attractions when it was presented in the United States in 1940. John Martin wrote:

> It is now more than thirty-five years since Fokine began to compose ballets, but though times have changed and fashions have succeeded fash-

256

ions, his latest work is so fresh and vital that it puts to shame the majority of creations in the *dernière mode*.

Fokine's use of the stage is magnificently authoritative, and what he accomplished in the fantastic opening scene is little short of a theatrical miracle. The interrupted idyll of the second scene provided more formal choreographic opportunities, and in the dance of the terrified maiden (superbly realized by Tatiana Riabouchinska) he has made a brilliant composition. The final scene is the least effective, partly because it is a little long in coming to its conclusion.[11]

Irving Kolodin was also enthusiastic:

Considering that the faintly incredible Paganini was a virtual contemporary of Hector Berlioz, it is reasonable that some of the passionate romanticism which vitalized Massine's "Symphonie Fantastique" should also have a part in this work. But Fokine's superlatively imaginative realization of the essence of Paganini in terms of dance, his masterful blending of theatrical and choreographic elements is enough to remind us again of the inescapable truism—there is no substitute for genius. Fokine's amazing capacity for making every dance movement the counterpart of a spoken phrase, and finding for every unspoken phrase a perfect counterpart in choreographic terms is the life blood of this ballet—and it flows insistently from the beginning to end.[12]

257

Other critics, though, felt the ballet's highly romantic expressionism to be passé.

The ballet stayed in the repertory throughout the years in South America and was presented again in the United States when the company returned after the war and in Europe during the 1947–48 performances. The role of Paganini was danced by Dokoudovsky. During the 1947 Covent Garden engagement Riabouchinska was the only member of the original cast to return to London. Of her Florentine Beauty then, Haskell commented: "The memories of the past, so often exaggerated ones, have not impaired the wonderful impression of this performance. If anything, it seems to have gained."[13]

In February 1986, Dokoudovsky staged a production for the Tulsa Ballet Theatre in Oklahoma, with the assistance of its directors, ex–Ballets Russes dancers Roman Jasinski and Moscelyne Larkin (Larkina). According to Lynn Garafola, few changes took place from the original production: the cast was reduced from forty-four to thirty-four; the sixty-by-fifty-foot platform was replaced by a smaller podium; the cardboard "audience" was tossed out; the green lights inside the violins in the last scene were also eliminated. However, these changes had already been made during the mid-forties. About this revival Garafola commented that "the 'hobble-goblins' do look dated and occasionally silly, but the pure dance passages do not. They speak their truth classically.''[14] This production, supervised by dancers who knew and danced the ballet for almost a decade—Larkina had performed Guile during the forties—is faithful to Fokine in style. Unfortunately, however, Tulsa Ballet Theatre did not refer to the surviving black-and-white 16mm excerpts of the ballet's three scenes, shot by Dr. Ringland Anderson in Australia and donated to the Australian Ballet Foundation; nor did they use excerpts in the Laird Goldsborough films donated to the Dance Collection in New York City or the color 16mm excerpt of the Florentine Beauty variation in Riabouchinska's collection.

GRADUATION BALL

Ballet in one act; music by Johann Strauss, arranged and orchestrated by Antal Dorati; libretto and choreography by David Lichine; set and costume design by Alexandre Benois; premiere March 1, 1940, at the Theatre Royal, Sydney, conducted by Antal Dorati.

ORIGINAL CAST

The Headmistress	Borislav Runanine
The Junior Girls	Tatiana Riabouchinska, Mlles Denisova, Leskova, Moulin, Svetlova, Leontieva, Bechenova, Bounina
The Senior Girls	Mlles Orlova, Lvova, Popova, Gontcharova, Smirnova, Golovina, Sobinova, Couprina
The Old General	Igor Schwezoff
The Junior Cadets	David Lichine, MM. Toumine, Alonso, Algeranoff, Alexandroff, Andahazy, Belsky, Irman, Nicolaieff, Matouchak, Wassilkovsky, Unguer
The Senior Cadets	MM. Ivangine, Skibine, Tupine, Vlassoff

Divertissement

The Mistress of Ceremony	Tatiana Riabouchinska
No. 1—The Drummer	Nicolas Orloff
No. 2—La Sylphide and the Scotsman	Natasha Sobinova and Paul Petroff
No. 3—Impromptu Dance	Tatiana Leskova
No. 4—Dance-step Competition	Alexandra Denisova and Geneviève Moulin
No. 5—Mathematics and Natural History Lesson	Marina Svetlova, Helene Lineva, Maria Azrova
No. 6—Perpetuum Mobile	Tatiana Riabouchinska and David Lichine
Mazurka Flirtation	Igor Schwezoff and Borislav Runanine
Grand Finale	Artists of the Ballet

According to Riabouchinska, the idea for *Graduation Ball* had come to Lichine in a dream in which he recalled his days in a military academy in Peschers, Bulgaria, when he was twelve years old and in exile. After the company's 1938 Copenhagen engagement, Lichine and the conductor Antal Dorati went to the Vienna State Library in search of unpublished Strauss scores to use for this ballet. When they returned to Paris, they brought with them a series of pieces that could be orchestrated and arranged to fit the story, which at that point existed only as a general outline. At the suggestion of Serge Grigoriev, Lichine engaged Alexandre Benois to design the scenery and costumes. Benois, as a collaborator, discussed the ballet with Lichine and the advice and criticism he offered were valuable in helping Lichine give the ballet its final form.

Music Dorati achieved one of the most successful arrangements of a ballet score. He compiled and orchestrated several pieces by Johann Strauss the Younger, two of which, "The Acceleration Waltz" and "Perpetuum Mobile," were familiar. The rest of the score consisted of unknown marches, waltzes, and mazurkas.

Action The curtain rises to reveal the scarlet plush and gilt salon of a Viennese girls' school during the 1840s. There is great activity as the girls prepare for their graduation ball and the arrival of a group of cadets from the neighboring military academy.

The younger girls (dressed in pinafores) and the seniors (in simple ball gowns) are frolicking with a powder puff, when the Headmistress (a comic travesty role) enters and snatches it away from them. She is, however, unable to resist experimenting with it herself, and just as she begins to do so, there is a flourish of military music announcing the arrival of the cadets, led by their impressively whiskered and gold-braided General. Girls and cadets are presented to one another in an atmosphere of ceremonious formality.

Once the introductions are over, the Headmistress and the General exit, leaving the students free to dance, but, though they are all obviously taken with one another, no one is able to pluck up the courage to make the first move. Finally, one of the younger girls, a tomboyish creature in pigtails, falls on the floor in front of the cadets. The ice has been broken and the students begin to dance under the light of a great crystal chandelier.

The General and the Headmistress return for the formal part of the evening's entertainment, a series of charming divertissements, during the course of which it becomes evident that no greater infatuation has taken place than that which has suddenly sprung up between the General and the Headmistress. The lead junior girl serves as mistress of ceremonies and introduces the numbers to the spectators who gather to each side of the stage; the General and the Headmistress preside, with the girls seated on chairs, the cadets standing behind them. The curtain of the center archway is drawn and the drummer appears. His variation is followed by a romantic pas de deux, "La Sylphide and the Scotsman." After the pas de deux, the pigtailed girl walks with her chair to center stage as if hypnotized, but soon becomes euphoric; then, a bit embarrassed at first, she dances her variation. Two barres are brought in and the young people divide into two factions behind them. The two competing girls

259

ABOVE: The arrival of the cadets. BELOW: The First Cadet (Lichine) approaches the Junior Girls.

ABOVE: The Junior Girls and an alarmed First Cadet. BELOW: Stroganova as the Pigtail Girl in a 1940s South American revival.

ABOVE: The fouetté competition: Moulin and Denisova.
BELOW: Finale of the 1940s South American revival.

do exercises at the barres and challenge each other in a series of complicated fouettés. Next, three students mimic a class of mathematics and a natural history lesson, and the divertissement ends with a circus number. Left alone while the students are having supper, the General and the Headmistress perform a mazurka in which any pretense of decorous behavior is thrown aside.

The merrymaking continues after the students have returned, until the older couple declares the ball to be over. The cadets take their leave, but their leader returns for one last moment with his young flame, only to be interrupted and shooed off by the Headmistress, who then exits with her pupil in tow, leaving behind a dark and empty stage.

Scenery and Costumes The decor depicted a rococo Viennese ballroom with ivory columns trimmed in gold, gilt chairs, and a crystal chandelier. The backdrop had a tall archway in the center with a red velvet curtain through which the cadets enter and exit; the same backdrop was used for the divertissement. To each side of the center arch was a smaller arch, also with a red velvet curtain; portraits of the emperor and empress hung over the arches.

For the first scene, the junior girls wore blue pinafores over their white dresses; the pinafores were discarded before the cadets arrived. The senior girls were dressed in simple ball gowns in pale yellow, pink, and green. The junior cadets had white pants and blue military jackets with white sashes across the shoulders. The General was in red and white with gold braid, and the Headmistress wore shades of brown and white. For the divertissement, the drummer wore a red military jacket and a cap, the Scotsman a kilt, and La Sylphide a romantic tutu; the fouetté girls were in short lace tutus, tiny bonnets, and had red sashes across their shoulders; the circus couple had flashy red outfits.

Rehearsals By the time the company returned to London in 1939, after their Australian tour, *Graduation Ball* had taken on a definite form; Lichine had experimented on the choreography with Riabouchinska during the tour. In London he did research on Viennese society of the period. He discussed the ballet with Cyril Beaumont and inquired about the right period style for the divertissement number "La Sylphide and the Scotsman." Beaumont sent the choreographer a collection of prints of the Romantic era to assist him in reproducing the right poses.[1]

The ballet was tentatively scheduled for the Berlin season in September of 1939, with the title *Perpetuum Mobile*, but the outbreak of war delayed the premiere to the spring of 1940 in Sydney.

The actual choreographing of *Graduation Ball*, as the ballet was finally called, was intensive. Although Lichine had staged some of the solo numbers on the voyage to Australia, no company rehearsals had ever been conducted. During the first months in Sydney all the rehearsal time was allotted to the general repertory, to accommodate the many new dancers. However, since de Basil insisted on having a premiere before leaving Sydney, they had only the one week before the end of their stay there to do everything. Funding for the new production was obtained through a committee of sponsors who donated one hundred pounds each. Even though de Basil, in his administrative capacity, was responsible for the fund-raising, Lichine was the one instrumental in making the contacts, since he already knew many people in Sydney and was very popular.

In the midst of the Second World War, *Graduation Ball* was an exuberantly gay work. The ballet received an enthusiastic reception in Sydney; there were twenty-five curtain calls.[2]

Choreog-
raphy

Graduation Ball is a divertissement-ballet, but with a difference. In the traditional Petipa divertissements, the suite of dances is independent of the story line. In Massine's approach, the divertissement is part of the structure of the drama, and each dance helps to develop the action. In Lichine's ballet the divertissement at first seems to be intended purely as entertainment. But then the spectators on the stage begin to respond and react emotionally to the dances, and insert themselves into the divertissement. For instance, after the first two numbers of the drummer variation and "La Sylphide and the Scotsman," the naughty girl rises from her chair and performs her own Impromptu Dance, switching from spectator to performer and back again, thus obliterating the line between divertissement and dramatic-dance action.

Critics

After the premiere, the *Sydney Morning Herald* reported: "These romping creatures had been imagined with uncommon penetration into juvenile psychology. Their pranks had an innocent, darting animation, which enkindled the ballet from the very beginning." It went on to compliment the dancers: "Lichine himself made a brilliant impression as a mischievous cadet with a bashful but amorous eye. The facial expressions, the swift attitudes, built up a first-rate comic character-study. . . . Riabouchinska performed her task with the radiance she always brings to the stage." It praised the whole cast individually and added, "It was an evening of splendid dancing in small parts. These were provided, not only in the body of the ballet, but also in a series of charming divertissements."[3]

264

In the United States *Graduation Ball* became the company's bread and butter. However, between the Antipodes and Los Angeles, a few changes had taken place. In the divertissement a variation for Riabouchinska was added to music composed by Dorati, in the manner of Strauss, immediately following the Impromptu Dance, and the "Mathematics and Natural History Lesson" was cut from the program. The "Perpetuum Mobile," originally consisting of a circus number for Riabouchinska and Lichine, was replaced by a youthful dance performed by the same dancers with two junior girls. Riabouchinska's strong objections had prompted these changes. Besides despising her costume, a sort of flashy red bell-like tutu, she believed the number, although well crafted and effective, was out of place, giving the ballet a vaudeville dimension. From its first performance in 1940, *Graduation Ball* became the company's signature piece, as *Le Beau Danube* in the thirties had been the finale of most evenings. During the nine-week engagement in New York, *Graduation Ball* was given thirty-seven times. John Martin wrote in the *New York Times*: "His [Lichine's] 'Graduation Ball' is a work of undeniable talent, fresh in spirit, full of spontaneous invention and totally without swank or pretense. One can think of no other ballet so truly youthful in design and performance."[4]

Today, *Graduation Ball* is in the repertories of many companies, including the Royal Danish Ballet, La Scala Opera Ballet, the London Festival Ballet, Les Grands Ballets Canadiens, the National Ballet of Cuba, the Australian National Ballet, the Dance Theater of Harlem, and many others. Its international popularity began when Lichine staged it for Ballet Theatre in 1944, with himself and Riabouchinska heading the cast. For this revival further changes were made. "La Sylphide and the Scotsman" was replaced by a virtuoso classical pas de deux to exploit the technique of the young Alicia Alonso.

In spite of the popularity of the ballet, revivals present problems. Its light-hearted humor can easily become burlesque if over-exaggerated, especially the passages between the Headmistress and the General. Also, the choreography is sometimes simplified, especially in the fouetté competition, where today most companies perform regular fouettés en tournant. Originally, Denisova and Moulin performed a variety of single and double fouettés combined with pirouettes en attitude, à la seconde, en arabesque, and so on, with different arm positions. In the United States the ballet is a favorite among regional companies. When Riabouchinska and Lichine were guests with the Teatro Colón Ballet in Buenos Aires in 1947, he created a sequel, *Sueño de Niña (Girls' Dormitory)*, to Offenbach music orchestrated by Dorati. This ballet, led by Riabouchinska, was never seen outside of Argentina.

Lichine and Riabouchinska in the "Circus" pas de deux, performed only in Australia.

The ballerinas in their dressing rooms. TOP LEFT, Riabouchinska; TOP RIGHT, Baronova; ABOVE, Toumanova.

October 1940– December 1941

FTER the midnight farewell performance in Sydney, the company sailed for Los Angeles on September 19, aboard the S.S. *Monterey,* arriving there on October 7. The Los Angeles season at the Philharmonic Auditorium that was to start on the tenth was sponsored by the company's general manager, Sol Hurok, and San Francisco impresario L. E. Behymer. For this tour Baronova, now under personal contract to Hurok, joined de Basil, while Fokine, who had left the company after the last Covent Garden engagement, would once more supervise his works in the repertory. Boris Romanov, ballet master of the Metropolitan Opera, was engaged to stage *Giselle,* whose hundredth anniversary would be celebrated during 1941, with the intention of presenting it during the forthcoming New York engagement—an event, however, that never materialized.[1] Other staff choreographers included Lichine, Schwezoff, and Verchinina, with Anatole Oboukhov as ballet master.

Opening night at the Philharmonic featured *Aurora's Wedding,* with Toumanova-Petroff and Riabouchinska-Jasinski; *Le Coq d'or,* with Riabouchinska, Baronova, Rostoff as Dodon, and Algeranoff as the Astrologer; and *Graduation Ball,* led by Riabouchinska, Leskova, and Lichine. It marked the triumphant return of the company to the United States after the 1937–38 tour, and the reunion of Baronova, Riabouchinska, and Toumanova, who in previous seasons, as the "baby ballerinas," had been the backbone of the company's publicity campaign.

In the view of *The American Dancer,* the Original Ballet Russe (as the company had been known since its opening in Australia in 1939) was at its peak:

Aurora's Wedding: Toumanova and Petroff.

For years we have had the questionable delight of seeing a company [Ballet Russe de Monte Carlo] who has been on tour an entire season, and we have had to see the good shine through taut, tired nerves, jaded enthusiasm and filthy ragged costumes. This company is fresh, filled with the excitement of a new American tour, costumes are spotless, crisp and beautiful. Dancers are rested and seem to perform the most arduous *tours de force* with effortless ease, never reaching, but always having untouched reserves of energy.[2]

The artistic deterioration of Denham's Ballet Russe de Monte Carlo sealed Hurok's decision to join forces again with de Basil.[3] John Martin remarked:

The auspices are perhaps unusually fortunate for the success of the Original Ballet Russe, not only because it has been absent for a time but also because it comes on the heels of what is undoubtedly the least distinguished season Massine's company has given. Just what the trouble has been it would be hard to say. Its first season had shortcomings which were

easily forgiven because it was a first season; its second season was seriously handicapped by the outbreak of the war just at sailing time. This year
it was apparently bad luck.[4]

De Basil's recent successful engagements in London and Australia convinced
Hurok that this company would compensate for the Monte Carlo's losses. In view of
the deteriorating relationship between Denham and Massine, the latter's obvious
fatigue resulting from an accumulation of pressures, and the company's failure to live
up to its own artistic standards of 1938–39, Hurok had wisely removed the exclu-
sivity clause from his contract[5] with Universal Art, in his own words "to be free to
experiment."[6] His relationship with Denham worsened as it became clear that Denham was not someone he could manipulate as he wished.

In Los Angeles, Walt Disney based the dance sequences of *Fantasia* on Ballets
Russes dancers, and Ostrich Upanova, Hyacinth Hippo, and Ben Ali Gator were
sketched after Baronova, Riabouchinska, and Lichine. After Los Angeles there were
bookings in Minneapolis and Chicago, after which the Fifty-first Street Theatre in
New York was reserved for an indefinite season. The anticipation was especially great
because of the reappearances of Baronova, Riabouchinska, and Toumanova, as well as
the younger dancers Denisova, Svetlova, Moulin, Stepanova, Leskova, Skibine, and
Tupine, a whole new generation who had never performed in the States, as well as
Nemtchinova. With few exceptions, the company included most of the principal
dancers and personnel introduced in 1933. In New York there was an important addition to the roster: Balanchine, who was invited to rehearse *Cotillon*. If on those previous trips de Basil had been without competition, audiences now would be able to
make comparisons with Denham's company and the recently formed Ballet Theatre.

From the opening performance, it became clear that de Basil's was the leading
company. John Martin noted its excellence in repertory and ballerinas, and although
the Monte Carlo surpassed it in classical danseurs nobles, he praised de Basil's group
for having "more body and unity as a company."[7] The efforts of Yola Miller as lighting director were noted, and Martin saluted the management for having "had the
good sense to engage a lighting expert to give its productions not only scenic atmosphere but simple visibility."[8]

The December issue of *Dance*, dedicated to the Original Ballet Russe, stated:

> Col. de Basil's current sojourn in the United States is nothing short of
> a triumphant return. His company, now as before, is still the Number One
> ballet company—unbeaten and untied, as they say in football.
>
> The personnel of the Original Ballet Russe, especially its feminine
> part, is high above anything that has been seen hereabouts in a long while.
> It includes the three ballerinas, Irina Baronova, Tamara Toumanova and
> Tatiana Riabouchinska . . . who have matured, perfected themselves,
> acquired individual styles which are as distinct and as different as their
> personal appearances.[9]

Eight of the thirty works in the touring repertory (*Cendrillon, Quest* [premiered in Australia as *Etude*], *Eternal Struggle, Graduation Ball, Paganini, Pavane, Prodigal Son,* and *Protée*) were new. Balanchine's *Balustrade* was the only world premiere, while for those works originated by de Basil's company, casting always featured the original artists if they were still with the company. Eugenia Delarova rejoined on November 14, dancing her role of Felicita in *Scuola di ballo,* now called *Ballet School,* as all titles were now known by their English translation.

David Lichine was the choreographic revelation of the season. John Martin wrote in the *New York Times:*

> With the state of the ballet what it is, both as an art and as an institution, the case of the young choreographer is a perplexing one. . . . All the more honor then, to David Lichine, who in the comparatively brief space of seven years has pulled himself up from tentative beginnings with a fantasy called "Nocturne," in 1933, to a position where his accomplishments as a choreographer demand not only acknowledgement but respect. . . . Both "Graduation Ball" and "The Prodigal Son" show skill and authority, but what they show that is of greater moment, perhaps, is an individual approach that is rare and eminently worth cultivating. In this day of widespread anemia, it is enheartening to find a choreographer marching into the field with strength and heartiness, humor and a good, lusty sense of the flesh and the devil.[10]

270

Jealousy and rivalry have traditionally been intimately associated with life in the theater, especially opera and ballet, and both had been rampant in de Basil's company from its very inception. However, the intrigues that gave zest and drama to backstage life never made it into the spotlight until the engagement at the Fifty-first Street Theatre. A disturbing incident occurred when, during a performance of *L'Oiseau de feu,* Baronova's shoulder straps broke as she came onstage for her long and difficult solo. Her upper body was almost entirely exposed, and the audience was in an uproar —people were betting on her chances of making it through her variation. But with her customary aplomb, Baronova continued to dance, acting as unconcerned as possible. During the pas de deux, Petroff did his best to hold her costume together. A later examination showed that the straps had been slit to the breaking point with a razor.

Two benefits were scheduled during this engagement, one for the Tolstoy Foundation on December 5 and the other for the British War Relief Fund on December 11. The latter was to consist of *Les Sylphides, Coq d'or,* an address by Dame Adeline Genée, *Suite des danses classiques* to music by Tchaikovsky, with Markova and Dolin as guest artists, and *Graduation Ball.* However, after all the publicity had been done, Hurok canceled the benefit. There were numerous possible motives for the impresario's decision; however, Irving Deaken, who at the time represented Markova and Dolin, believed that the real reason was Hurok's rage against Markova and Dolin (the originators of the benefit idea) because they had not signed the contracts that Hurok had given them, which would have placed them under his personal management.[11] It was very important for Hurok to have these two under his control because his contract with the Ballet Russe de Monte Carlo contained a clause that stipulated that Denham had to guarantee Markova's appearances. According to Deaken, if Markova signed with Hurok when her contract expired in February 1941, Denham would no longer be able to honor that clause, and Hurok would be able to drop the Ballet Russe de Monte Carlo altogether. Dolin, now a major force behind the newly formed Ballet Theatre, was no less important. If he came under personal contract to Hurok, the impresario could send him to any company under his management, taking him away from Ballet Theatre. This was precisely what Dolin, who did not want to rejoin de Basil's company, feared.

The success of the New York engagement stirred up understandable resentment among those who were striving to establish an indigenous American ballet. The hos-

A caricature by Alex Gard captioned "De Basil's company at the 51st Street Theater, New York: Top left, Grigorieva as Guile disturbs the music of *Paganini* (Rostoff). Top right, Toumanova and Skibine as Illusion and Youth in *The Eternal Struggle.* Center, Baronova as the *Firebird.* Below, Lichine dances the title role in his ballet *The Prodigal Son;* Riabouchinska becomes a demure *Cinderella;* Leskova sets out to find a cadet in *Graduation Ball.*"

271

tility went back to the thirties, and it was openly manifested in *Blast at Ballet,* a pamphlet published in 1938 by Lincoln Kirstein (a co-founder of Balanchine's School of American Ballet in 1934), in which the author attacked the Russian ballet. Now, while the press acclaimed the Original Ballet Russe performances at the Fifty-first Street Theatre, Kirstein again took the Russian ballet to task. Throughout the season he kept up the bombardment: "It is not unfamiliar to hear people praise the Silly Symphonies."[12] In a letter to the editor of the left-wing *P.M.*, under the headline LINCOLN KIRSTEIN SMACKS THE BALLET RUSSE, he continued his devastating and embittered comments: ". . . *Le Coq d'or,* for example, which is a large bore, but full of so much Russian Tea Room decor and properties."[13] His tone was always destructive and negative. But the public obviously didn't agree with Kirstein: the open-ended season lasted a record seventy-nine performances and, when added to the previous three weeks offered by the Monte Carlo company, totaled an unprecedented twelve consecutive weeks of ballet in New York. With Europe at war, New York had become the undisputed ballet capital of the world.

Shortly before the Canadian tour was to begin, three dancers, Sono Osato, Alexandra Denisova, and Alberto Alonso, left the company for personal reasons.

Following Montreal, the company played Toronto, Springfield, Boston, Washington, Baltimore, and Philadelphia. Here, on March 2, upon the expiration of her contract, Toumanova left to join Denham's company.

After a matinée performance in Philadelphia for the benefit of the British War Relief Fund, the Original Ballet Russe traveled to Mexico City, where it opened on March 5 at the Palacio de Bellas Artes. Baronova and Sevastianov, Hurok's tour representative, flew to Mexico City from New York. Extra chairs had to be placed in the aisles to accommodate the overflow audience. It was in Mexico that Lifar's arrangement of *Le Beau Danube* was restored to the repertory.

After twelve performances the company left for Havana via Vera Cruz for a five-day engagement of seven performances, beginning on March 20; Baronova and Sevastianov also flew to Havana. The proposed schedule was then to move on to Panama, proceeding to Lima for the first Pan American tour, which included Peru, Venezuela, Brazil, Chile, and Argentina, all under Hurok's management.[14] Only in Mexico and Cuba did the Sociedad Musical Daniel—a Mexico City–based theatrical management corporation run by impresario Ernesto Quesada—co-sponsor the tour.

In Havana the company experienced its greatest crisis, from which it was never to recover. Lazowski recalled that in Mexico the dancers had been called individually into the office by Vova Grigoriev, the company's secretary, and informed of salary reductions. According to *Variety,*[15] Hurok had reduced the payroll from the usual $5,750 a week to a total of $3,400 a week; the roster was also reduced from the eighty-two people who toured the United States and Canada to sixty-four. Throughout the United States–Canada tour, corps dancers had earned a minimum of $180 a month, in accordance with AGMA scale (the company signed with the union when they arrived from Australia). In Mexico, de Basil was reducing their salaries to an average of $108 a month.[16] On March 18 the dancers presented a letter to Vova Gri-

272

goriev and Alexander Philipoff, the assistant director, demanding $140 per month for South America and $180 per month for Cuba; otherwise they would go on strike in Havana.[17] According to Lazowski, plans for the strike matured on the voyage from Vera Cruz to Cuba. In Havana, Philipoff refused to sign the letter in de Basil's absence, claiming that he lacked authority, and he asked the dancers to perform on opening night at the Teatro Auditorio and wait for de Basil to arrive from New York. But the dancers carried out their threat. The strikers, listed on the statement to AGMA (April 23, 1941), were Borislav Runanine, Serge Berlinraout Ismailoff, Betty Louise Ismailoff, Yvonne Louise Leibbrandt [Irina Zarova, later Ivonne Mounsey], Vladimir Irman, Nicholas Orloff, Oleg Tupine, Cyril Bernstam [Kiril Vassilkovsky], Jean Hunt [Kira Bounina], Mrs. H. Hunt [Jean's mother], M. Tupine, Vassily Tupine, Marcyz Matouchak, Gladys Godby [Nina Golovina], Georges Skibine, Shirley Bridge Andahazy [Anna Adrianova], Lorand Andahazy, Betty Low Weisser [Ludmila Lvova], Robert Weisser [Anton Vlassove or Robert Pagent].

The non-strikers formed a coalition in the midst of the chaos, and the show went on. The opening night program featured *Les Sylphides, Le Coq d'or,* and *Graduation Ball,* with Tchernicheva, Grigoriev, Lichine, Verchinina, Morosova, and many others replacing missing dancers. Riabouchinska, who that night danced a lead in each ballet, joined the corps de ballet in subsequent performances of *Symphonie fantastique* and *Prince Igor.*

When de Basil reached Havana, he offered the striking dancers the chance to return to the company, promising to discuss the matter with each one individually. But the situation worsened when Hurok decided to withdraw his sponsorship because of the internal conflicts, and Baronova, who was under personal contract to him, left after dancing in the third performance. For the following matinée, Riabouchinska replaced her in *Swan Lake* Act II.[18] Denisova was in Havana with her husband, Alberto Alonso, and was invited to take over Baronova's roles as a guest artist. The final performance of the season saw Denisova in *Les Cent Baisers, Les Présages,* and *Graduation Ball.* Cuban president Fulgencio Batista attended with the minister of state, members of the diplomatic corps, and members of the Inter-American Bar Association Conference, then being held in Havana.[19]

Surprisingly, perhaps through the influence of Laura Rayneri de Alonso (president of Pro-Arte Musical, and mother of Alberto), Havana's daily newspapers, in both Spanish and English, reviewed the performances, avoiding any mention of the critical circumstances, while in New York the events in Cuba were followed closely by the dance community. In retrospect, the strike appears paradoxical. From its beginning, many company members suspected that Hurok had a lot to do with it. After his decision to withdraw, most believe that he had engineered it himself to eliminate de Basil and to break the two-year contract that both men had signed. The presence in Havana of Sevastianov, at the time representing Hurok and closely linked with the strikers, made many suspect that he was Hurok's accomplice in the affair.

On April 28 a meeting was scheduled at the Hotel Victoria in New York by AGMA to discuss the position of the dissidents, who were stranded along with the

273

rest of the company in Havana. A letter signed by the nineteen strikers was circulated among the AGMA members, explaining the situation. This letter was also accompanied by a series of questions about AGMA's position in respect to the strikers in view of the union's recent announcement that the strike was unauthorized, since its agreement with de Basil's dancers covered only the United States and Canada. According to the dancers' statement, they could not obtain their passports, which de Basil had in his possession.[20] According to Charles Payne, when Sevastianov arrived in New York, he "pressed the strikers' case with AGMA and continued to do so through correspondence to direct their activities in Havana."[21]

It is hard to ascertain whether or not Hurok was behind the strike from the beginning or simply took advantage of the dancers' decision. There certainly was motivation for both: Hurok's new interest in Ballet Theatre, and his wish to oust de Basil, for which there had been precedent in London in 1938, and which would enable Hurok to take over the company. The Original Ballet Russe was superior to any other ballet company of the time and it seems unlikely that Hurok would have risked such an opportunity in favor of any patriotic leanings towards Ballet Theatre. It is clear that Ballet Theatre was not Hurok's top priority and that ever since the unsuccessful merger attempts in 1938 he had been aiming towards one company under one management, all of which is confirmed by the Irving Deaken–Anton Dolin correspondence. Deaken reports to Dolin Hurok's remarks that Ballet Theatre is a "flop." Hurok threatens Dolin and Ballet Theatre by saying to Deaken, "If they are not careful, there's going to be only one ballet company and that will be my ballet company. I'll see to that."[22] As late as May 5, David Lichine received a telegram in Havana indicating Hurok's willingness to proceed with the tour, with extra stars (under personal contract to Hurok), if de Basil would let his company go.[23] De Basil was in New York then and had already categorically refused any form of relinquishment, while Lichine and Riabouchinska similarly declined to answer any such offers.

By June, Hurok, free of any obligations towards the Original Ballet Russe, signed with Ballet Theatre, taking with him Sevastianov and some of the strikers. He also refused to pay those stranded in Cuba for their final four performances or to provide return transportation.[24] De Basil filed a lawsuit in New York, charging conspiracy, against both Hurok and Sevastianov. According to de Basil's charges in *Variety,* "Hurok never provided payments for the company for the last four Havana performances and withdrew the bond guaranteeing return transportation."[25] *Variety* added: "AGMA states return bond was never posted with it as its jurisdiction outside of the U.S. is doubtful because pact between producer and impresario was negotiated in Australia."[26] According to Charles Payne, after de Basil accused Hurok and Sevastianov of sabotage and filed charges, Hurok's first decision was to settle out of court, but Harry Zuckert, Ballet Theatre's legal consultant, "insisted that since Ballet Theatre (and presumably Hurok) was innocent of charges, it could not admit to even partial guilt, which would be implicit in the settlement."[27] The charges were dismissed on the technicality that de Basil, now in South America, was not present in court. Payne feels that "it seems incredible that such astute lawyers as Harry M. Zuckert, Morris Permut and John Wharton should have been confident that the court would decide in favor of Ballet Theatre."[28] In hindsight, Payne, then secretary-treasurer of Ballet Theatre, finds it unbelievable that he himself accepted this "version of the affair and [was] convinced that Ballet Theatre was not even unknowingly involved in a conspiracy."[29]

According to Fortune Gallo, Hurok saved himself $38,500 by canceling de Basil's contract. Gallo goes on to say:

> Hurok had the Ballet Russe booked in this country twenty weeks according to his contract but only gave them seventeen weeks, thereby saving himself 5,500 dollars each of the three weeks, or 16,500 dollars. He was to pay the Colonel at the end of twenty weeks in this country 10,000 dollars according to the contract, so the Colonel could move his company wherever he wished, and this was not paid. Then again, if Mr. Hurok exercised his option for the season 1941–42, which he did, he was to pay the Colonel another 12,000 dollars, but this was not paid. The above 38,500 dollars Hurok saved by making a new contract with the Colonel to take the ballet down to South America but at the end of three weeks he cancelled it, leaving the company in Havana, and saving himself 38,500 dollars.[30]

For five months the members of the Original Ballet Russe were stranded in Havana, scattered around town in inexpensive lodgings. De Basil had permitted performing groups to be organized using the company's music and costumes to present divertissement programs. One of these groups was headed by Lazowski, and another by Algeranoff. Señora Alonso scheduled four performances at the Teatro Auditorio on April 22, 23, and 24, for which occasions Denisova rejoined the company.

On April 21, Lichine opened an Afro-Cuban dance act called *Conga Pantera* at the Tropicana nightclub. The ballet was led by Leskova as the panther, with an ensemble of black dancers, and was the highlight of Havana's nightlife for many months. It was presented in the nightclub's famous garden theater restaurant, which provided an exotic setting of tropical vegetation. Lichine received a modest salary, but negotiated with the management to ensure that the dancers were given dinner in the casino during the entire run.

On July 25 and 26, the Sociedad Pro-Arte sponsored another two performances in the Teatro Auditorio. All the Pro-Arte programs were conducted by Dorati, but Lichine and Riabouchinska did not participate in this last engagement, for they had departed for their farm in New Jersey, partly to liquidate certain valuables to help pay off the Cuban debts.

While these events were taking place in Havana, in New York de Basil was finding the way to bring the company back to the States. He negotiated through Nicholas Koudriavtzeff, who at one time was Hurok's representative in Canada, to arrange a tour of Canada under the management of Frank Benedict. Also in New York de Basil negotiated with Fortune Gallo, who had previously shown interest in sponsoring the company's 1938–39 American tour, to represent the company in the United States. A shareholding corporation, Ballet Art, Inc., was set up in New York with de Basil as president and Gallo as treasurer, secretary, and chairman. De Basil was responsible for hiring the personnel, and Gallo was to book and advertise the company in the United States, and possibly organize a tour of South America to begin in April 1942. De Basil freed Gallo from any of the company's past debts, and Gallo in turn would pay de Basil $3,000 to transport the company back to New York.[31] In New York, de Basil engaged Nana Gollner, from Ballet Theatre, and Nemtchinova to share with Riabouchinska the status of ballerina. Other recruits included Moussia Larkina (Mouscelyne Larkin), Leon Danielian, and Kenneth Mackenzie.

The first performances under Gallo's management took place at the Watergate Theatre in Washington, August 23 to 29. Nijinska joined as ballet mistress and Alexander Smallens replaced Dorati as conductor. Following this came successful engagements in Canada under the management of Frank Benedict. On September 19, the company gave a ball at Toronto's Eaton Auditorium for the benefit of the *Evening Telegram* British War Victims' Fund, and on September 22, the season opened in Massey Hall. The Original Ballet Russe followed immediately after the engagement of the Ballet Russe de Monte Carlo at the Royal Alexandra, a situation that prevented either company from having full houses. De Basil's company opened in Ottawa on September 29, in Montreal on October 1 (where the *Standard* reported that it had been "the most successful stage event in Canadian history" and that the company's "gross receipts shatter all Montreal records for any stage production"[32]), and in Quebec on October 14. From Canada the company traveled to Chicago, where it opened on October 20, and from there to Detroit for a November 2 opening, again under the aegis of Fortune Gallo.

At this point the prospects of a cross-country tour became unlikely, as Hurok had monopolized bookings with his priority through the National Broadcasting Company. There were talks concerning a merger between the two impresarios in order to avoid interference in booking their respective companies. This never materialized, and right after the Canadian season the relationship between Gallo and de Basil began to deteriorate. Gallo felt that the corporation should have received four percent of the Canadian earnings, amounting to $15,000. He complained that the company was costing him $5,000 and not the $3,500 to $4,000 that de Basil had reported to him. He also felt that Hurok was doing his best to obstruct his progress.[33] After Detroit, the tour of the West Coast was canceled and the company moved to New York, where the dancers' headquarters was established at the Park Central Hotel. With no possibility of remaining in the United States, de Basil arranged an engagement in Mexico. With the help of Mario Gallo, the impresario's nephew, Vova Grigoriev organized the transportation of the company and properties to Mexico City.

On December 12, 1941, René Blum was interned at the concentration camp of Royallieu. Later, he was transferred to Drancy, where, on September 23, 1942, he boarded a train with eighty other French intellectuals and was set on the road of deportation without return.

BALUSTRADE

Ballet in four movements; music by Igor Stravinsky, Concerto for Violin and Orchestra; choreography by Balanchine; set and costume design by Pavel Tchelitchev; costumes executed by Madame Karinska; premiere January 22, 1941, at the Fifty-first Street Theatre, New York, conducted by Igor Stravinsky.

ORIGINAL CAST

Toccata	Tatiana Leskova, Roman Jasinski, and corps de ballet	Aria II	Tamara Toumanova, Roman Jasinski, Paul Petroff
Aria I	Galina Razoumova, Paul Petroff, Sonia Orlova, Irina Zarova, and corps de ballet	Capriccio	Entire Cast

During the American tour of 1940–41, Balanchine returned as a guest choreographer, to collaborate with de Basil for the first and last time since his departure in 1932. The project promised to be memorable, not least because it would include two other great artists, Stravinsky and Tchelitchev. According to Parker Tyler, Tchelitchev's biographer, Balanchine approached the designer, who was recovering from ill health, and persuaded him to undertake the set and costume design.[1] Even though the ballet was without plot, Tchelitchev suggested through his decor and costumes an enchanted, surrealistic garden inhabited by fantastic creatures and birds. This idea was most likely Tchelitchev's, for Balanchine is quoted in the *New York Times* as saying that the ballet "has no story but is a contrast of moods in movement and color. It is not an illustration but a reflection of Mr. Stravinsky's music."[2] There was no scenario, but there were, certainly, suggested atmosphere and characters, on which the three collaborators agreed and set to work immediately after the new year.

As *Cotillon* had been in the thirties, *Balustrade*—the title inspired by Tchelitchev's decor—was a milestone in Balanchine's development. It inaugurated the forties, a prolific decade during which he was to establish definite stylistic preferences and choreographic syntax. This ballet possessed no story and its only concern was for movement as a physical expression of the music. It is of interest to note that Balanchine's two previous ballets, *Le Baiser de la fée* and *Jeu de cartes,* both created in 1937, had libretti, as did most of his works produced since his arrival in the United States (with the notable exception of *Serenade*).

Edwin Denby wrote: "Since 1940, it seems to me, Balanchine's choreographic style has more and more clarified the dancer's momentum in motion. . . . The spring of the steps and the thrust of the gesture clarify and characterize the dancer's changing impetus. . . . His present style is not an oblique neo-classicism, it is a direct new classicism."[3]

Music

Balustrade was the first ballet version of Stravinsky's violin concerto. The concerto was dedicated to Samuel Dushkin, who collaborated with the composer, advising him on the technique of the instrument. Its orchestral premiere took place in 1931 with Dushkin playing and Stravinsky at the podium. The concerto was divided into four movements: Toccata, Aria I, Aria II, and Capriccio.

Scenery and Costumes

Tchelitchev's poetic scenery suggested a fantasy garden, and the costumes, fabulous garden creatures. The decor consisted of a low, white balustrade in perspective with two (in Lillian Moore's words) "pale, macabre, skeleton trees of which the artist is so fond"[4] lit in red against a black background.

The corps de ballet wore grey silk tights, tops with batlike wings, and bandeau-like headpieces with two circles suggesting owl-like eyes. The female lead for the Toccata wore a blue dress with painted veins and a tree branch headpiece. The female lead for Aria I was dressed in a chiffon dress in shades of pink and grey. The male leads for the first two movements wore jackets with veins painted on the puffed sleeves, small headpieces with leaf motifs, and tights. The woman in the Aria II wore a black sleeveless dress, with a georgette skirt fringed down the center, and long black gloves. The bodice of her dress, the gloves, and the toe shoes were ornamented with rhinestones; a small crescent moon crowned her head. Her two companions had turtlenecked black leotards and tights and visorless caps. The caps, the turtlenecked collars, the belts, and slippers were also adorned with rhinestones. In the fourth movement, the dancers from Aria II again wore the black outfits.

278

Choreography

Balustrade was set entirely in terms of dance movements, an enterprise not new to Balanchine; however, the structure of the choreography was very intricate. With the exception of Aria II, a pas de trois, Balanchine used the interweaving of individual dancers and groups to create geometrical patterns. At times the soloists detached themselves from large groups. At other times the soloists appeared as individual units that would merge with other units, eventually to create a new mass. It was a continuous process of assembling and fragmenting, dominated by a strong sense of organizational structure but achieved with such speed and precision that the spectator was taken by surprise with each new formation. And yet, there was also an elaborate construction that provided a feeling of slow motion that enhanced the work's duality.[5]

For Toumanova, the center of the production, *Balustrade* marked a continuation of the method Balanchine had formulated in *Cotillon*: "Many of the peculiarities of *Balustrade* were in embryo form in *Cotillon*, and in 1941 he developed them further. First there was his 'dentellisme' (lace work)—very intricate pointe work, as if the toes were weaving the most complex designs. Some of these steps and other choreographic motifs recurred throughout the ballet. There was also a more accentuated concern for line. Not only the line of the individual movement of each dancer, but the overall geometrical construction of the groups."

ABOVE: Pas de trois: Toumanova, Petroff, and Panaiev. LEFT: Jasinski, Toumanova, and Petroff. BELOW: Final movement: Leskova, Panaiev, Toumanova, Petroff, and Razoumova.

279

Denby, reviewing the ballet, wrote: "I noticed two elements or 'motifs': the upstretch on the downbeat; and one knee slipping across the other in a little gesture of conventional shame. The first syncopic element Balanchine enlarges into the liveliest and lightest ensemble dances; the second element—one of gesture—he elaborates into a long acrobatic trio in which all sorts of 'slippings across' are tried—of legs, of bodies, of arms; and this trio ends by a separation, the girl looking reproachful, the boys hanging their heads in shame. How strangely such a concrete moment tops the abstract acrobatics before it; a discontinuity in one's way of seeing that is bridged by the clearness of placing and the sureness of timing."[6]

The work was built around the four parts of the violin concerto. The first movement had two soloists, Leskova (in the role originally announced for Riabouchinska, who left soon after rehearsals began) and Jasinski. The second movement had Razoumova (intended for Baronova, who also left shortly after rehearsals started) and Petroff joined by Orlova and Zarova (Ivonne Mounsey). The third was a pas de trois for Toumanova, Jasinski, and Petroff, while in the fourth, the corps de ballet was led by the soloists of the previous movements.

The most controversial movement was the pas de trois, for which Balanchine devised fantastic designs of bodily weaving full of sensual suggestiveness. Toumanova, Petroff, and Jasinski performed a trio in which the female dancer's legs hooked in various positions around her partners' waists; the dancers wore black outfits that became lost against the black background, so that the audience could discern only heads with rhinestone-studded headpieces and black toe shoes and elbow-length gloves also ornamented with light-reflecting gems. This unusual choreographic design inspired boos, cheers, applause, and laughter from the audience.

The finale departed considerably from Balanchine's early works. It was a grandiose formation of dancers collectively performing with great impetus a continuous sequence of movements that were fascinating in their powerful and breathtaking effect. For Toumanova, "it was like an ocean, a crescendo of waves composed by dancers in motion, but always with a strong sense of symmetry."

Perhaps it was not only the sensual acrobatics of the pas de trois that were shocking but the whole choreographic concept explored in the work. The pas de trois functioned as a sort of exorcism to provide some relief for the audience from the disturbing effect of the ballet. Anatole Chujoy said, "If some of Balanchine's work can be described as nervous, then this one is a nervous breakdown."[7]

The female role in *Balustrade* was expanded from the one in *Cotillon,* resulting in the transformation of the enigmatic adolescent into an enigmatic woman. While *Cotillon* contained implicit sexual overtones, in *Balustrade* they found more open expression.

Concerning these roles, Toumanova felt: "*Cotillon* and *Balustrade* exploited my personality at two different epochs of my life, not only psychologically, but physically as well. . . . *Balustrade* was imbued with a femininity that was alien to me in 1932." Walter Terry said: "Toumanova was beautiful to look at and danced with sureness, ease and electric manner."[8] And Anatole Chujoy remarked: "She, perhaps, more than any other dancer I can think of, is the perfect exponent of Balanchine's choreographic inventions."[9] She appeared as a statuelike figure with, in Denby's words, her "deadly face,"[10] incomparably regal, puzzling, and sinister. She enhanced the choreography with her dazzling legs, swordlike toes, high leg extensions, sharp pirouettes, and long-poised balances.

Nor is it possible to overlook the invaluable contribution of Tchelitchev's costumes and scenery, though Denby found the costumes "elegant but annoying . . . obscuring the differentiation of steps and messing up the dance."[11]

Critics
Reaction to the work was widely divergent. According to Kolodin in the *New York Sun,* Balanchine "has exceeded himself in the designing of intricate weavings of hands and legs and stunty groupings. But if he has done any more than this, it has escaped the notice of this onlooker. To be sure, one is hardly so naive as to expect meaning or significance from a ballet, especially one that uses Stravinsky's acidulous and banal violin concerto as a point of departure."[12]

John Martin, in the *New York Times,* merely quoted the program and added: "Beyond the recording of these simple facts, the event need not detain us. Nobody involved in it can have been very serious about it, so there seems little reason for anybody else to be."[13] He resented that "while gifted American artists are starving in the effort to bring their work before the public, there is money available for the production of European importations of this calibre."[14]

Virgil Thomson joined Denby in praising the work, writing in the *New York Herald Tribune*:

281

> It is exactly because of its lack of any floating cantilena, and of sparkling passage work, cadenzas, show-off matter in general that it is ideal for continuous choreographic composition. It is as tightly knit and woven as a bird cage. As four bird cages to be exact . . .
>
> [The ballet's] accentuated emotional quality . . . concentrated in and expressed by a structural ingenuity, seems to have given Mr. Balanchine his first chance in several years to do what he loves to do best, to build long choreographic "variations," as the dancing world calls them, over tightly knit continuity. . . . They seem to have come out of the music and to walk in closed communion beside it, the closeness of this communion providing an independence so characteristic of Balanchine, that relieved the dancers from any pedestrian obligation to keep step with the measure.[15]

Stravinsky himself considered *Balustrade* to be "one of the most satisfactory visualizations of any of my theatre works. . . . a dance dialogue in perfect co-ordination with the dialogues of the music."[16]

In 1972 Balanchine created a new ballet to the same score for the New York City Ballet, entitled *Stravinsky Violin Concerto.*

The company's ballerinas during the South American years. Clockwise from top: Morosova, Stroganova, Stepanova, and Moulin.

January 1942–
August 1946

ON JANUARY 5, 1942, the Original Ballet Russe began a season (ending on January 25) at Mexico City's Palacio de Bellas Artes, sponsored once more by Ernesto de Quesada from the Sociedad Musical Daniel. Eugene Fuerst joined the company as principal conductor. The opening program consisted of *Swan Lake* Act II, *Paganini, Protée,* and *Prince Igor.* Riabouchinska, Lichine, Nina Stroganova, and Vladimir Dokoudovsky drove all that night in order to arrive in Mexico City the following morning. (Stroganova and Dokoudovsky both came to de Basil via Ballet Theatre, after auditioning for him and Lichine in New York.) Stroganova and Dokoudovsky were scheduled to rehearse their new repertory immediately upon arrival. Many long hours of rehearsal later, they made their debut in the company's second performance, when Stroganova took Denisova's part in the *Graduation Ball* fouetté competition and Dokoudovsky performed the pas de deux in "La Sylphide and the Scotsman," the role originally created by Petroff. This production of *Graduation Ball* featured a rare appearance by Lichine as the Drummer.

The company's success during its previous visit ensured an even more enthusiastic response from the Mexican public and the press. The major daily newspapers featured long and detailed reviews that indicated a conscientious effort at cultivation of the art of ballet. Among the assiduous ballet-goers who lent glamour to the season were two London admirers from the pre-war days: Carol, former king of Rumania, and Mme Lupescu.

When the Mexico City engagement ended, the company moved on to the Teatro Degollado in Guadalajara, from January 23 to 27, to celebrate the four-hundredth anniversary of that city. Riabouchinska and Lichine had returned to New York from Mexico City.

De Basil celebrated his company's tenth anniversary in somewhat gloomy and uncertain circumstances. Cut off from Europe because of the war, and from the United States as the result of the latest developments with Hurok, the Ballets Russes was without future prospects. Fortunately, de Basil was able to arrange a first tour to South America, to open on April 10, at the Teatro Municipal in Rio de Janeiro.[1]

In Rio, Shabelevsky, who had left de Basil's company at the beginning of the 1938–39 Australian tour for personal reasons, returned now as a guest artist. The roster included Tchernicheva, Gollner, Grigorieva, Morosova, Volkova, Moulin, Leskova, Stepanova, Stroganova, Larkina, Obidenna, Jasinski, Tupine, Mackenzie, Petroff, Rostoff, Orloff, Algeranoff, Ladré, Dokoudovsky, and Matouchak.

The company toured through South America twice, starting in Brazil, from April 10 to May 25, first at the Teatro Municipal in Rio and then at the Teatro Municipal in São Paulo. The next stop was Buenos Aires at the Teatro Politeama Argentino from June 12 to July 12. Balanchine, who was engaged at the Teatro Colón to choreograph a new work to a Mozart Violin Concerto and to restage *Apollo*, attended these performances. He asked Leskova to join him at the Teatro Colón, where Shabelevsky was now guest artist, but even though she did attend some of the rehearsals there, de Basil did not free her from her contract. From Buenos Aires they visited Montevideo, where they performed at the S.O.D.R.E. from July 15 to August 2. The company returned to Argentina to tour Rosario (Teatro Municipal), Córdoba (Teatro Rivera Indarte), and Mendoza (Teatro Municipal) from August 5 to 27. They performed in Chile from September 1 to October 4 at the Teatro Municipal in Santiago and at the Teatro Municipal in Viña del Mar, returning to Buenos Aires for their first season at the Teatro Colón from October 15 to November 28.

Backstage after a performance of *Aurora's Wedding*. Left to right: Andreyev, Bechenova, Dokoudovsky, Moulin, Stepanova, Tupine, Stroganova, Mackenzie, Ladré.

The company in Montevideo. Back row: third from left, Hawtrey; fifth from left, Celada; seventh from left, Yurikov; ninth from left, Stepanova; Terekov, Psota. Front row: Bechenova (in profile), Pereyra, Galval, unidentified, Larkina, Tchernicheva, Grigoriev, Moulin, Dokoudovsky, Stroganova.

285

After the Ballets Russes engagement at the Politeama, Margarita Wallmann, head of the Colón Ballet, invited the troupe to collaborate in the forthcoming season at the Colón.[2] For the occasion both companies performed one or two ballets in each of the twice-weekly programs, and dancers of both companies alternated roles in order to learn both repertories. With two directors, two companies, and two repertories under one roof, the collaboration was not successful.

After the Teatro Colón the company returned to Córdoba (Teatro Griego), from December 4 to January 11, 1943. The next stop was again Viña del Mar, from January 16 to February 16, and then, for the first time, to Lima (Teatro Municipal), from March 14 to April 4, and on to La Paz (Teatro Municipal), from April 13 to 18. From Bolivia the company returned to the Teatro Colón in Buenos Aires, from April 22 to November 28, for a joint season with its resident company. This time, with Wallmann absent owing to prior commitments in Europe, de Basil's collaboration with the resident ballet and opera went smoothly, and he was billed as director of the ballet.

Next they visited Montevideo, where they inaugurated the Teatro Municipal de Verano and participated in the opera season at the S.O.D.R.E., from December 29 to March 31, 1944.

The second transcontinental tour, mostly represented by N. Loutchinsky,[3] with limited support from national ministries of education and culture, began in Brazil (Rio and São Paulo), from April 10 to June 21. The company returned then to S.O.D.R.E., from June 30 to August 20, and then went on to Buenos Aires (Teatro Avenida), from August 28 to October 1. After Buenos Aires they visited Santa Fe (Teatro Municipal) and Rosario (Teatro Municipal) and left Argentina to open their second season in Santiago (Teatro Municipal), from October 11 to 17. The Christmas and New Year holidays of 1944 saw them performing at the Teatro Municipal of Lima, from December 16 to January 16, 1945. They visited Ecuador for the first time, from January 30 to February 24, performing in Guayaquil (Teatro Nueve de Octubre) and Quito (Teatro Municipal). A tour of Colombia followed, from March 6 to April 20: Bogotá (Teatro del Colón), Medellín (Teatro Bolívar), Barranquilla (Teatro Apolo), and Cartagena (Teatro Heredia). They performed in Caracas (Teatro Municipal), from mid-July to August 19.

Their first tour through Central America began in Panama, from September 2 to October 13, and on to San José, Costa Rica, from October 15 to November 9; Tegucigalpa, Honduras, from November 11 to 13; San Salvador and Santa Ana, El Salvador, from November 14 to December 3; and Guatemala, from December 4 to 31. They returned to Mexico in 1946 for a national tour, and then went to Havana (opening there on May 14) before returning to Brazil for the last time.

During the four-year tour new members joined, including April Olrich, Carlota Pereyra, Miguel Terekov, and the conductor William McDermott. Much to de Basil's dismay, however, his most outstanding artists defected in search of better opportunities. These included Grigorieva, Leskova, Volkova, Petroff, and Gollner.

286 The reception of the Ballets Russes in Latin America was spectacular and of paramount importance to the artistic life of the cities visited, especially São Paulo, Rio de Janeiro, and Buenos Aires, where the company found instant acceptance into the mainstream of cultural life. Because of the constant flow of ballet guest artists and companies, these cities had already developed a true appreciation of the art. When the company made its debut in Buenos Aires at the Teatro Politeama Argentino in 1942, they had the support of the city's intellectuals and the upper classes because the achievements of the thirties had been chronicled by the leading newspaper, *La Nación*. In Buenos Aires there was also a large community of European emigrants from the Second World War, as well as refugees from the Spanish Civil War, who had been previously acquainted with the Ballets Russes. Among the Spanish intellectuals and artists in exile who had always admired de Basil's repertory was Diaghilev's former collaborator Manuel de Falla. Now, despite the absence of some of the more familiar names in the company, they, too, offered their support. Ballet was well established in Buenos Aires; its great opera house, the Teatro Colón, had engaged Fokine, Nijinska, and, in 1942, Balanchine.

The war years in South America deserve a book of their own. Under precarious conditions, the travel-weary dancers journeyed from the sophistication of such cities as Rio de Janeiro, Buenos Aires, and Santiago across jungles, pampas, and the Andes to smaller, often quasi-primitive towns. There was, however, a special feeling of satisfaction in what they were doing. Not since the days of Diaghilev and Pavlova had the larger cities seen dancing of such high caliber; indeed, some of the smaller communities had never seen any ballets at all. In several countries the Ballets Russes performances inspired local groups to found their own schools and companies. And, as in Australia, some of de Basil's dancers stayed behind to help establish these new ventures.

In Latin America, de Basil, encouraged by the American popularity of *Union Pacific*, relied once more on the use of national themes in new works. This had become an effective maneuver to infiltrate local artistic circles and gain private funding.

The first work produced in South America was *Fue una vez*, created for the company's debut at the Teatro Colón. The music was by Carlos Gustavino, the scenery and costumes by Ignacio Pirovino, the sets executed by Constantino Popoff and the costumes by Maria Tcherpennikova. It had its premiere at the Teatro Colón on November 27, 1942, conducted by Eugene Fuerst.

The ballet was based on the life and customs of Buenos Aires in 1830, inspired by the lithographs (1829–30) of Cesar Hipolito Baclo and the watercolors of Carlos Pellegrini.[4] The choreography was credited to Sylvia Pueyrredon de Elizalde and the mise en scène to Vania Psota. The lead dancers were Nana Gollner, Roman Jasinski, Kenneth Mackenzie, and Lara Obidenna. According to the dancers, Señora Elizalde never rehearsed them and probably was responsible only for securing the funding; Psota rehearsed the dancers, and most likely did the choreography, incorporating some of Señora Elizalde's ideas. Sorley Walker claims that "the company gossip was that she was pregnant, and believed that if she worked on a ballet her child would be a choreographer."[5]

The second creation, a co-production with the Colón ballet, also boasted a regional theme. *El Malón* had a commissioned score and scenario by Hector Iglesias Villoud, and was choreographed by Psota. The scenery and costumes were by Hector Basaldua, resident designer of the Colón; the costumes were executed by Juan Mancini. The story revolved around an Indian attack on a village just as two of its inhabitants are about to celebrate their marriage.

In 1936 Psota had left de Basil to become ballet master in Brno, Czechoslovakia, where he remained from 1936 through 1941. In 1941 he arrived in the United States and became ballet master of Ballet Theatre, where he created *Slavonica* to Dvořák's Slavonic Dances, with little success. He rejoined de Basil in 1941 and became the company choreographer. *El Malón* was his second ballet and proved to be unsuccessful also. Antonio Barceló assisted Psota with the choreography of the Argentinian folk dances so that the dance steps would be authentic. The leading roles were danced by Esmeralda Agoglia (a seventeen-year-old Colón dancer), Angel Eleta, and Kenneth Mackenzie. The ballet was first presented at the Teatro Colón on July 16, 1943, with Iglesias Villoud conducting the orchestra and Rafael Terragnolo directing the choir.

During the company's second visit to Montevideo, it inaugurated the open-air Teatro Municipal de Verano at Rodo Park. It also participated in the opera season, and performed as well at the Teatro S.O.D.R.E. At the S.O.D.R.E. Psota collaborated in

287

Les Femmes de bonne humeur: Stepanova, Stroganova, Larkina,
Morosova, Bechenova, and Dokoudovsky.

the creation of *La Isla de los Ceibos*, with composer Eduardo Fabini and Jacob Anchu-
tin, the company scene painter, who this time designed the scenery and costumes.
The scenario—an ode to the native ceiba tree—was provided by Roman Vignoly
Barreto. Leading roles were taken by Stepanova, Volkova, Larkina, Mackenzie, and
Tupine. The premiere took place on February 11, 1944.

In 1945 a divertissement was added to the permanent repertoire of the company. It included *Pas de Deux* (music by Chabrier; choreography by Balanchine; performed by Olga Morosova and Kenneth Mackenzie); *Farruca* (music by Falla;
choreography by Eleta; performed by Angel Eleta); *Pas de Deux classique* (music by
Tchaikovsky; choreography by Petipa; performed by Geneviève Moulin and Roman
Jasinski); *Vienna 1860* (music by J. Strauss; choreography by Dokoudovsky; performed by Nina Stroganova); *Danza-Romanza* (music by Segundo Moreno; choreographed by Mackenzie; costumes by Lloyd Wulf; performed by Carlota Pereyra and
Kenneth Mackenzie); *Mazur-Obertas* (folkloric dance arranged by M. Ladré; music
by Lewandowski; performed by Tatiana Bechenova, Marian Ladré, and Angel Eleta);
Bufones Rusos (music by Rimsky-Korsakov; choreography by Dokoudovsky; performed by Kiril Vassilkovsky, Celada, Fedoroff, Thomson, and Yurekoff); *Gai Paris . . .*
(music by Offenbach; choreographed by Dokoudovsky; performed by Nina Stroganova and Vladimir Dokoudovsky).

Some of these numbers had originally been choreographed for a divertissement
presented on November 3, 1943, at the Teatro Colón in a gala to benefit the Junta
Protectora de Obras Sociales de la Republica Argentina y del Patronato de Leprosos
(Council for the Preservation of the Social Welfare of the Argentinian Republic and
the Guardianship of Lepers). This gala included the following divertissement: Pas de
Deux from *Swan Lake*; *Vienna 1860*; Drummer Variation from *Graduation Ball*; scene
from *The Good-Humoured Ladies*; *Gai Paris . . .*; Grand Pas classique from *Coppélia*;
"The Three Ivans" from *Aurora's Wedding*.

Before returning to Mexico, the company stopped in Guatemala, where Psota produced another ballet, *YX-KIK*, based on a Maya-Quiche legend by Ricardo and Jesus Castillo. So ephemeral was the ballet that most dancers have no memory of its short life.

From January until April the company gave performances at the Palacio de Bellas Artes and the Plaza de Toros (bull ring) and toured Monterrey, Laredo, Guadalajara, Vera Cruz, and Jalapa. Lichine premiered *Cain and Abel* at the Bellas Artes on April 16.

When the company arrived in Mexico City in January 1946, it marked the first reunion since 1941 of such old members as Baronova, Riabouchinska, Lichine, and Sevastianov.

Although Baronova had participated in Massine's short-lived Ballet Russe Highlights, she had remained virtually inactive since her last association with Ballet Theatre. She was to join de Basil as a guest artist in Cuba and had come to Mexico in order to start rehearsals. Sevastianov, now pursuing other business interests, accompanied her.

Even though Riabouchinska and Lichine had elected to remain in the United States, they always maintained close correspondence with de Basil.[6]

$\mathcal{F}$OR the 1946 Mexican tour, Riabouchinska's appearance was to be limited since she was five months pregnant, and the only role she performed was her legendary prelude in *Les Sylphides*. Dancers who had not seen it before crowded the wings to observe how she glided, with her back to the audience, in bourrée from back stage center to front center in a cambré position. This had left such an impression that when the company moved on to Havana, after a five-year absence, critics immediately noticed that Moulin had omitted it.[7]

289

Moulin and Jasinski in Havana.

The ensuing Cuban engagement was sponsored by the Sociedad de Amigos de la Música, under the presidency of Señora May MacCarthy de Gomez Cueto.[8] Although the season, which began on May 14, took place at the Teatro Auditorio, headquarters of Pro-Arte, this organization was not involved in the engagement. This was probably to a great extent due to the achievements of Pro-Arte's dance school, which was by then presenting ballet seasons throughout Cuba. Alexandra Denisova and Alberto Alonso, directors of the school since 1941, figured prominently in its development. Denisova left in 1944 after divorcing Alonso.[9]

After a successful run at the Auditorio, the company traveled to Rio de Janeiro in a ship sent especially by the Brazilian government. Baronova came to Rio but almost immediately returned to England, where she was to star in the play *A Bullet in the Ballet*. Her short association with de Basil did not fulfill its promise. The ballerina was going through a personal and professional crisis that was soon to lead to her divorce from Sevastianov and her final retirement from the stage.

For its return to Brazil, the Original Ballet Russe was represented by Count Jean de Beausacq, the future husband of Verchinina, under the partial management of N. Viggiani.[10] The company was scheduled to perform in Rio de Janeiro (from June 10 to July 10), São Paulo (from July 18 to August 4), and then again in Rio (from August 10 to 31), before coming to the United States. The only novelty for the first season in Rio that was highly praised was *Cain and Abel*, and among the works that attracted considerable attention was *Paganini*.

In São Paulo, the Original Ballet Russe created its finest ballets of the South American period in Verchinina's *Valse triste* and Psota's *Yara*.

Valse triste was not based on any regional or folk tale but instead was a choreographic poem to melancholy: though man strives to achieve happiness, his soul is always overcome with sadness. The ballet was set to Sibelius's piece of the same name, and the scenery and costumes were designed by Jan Zach, a Czech artist resid-

Yara: Dokoudovsky and Stroganova as the Black Couple.

Yara: Finale.

ing in São Paulo. Verchinina danced the leading role of Melancholy, with April Olrich as Life. *Valse triste* was an amplification of Verchinina's personal choreographic vocabulary already explored in *Quest*, blending classical ballet with modern dance. It was presented on July 26, 1946, at the Teatro Municipal in São Paulo, with the orchestra under the direction of McDermott.

The premiere of *Yara* was one of the most important artistic events in Brazil in 1946, marking the close collaboration of Guilherme de Almeida, Francisco Mignone, and Candido Portinari. The ballet was based on a scenario by de Almeida concerning Yara, the rain goddess, who, dominated by the Sun, induces a drought, causing disaster to farmers until she reappears. Mignone's score was inspired by strongly rhythmical Afro-Brazilian dances and rituals, in the same style as "Congada," from *Os contratados dos diamantes*, which had been introduced in New York by Toscanini in 1940. When the curtain went up, Portinari's decor received thunderous applause, but Psota's choreography, although his best in South America, could not match the artistic level of his collaborators. The leading roles were created by Stepanova, Moulin, Stroganova, Tupine, Mackenzie, and Dokoudovsky. The ballet was first performed on July 31, 1946, at the Teatro Municipal, conducted by the composer.

When the ballet was presented in New York, Denby remarked that it had "no dance interest,"[11] and John Martin wrote:

> *Yara* is a long, involved and inept work based on Brazilian folklore, and though its music is by Francisco Mignone and its decor by Candido Portinari, both prominent artists of Brazil, there is no use going into it here. It won't be around much longer, anyway.[12]

CAIN AND ABEL

Ballet in one act; music by Richard Wagner, assembled by William McDermott; libretto by David Lichine after the biblical theme; choreography by David Lichine; set and costume design by Miguel Prieto; set executed by Jacob Anchutin; premiere April 16, 1946, at the Palacio de Bellas Artes, Mexico City, conducted by William McDermott.

ORIGINAL CAST

Cain	Kenneth Mackenzie	Good	April Olrich
Abel	Oleg Tupine	Evil	Carlota Pereyra
Eve	Anna Miltonova		

292

Now a guest artist with the company, David Lichine was commissioned to create a new ballet in 1946. The idea of a piece based on Cain and Abel had been in Lichine's mind ever since his success with *The Prodigal Son* (he was an avid reader of the Old Testament). He was not interested in creating a spectacle ballet like *Francesca da Rimini* but, rather, a work of moods in which emotions could be intensified through the use of an intimate scale, with few dancers, as he had done in *Protée*. The Wagner music, from *Siegfried* and *Götterdämmerung*, was arranged by William McDermott; the scenery designed by Miguel Prieto was executed by Jacob Anchutin, who traveled with the company throughout Latin America.

Action From the synopsis in the Original Ballet Russe souvenir program for the 1946–47 Met season:

The ballet opens with the birth of the children. Eve, an anxious mother, unwittingly nourishes Abel with Good and Cain with Evil. In a valley Abel is delighted by his voice's echo. Cain is jealous because no echo answers his call.

Abel gives thanks to God with an offering of fruit from the work of his own hand. Cain, to surpass this gift, sacrifices Abel's kid. Abel forgives him and they lie down to rest. While Abel sleeps, Cain plots to kill him. Abel awakes and comforts his disturbed brother. They realize the displeasure of God is on Cain. As Abel goes to his mother for comfort, Cain watches them jealously.

Incited by Evil, Cain decides to placate God's anger by sacrificing his brother. He pushes the unresisting Abel over a precipice. Suddenly, he is overcome by remorse. Eve tries to soothe him. Cain, aware that he bears a curse upon him, goes forth on his eternal wanderings.

The characters remain onstage all the time and the action evolves in a series of dramatic solos and ensembles.

Scenery and Costumes

The mise en scène was a barren grey decor of rocks and cliffs that suggested a mythical world. Ramps of various heights gave the dancers access to different levels across the stage.

The costumes anticipated the avant-gardism of the fifties and sixties, with the men practically naked and the women wearing very tight, short, sleeveless dresses, their long hair flowing free.

Choreography

The only characters were Cain (Mackenzie), Abel (Tupine), Eve (Miltonova), Good (Olrich), and Evil (Pereyra). Through Eve and Good and Evil the choreographer focused on the dual concept of sin, hereditary and willed.

There was much use of the floor as an expressive element: dancers rolled down the stage, on top of one another, and dragged themselves or others all over the stage. The effect was striking, especially with the four or five levels of simultaneous action provided by Prieto's decor, which supplied a feeling more operatic than balletic. The intertwining of limbs and movements of a similar sensuousness provoked an outcry from some conservative quarters. Edwin Denby, in a general criticism of the Ballets Russes repertory, wrote:

293

> *Cain and Abel* stressed manly Body Beautiful poses by two rugged boys in tiny trunks, and sexy entanglements with two girls called Good and Evil; Cain and Abel also bumped around together on the floor a good deal and perspired freely. A wit called it "Tarzan in a Turkish Bath" and the orchestra played *Siegfried* to it.[1]

Critics

Although controversial, the ballet was extremely well received in Mexico, Havana, and Rio de Janeiro. In the United States it was severely attacked by the critics, which only contributed to its general popularity.

John Martin wrote in the *New York Times*:

> Though [Lichine] has aimed at simplicity of style, and has chosen Richard Wagner for his composer, he never manages to hit the epic mood which the subject of the primordial murder demands.

He reacted prudishly to the daring passages:

> For lack of taste, indeed, it must set some sort of record. Not only are we subjected once again to those obstetrical details with which the ballet

TOP LEFT: left to right, Miltonova, Pereyra, and Olrich; Tupine and Mackenzie. BOTTOM LEFT: Tupine and Mackenzie. ABOVE: top, Olrich; below, left to right, Miltonova, Pereyra, Tupine, and Mackenzie.

these days is so much concerned, but once Eve has borne her two sons (they are twins in this version), we are regaled with the nursing of them.

For the stylized nursing scene, Eve had her two hands act as extensions of her breasts, which both brothers suckled.

Martin went on:

> It is pretty gauche. Nevertheless, the dancers work hard and seriously, and Kenneth Mackenzie as Cain turns in a sturdy and admirable performance. Both boys look handsome in their trunks and "bole Armenia"; the girls, unhappily, after they have crawled around the dirty floor in their blue non-descripts, appear to have been designed by Thurber. It is to be feared that "Cain and Abel" has neither cleanliness nor godliness to recommend it.[2]

He nevertheless admitted that the work "had moments of inventiveness."[3]

Anatole Chujoy objected that "five dancers, no matter how much they jump, roll on the floor, drag each other, beat their breast and go through assorted contortions, cannot fill the huge stage of the Metropolitan."[4] However, Walter Terry pointed out that "it should serve to remind the ballet choreographer that a substantial portion of male dance possibilities has been left untouched."[5]

Dancers reacted enthusiastically, and throughout the United States tour Lichine received many letters of support from members of other companies, expressing their high opinion of the work and condemning the critics' lack of sensitivity. John Taras still has a vivid memory of it and has said, "I don't know how it would look today, but then it had a good theatrical flair, it was effective and the dancers were good in it." Markova feels that it was ahead of its time, Dokoudovsky that it was a good and powerful work, and Riabouchinska agrees with Markova that it was too modern and daring, especially some of the passages between the two male dancers, the nursing scene, and the groupings.

Pas de Quatre at the Metropolitan Opera House, New York, 1946. Left to right: Stroganova, Morosova, Markova (kneeling), and Hightower.

September 1946- November 1948

HILE the Original Ballet Russe was touring Central Amer-
ica, de Basil went to New York to explore the possibility of bringing his company
back to the United States.[1] Once there, he contacted Nicholas Koudriavtzeff, a Russian-
born personality of Montreal's art world and husband of Tatiana Lipkovska, former
Diaghilev and de Basil dancer. Koudriavtzeff wanted very much to help de Basil,
but unfortunately his contacts outside Montreal's theatrical circuit were limited.
Consequently, he contacted Hurok to inquire whether he would take an interest
in de Basil's company.[2]

Hurok, after he had broken with de Basil during the Cuban strike, had become
the manager of Ballet Theatre. Lucia Chase and Oliver Smith, appointed administrative directors in April 1945, replacing J. Alden Talbot, bitterly protested the impresario's imposition of the star system—something they themselves, ironically, would
perpetuate until the end of their association with that company. Hurok earnestly
believed that stars were necessary; he was conditioned to a general audience that
responded more to personality than to any other aspect of a production. Another
point of contention was Hurok's privilege of accepting or rejecting proposals for new
works, a further source of friction between him and Ballet Theatre.[3] Under Hurok's
contract with Ballet Theatre, the impresario guaranteed the company a weekly fee,
and the company committed itself to engage international stars and to produce four
productions a year, two major and two minor—but the choosing of the stars and productions was subject to Hurok's approval. By 1945 the partnership had deteriorated,

and even though the contract ran until October 10, 1947, a settlement was reached in April 1946 and the agreement between Hurok and Ballet Theatre was canceled.

This separation presented a problem for Hurok. In 1935, when ballet proved to be a popular art and a viable business proposition in the United States, he had signed a three-year lease with the Metropolitan Opera. At its termination in 1938, a new ten-year lease was negotiated and signed;[4] so, when Hurok ceased to represent Ballet Theatre, his lease with the Met still had two more years to go. As was his custom, he had already booked the theater a year in advance for the fall of 1946 and the spring of 1947. As a first solution to the problem Hurok had taken the Markova-Dolin Ballet under his wing. Now de Basil appeared a likely alternative.

Before de Basil left the United States, he held discussions with Hurok and Koudriavtzeff. As an agreement began to take shape, the three men were joined by de Basil's lawyers, Jacques Lidji and Asa Sokoloff, and Hurok's legal advisor, Elias Lieberman. During these negotiations, Hurok cabled the Marquis de Cuevas in Paris to inform him of his new decision to associate himself once again with de Basil, and to ask for his collaboration and, principally, for financial support.[5]

The picturesque Chilean-born Marquis George de Cuevas married Margaret Strong, a granddaughter of John D. Rockefeller, and with his wife's money became an entrepreneur in the arts. He sponsored the Masterpieces of Art exhibition at the New York World's Fair (1939–40); however, his first and lasting love was the ballet. In 1943 he established the Ballet Institute to promote the advancement of the art; this led, in 1944, to the leasing of the Park Theatre, which he renamed Ballet International. Eventually, it became the headquarters for his company of the same name, but that lasted only one season, October 30–December 23. He incurred a loss of about $800,000, but the company did enjoy a *succès d'estime*, presenting works by Massine and Nijinska; moreover, it gave choreographic opportunities to Edward Caton, William Dollar, and Antonia Cobos.

According to Hurok, de Cuevas had seen the Original Ballet Russe dance in Mexico City in 1946 and had informed him of his intentions to invest in the company. Hurok dissuaded him from such a project. De Cuevas seems to have been interested in the possibility of creating a sort of Ballet Russe company, since the Mexican press publicized in early 1945 a March engagement by a company called Ballet Russe–Ballet International, of which de Cuevas was founder and director. Riabouchinska was announced as ballerina, Lichine as choreographer, and the repertory was to include, besides new and old works by Lichine, *Symphonie fantastique, Tristan Fou, Paganini, L'Après-midi d'un faune,* and works from the repertory of Ballet International.[6] For the return of the Original Ballet Russe to the United States in 1946, Hurok offered de Cuevas the title of artistic director and, in addition, a promise to revive some of his 1944 works from Ballet International, and to recruit some of his dancers. For Hurok this was the hope of a new beginning, now that his connections with Ballet Theatre had been severed.

According to John Taras, Hurok, back in New York from a short trip to Paris to discuss matters with the Marquis de Cuevas, enlisted a group of dancers and sent them along with Tcherhassky to Rio de Janeiro to strengthen de Basil's company and to learn the repertory before their arrival in New York. For the New York engagement he had organized another nucleus of dancers, also under personal contract to him, to join the company: Markova, Hightower, Dolin, Eglevsky, Skibine, Moncion. Antonia Cobos joined in order to revive her ballet *The Mute Wife*, originally created for Ballet International. Even though the impresario managed companies and dancers independently, usually the stars that he represented were asked to appear as guest artists with those same companies; that had been the case with Baronova's engagement with de Basil in 1940–41. According to Rosella Hightower, Hurok added guest stars to the Original Ballet Russe roster for the 1946–47 American tour to secure large audiences, since most of de Basil's dancers were not known in the United States.

To avoid conflict between the two groups and to save rehearsal time, two repertories were devised: de Basil's own, performed by his company, and works by the newly acquired company, which included *The Mute Wife* (October 4, 1946), *Pas de Quatre* (October 7, 1946), *Sebastian* (October 13, 1946), *Constantia* (October 16, 1946), *Pictures at an Exhibition* (March 25, 1947), the Black Swan pas de deux, *Nutcracker* pas de deux, and *Don Quixote* pas de deux, all performed by Hurok's personal artists. Only in Dolin's *Pas de Quatre* and in some of the classics did dancers alternate in both repertories. *Giselle* (October 11, 1946) was staged by Dolin as a vehicle for Markova and himself, offering balletomanes the opportunity to compare them with Alonso and Youskevitch, appearing in *Giselle* that season at Ballet Theatre. *Camille* (October 1, 1946), with choreography by Taras, was the only world premiere, and Lichine's *Cain and Abel* (October 2, 1946) and Psota's *Yara* (October 8, 1946) were presented in the United States for the first time.

299

The opening of the Original Ballet Russe at the Metropolitan coincided with that of Ballet Theatre at the Broadway Theatre, allowing New York to witness a ballet battle reminiscent of those of pre-war London, as reported in *Ballet* by Paul Tassovin:

> The whirl of the season certainly gave the Press boys a spate of dope such as they have not landed since the good old days, and they let off the fireworks with both hands. At the sensational opening night of September 30th it was reported that between two and four thousand first nighters were turned away from the Metropolitan box-office. The galaxy of socialites and other fashionable celebrities who managed to get their bodies inside were voted to be a "queerer audience than heretofore."* "Predominantly male, the balletomanes hung over the Met's double staircase like soggy dish-towels, and chattered like magpies. What they lack in numbers the gals made up for in costumes. One bony structure had an entire cornfield growing out of her hair-do and another was certainly Maha[t]ma Gandhi's true girl friend. . . ." All of which goes to show that curiosity was keen for de Basil combinations, absent these five years past in South

* [From] authentic but unidentified press cutting.

America. The Broadway Theatre was also filled to capacity on the following evening to greet Ballet Theatre. . . .

Be that as it may, the Original Ballet Russe won the battle of the box
office with reputed takings of $50,000 gross weekly. The Ballet Theatre in
the smaller recesses of Broadway Theatre was far away behind averaging
between $16,000 and $22,000. As is usual in modern warfare, neither side
benefited greatly. The winner may have managed to pay his way; the loser
was decidedly out of pocket. Ballet Theatre wound up their season with a
deficit, but artistically they gained the critic's verdict. . . .[7]

After the Met engagement, the Original Ballet Russe toured the most important
cities in the country, returning to the Met for the 1947 spring season, March 20–29,
for which Jerome Robbins created *Pas de Trois* for Markova, Dolin, and Eglevsky, to
Berlioz's *Minuet of the Will o' Wisps*. Owing to an injury suffered by Markova, it was
premiered (March 25, 1947) with Hightower, who also replaced Markova in *Giselle*.

There were many reasons for the lower artistic standards of the new enterprise.
After four years of a nomadic existence in South America, the company arrived in the
United States exhausted. A number of dancers had been recruited in South America
and had not yet had the opportunity to blend into the style of the works, nor were the
conditions propitious for rehearsing and performing. Hurok further fragmented the
company by adding to it two other, outside groups. Obviously, his concern was to
produce a company that could fulfill his engagement with the Met and could provide
the glamour of a few big stars.

According to Denby, the company "had no collective vitality or style."

There were times when these pre-war Ballet Russe productions
evoked a ghost of the company's pre-war grand manner—evoked as in a
parody the former sweep of phrase, the former temperament, the former
gift for color and impersonation. . . . That there was talent buried under
these ruins only made the spectacle more morbid. If the Ballet Russe section of the Original is to be revivified as a company, it will take a year of
rigorous classwork and new repertory to do it.[8]

In de Basil's repertory the problem was not choreographic authenticity but
atmosphere and unity of style. As Markova remembers, "The pre-war ballets that had
made a sensation before were still in the repertory, and the choreography was well
performed under the supervision of Grigoriev." But the talented young recruits
immersed themselves in the pre-war repertory without the historical awareness that it
had been the product of an era that, although recent, had ended. They were not given
the opportunity to develop an understanding of these ballets, and erroneously gave
them a contemporary interpretation. Unfortunately, most of the dancers who intuitively embodied the nuances of that era, having been a product of it, such as Baronova, Riabouchinska, Toumanova, Verchinina, Grigorieva, Lichine, Lazowski, and

Shabelevsky, were no longer on the scene. The individual efforts of the few who remained could not raise the quality of a performance that depended on a collective one. This does not mean that the works themselves were démodé.

When de Basil's company left the United States in the spring of 1947, a chapter of twentieth-century ballet history slipped into oblivion.

CAMILLE

Ballet in one act; music by Franz Schubert, arranged by Vittorio Rieti; libretto by John Taras, after Alexandre Dumas fils; choreography by John Taras; set and costume design by Cecil Beaton; sets executed by Eugene B. Dunkel Studio; costumes executed by Madame Karinska; premiere October 1, 1946, at the Metropolitan Opera House, conducted by Eugene Fuerst.

ORIGINAL CAST

Camille	Alicia Markova	Nanine	Mattlyn Gevurtz
Armand	Anton Dolin		
Armand's Father	Miguel Terekov		Corps de Ballet

For the return of de Basil's company to the Metropolitan Opera House, after a five-year absence from New York, Hurok wanted a world premiere, to stimulate audience interest. The new ballet was to be sponsored by Ballet Associates (later to become Ballet Associates in America), founded in 1941 by John Alden Talbot; in 1946 he was the treasurer. This organization contributed large sums of money to further the creation and performance of American ballet and had previously sponsored Tudor's *Pillar of Fire* and *Romeo and Juliet*, de Mille's *Tally-Ho!*, and Dolin's *Romantic Age*, among others. It counted among its members such personages as Elsa Schiaparelli and Contessa Mercati, a prominent socialite who was the mother of Michael Arlen; Isabelle Kempt was also a contributing member.

The new work was commissioned from John Taras, who had choreographed his first ballet, *Graziana*, for Ballet Theatre in 1945. It was to be a vehicle for guest artist Alicia Markova. Taras had worked with Markova at Ballet Theatre and the Markova–Dolin Ballet, and he felt that Dumas fils' heroine, *La Dame aux Camélias*, would provide her with a role that would exploit her style.

The first rehearsals of the principals were conducted at the small studio of Ana Simpson (known professionally as Ana Ricarda), a friend of the choreographer, as

Markova and Dolin.

there were no other studios available at the time. Initially the role of Armand was given to George Skibine. Besides being physically ideal for the role, Skibine had already developed a close rapport with Markova, with whom he had previously worked in *Les Sylphides* and *Bluebeard* for Fokine, and *Aleko* for Massine. But he was soon replaced by Dolin, since Hurok had decided to send Skibine to Rio de Janeiro. Since the Met's studio was still not available, rehearsals were scheduled in other studios around Manhattan, most often at Carnegie Hall.

The preparations for *Camille* were plagued by trouble from the beginning. Rehearsals with the principals progressed in New York; however, Taras could not work on the whole production because the company was still in South America. He was sent to Rio to stage the ensembles there, but when a general transportation strike prevented the company from leaving for the United States, Taras was summoned back to New York by plane. His immediate task was to improvise a company to open at the Met as the Original Ballet Russe. By now Hurok's publicity campaign had been in full force for over three months and the impresario could not postpone the engagement. For the newly assembled company, Taras, in his own words, "selected some of the best dancers from the School of American Ballet and from other sources in New York. When the group was assembled, I was finally able to insert the solo parts and work on the ballet as a whole."

Taras was the first choreographer to create a ballet based on *La Dame aux Camélias* in the twentieth century. Not wishing to use Verdi's *Traviata* music without the voices, he decided on music by Schubert, arranged and orchestrated by Vittorio Rieti. For the scenery and costumes he chose Cecil Beaton, who had come to New York to design Ballet Theatre's production of Ashton's *Les Patineurs*. Beaton had shown with his previous contributions to Ashton's *Apparitions* and Lichine's *Le Pavillon* a special sensitivity and elegance in taste for romantic themes.

Scenery and Costumes

To make the changes of scene smoothly, especially since Taras's intention was to re-create Camille's life as a dreamy reminiscence from her deathbed, Beaton employed transparent screens; the bedroom scene was the simplest in conception. For the ball scene that followed he designed a magnificent period ballroom with a slanted ceiling that when lit up was transformed into the garden of the third scene.

John Martin acclaimed Beaton's contribution:

> In all this, the thing most worthy of note is Cecil Beaton's setting for *Camille*, which is not only eye-pleasing but theatrically imaginative. Aside from the ingenuity with which it achieves a change of milieu, employing a method entirely in keeping with the dream psychology of Camille in the deathbed flashback approach of the scenario, it also establishes an admirably three-dimensional stage. For a change, a ballet is performed within a setting instead of in front of it.[1]

For the costumes Beaton chose an earlier historical period that provided more stylistic options. The whole was magnificently executed by Mme Karinska, with the designer supervising every detail. Markova remembers how "after rehearsals I would come around 9 p.m. to Karinska's studio where the fittings took place. There were long sessions in which we discussed the style, period and the choreography as well. For my hair I did not want to wear a wig and Cecil devised a half wig that only consisted of the curls, the front being my own. The costumes were large, but so light and fragile that it was not difficult to dance with them."

Markova appeared throughout the ballet dressed in white. Taras has commented that it was the designer's intention. However, Markova remembers that Beaton had designed a beautiful geranium-colored outfit with pink camellias, for a scene in which she was that was cut after the dress rehearsal, for the ballet had become too long.

De Basil's company arrived in New York the day before the Metropolitan opening. Fortunately, by then Taras had finished rehearsing the substitute company in other works from the old de Cuevas repertory from Ballet International. The premiere of *Camille* was performed entirely by the improvised company. Taras is convinced that using two different corps de ballet during the gestation of the work was detrimental to its cohesiveness.

Music   For the score Rieti assembled and orchestrated various piano pieces by Schubert. Although the "Death and the Maiden" theme was used as a leitmotiv throughout the ballet, Rieti also employed various bits from *Moments musicaux*, op. 94; *Last Waltzes*, op. 127, for the ballroom scene; *Impromptu Elégiaque*, op. 90, no. 3, for the grand pas de deux of Camille and Armand; and *Variations*, op. 82, no. 2, for the country scene.

Action   The story, as in Dumas's book, was told in retrospect. From Camille's deathbed the ballet proceeds in flashback to the ballroom and then to the country, and then returning to the deathbed. The first three scenes, until the father's appearance, are realistic in approach, while the last one reflects the heroine's state of mind: a nightmarish depiction of the lovers separated by destiny and in search of each other. In the tragic dénouement, the heroine dies in Armand's arms.

Taras tried to express the emotional force of the self-sacrifice, the misunderstanding between the lovers, and the hopeless reconciliation. Unfortunately, the choreography did not sustain the romantic tension.

Critics   In *Dance News* Anatole Chujoy commented: "The weakness of the ballet is not in the treatment but in the fact that the choreographer abstracted the story to such a degree that the audience is not prepared to follow it."[2]

John Martin concluded: "Not even Alicia Markova with all her artistry can give it body and validity. Its scenario omits all detail, all episode, from the famous tale, and gives only a faint whiff of its central situation." Martin also felt that the music did not provide "an atmosphere for the dying emotionalism of a romantic, Parisian, nineteenth century, demi mondaine."[3]

304

Although the work was not enthusiastically received, Markova's Camille was praised as the embodiment of the romantic heroine. Dolin, less convincing as young Armand, nevertheless gave a commendable interpretation, in the opinion of Taras and the majority of the press. Miguel Terekov imparted a menacing quality to his interpretation of the father.

The work stayed in the repertory of the Original Ballet Russe until the end of the United States tour, when Markova left with Dolin to organize once again the Markova–Dolin company. For this company Dolin, with Markova's assistance, choreographed a new production of *La Dame aux Camélias*, designed by Castellano to Verdi's music arranged by Robert Zeller. As in *La Traviata*'s first act, this ballet began with the ballroom scene. It was premiered in Mexico and later was presented in New York during the Markova–Dolin company's United States tour.

Beaton's scenery and costumes were donated by Ballet Associates to the New York City Ballet so that Antony Tudor could create a new version to Verdi's music. Tudor's work was presented for the first time on February 28, 1951, with Diana Adams and Hugh Laing in the leading roles. Unfortunately, the City Ballet's warehouse caught fire and the costumes and decors were lost. In 1963 Beaton designed another production of *La Dame aux Camélias*, for Ashton's *Marguerite and Armand*, with music by Liszt, for the Royal Ballet, with Fonteyn and Nureyev.

As the last engagement, March 20–29, of the Original Ballet Russe drew to a close at the Met, de Basil traveled to Europe in order to renew his connections there and arrange his company's return to the Continent. In England he contacted Julian Braunsweg and Bruce Ottley, one of his foremost pre-war supporters in London. (To de Basil's distress, Ottley died on July 21, 1947, a day before the company's opening at Covent Garden. Braunsweg, a familiar figure in ballet since the twenties, was later to become even better known as the founder and impresario of London's Festival Ballet.) De Basil also visited Paris, where he met once more with the concert agent Nadine Bouchonnet. After the war Mme Bouchonnet had opened a theatrical agency called Office Artistique Continental, a continuation of her pre-war agency Office Théâtral Européen, which had presented artists such as Vladimir Horowitz. De Basil engaged her to book the company in Paris and to act as his European representative. He returned to London in March to explore the possibility of a future engagement there.

According to Braunsweg's memoirs, de Basil then returned to America, and from there cabled Braunsweg to arrange a European tour for the Original Ballet Russe.[1] Whether or not, as Braunsweg claims, he was instrumental in getting David Webster, general administrator of the Royal Opera House, to book the Original Ballet Russe at Covent Garden, the arrangements were carried out in May between Webster and de Basil while the latter was still in London, residing at the Savoy Hotel. On May 14, Webster sent de Basil a contract securing a six-week season beginning in July, and allowing for a possible extension. Nine works—*Symphonie fantastique, Francesca da Rimini, Firebird, The Good-Humoured Ladies, Les Présages, Paganini, Scuola di ballo, Prince Igor,* and *Le Coq d'or*—were listed as obligatory items in the repertory.[2]

Before leaving the United States, de Basil suffered numerous losses in personnel. Some of the old members, like Stepanova and Tupine, decided to remain in America, while the majority of those who had previously been with Ballet International were readying themselves to rejoin the Marquis de Cuevas, who had negotiated a contract with the Monte Carlo Opera to establish Le Grand Ballet de Monte Carlo under his direction. Once again the company had to be reassembled, with performers who had not been trained in the style of the Russian ballet and who did not have the necessary rehearsal time with the company to understand the nuances of the repertory. De Basil's repertory was eclectic, consisting of works by choreographers as diverse as Petipa, Fokine, Massine, and Lichine, whereas the new recruits in Paris had come up through the Paris Opéra, the Ballets des Champs-Elysées, and choreographers such as Roland Petit (from whom Dokoudovsky suggested to de Basil that he commission a new work—wise advice that was not followed). Because Paris was having a great ballet renaissance at the time, de Basil felt that French dancers were probably by style (the Russian teachers were still in Paris) and temperament more compatible with the Russian ballet than dancers that might be recruited in London. Among the most important additions to the roster in Paris were Renée (Zizi) Jeanmaire and Vladimir Skouratov. Skouratov, a pupil of Preobrajenskaya in Paris, had joined the Nouveau Ballet de Monte Carlo in 1946, where he partnered Jeanmaire in Lifar's *Aubade*. He was a very strong technician with great speed, lightness, and elevation. Hélène Komarova, who was the American Hélène Constantine and danced with de Basil's company in the 1941 corps as Hélène Muselle, was also taken on in Paris.[3] Taras recalls that he was engaged to travel with the company as ballet master and to dance character roles, notably the General in *Graduation Ball*. Riabouchinska and Lichine were to join for the first eleven days of the London season before traveling to Buenos Aires to appear as guests at the Teatro Colón. The company roster also included Morosova, Moulin, Larkina, Olrich, Barbara Lloyd (a protegée of Lichine), Dokoudovsky, and Jasinski.

On July 22, de Basil opened his only post-war engagement at Covent Garden, achieving throughout the season a *succès d'estime*. Some of the productions were adequately revived and managed to create a good impression, but the programs lacked consistency; at times, only one of the three ballets was properly presented. The standard of dancing was good, especially that of the principals, but the individual accomplishments of some of the lead dancers and soloists were not sufficient to offset the weaknesses in atmosphere and style: the dancers were so pressed for time that they were lucky just to learn the choreography. In addition, Grigoriev and Tchernicheva were struggling to teach the steps and could not devote much time to coaching. The repertory was by this time considered passé, inviting comparison with the legendary performances given by the company in 1933–39. For Cyril Beaumont the present company had no relationship to the previous one: "The ballet-goers of recent adherence must rid themselves from the impression . . . that they are now seeing the ballets, familiar to them by name, as they were presented then."[4] He felt that only Riabouchinska and Lichine were responsible for maintaining the style and the atmosphere of the earlier era. The critic for the *Manchester Guardian* agreed:

> It must indeed be owned that without Riabouchinska and Lichine the occasion last night would have been no great one. Riabouchinska in 1933 was one of the youngest of ballerinas; when she gave her familiar and lovely performance last night in the prelude of "Sylphides" it was clear that she has lost none of her fluent lyricism and that she had acquired a new sureness of technique. She danced in all three ballets last night; in each one she was in a class of her own.[5]

(On that opening night the three ballets were *Les Sylphides, Paganini,* and *Graduation Ball.*)

The only new works unveiled in London were *Graduation Ball, La Légende du Bouleau,* and *Piccoli;* the latter two, both by Kniaseff, were presented just before the

ABOVE: Larionov, an assistant, and Lichine. Larionov was hired by de Basil to refurbish the sets when the company came to London. BELOW: Lichine and Riabouchinska rehearse *Graduation Ball* as the charwomen clean the floor of the Covent Garden stage (London, 1947).

company left for Paris. From the outset, *Graduation Ball* was enthusiastically received by the critics as well as by the audience.

This was not Boris Kniaseff's first association with de Basil's company. He had been part of the 1934 season in Monte Carlo when Nijinska had been in charge of a second company responsible for fulfilling de Basil's engagements there while the parent company remained in the United States. Kniaseff had been a pupil of Kasyan Goleizovsky in St. Petersburg, and was the ballet master of the Opéra-Comique in 1932–34. As a teacher he was famous for his *barre par terre*, with the dancers lying on the floor; among his pupils were Yvette Chauviré, Zizi Jeanmaire, and Youly Algaroff.

La Légende du Bouleau (September 11, 1947) had first been created in July 1930 with Valentina Blinova (originally intended for Kniaseff's wife, Olga Spessivtseva) for performance at a gala organized by the choreographer at the Opéra-Comique that would present, among other dancers, Lichine, Shabelevsky, Jasinski, and Petroff. There had been various revivals throughout the thirties—by Kniaseff's group in Monte Carlo in 1932 as *Légende de Berioska* and as *Biroska* by the Ballets de Leon Woizikowski—and in December 1940 a second version was created, this time for Chauviré and Kniaseff himself, at the Théâtre Marigny.[6] This was the version that he staged for de Basil's company.

This ballet derives from a Russian legend about a silver birch tree that grows in soil that had previously been sterile. To music by Tchaikovsky, the winds uproot the tree and it dies. Once dead, the tree acknowledges the love the land had for it. The scenery and costumes were by Monique Lancelot, and the leads were danced by Geneviève Moulin (the tree) and Milorad Miskovitch (the land).

Piccoli (September 12, 1947) had received its world premiere at the Théâtre Marigny in December 1940, together with the revival of *La Légende du Bouleau* for Chauviré. Kniaseff's scenario concerned a dance teacher who discovers his wife with a lover, murders them, and then brings in his mistress. Danced to music of Rossini, and with scenery and costumes by Gontcharova, the ballet was led by Jeanmaire and Dokoudovsky, both of whom garnered high praise for their interpretations. Of the two revivals, only this one attracted any serious attention.

With the season in London nearing its close, the company earned praise for its improvement in uniformity and cohesiveness, the result of six weeks of continuous performing. Arnold Haskell wrote:

> In the last fortnight they caught a glimpse once again of the old de Basil. . . . Morosova revealed something unexpected in what was an excellent revival of *The Firebird*, Skouratoff gave a magnificent performance in *Schéhérazade* and was memorable in *Les Sylphides*, and Komarova showed herself a Zobeïde in the grand manner. Jeanmaire's Aurora, always brilliant technically, greatly gained in the classical certainty of its presentation, Dokoudovsky's *Blue Bird* soared and Orloff thrilled us as Ivan. If I do not mention Jasinsky, it is because he showed himself a mature artist throughout the season.[7]

ABOVE: Colonel de Basil and Arnold
Haskell (London, 1947). BELOW: left
to right, Jeanmaire, Kniaseff, Komarova,
and Dokoudovsky, in *Piccoli*.

For Haskell, the forthcoming visit to Paris by de Basil was cause for great optimism:

> Now, after a long interval, de Basil is to visit Paris once again, a new Paris that is enjoying a dancing renaissance. . . . De Basil's company will benefit enormously through contact with Paris, and the French dancers through seeing a well disciplined company with a strong and varied repertory. Much may come of this visit which should halt the Americanisation of Russian Ballet and give it a new lease of life.[8]

The Original Ballet Russe opened its Paris season at the Palais de Chaillot on October 7, 1947, presented by Jules Borkon and Nadine Bouchonnet of the Office Artistique Continental. On this opening night the magic of the name, along with the attendant memories of a glorious past, attracted *le tout Paris* from the Aga Khan to Madeleine Renaud.[9] During the first week enthusiasm was lacking, but by the second week the reviews had improved and the company began to be a box office success. *Symphonie fantastique, Paganini, The Prodigal Son,* and *Graduation Ball,* none previously seen in Paris, attracted the greatest attention.

According to the ballet historian Pierre Michaut, *Symphonie fantastique* and *Paganini* did not succeed owing to the technical limitations of the theater. *Paganini* suffered the most, for in the first scene it was impossible to reproduce the double row of "spectators" and the second level of action for Paganini. The elimination of these devices destroyed the effect of "theater within a theater," so vital in heightening the distance of the main character from the real audience—the public. In the third scene the much anticipated transparent violins could not be used. However, despite the difficulties of presentation, both ballets were praised by Michaut: "Ce sont l'un et l'autre de grands ouvrages conçus et developpés avec ampleur et puissance, une grande sureté de métier, une habilité accomplie dans l'animation des masses" ["Both are works conceived and developed with fullness and power, great sureness in craftsmanship, accomplished skill in moving the masses"].[10] The greatest successes of the season were *The Prodigal Son* and *Graduation Ball.*

From Paris the company moved to the Alhambra Theatre in Brussels for a short season (without Taras, who remained in Paris, stricken with meningitis). From Belgium they returned to Paris to prepare for a tour of Spain.

When the company opened, after a twelve-year absence from Barcelona, at the Teatre Liceu (April 20, 1948), it was welcomed ecstatically. For this engagement Riabouchinska, Verchinina, and Lichine joined de Basil, and while there Verchinina restaged her *Valse triste,* now with scenery and costumes by Manuel Muntanola.

The extensive tour of Spain and Portugal took the company to Madrid (Zarzuela Theatre), Bilbao, San Sebastián, Madrid (Albeniz Theatre), Lisbon, Pôrto, Valencia, Madrid (Retiro Park), Bilbao, Santander, Salamanca, Málaga, Tangier, Tetuán, Barcelona (Tivoli Theatre), and, finally, Mallorca.[11]

During the second visit to Bilbao in September, Riabouchinska and Lichine left in order to fulfill their contract with de Cuevas and Kochno and his Ballets des Champs-Elysées. The sole novelty presented in Spain was Verchinina's *Suite chorégraphique*, to music of Gounod, with scenery and costumes by Odette de Santos. It was presented around September 14, during the second appearance in Bilbao.[12]

During the final visit to Barcelona, at the Tivoli Theatre, de Basil announced a new project: the creation of an Academia Nacional, to develop Spanish ballet. Prominent Spanish personalities in the arts, such as Turina, Escudero, and Juan Magrina, became involved. Two Dokoudovsky ballets, *La Celestina*, with music by Pedrell and scenery and costumes by the Portuguese artist Hugo Manoel, and *Istar*, with music by D'Indy and scenery and costumes by Federico Calderón, were then in the planning stages.[13]

From Barcelona the company sailed to Mallorca to appear at the Sala Augusta. Upon the completion of their season there they traveled back to the mainland and then Paris, where new bookings were to be arranged by de Basil. No one suspected that the last performance on the Mediterranean island, on November 8, 1948, was to mark the abrupt end of the company's sixteen-year existence.

311

Epilogue

ROM Spain the company returned to Paris. As there were no immediate bookings, the dancers scattered, while de Basil tried to find new engagements and funds to reassemble the troupe One of his main concerns at this time was to establish new headquarters and find a way to become more integrated with a national artistic life, an effort already evident in his attempt to organize the Academia Nacional in Spain. In Paris de Basil planned new productions: one, *The Abyss*, was a ballet by Dokoudovsky based on the story of the same title by Leonid Andreyev, for which de Basil approached Alexander Tcherepnin to compose the score. There were also discussions about reviving an old project—a ballet on the myth of Niobe that had been projected in the late thirties, for which de Chirico had at the time completed the designs.

In the spring of 1949, de Basil signed a contract with Tadié-Cinema to produce thirteen ballet films under the direction of Boris Zatourov. Dokoudovsky, then the Colonel's right hand, was in charge of scheduling auditions; rehearsals began on May 19. The first ballets to be rehearsed were *Swan Lake* Act II, *Graduation Ball*, *Petrouchka*, and *Firebird*. However, only the first two materialized: *Swan Lake* Act II, filmed at the Parc de Bagatelle, and *Graduation Ball* at the Musée des Arts Décoratifs.

In the meantime, de Basil visited London during April and May to negotiate the appearance of his company with Markova and Dolin at the Harringay arena, in August. He proposed to present the two new ballets previously planned for the Academia Nacional: *Ishtar* and *La Celestina*. Nothing came of this, and the Ballet Rambert

 313

shared the spotlight at Harringay. The plans for a projected Spanish tour did not materialize either, and by July 15 the company had disbanded.

Despite the odds, de Basil did not abandon his efforts to revive the Original Ballet Russe, and now he joined forces with George Kirsta, the Ukrainian theatrical designer. By 1951, however, the Colonel's desperate financial situation forced him to become the manager of the Spanish folk dance company Coros y danzas de España, with which he had become acquainted during his last tour of Spain. He took the group to France, Belgium, and Italy, and during an engagement in Milan he contacted Toumanova, who was at La Scala creating Strauss's *La leggenda di Giuseppe* with choreography by Margarita Wallmann. Toumanova and her mother accepted de Basil's invitation to visit the theater where his group was performing. According to Toumanova it was a sad occasion. De Basil, looking like an Emil Jannings character, introduced her to everyone from stagehands to dancers, reiterating to each that this famous ballerina dancing at La Scala was his child prodigy.

Back in Paris de Basil's health deteriorated rapidly. However, he continued to work almost compulsively to revive his company. His intense preoccupation with the survival of the Russian ballet bordered on the obsessive. Now, through the path of adversity—as he had persisted before through success and the uncertainty of the war years—he remained faithful to his ideal. On July 24 he suffered a first heart attack; on the twenty-seventh, he suffered a second, fatal one. The funeral services were conducted at the Russian Orthodox church on the rue Daru. Friends and colleagues gathered to pay their last respects: Kchessinskaya, Kochno, Toumanova, Riabouchinska, Lichine, Lifar, the Grigorievs, Dokoudovsky, Stroganova. A wreath sent by Lichine was inscribed "From Irina, Tania, Tamara, and David." De Basil was buried at the Russian cemetery of St. Geneviève du Bois.

On the day of de Basil's death, Thomas Bischoff, of Bischoff Coxe and Company, senior operating director of the Original Ballet Russe, Ltd., and the Russian Ballet Development Company, Ltd., died in London. The other solicitors resigned, and the Greek financier Anthony Diamantidi took control of both companies. Diamantidi had been a friend of de Basil's since the thirties, and when the Colonel returned to Europe after the war they had resumed their friendship. As executor of de Basil's estate he became director of the Original Ballet Russe, Ltd., and the Russian Ballet Development Company, with Morosova as co-director.

A month after de Basil's death, Kirsta revived the Original Ballet Russe. In August 1951, Universal Ballet, Ltd., was registered in London as a subsidiary of Continental Opera and Ballet Entertainments, Ltd., of which Middleton d'Este and Ellerie Fricker were directors. The new company had Kirsta as artistic director, Vova Grigoriev as general director, Grigoriev and Tchernicheva as régisseur and ballet mistress, and Joseph Horowitz and Colin Davis as conductors. Even though Riabouchinska and Lichine were announced, the only previous members to appear were Dokoudovsky, Stroganova, and Vassilkovsky. The repertory included *Aurora's Wedding, Swan Lake* Act II, *Le Coq d'or, Paganini, Prince Igor, Graduation Ball,* and *Les Présages.*

314

After an insufficient four-week rehearsal period, the Original Ballet Russe opened on October 1, 1951, at Wimbledon Theatre. Except for complimentary notices for some of the principals, the critical reception was disastrous. From Wimbledon the company moved to the Coventry Hippodrome and then to Manchester, Sheffield, Oxford, Bolton, Newcastle, and Glasgow. December 26 was opening night at London's Royal Festival Hall. The only new creation, *Femmes d'Alger*, was presented on January 3, 1952; libretto and designs were by Kirsta after paintings by Delacroix; music by Joseph Horowitz; choreography by Dokoudovsky. On January 16, by arrangement with Jack Hylton (Musical Plays, Ltd.), the company opened at the Adelphi Theatre, on the Strand. A few days later, increasing financial difficulties forced them to close, and Hylton impounded the scenery and costumes to cover the debt. According to Hylton's solicitor, Oscar Beuselinck (as narrated by Sorley Walker), the following events took place:

> Continental Opera and Ballet Entertainments Ltd. sued Jack Hylton (Musical Plays Ltd.) for recovery of the scenery and costumes left at the Adelphi Theatre. Bischoff and Co., representing the holding companies of the Original Ballet Russe Ltd. and the Russian Development Company, intervened, saying that as no royalties had been paid, the rights had reverted to them, and they owned the scenery and costumes of these ballets. Before the main case against Jack Hylton could go forward, the case for settlement of title was heard. Master Clayton, presiding, found for Continental Opera and Ballet and then, whilst working out the judgement, changed his mind and found for Bischoff and Co. Middleton d'Este, for Continental Opera and Ballet, appealed to the Divisional Court and the appeal was heard by Lord Goddard, Mr. Justice Slade and a third Justice, with a two-to-one result in favour of Bischoff. D'Este pursued it to the Court of Appeal where Mr. Justice Singleton found in his favour. . . . D'Este returned to the proceedings he initiated in 1952 against Jack Hylton. This case came up at the end of January 1956. D'Este was represented by Stockton, Jack Hylton by Claude Duveen, QC, and Mark Littman. Jack Hylton won the case and costs were set at £1000, but there was no money to pay this and Continental Opera and Ballet went into liquidation.[1]

The Original Ballet Russe, Ltd., and the Russian Ballet Development Company, Ltd., had an obscure fate. According to Mme de Basil (Olga Morosova), after de Basil's death Diamantidi rented a studio for her, but after she signed the documents giving him complete control of the companies, he sold the lease. Had not her sister, Verchinina, sent aid from Rio de Janeiro, she would have been on the street. Diamantidi formed the Diaghilev and de Basil Ballet Foundation from both companies. In 1967, he contacted Sotheby and Company and Richard Buckle to arrange a sale of the Ballets Russes properties in storage in Montrouge. The first historic sale of the material took place in July 1968. Afterwards, Diamantidi sent a balance statement to

Mme de Basil indicating that she was to receive no money. Mme de Basil could not verify the account and could not afford to pursue legal action against Diamantidi (also, he was a Greek citizen, which would have made litigation terribly difficult). The 1968 sale was followed by another in December 1969 and still another in March 1973, of which Mme de Basil was not even informed.

Today the maquettes, scenery, curtains, and costumes of the Ballets Russes have found their way to numerous museums and collections all over the world. However, one of the greatest legacies of the Ballets Russes was de Basil's pioneering work and the various ballet schools and companies founded by many of the former members of his company. In Australia, Kirsova opened a studio in Sydney and created the Kirsova Ballet, the first professional ballet company there. Borovansky opened a school in Melbourne and later founded a company that became the Australian National Ballet. In Latin America: Grigorieva and Matouchak stayed in Argentina; Verchinina, Leskova, and Shabelevsky in Brazil; Rostoff stayed many years in Peru; Leontieva taught in Cuba until her death. In the United States: Riabouchinska and Lichine opened a school in Beverly Hills, and directed several performing groups, including the first Los Angeles Ballet in 1953; Panaiev taught in Los Angeles until his death, and Denisova (Patricia Denise) and Kosmovska still teach there; Jasinski and Larkina settled in Tulsa, Oklahoma, where they teach and direct a regional ballet company; Lara Obidenna and the late Marian Ladré settled in Seattle; Stroganova and Dokoudovsky in New York; Oleg Tupine in Springfield, Virginia; Adrianova and Andahazy in Minneapolis. Lazowski and Zoritch had more itinerant careers in the United States. In Canada, Sabinova (Rosemary Doveson) teaches in Vancouver. Geneviève Moulin returned to France. Baronova taught at the Royal Ballet School and appears as guest teacher all over the world. The list is extensive. The work of these devoted artists is instrumental in passing from generation to generation a tradition that has enriched the knowledge and served as an indispensable foundation for today's dancers.

NOTES

BIBLIOGRAPHY

INDEX

NOTES

August 1929–December 1932

1. Letter from John Martin to Léonide Massine, November 28, 1930, Massine Collection, Isole dei Galli.
2. Letter from E. Ray Goetz to Léonide Massine, May 28, 1932, Massine Collection.
3. Such as Kathrine Sorley Walker in *De Basil's Ballets Russes* (London: Hutchinson, 1982), 3.
4. Letter from René Blum to Léonide Massine, July 8, 1931, Massine Collection.
5. Letter from René Blum to Léonide Massine, August 18, 1931, Massine Collection.
6. Letter from Léonide Massine to Colonel de Basil, December 8, 1931, Mme de Basil Collection, Paris.
7. Bernard Taper, *Balanchine* (New York: Macmillan, 1974), 144.
8. Letter from Léonide Massine to W. de Basil, December 8, 1931, Massine Collection.
9. Contract dated January 2, 1932, Mme de Basil Collection.
10. Contracts in the Mme de Basil Collection.
11. Unsigned contract in the Mme de Basil Collection.
12. The repertory of Nijinska's company during this season is rarely given correctly in printed sources. It consisted of *Les Variations* (Beethoven), *Bolero* (Ravel), *Princess Cygne* (Rimsky-Korsakov), *Les Biches* (Poulenc), *Etude* (Bach), *Le Comédien Jaloux* (Scarlatti), *Miniature Chorégraphique* (Lanner, Borodin, Moussorgsky, Dargomijsky), *Hamlet* (Liszt), *Divertissement des Dances* (Glinka, Tchaikovsky, Liadov, Rubinstein), and *Baiser de la fée* (Stravinsky).
13. Letter from Ernest Ansermet to Boris Kochno, Mme de Basil Collection.
14. Sorley Walker mistakenly says that David Lichine's uncle provided the transportation, but the buses were rented from a Monsieur Laroche, proprietor of the Garage Pigalle, who specialized in buses for theatrical tours.

COTILLON

1. David Lichine's role was first performed by Balanchine at a gala in honor of Prince Louis II de Monaco.
2. The role created by Blinova was soon given to Riabouchinska, who monopolized it thenceforth.

3. Sono Osato, *Distant Dances* (New York: Alfred A. Knopf, 1980), 106.
4. A. V. Coton, *A Prejudice for Ballet* (London: Methuen & Co., 1938), 75.
5. Ibid., 74.
6. Ibid., 74–75.
7. André Levinson, "The New Ballet versus the Old," in *Ballet Old and New*, trans. Susan Cook Summer (New York: Dance Horizons, 1982), 72.
8. Coton, *A Prejudice for Ballet*, 76.
9. André Levinson, *Les Visages de la danse* (Paris: Editions Bernard Grasset, 1933), 75–76.

LA CONCURRENCE

1. *Diaghilev: Les Ballets Russes* (Paris: Bibliothèque Nationale, 1979), 85.
2. André Levinson, *Les Visages de la danse* (Paris: Editions Bernard Grasset, 1933), 70–71.
3. Georges Hilaire, *Derain* (Geneva: Pierre Cailler, 1959), 23.
4. Levinson, *Les Visages de la danse*, 70.
5. *Sunday Times*, London, July 9, 1933.

JEUX D'ENFANTS

1. A. V. Coton, *A Prejudice for Ballet* (London: Methuen & Co., 1938), 71–72.
2. Ibid., 70–71.
3. Letter from Miró to Grigoriev, May 26, 1934, Dance Collection, New York.
4. Letter from Miró to Riabouchinska, March 24, 1978, Riabouchinska Collection.
5. André Levinson, *Les Visages de la danse* (Paris: Editions Bernard Grasset, 1933), 75.
6. *Sunday Times*, London, July 16, 1933.
7. Irving Deaken, *Ballet Profile* (New York: Dodge Publishing Co., 1936), 262.
8. Arnold Haskell, *Balletomania, Then and Now* (New York: Alfred A. Knopf, 1977), 182.
9. *Daily Telegraph*, July 9, 1937.
10. *Sunday Times*, London, July 11, 1937.

NOTES

LE BOURGEOIS GENTILHOMME

1. Norman del Mar, *Richard Strauss: A Critical Commentary on His Life and Works* (London: Barrie and Rockliff, 1969), 93–94.
2. André Levinson, *Les Visages de la danse* (Paris: Editions Bernard Grasset, 1933), 76.
3. Ibid., 76.
4. Pierre Michaut, *Le Ballet contemporain* (Paris: Librairie Plon, 1950), 74.
5. Levinson, *Les Visages de la danse*, 76.

January 1933–April 1934

1. Letter from Joan Miró to Colonel de Basil, October 9, 1932, Mme de Basil Collection.
2. Agreement between Ray Goetz, Colonel de Basil, and Léonide Massine, January 29, 1933, Mme de Basil Collection.
3. Sale authorization, November 8, 1933, Mme de Basil Collection.
4. Agreement, August 10, 1934, Mme de Basil Collection.
5. Agreement, April 15, 1933, Mme de Basil Collection.
6. Letter from Colonel de Basil to B. Schott, December 5, 1933, Mme de Basil Collection.
7. Agreement between the Ballets Russes de Monte Carlo and Michel Kachouk, May 8, 1933, Mme de Basil Collection.
8. Letter from Ernest Ansermet to Colonel de Basil, March 13, 1933, Mme de Basil Collection.
9. Agnes de Mille, *Dance to the Piper* (Boston: Little, Brown, 1952), 152.
10. Cable from Sol Hurok to Colonel de Basil, November 12, 1933, Mme de Basil Collection.
11. Bernard Taper, *Balanchine* (New York: Harper & Row, 1974), 147.

LES PRÉSAGES

1. Letter from Masson to de Basil, January 23, 1933, Mme de Basil Collection.
2. Letter from de Basil to Masson, January 27, 1933, Mme de Basil Collection.
3. Letter from Masson to de Basil, May 29, 1936, Mme de Basil Collection.
4. Massine, conversations, 1978.
5. André Masson, *Peindre et une gageure, Le Plaisir de peindre*, p. 13.
6. Léonide Massine, *My Life in Ballet* (London: Macmillan, 1968), 187.
7. Alexander Gorsky had already produced a ballet to Glazunov's Fifth Symphony in 1916.
8. *Gazette de Monaco et de Monte Carlo*, April 15, 1933.
9. *Sunday Times*, London, July 9, 1933.

10. *New York Times*, New York, March 9, 1989.
11. Ibid.

LE BEAU DANUBE

1. A. V. Coton, *A Prejudice for Ballet* (London: Methuen & Co., 1938), 68.
2. Ibid., 67.
3. Ibid., 68.
4. Irving Deaken, *To the Ballet* (New York: Dodge Publishing Company, 1935), 116.
5. *L'Eclaireur*, February 3, 1933.
6. *Dance Magazine*, March 1952, p. 20. An open letter to the magazine from Alexandra Danilova.

BEACH

1. André Levinson, *Les Visages de la danse* (Paris: Editions Bernard Grasset, 1933), 86.
2. *New York Times*, January 2, 1934.

SCUOLA DI BALLO

1. *Mercury*, London, September 1933, pp. 453–54.
2. Léonide Massine, *My Life in Ballet* (London: Macmillan, 1968), 29.
3. Skibine, conversations, 1979.
4. André Levinson, *Les Visages de la danse* (Paris: Editions Bernard Grasset, 1933), 89.
5. *Sunday Times*, London, July 16, 1933.
6. *New York Times*, January 3, 1934.

NOCTURNE

1. *The Musical Times*, London, September 1933; the review was signed W.E.A.

CHOREARTIUM

1. "Choreartium" might be translated as "Chorus of the arts." *Chorea* was a type of classical dance performed in circles; *artium* is the Latin genitive plural of "art."
2. *Sunday Times*, London, July 19, 1936.
3. Léonide Massine, *My Life in Ballet* (London: Macmillan, 1968), 191.
4. Interview with Vera Zorina, conducted by John Gruen in 1972. Dance Collection, New York Public Library at Lincoln Center.
5. Parker Tyler, *The Divine Comedy of Pavel Tchelitchev* (New York: Fleet Publishing Corporation, 1967).
6. John Pearson, *The Sitwells* (New York and London: Harvest/HBJ Books, 1980), 123.

7. *Sunday Times*, London, July 5, 1936.
8. Ibid.
9. Ibid.

UNION PACIFIC

1. Nicolas Nabokov, *Bagázh; Memoirs of a Russian Cosmopolitan* (New York: Atheneum, 1975), 190.
2. Léonide Massine, *My Life in Ballet* (London: Macmillan, 1968), 197.
3. Nabokov, *Bagázh,* 192.
4. Massine, *My Life in Ballet,* 198.
5. A. V. Coton, *A Prejudice for Ballet* (London: Methuen & Co., 1938), 108.
6. *Sunday Times*, London, July 25, 1937.
7. Nabokov, *Bagázh,* 193–94.
8. Ibid., 194.
9. Lincoln Kirstein, *Ballet, Bias and Belief* (New York: Dance Horizons, 1983), 182.
10. Grace Robert, *The Borzoi Book of Ballets* (New York: Alfred A. Knopf, 1946), 346.
11. *Sunday Times*, London, July 25, 1937.
12. Coton, *A Prejudice for Ballet,* 108.
13. *Candide*, June 14, 1934.
14. Coton, *A Prejudice for Ballet,* 108.

May 1934–May 1935

1. Offer from Geoffrey Toye to Bruce Ottley acting as representative of de Basil, December 22, 1933, Mme de Basil Collection.
2. Letter from Geoffrey Toye to Bruce Ottley, January 1, 1934, Mme de Basil Collection.
3. Letter from Bruce Ottley to Colonel de Basil, April 6, 1934, Mme de Basil Collection.
4. Ibid.
5. Agreement between de Basil and Michel Kachouk, August 3, 1933, Mme de Basil Collection.
6. Agreement between Nijinska and Michel Kachouk, December 8, 1933, Mme de Basil Collection.
7. Letter from René Blum to Colonel de Basil, May 24, 1934, Mme de Basil Collection.
8. In a letter to Miró dated October 10, 1933, de Basil openly expressed his views regarding the rejection of the artist's program design: " . . . en mettant Monte Carlo en evidence trop marquée, tandis que pour nous ce mot joue un rôle secondaire, pour ne pas dire plus et l'idée, comme vous le savez, est de lancer le nom de Ballets Russes d'abord et même uniquement." (" . . . placing Monte Carlo too prominently, whereas for us that word plays a secondary role, to say the least, and as you know, our idea is to launch the name of Bal-

lets Russes exclusively and above all . . .") Mme de Basil Collection.
9. Letter from René Blum to Colonel de Basil, May 24, 1934, Mme de Basil Collection.
10. Letter from Bruce Ottley to Colonel de Basil, February 12, 1934, Mme de Basil Collection.
11. Letter from René Blum to Colonel de Basil, May 31, 1934, Mme de Basil Collection.
12. Agreement, René Blum to Colonel de Basil, August 16, 1934, Mme de Basil Collection.
13. Letter from Geoffrey Toye to Colonel de Basil, July 28, 1934, Mme de Basil Collection.
14. Document dated August 14, 1934, Mme de Basil Collection.
15. Letter from Erlangers, Ltd., to Colonel de Basil, September 11, 1934, Mme de Basil Collection.
16. Letter from Colonel de Basil to Baron d'Erlanger, September 11, 1934, Mme de Basil Collection.
17. Letter from Bruce Ottley to Colonel de Basil, April 6, 1934, Mme de Basil Collection.
18. Letter from Bruce Ottley to Colonel de Basil, January 2, 1934, Mme de Basil Collection.
19. Letter from Bruce Ottley to Colonel de Basil, March 14, 1934, Mme de Basil Collection.
20. Cable from Bruce Ottley to Colonel de Basil, March 28, 1934, Mme de Basil Collection.
21. Cable from Lord Keynes to Colonel de Basil, February 25, 1934, Mme de Basil Collection.

LES IMAGINAIRES

1. *Excelsior*, June 14, 1934.
2. *Paris-Midi*, June 12, 1934.
3. *Daily Telegraph*, August 1, 1934.
4. *Excelsior*, June 14, 1934.

JARDIN PUBLIC

1. Vernon Duke, *Passport to Paris* (Boston: Little, Brown, 1955), 298. All subsequent references to the history of the production are from this book.
2. Synopsis by Dukelsky and Massine. Souvenir program, American tour, 1935–36.
3. *Sunday Times,* London, July 28, 1935.
4. *Sunday Referee*, July 28, 1935.
5. Ibid.
6. *Sunday Times*, London, July 28, 1935.

June 1935–May 1936

1. Edinburgh *Evening News*, June 11, 1935.
2. Lazowski, conversations, 1980.
3. Edwin Denby, *Looking at the Dance* (New York: Pellegrini and Cudahy, 1949), 156.

4. *The Dancing Times*, August 1935.
5. Michel Fokine, *Memoirs of a Ballet Master*, trans. Vitale Fokine (Boston: Little, Brown, 1961), 157.
6. *The Dancing Times*, February 1976.
7. Irving Kolodin, *The Metropolitan Opera 1883-1935* (New York: Oxford University Press, 1936), 464.
8. Agnes de Mille, *Dance to the Piper* (Boston: Little, Brown, 1952), 220.
9. *Time* magazine, April 20, 1936.
10. Arnold L. Haskell, *In His True Centre* (London: Adam and Charles Black, 1951), 134–35.
11. *New York Times*, April 21, 1936.
12. *New York Sun*, April 21, 1936.

LES CENT BAISERS

1. *Times*, London, July 19, 1935.
2. *Sunday Times*, London, July 21, 1935; *Daily Mail*, July 19, 1935.
3. Vasilieva, conversations, 1982.
4. André Levinson, *Les Visages de la danse* (Paris: Editions Bernard Grasset, 1933), 55.
5. Edwin Denby, *Looking at the Dance* (New York: Pellegrini and Cudahy, 1949), 69.
6. Kochno, conversations, 1982.
7. Jean Hugo. Manuscript in the possession of the author.
8. Ibid.
9. Ibid.
10. Ibid.
11. *Daily Telegraph*, July 19, 1935.
12. *Sunday Referee*, July 21, 1935.
13. *Daily Telegraph*, July 19, 1935.
14. *New York Times*, October 23, 1937.
15. Grace Robert, *The Borzoi Book of Ballets* (New York: Alfred A. Knopf, 1946), 193–94.

June 1936–April 1937

1. Letter from René Blum to George Balanchine, November 5, 1935, Dance Collection, New York.
2. Letter from George Balanchine to René Blum, November 21, 1935, Dance Collection, New York.
3. Letter from E. J. Tait to Léonide Massine, March 22, 1927, Léonide Massine Collection.
4. Arnold Haskell, *Dancing Around the World* (New York: Dodge Publishing Co., 1938), 22.
5. Tchinarova, conversations, 1982.
6. Ibid.
7. Kolodin, conversations, 1982.

SYMPHONIE FANTASTIQUE

1. Antal Dorati, *Notes of Seven Decades* (London: Hodder and Stoughton, 1979).
2. Letter from Ansermet to Massine, January 15, 1933, Mme de Basil Collection.
3. Vera Newman, *Ernest Newman, A Memoir by His Wife* (New York: Alfred A. Knopf, 1964), 155.
4. *Evening News*, July 25, 1936.
5. *Sunday Times*, London, August 2, 1936.
6. *Sunday Times*, London, August 2, 1936.
7. *Sunday Referee*, August 2, 1936.
8. Grace Robert, *The Borzoi Book of Ballets* (New York: Alfred A. Knopf, 1946), 328.
9. *Sunday Times*, London, August 2, 1936.
10. *Dance*, January 1937.
11. Robert, *The Borzoi Book of Ballets*, 328.

LE PAVILLON

1. *Sunday Times*, London, July 4, 1937.
2. *Evening Standard*, London, August 12, 1936.
3. Cecil Beaton, *Ballet* (London and New York: Wingate, 1951), 45.
4. Ibid., 46–47.
5. *Sunday Times*, London, July 4, 1937.
6. *Times*, London, August 12, 1936.
7. *Daily Telegraph*, London, August 12, 1936.
8. *New York Times*, October 31, 1936.
9. *Daily Telegraph*, London, August 12, 1936.
10. *Sunday Times*, London, July 4, 1937.

May 1937–May 1938

1. *Times*, London, February 23, 1938.
2. *Evening News*, June 18, 1937.
3. *The New Yorker*, July 24, 1937.
4. *Times*, London, October 11, 1937.
5. *The Observer*, October 10, 1937.

FRANCESCA DA RIMINI

1. Interview with David Lichine, *Theatre News*, October 18, 1938.
2. Ibid.
3. Will Durant, *The Renaissance*, vol. 5, *The Story of Civilization* (New York: Simon & Schuster, 1953), 339–40.
4. *Times*, London, July 16, 1937.
5. *Daily Telegraph*, July 16, 1937.
6. Grace Robert, *The Borzoi Book of Ballets* (New York: Alfred A. Knopf, 1946), 140.

7. *Francesca da Rimini*, 16mm silent film in color, Riabouchinska Collection.
8. *Times*, London, July 16, 1937.
9. *Daily Telegraph*, July 16, 1937.
10. *Morning Post*, July 16, 1937; review was signed F.T.

LE COQ D'OR

1. Andrei Rimsky-Korsakov outlined these objections in a letter to the *Times*, London, June 24, 1914.
2. *Sunday Times*, London, September 26, 1937.
3. *Daily Telegraph*, September 24, 1937.
4. *New York Times*, October 31, 1937.
5. *Sunday Times*, London, September 26, 1937.
6. *New York Sun*, October 25, 1937.
7. Letter from Michel Fokine to the *Times*, London, September 30, 1937.
8. Arnold Haskell, *Daily Telegraph*, September 24, 1937.
9. Grace Robert, *The Borzoi Book of Ballet* (New York: Alfred A. Knopf, 1946), 100–101.
10. *New York Times*, September 2, 1942.
11. In early January the Metropolitan Opera House replaced the 1918 *Le Coq d'or* production, one of Gatti's most lavish spectacles, with a simplified version staged by Fokine in which Lily Pons sang and danced the role of the Queen.
12. Peter Williams, *Dance and Dancers*, June 1976.

LES DIEUX MENDIANTS

1. The pseudonym Sobeka was *S* for Sauguet, *B* for Balanchine, and *K* for Kochno. When Kochno wrote his libretto for *La Chatte*, he wanted to adopt a pseudonym in which to incorporate the first letter of the names of his collaborators, as a desire to express the teamlike atmosphere that existed among the three. When he arrived at the word *Sobeka*, he liked it immediately because it so closely resembled the word *sovaka*, which in Russian means watchdog, a term Diaghilev often used in referring to him. Later on, he adopted the same pseudonym for *The Gods Go a-Begging*.
2. Interview with David Lichine, *Theatre News*, October 18, 1938, p. 3.
3. *Times*, London, September 18, 1937.
4. *The Observer*, September 19, 1937.
5. *Times*, London, September 18, 1937.
6. A. V. Coton, *A Prejudice for Ballet* (London: Methuen & Co., 1938), 190.

LE LION AMOUREUX

1. "Sitter Out," *The Dancing Times*, October 1937.
2. Prince Franz Hohenlohe, *Steph, the Fabulous Princess* (London: New English Library, 1976), passim.

3. *Times*, London, October 7, 1937.
4. A. V. Coton, *A Prejudice for Ballet* (London: Methuen & Co., 1938), 195.
5. *The Dancing Times*, November 1937, p. 137.
6. Arnold Haskell, *The Daily Telegraph*, October 7, 1937.
7. Coton, *A Prejudice for Ballet*, 195.
8. *Times*, London, October 7, 1937.
9. *Daily Telegraph*, October 7, 1937.

June 1938–May 1939

1. *New York Times*, April 24, 1938.
2. *Times*, London, April 20, 1938.
3. Sol Hurok, *Impresario* (New York: Random House, 1946), 204.
4. *Times*, London, April 20, 1938.
5. *Evening Standard*, June 21, 1938.
6. Immigration permits. Royal Opera House, Archives.
7. *Daily Sketch*, June 1938.
8. *Birmingham Post*, June 22, 1938.
9. *The Bystander*, July 13, 1938.
10. *The Observer*, June 19, 1938.
11. *Daily Telegraph*, July 1, 1938.
12. *The Observer*, July 3, 1938.
13. *Times*, London, June 21, 1938.
14. *The Bystander*, July 27, 1938.
15. Ninette de Valois, *Invitation to the Ballet* (Oxford: Oxford University Press, 1938), 145.
16. Antal Dorati had sailed for Australia on August 5 to recruit the orchestra before the company's arrival. Franz Allers replaced him at Covent Garden until the end of the season.
17. The Australian tour allowed Fokine to stage his elaborate *Paganini*. Also he began to revive his *Bacchanale* with music from Wagner's *Tannhäuser*, previously staged as *Grotto of Venus* in 1910 for a benefit of the Ladies' Patriotic Society at the Maryinsky Theatre. He tried to revive it first on Baronova and then on Grigorieva and Denisova, but finally did not pursue it. The ballet was supposed to be premiered during the 1939 Berlin season at the Scala. Baronova feels that the work was very much rooted in Duncan's style and would not have been relevant for the times.
18. Nicolson, Harold, *Diaries and Letters, 1930–1964* (New York: Atheneum, 1980), 131.

PROTÉE

1. *Mercury*, August 1938.
2. *Daily Telegraph*, July 6, 1938.
3. Ibid.

CENDRILLON

The description of the action of *Cendrillon* is based on the excerpts from the ballet in the Riabouchinska film collection shot by Dr. Ringland Anderson and Laird Goldsborough.

1. *Sunday Times*, London, July 24, 1939.
2. *Ballet*, July–August 1939.
3. *Sunday Times*, London, July 24, 1938.
4. *The Daily Mail*, July 20, 1938.
5. *Times*, London, July 20, 1938.
6. *Daily Telegraph*, July 20, 1938.
7. *Sunday Times*, London, July 24, 1938.
8. *Daily Telegraph*, July 20, 1938.
9. *Sunday Times*, London, July 24, 1938.
10. Ibid.
11. *Daily Telegraph*, July 17, 1939.
12. Irving Deaken, *Ballet Profile* (New York: Dodge Publishing Co., 1936), 311.
13. *The Dancing Times*, September 1938.
14. Ibid.
15. *New York Herald Tribune*, November 16, 1940.
16. Grace Robert, *The Borzoi Book of Ballets* (New York: Alfred A. Knopf, 1946), 78.

THE PRODIGAL SON

My observations of Lichine's version were based on the 16mm black-and-white film of the ballet with Jasinski and Stepanova. This film was made by Laird Goldsborough during a performance at the Met in 1946. Although some scenes were abridged in the editing, the ballet is quite complete. In an excerpt in the Riabouchinska film collection, shot in Australia by Dr. Ringland Anderson, there is a closer view of the pas de deux performed by Dolin and Osato.

1. *Sydney Morning Herald*, May 19, 1940.
2. Agnes de Mille, "Acrobatics and the New Dance," *Theatre Guild*, January 1930.
3. Anton Dolin, *Divertissement* (London: Sampson Law, Marston, 1931).
4. *Sydney Morning Herald*, May 19, 1940.
5. *The Bystander*, July 5, 1939.
6. *The Dancing Times*, February 1939.
7. *New York Times*, November 27, 1940.
8. *New York Sun*, November 27, 1940.
9. *New York Times*, December 1, 1940.
10. *New York Sun*, October 18, 1946.

June 1939–September 1940

1. *News Chronicle*, June 2, 1939.
2. *Sunday Dispatch*, June 18, 1939.
3. *The Bystander*, July 5, 1939, p. 9.
4. *Ballet*, July–August 1939.
5. *The Dancing Times*, June 1939.
6. *The Bystander*, July 5, 1939.
7. *Times*, London, June 30, 1939.
8. *The Dancing Times*, June 1939.
9. *The Bystander*, July 5, 1939.
10. *The Dancing Times*, June 1939.
11. *The Observer*, July 30, 1939.
12. Ibid.
13. Ibid.
14. *The Observer*, August 13, 1939.
15. *The Observer*, July 30, 1939.
16. Ibid.
17. *The Dancing Times*, August 1939.
18. Baronova, conversations, 1983.
19. Kathrine Sorley Walker, *De Basil's Ballets Russes* (London: Hutchinson, 1982), 96.
20. Ibid.
21. Edward Pask, *Enter the Colonies Dancing: A History of Dance in Australia, 1835–1940* (Melbourne: Oxford University Press, 1979).
22. Costume and scenery inventory, Mme de Basil Collection.

PAGANINI

The description of the action of *Paganini* is based on the film of the ballet in the Riabouchinska film collection shot in Australia by Dr. Ringland Anderson.

1. Michel Fokine, *Memoirs of a Ballet Master*, trans. Vitale Fokine (Boston: Little, Brown, 1961), 281.
2. David Vaughan, *Frederick Ashton and His Ballets* (New York: Alfred A. Knopf, 1977), 171.
3. Arnold Haskell, *Balletomania* (New York: Alfred A. Knopf, 1977), 86.
4. *Times*, London, July 1, 1939.
5. *Daily Telegraph*, July 1, 1939.
6. *The Bystander*, July 12, 1939, p. 42.
7. *Daily Telegraph*, July 1, 1939.
8. *The Bystander*, July 12, 1939.
9. Grace Robert, *The Borzoi Book of Ballets* (New York: Alfred A. Knopf, 1946), 209–10.
10. *The Bystander*, July 12, 1939, p. 42.
11. *New York Times*, November 9, 1940.
12. *New York Sun*, November 9, 1940.
13. Arnold Haskell, *The Ballet Annual* (London: Adam and Charles Black, 1948), 42.
14. Lynn Garafola, "Fokine's 'Paganini' Resurrected," *Ballet Review*, Spring 1986.

GRADUATION BALL

The description of the action of *Graduation Ball* is based on the complete film of the first version of the ballet in the Riabouchinska film collection shot in Australia by Dr. Ringland Anderson.

1. Letter from Beaumont to Lichine, July 18, 1939, Riabouchinska Collection.
2. *The Sydney Morning Herald*, March 2, 1940.
3. Ibid.
4. *New York Times*, November 17, 1940.

October 1940–December 1941

1. *Los Angeles Times*, October 13, 1940.
2. Dorathi Bock Pierre, *The American Dancer*, November 1940.
3. S. Hurok, *S. Hurok Presents the World of Ballet* (London: Robert Hale, 1955), 130.
4. *New York Times*, November 3, 1940.
5. *S. Hurok Presents the World of Ballet*, 131–32.
6. Ibid.,130.
7. *New York Times*, November 17, 1940.
8. Ibid.
9. *Dance*, December 1940, p. 8.
10. *New York Times*, December 1, 1940.
11. Letter from Irving Deaken to Anton Dolin, December 2, 1940, Irving Deaken Papers, Dance Collection, New York Public Library.
12. Lincoln Kirstein, *Dance*, December 1940.
13. Lincoln Kirstein, *P.M.*, December 1, 1940.
14. Press release from Hurok's office, March 1, 1941, Riabouchinska Collection.
15. *Variety*, April 16, 1941.
16. Strikers' statement to AGMA, April 25, 1941, Original Ballet Russe Papers, Dance Collection, New York Public Library.
17. Kathrine Sorley Walker, *De Basil's Ballets Russes* (London: Hutchinson, 1982), 108.
18. *El Avance Criollo*, March 24, 1941.
19. *The Havana Post*, March 25, 1941.
20. Letter from AGMA, April 28, 1941, Riabouchinska Collection.
21. Charles Payne, *American Ballet Theatre* (New York: Alfred A. Knopf, 1978), 112.
22. Carbon copy of letter from Irving Deaken to Anton Dolin, December 2, 1940, Irving Deaken Papers, Dance Collection, New York Public Library.
23. Telegram from Saltus to Lichine in Havana, May 5, 1941, Riabouchinska Collection.
24. Sorley Walker, *De Basil's Ballets Russes*, 110.
25. *Variety*, April 16, 1941.
26. Ibid.
27. Payne, *American Ballet Theatre*, 112.
28. Ibid.
29. Ibid.
30. Sorley Walker, *De Basil's Ballets Russes*, 112 (quoting the Gallo Papers, Verdac Collection).
31. Ibid., 110.
32. *The Standard*, October 11, 1941.
33. Sorley Walker, *De Basil's Ballets Russes*, 114.

BALUSTRADE

1. Parker Tyler, *The Divine Comedy of Pavel Tchelitchev* (New York: Fleet Publishing Corporation, 1967), 435.
2. *New York Times*, January 19, 1941.
3. Edwin Denby, *Looking at the Dance* (New York: Pellegrini and Cudahy, 1949), 113.
4. Lillian Moore, *The Dancing Times*, April 1941.
5. From *Balustrade*, an eight-minute 16mm film containing black-and-white and color excerpts of two performances at the Fifty-first Street Theatre in New York City. Filmed by Laird Goldsborough in 1941; donated to the Dance Collection of the New York Public Library by Mrs. Goldsborough.
6. Denby, *Looking at the Dance*, 226–27.
7. *Dance*, March 1941.
8. *New York Herald Tribune*, January 23, 1941.
9. *Dance*, March 1941.
10. Denby, *Looking at the Dance*, 156.
11. Ibid., 227.
12. *New York Sun*, January 23, 1941.
13. *New York Times*, January 23, 1941.
14. Ibid.
15. *New York Herald Tribune*, January 23, 1941.
16. George Balanchine and Francis Mason, *Balanchine's Complete Stories of the Great Ballets* (New York: Doubleday, 1977), 713.

January 1942–August 1946

1. Sorley Walker names Ernesto de Quesada as the impresario concerned with this tour.
2. Margarita Wallmann, *Les Balcons du ciel* (Paris: Editions Robert Laffont), 91.
3. *El Tiempo*, Bogotá, December 2, 1944.
4. Marta Giovanni, *Ballet Argentino en el Teatro Colón* (Buenos Aires: Editorial Plus Ultra, 1973), 149.
5. Kathrine Sorley Walker, *De Basil's Ballets Russes* (London: Hutchinson, 1982), 125–26.
6. Unfortunately, the correspondence has not survived, with the exception of short notes accompanying the press notices de Basil sent to Lichine and Riabouchinska from South America, which Riabouchinska kept in scrapbooks.

7. *Diario de la Marina*, May 16, 1946.
8. *El Avance Criollo*, May 4, 1946.
9. Celida Parera y Alonso, *Historia concisa del Ballet en Cuba*.
10. *A Noite*, São Paulo, July 31, 1946.
11. Edwin Denby, *Looking at the Dance* (New York: Pellegrini and Cudahy, 1949), 203.
12. *New York Times*, October 13, 1946.

CAIN AND ABEL

1. Edwin Denby, *Looking at the Dance* (New York: Pellegrini and Cudahy, 1949), 203.
2. *New York Times*, October 5, 1946.
3. *New York Times*, October 13, 1946.
4. *Dance News*, November 1946.
5. *New York Herald Tribune*, October 3, 1946.

September 1946–November 1948

1. Mme de Basil, conversations, 1979. Sorley Walker dates the trip right after Panama.
2. Sol Hurok, *S. Hurok Presents the World of Ballet* (London: Robert Hale, 1955), 179.
3. Ibid., 161.
4. *Variety*, November 5, 1947.
5. *S. Hurok Presents the World of Ballet*, 173.
6. Unidentified clippings in Riabouchinska's files. Riabouchinska has only vague memories of this venture, since it was Lichine who always dealt with the Marquis de Cuevas about contracts.
7. *Ballet*, London, December 1946, 19–21.
8. Edwin Denby, *Looking at the Dance* (New York: Pellegrini and Cudahy, 1949), 202–3.

CAMILLE

1. *New York Times*, October 13, 1946.
2. *Dance News*, November 1946.
3. *New York Times*, October 13, 1946.

APRIL 1947–NOVEMBER 1948

1. Julian Braunsweg, *Ballet Scandals* (London: George Allen and Unwin, 1977), 96.
2. Contract sent to de Basil by David Webster, May 14, 1947, Mme de Basil Collection.
3. Braunsweg, *Ballet Scandals*, 97.
4. *Ballet*, London, September 1947.
5. *The Manchester Guardian,*, July 24, 1947; column signed J.H.M.
6. Boris Kniaseff, *25 Années de danse, 1918–1943* (Paris: Les Editions-Publicité, 1943), unpaginated.
7. Unidentified press clipping.
8. Ibid.
9. *Le Figaro*, October 8, 1947.
10. Pierre Michaut, *Le Ballet contemporain* (Paris: Librairie Plon, 1950), 331.
11. I have not found records for those in Seville and Granada mentioned by Sorley Walker.
12. Sorley Walker also mentions *Danzas eslavas* with choreography by Anatole Joukovsky.
13. *Solidaridad Nacional*, October 26, 1948.

Epilogue

1. Kathrine Sorley Walker, *De Basil's Ballets Russes* (London: Hutchinson, 1982), 162.

BIBLIOGRAPHY

Balanchine, George, and Francis Mason. *Balanchine's Complete Stories of the Great Ballets.* New York: Doubleday, 1977.

Beaton, Cecil. *Ballet.* London and New York: Wingate, 1951.

Beaumont, Cyril W. *Complete Book of Ballets.* Garden City, N.Y.: Garden City Publishing Co., 1941.

———. *The Monte Carlo Russian Ballet.* London: C. W. Beaumont, 1934.

Brahms, Caryl. *Footnotes to the Ballet.* London: Lovat Dickson, Ltd., 1936.

Braunsweg, Julian. *Ballet Scandals.* London: George Allen and Unwin, Ltd., 1977.

Buckle, Richard. *Diaghilev.* New York: Atheneum, 1979.

Cabrera, Miguel. *Orbita del Ballet Nacional de Cuba.* Havana: Editorial Orbe, 1978.

Chujoy, Anatole. *Ballet.* New York: Robert Speller Publishing Corp., 1936.

———. *The Dance Encyclopedia.* New York: A. S. Barnes, 1949.

Clarke, Mary. *The Sadler's Wells Ballet.* London: Adam and Charles Black, 1955.

Coton, A. V. *A Prejudice for Ballet.* London: Methuen & Co., 1938.

Deaken, Irving. *Ballet Profile.* New York: Dodge Publishing Co., 1936.

———. *To the Ballet.* New York: Dodge Publishing Co., 1935.

De Mille, Agnes. *Dance to the Piper.* Boston: Little, Brown, 1952.

Denby, Edwin. *Dancers, Buildings, and People in the Streets.* New York: Popular Library, 1965.

———. *Looking at the Dance.* New York: Horizon Press, 1968.

De Valois, Ninette. *Invitation to the Ballet.* Oxford: Oxford University Press, 1938.

Dorati, Antal. *Notes of Seven Decades.* London: Hodder and Stoughton, 1979.

Drinker Bowen, Catherine, and Barbara von Meck. *Beloved Friend: The Story of Tchaikovsky and Nadejda von Meck.* New York: Random House, 1937.

Duke, Vernon. *Passport to Paris.* Boston: Little, Brown, 1955.

Durant, Will. *The Renaissance.* New York: Simon and Schuster, 1953.

Fokine, Michel. *Memoirs of a Ballet Master.* Boston: Little, Brown, 1961.

Garcia Victorica, Victoria. *El Original Ballet Russe en America Latina.* Buenos Aires: Ediciones Arturo Jacinto Alvarez.

Giovanni, Marta, and Amelia Foglia de Ruiz. *Ballet Argentino en el Teatro Colón.* Buenos Aires: Editorial Plus Ultra, 1973.

Grigoriev, S. L. *The Diaghilev Ballet.* London: Penguin Books, 1960.

Haskell, Arnold. *Ballet.* London: Penguin Books, 1938.

———. *Balletomane's Album.* London: Adam and Charles Black, 1939.

———. *Balletomania, Then and Now.* New York: Alfred A. Knopf, 1977.

———. *Ballet Panorama.* London: B. T. Batsdorf, Ltd., 1938.

———. *Dancing Around the World.* London: Victor Gollancz Ltd., 1937.

———. *Diaghilev, His Artistic and Private Life.* New York: Simon and Schuster, 1935.

———. *In His True Centre.* London: Adam and Charles Black, 1951.

Hilaire, Georges. *Derain.* Geneva: Pierre Cailler, 1959.

Hohenlohe, Prince Franz. *Steph, the Fabulous Princess.* London: Methuen & Co., 1976.

Hurok, Sol. *Impresario.* New York: Random House, 1946.

———. *S. Hurok Presents the World of Ballet.* London: Robert Hale Ltd., 1955.

Kierkegaard, Sören. *The Concept of Anxiety.* Princeton, N.J.: Princeton University Press, 1980.

Kniaseff, Boris. *25 Années de danse, 1918–1943.* Paris: Les Editions-Publicité, 1943.

Kochno, Boris. *Diaghilev and the Ballets Russes.* New York: Harper & Row, 1970.

———. *Le Ballet.* Paris: Hachette, 1954.

Kolodin, Irving. *The Metropolitan Opera, 1883–1935.* New York: Oxford University Press, 1936.

Krokover, Rosalyn. *The New Borzoi Book of Ballets.* New York: Alfred A. Knopf, 1956.

Lambranzi, Gregorio. *New and Curious School of Theatrical Dancing.* Edited by Cyril W. Beaumont. London: The Imperial Society of Teachers of Dancing, 1928.

Levinson, André. *Ballet Old and New.* New York: Dance Horizons, 1982.

Levinson, André. *Les Visages de la danse*. Paris: Editions Bernard Grasset, 1933.

Massine, Léonide. *My Life in Ballet*. London: Macmillan, 1968.

Masson, André. *Peindre et une gageure, Le Plaisir de peindre*. Paris, n.d.

Meyer, Denise, and Pierre Souvtchinsky. *Roger Désormière et son temps*. Monaco: Editions du Rocher, 1966.

Michaut, Pierre. *Le Ballet contemporain*. Paris: Librairie Plon, 1950.

Milford, Nancy. *Zelda*. New York: Avon Books, 1970.

Nabokov, Nicolas. *Bagázh*. New York: Atheneum, 1975.

Nicolson, Harold. *Diaries and Letters, 1930–1964*. New York: Atheneum, 1980.

Obolensky, Serge. *One Man in His Time*. New York: McDowell, Obolensky, 1958.

Osato, Sono. *Distant Dances*. New York: Alfred A. Knopf, 1980.

Pask, Edward. *Enter the Colonies Dancing*. Melbourne: Oxford University Press, 1979.

Pearson, John. *The Sitwells*. New York and London: Harvest/HBJ Books, 1980.

Robert, Grace. *The Borzoi Book of Ballets*. New York: Alfred A. Knopf, 1946.

Roslavleva, Natalia. *Era of the Russian Ballet*. London: Victor Gollancz Ltd., 1966.

Rubin, William. *André Masson*. New York: Museum of Modern Art, 1976.

Shirer, William. *The Rise and Fall of the Third Reich*. New York: Simon and Schuster, 1960.

Soby, James Thrall. *Joan Miró*. New York: Museum of Modern Art, 1959.

Sorley Walker, Kathrine. *De Basil's Ballets Russes*. London: Hutchinson, 1982.

Steinberg, Cobbett. *The Dance Anthology*. New York: New American Library, 1980.

Stokes, Adrian. *Russian Ballets*. London: Faber and Faber, 1946.

_____. *To-Night the Ballet*. London, 1935.

Taper, Bernard. *Balanchine*. New York: Macmillan, 1974.

Tyler, Parker. *The Divine Comedy of Pavel Tchelitchev*. New York: Fleet Publishing Corp., 1967.

Vaughan, David. *Frederick Ashton and His Ballets*. New York: Alfred A. Knopf, 1977.

Wallmann, Margarita. *Les Balcons du ciel*. Paris: Robert Laffont, 1977.

Wolff, Stephane. *L'Opéra au Palais Garnier*. Paris: L'Imprimerie Maison-neuve, 1962.

INDEX

Note: Page numbers in *italics* refer to illustrations.

PHOTO SOURCES

All photos are from private collections, with the exception of the following:

BBC HULTON PICTURE LIBRARY: 60 *bottom*, 122, 181 *bottom*, 182 *left*, 205, 228, 229, 236 *upper left*, 307 *top*, 309 *top*; BIBLIOTHÈQUE NATIONALE: 15 *top*, 16 *top*, 40 *middle*, 102; DANCE COLLECTION OF THE NEW YORK PUBLIC LIBRARY, ASTOR, LENOX AND TILDEN FOUNDATIONS: 10, 43, 45, 47, 50, 69, 93 *bottom*, 94 *bottom*, 111, 116, 117 *right*, 143 *bottom*, 148, 164 *top right*, 165 *top left and bottom*, 174, 179, 195, 197 *top*, 203 *top*, 208, 218 *bottom*, 242, 254 *top*, 255 *top*, 266, 271 *top right*, 279 *middle*, 302; PARIS OPÉRA: 16 *bottom*, 22 *top*, 40 *bottom*, 41, 75; ROGER-VIOLLET: 79 *top*.

PHOTOGRAPHERS

ANTHONY: 165 *top right*, 170, 211; DAN BALE: 60 *bottom*, 122, 164 *bottom right*, 181, 182 *left*, 187 *left*, 205, 228, 229, 236 *top left*, 255 *bottom*, 307 *top*; RAOUL BARBA: 7, 22 *top*, 32 *bottom*, 33 *top*, 40 *top*, 61 *top*, 75; BARON: 307 *bottom*; BBC STUDIOS: 179; CECIL BEATON: 17 *bottom*; CONSTANTINE: 195 *bottom*; COSMO-SILEO ASSOCIATES: 279 *middle*; PEGGY DE LUIS: 196 *middle*; MME. S. GEORGES: 95 *top*; BOB GOLBY: 268; HUGH P. HALL: 15 *bottom*, 60 *bottom*, 68 *top*, 143 *top*, 197 *top*, 218 *top*, 222, 223, 254 *bottom*, 260 *top and bottom*, 261 *top*, 265; NANETTE KUEHN: 203 *bottom*; STUDIO LIPNITZKI: 79 *top*; LIONEL LUNN: 262 *bottom*; MOORE & THOMPSON: 217; GEORGE SANDERSON: 266 *top right*; MAURICE SEYMOUR: 47, 117 *bottom*, 136, 143 *bottom*, 203 *top*, 218 *bottom*, 242, 246, 302; T. N. WICKENS: 60 *top*.

A Note About the Author
Vicente García-Márquez is a cultural historian who was born in Cuba and educated in the United States, France, and Spain. He was consultant to the Paris Opéra for its 1989 revival of the ballet Les Présages, *and was director of "Spain and Diaghilev's Ballets Russes," a congress and exhibition which was part of the 1989 Granada Festival of Music and Dance. He lives in Los Angeles.*